The Church of North Africa has mushroomed from almost nothing to tens of thousands within the past few years, with the result that indigenous believers that are thrust into leadership have never seen a mature leader of their own ethnicity as a role model. Farida approaches the subject with the insight and respect achieved through leading to faith and nurturing hundreds of Muslims in France and North Africa. Drawing from the leadership styles in the cultures and history of the latter region, including its ancient and contemporary church, she examines them through the lens of biblical leadership values and discerns guidelines that are both culturally relevant and biblical.

J. Dudley Woodberry
Dean Emeritus and Senior Professor of Islamic Studies
School of Intercultural Studies
Fuller Theological Seminary

In the growing North African Church today, there is a vital need to reflect on a number of biblical, theological and practical issues. Few, if any, are more important than the question of the church's leadership. Dr. Saidi has done a remarkable job in advancing the reflection and proposing concrete and credible models, developed under the scrutiny of biblical teaching and deeply rooted in the history and culture of North Africa, with input from her vast and lengthy experience in the field. One would search in vain for another book on the subject with the same pertinence, depth of research, quality of presentation and practical outlook. Highly recommended.

Amar Djaballah
Dean and professor of Biblical Studies,
Faculté de Théologie Évangélique de Montréal, Affiliated with Acadia University

A Study of Current Leadership Styles in the North African Church

Farida Saïdi

MONOGRAPHS

© 2013 by Farida Saïdi

Published 2013 by Langham Monographs
an imprint of Langham Creative Projects

Langham Partnership
PO Box 296, Carlisle, Cumbria CA3 9WZ, UK
www.langham.org

ISBNs:
978-1-907713-80-4 print
978-1-907713-79-8 Mobi
978-1-907713-78-1 ePub

Farida Saïdi has asserted her right under the Copyright, Designs and Patents Act, 1988 to be identified as the Author of this work.

All rights reserved. No part of this publication may be reproduced, stored in a retrieval system or transmitted, in any form or by any means, electronic, mechanical, photocopying, recording or otherwise, without the prior written permission of the publisher or the Copyright Licensing Agency.

Scriptures taken from the Holy Bible, New International Version®, NIV®. Copyright © 1973, 1978, 1984, 2011 by Biblica, Inc.™

British Library Cataloguing in Publication Data
Saidi, Farida, author.
  A study of current leadership styles in the North African Church.
  1. Independent churches--Africa, North. 2. Clergy--
  Africa, North. 3. Leadership--Religious aspects.
  I. Title
  206.1'0961-dc23

ISBN-13: 9781907713804

Cover & Book Design: projectluz.com

Langham Partnership actively supports theological dialogue and a scholars right to publish but does not necessarily endorse the views and opinions set forth, and works referenced within this publication or guarantee its technical and grammatical correctness. Langham Partnership does not accept any responsibility or liability to persons or property as a consequence of the reading, use or interpretation of its published content.

To Bati and Mona

Contents

Abstract xv

Acknowledgements xvii

Part 1: Background 1

Chapter 1 3
  Introduction
    Rise and Decline of the Church in North Africa 3
    New Beginnings of the North African Church 8
    Purpose of Study 10

Chapter 2 13
  An Overview of Contemporary Leadership Theories
    Great-Man Theory 13
    Trait-Theory 14
    Behavioral Theories 15
    Contingency Theories 15
    Transactional Leadership 20
    Transformational Leadership 22
    Visionary or Charismatic Leadership 23
    Autocratic, Democratic and Laissez-Faire Leadership 25
    Servant Leadership 28
    The Relationship of the Leader with God 30
      Biblical Leadership Theories 30
      Spiritual Leadership Theories 37
      Islamic Leadership Theories 38
    Cultural Approaches to Leadership Styles 43
      Universal Versus Cultural 43
      Western Theories Measure Applied Globally 44
      Cultural Categories For Measuring Leadership Behaviors 44
      Leadership Styles in the Middle East and North Africa 45
    Conclusion 52

Chapter 3 55
  Methodology
    My Flowchart 55
    Existing Questionnaires? 56
    Measuring Leadership Styles 59

What Makes a Leadership Style?	59
Questionnaires and Interviews	60
Leadership Styles in Contingency Theory	61
Behaviors	61
Values	63
Leadership Legitimacy	67
Leadership Power and Influence	68
Metaphors and Definitions	68
Field Research	69
Informants	70
NAP Conference	71
Visits to North Africa	71
Data Analysis	73
Descriptive Study	75
Limitations of my Research	76

Part 2: Styles of Leadership in Islam and North African Culture and History 79

Chapter 4 81
Leadership Styles in Islam

    Pre-Islamic (*jahiliyya*) Leadership 83
        Leadership Roles 83
        Influence of Pre-Islamic Leadership on Islamic Leadership 89
        Conclusion 91
    Leadership in Early Islam 91
        God's Power versus Human Power 92
        Authority and Power 95
        Conclusion 98
        Muhammad 98
        Leadership Legitimacy 114
        Leadership Roles 116
    Conclusions and Recommendations 130

Chapter 5 133
Styles of Leadership in North African Culture

    Socio-political Leadership 134
        The Sheikh 134
        Leadership Patterns of President Boumediène (1932-1978) 137
    Family Leadership Style 138
        Traditional and Contemporary North African Families 139
        Grandparents Leadership Style 141

  Father Leadership Style 142
  Mother Leadership Style 146
  North African Family Values 148
 Religious Education 153
  Qur'anic School 154
  The *Talib* 154
  The *Wali* 156
  Marabouts in Contemporary North Africa 160
  North African *Zawiyas* 162
 Conclusion 163

Chapter 6 167
Styles of Leadership in North African History
 Augustine: Theologian and Church Father 168
  Augustine's Life and Legacy 168
  Augustine's Leadership Attributes and Behaviors 170
  Augustine's Leadership Styles 175
 Amir Abd el-Kader: Visionary and Father of the Nation 176
  Amir Abd el-Kader's Life and Legacy 177
  Amir Abd el-Kader's Leadership Attributes and Behaviors 178
  Amir Abd el-Kader's Leadership Style 182
 Cardinal Lavigerie: Contextual Missionary and Communicator 184
  Cardinal Lavigerie's Life and Legacy 184
  Cardinal Lavigerie's Leadership Attributes and Behaviors 186
  Cardinal Lavigeries' Leadership Style 191
 Ibn Badis: Doctor of the Muslim Community 192
  Ibn Badis' Life and Legacy 192
  Theologian 194
  Ibn Badis' Leadership Attributes and Behaviors 195
  Ibn Badis' Leadership Styles 200
 Conclusion 201

Part 3: Leadership Styles of Current North African Church Leaders ... 203

Chapter 7 205
Results of Questionnaires and Interviews
 Leadership Values 205
  Spiritual Values 206
  Human Values 206
  Moral Values 207
  Relational Values 207
  Other Responses on the Question on Values 209
  Conclusion 210

- Human Qualities 210
  - Accountability 211
  - Courage 211
  - Faithfulness 211
  - Forgiveness 212
  - Generosity 212
  - Humility 212
  - Justice 213
  - Love and Its Cognates 213
  - Loyalty 214
  - Patience 214
  - Trustworthy 215
  - Wisdom 215
  - Conclusion 216
- Moral Qualities 217
  - Blameless 217
  - Integrity and Its Cognates 218
  - Sanctity 219
  - Conclusion 219
- Legitimacy 220
  - Divine Legitimacy 220
  - Divine and Human Legitimacy 221
  - Self-Appointed Leaders 221
  - Conclusion 222
- Power-Influence 223
  - Authority 223
  - Consultation 226
  - Behavior-Modeling 229
  - Conclusion 231
- Relational Behaviors 232
  - Caretaking 232
  - Dying for One's Followers 233
  - Listening 234
  - Protection 234
  - Conclusion 235
- Spiritual Characteristics-Piety 235
  - Attached to God and Jesus 235
  - Bible-Centered 236
  - Charisma/Filled with the Holy Spirit 236
  - Prayer 238

  Submission to God 238
  Conclusion 239
 Leadership Skills 239
  Leading..239
  Accepting Responsibility...240
  Teaching 241
  Visionary 241
  Administration 241
  Conclusion 242
 Leadership Metaphors..242
  Father Metaphor..243
  Servant Metaphor 243
  Shepherd Metaphor 244
  Conclusion 245
 Biblical Leadership Styles 245
  Jesus 246
  Moses 246
  Timothy 248
  Paul 248
  Other Biblical Leaders 249
  Conclusion 250
 Chapter Conclusion..252

Chapter 8 257
Integration and Implications
 The Sheikhocratic Leadership Style 258
  Caretaking Characteristics 260
  Autocratic-Consultative Leadership Style............................260
  Charismatic-Visionary Leadership style 262
  Community-Oriented 262
  Competence 263
  Paternalistic Leadership Style..265
  Strengths and Weaknesses of the *Sheikhocratic* Leadership Style ... 265
 The Servant Leadership Style...267
  Greenleaf's Categories..268
  Biblical "Servant"...270
  Strengths and Challenges of the Servant Leadership Style 271
 The Shepherd Leadership Style..273
  Shepherd Metaphor 274
  Shepherd Style Characteristics 274
  Strengths and Challenges of the Shepherd Leadership Style 277

  The Holy Man Leadership Style 278
    Divine and Human Legitimacy 279
    Autocratic-Consultative Leadership Style 280
    Charismatic-Visionary Leadership Style 281
    Piety 282
    Competence 283
    Strengths and Challenges of the Holy Man Leadership Style 288
  Conclusion 290

Appendix A 295
 Pre-Islamic Leadership Characteristics

Appendix B 297
 Islamic Leadership Characteristics

Appendix C 303
 The Sheikh's Leadership Characteristics

Appendix D 305
 Family Leadership Characteristics

Appendix E 309
 The Talib Leadership Characteristics

Appendix F 311
 The Sufi-Marabout Leadership Characteristics

Appendix G 313
 Church Leadership Values

Appendix H 315
 Church Leadership Characteristics Used to Identify Church Styles

Appendix I 319
 Augustine's Leadership Characteristics

Appendix J 321
 Lavigerie's Leadership Characteristics

Appendix K 323
 Ibn Badis' Leadership Characteristics

Appendix L 325
 Abd El-Kader's Leadership Characteristics

Appendix M 327
 BIblical Leaders Identified by the Church Leaders

Appendix N 329
    Leadership Characteristics Quoted by More Than Ten Respondents

Appendix O 331
    Leadership Characteristics of Church Leaders

Appendix P 333
    Church Leaders' Characteristics Compared with Historical, Religious, and Cultural Characteristics

Appendix Q 341
    Research Flowchart

Glossary 343
    Arabic Transliteration of Terms

Bibliography.. 347

Index... 373

List of Tables

Table 1: Various Types of Authority 27
Table 2: Shepherd Leadership 36
Table 3: Instruments, Informants and Location 69
Table 4: Pre-Islamic Leadership Roles 88
Table 5: Leadership Values 208
Table 6: Human Qualities 216
Table 7: Moral Qualities 219
Table 8: Authority 225
Table 9: Consultation 228
Table 10: Behavior Modeling 230
Table 11: Recipients Of Caretaking 233
Table 12: Jesus' Leadership Characteristics 246
Table 13: Moses' Leadership Attributes 247
Table 14: Paul's Leadership Style 249
Table 15: Attributes Of Miscellaneous Leaders 250
Table 16: Comparing Church Leadership with the
   Sheikhocratic Leadership Style 259
Table 17: Comparing Church Leadership with the
   Servant Leadership Style 268
Table 18: Comparing Church Leadership with the
   Shepherd Leadership Style 275
Table 19: Comparing Church Leadership with the
   Holy Man Leadership Style 279

Abstract

Indigenous church leadership is a new phenomenon in North Africa. Until recently, non-Muslim background believers were the only leaders of churches in this region. With the current growth of national churches there are more and more leaders from a Muslim background. While a few researchers have explored the church in North Africa, no one has looked at the specific aspects of church leadership. This study is the first one to explore leadership styles of North African church leaders. After developing a thirty-four-item questionnaire from the study of contingency theory, this study measures the leadership values, behaviors, and qualities of fifty-five church leaders in North Africa. The findings are then compared with historical, cultural, and religious leadership styles from previous studies. Four leadership styles are identified: the Shepherd, the Sheikh, the Servant, and the Holy Man. After a detailed description of the specific elements that make up these four styles, there is a discussion on how they can impact congregations and the society for good. There is strong evidence that these leadership styles of current North African leaders have contextual elements and are clearly shaped by biblical principles. The study concludes with a biblical discussion on the implications of these four styles for the current North African church. It is recommended that North African leaders incorporate teaching about these four leadership styles in their leadership development and further explore the interface between them and the biblical teaching on leadership.

Acknowledgements

I want to first express my gratitude toward God. During the forty-six years I have been his disciple, he has always showed goodness, care and love, and has never forsaken me. He has been my Good Shepherd during this research.

This book would not have been possible without the support of many people. I would like to express my gratitude to my mentor, Dr. J. Dudley Woodberry, who was abundantly helpful. He supported me and guided during every step of this research. My deepest gratitude is also due to Dr. Douglas McConnell of the doctoral committee, without whose knowledge and guidance this book would not have been successful. I also extend my thanks to Dr. Amar Djaballah, an expert in the field, who served as an outside reader on this research and made extremely useful comments that will be a blessing for the church in North Africa.

Especially, I am deeply indebted to Dr. Evelyne Reisacher, who offered invaluable assistance, constantly stimulated my thinking and encouraged me during the entire time of my research and writing. Our collaboration in ministry for over thirty years amongst North Africans has deeply impacted my life and this research.

I would like to express my gratitude to all those whose scholarship has shaped my thinking, equipped me to serve others, and transformed my views on leadership for the better. I want to thank Dr. Robert Clinton, Dr. Wilbert Shenk, Dr. Betsy Glanville, and Dr. Shelley Trebesch.

I would also like to express my love and gratitude to my beloved family: my parents, my sisters and brothers, my nephews and nieces, for their understanding, support and endless love, through the duration of my studies.

This book would not have been possible without the financial help from a number of friends. I would like to thank Catherine Headington and her son, Gregory Headington, for faithfully supporting me financially and being part of the ministry to North Africans. I could never have accomplished this research without their help. I am also so grateful to my dear friends André and Evelyne Richir and their children. They have been exceedingly generous. They have encouraged me in so many ways. Najib and Nayla Bahous, my long-term partners in ministry have faithfully cared for me. Their friendship is invaluable. I want to further express my gratitude to Jean-Pierre and Deborah Adoul who walked with me during that journey and whose advice and support were precious. Finally, I want to thank the ScholarLeaders International, who chose me as one of their scholarship recipients.

Special thanks also to all my graduate friends and those who have been students before me and whose advice and scholarly experience have been so precious for my journey in the academic world: Barbara Lundsten, Mary McVicker, Ah Ki Lim, and Wilmer Villacorta. I am grateful that they generously shared their time, their knowledge, and gave me priceless assistance.

I am indebted to many colleagues and friends with whom I had great conversations about my research, with whom I spent refreshing times and who gave me much insight: Lucien and Huguette Accad, Yves and Sana Accad, Thierry and Hélène Huser, Henri and Ruth Aoun, Gwen Flemming, Margie Waldo-Simon, Jenny, Una Lucey, Claude and Monique Demaurex, Pierre-Alain and Catherine Matthey, Pierre and Nicole André, and Monique Legal.

I want to particularly thank my brothers and sisters from North Africa. This book is for them. Without their participation, this research would not exist. I am grateful that they were so open to share their values and practices in leadership. Their contribution will certainly bless not only North Africa, but people around the world.

Part 1

Background

This section includes three chapters, which are the introduction of my research, the literature review of contemporary leadership theories, and my methodology. Chapter 1 gives a brief overview of the history and current context of the North African church in which the study will be conducted. I also integrate in this chapter my research proposal.

Chapters 2 and 3 deal with background information on the dependent variable of my research which is the leadership styles of North African church leaders. I look at leadership styles in the context of two major disciplines: Islamic and leadership studies. To establish a theoretical framework, I look in chapter 2 at what I can learn from current leadership theories. The review of leadership theories provides me with the information about definitions and research data on leadership styles. It also lays the groundwork for my research.

Chapter 3 addresses the question of methodology. I describe the flowchart of my research and how I collected various sets of data through different methods conducting sometimes primary and secondary research. I also give a detailed description of my field research, which draws heavily on social sciences from a leadership perspective.

CHAPTER 1

Introduction

In order to explain why the study of North African leadership styles is important, I present here a brief overview of the historical and present context of the North African church. The assumptions that undergird the leadership worldview of North African church leaders are influenced by sociocultural, historical and biblical factors. Before I address these issues in the body of this study, I provide the reader with a brief overview of the historical development of the North African church and a short description of its current status. I finish this section by explaining what led me to conduct this research and present a summary of my research proposal.

Rise and Decline of the Church in North Africa

No one knows for sure when and how the gospel was preached in North Africa for the first time. The New Testament mentions Libyan inhabitants who heard the gospel at the first Pentecost in Jerusalem (Acts 2:10); Simon of Cyrene[1] who carried Jesus' cross (Matt 27:32) and the believers of Cyrene who brought the gospel to Gentiles in Antioch (Acts 4:11). The first written document showing the presence of Christians in North Africa relates the martyrdom of twelve believers[2] from Scillium[3] in AD 180 (Decret 1996: 17-18; Cuoq 1984). François Decret therefore believes that

---

1. Cyrene was a Libyan port.
2. The document that relates this martyrdom is called *Actes*.
3. Scillium was a city in La Proconsulaire, a region covering the Western part of present Libya and Tunisia.

Christian religion must have been public before this event. Robin Daniel, in his study of the early North African church, suggests the gospel "had probably reached all the major ports of Mediterranean Africa within fifty years of Christ's death" (Daniel 1992: 59). Whether it is in the first or the second century, there is consensus among scholars about an early presence of Christians in North Africa.

The North African churches expanded very rapidly. Decret quotes the North African church father Tertullian who wrote in 197-198, "We are but of yesterday, and we have filled every place among you—cities, islands, fortresses, towns, market-places, the very camp, tribes, companies, palace, senate, forum" (Decret 1996; Apology 37: 4). Decret (1996: 19) thinks Tertullian may have exaggerated when he said that, "our numbers are so great—constituting all but the majority in every city," but still believes thousands of men and women became Christians. Although it may never be possible to know the exact number of believers, the vitality of the early North African churches is evidenced by archaeological findings, the writings of church fathers like Cyprian, Tertullian and Augustine, as well as numerous synods and the rise of bishoprics—there were 92-95 bishoprics in the third century (Cuoq 1984)[4] and 600-700 bishoprics in fifth century (Djilani Sergy 1986).

After those strong beginnings, the church started its decline in the sixth and seventh century. The number of bishoprics decreased to 150-200 with only 30-40 left after the Arab conquest (Djilani Sergy 1986). Christianity was at its lowest point in the eleventh century. Leon IX states that in 1053 North Africa had only five bishops left (Decret 1996). In 1076 Cyriacus was the last bishop left in North Africa (Decret 1996).[5] For several centuries Christians continued to live in North Africa, but there are no traces of organized communities and bishoprics after the Hillalian invasions in 1050 (Jehel 2005).[6]

---

4. Pierre Maraval (2005: 127) gives the number of 87 bishops attending the council of Carthage convened by Cyprian.

5. According to Decret (1996), the Arab historian Ibn abd al-Hakam mentions Christians in the 1050s, Al-Bakri talks about a church in Tlemcen in the eleventh century and Ibn Khaldun mentions the presence of Berber Christians in North Africa.

6. During the conquest of Abd el-Moumen in the 12th century, the Carthage church was dispersed and its overseers went in exile (Watt 1991).

There is no general agreement amongst scholars on the reasons for this extinction of the church in North Africa. Most authors agree that Islam's arrival in North Africa in the seventh century played a role in Christianity's demise (Cuoq 1984). Joseph Cuoq describes this decline as slow, taking half a millennium,[7] saying:

> This prolonged agony can be explained by the relative tolerance by Islam of the "heavenly" religions, according to the phrase used by Muslims to describe Christianity and Judaism. Nevertheless this tolerance was relative and did not exclude numerous restrictions and encouraged a widespread and profound undermining of the people of the Book, who were obliged to live in ghettos to preserve their identity. (Cuoq 1984: 174)

Although most authors would agree that Islam played an important role in the decline of the church, there are also other reasons advocated for this. First, the state of the church, which had been dominant in the region until the middle of the seventh century, is believed to have accelerated its own downfall. The church compromised with the world (Daniel 1992; Djilani Sergy 1986). It had become secular in many regions (Djilani Sergy 1986). There were also internal divisions in the church.[8] The Donatist controversy played a major role in the decline of African Christianity (Djilani Sergy 1986).[9] Second, the lifestyle of individual believers may have also played a role in the decline. A large number of Christians had become nominal (Daniel 1992). Many had superficial beliefs and had not given up paganism. Third, the leaders may have played a role in the disappearance of

---

[7]. Pierre Maraval writes, "Christianity survived there for several more centuries, but was a small minority" (2005: 134).

[8]. For further details, see an example of division in Maureen A. Tilley (1996 and 1997).

[9]. Maraval (2005: 135) may not totally agree with the argument that the division of the church led to its decline, at least not in an early stage. He writes, "The most striking fact about African Christianity for the whole of the 4th century is its division into two separate and violently hostile Churches, the Catholic Church and the Donatist Church: a phenomenon which, however, does not seem to have hindered its development."

Christianity.[10] There were fewer and fewer church leaders after the arrival of Islam (Cuoq 1984). Furthermore, after the eighth century, no prominent spiritual leader played as significant of a role as Tertullian and Augustine. Cuoq says, "There is no theologian, not even a minor one, worth mentioning" and grieves the "poverty of thought in Christian communities" (Cuoq 1984: 176). Fourth, the use of Latin and Greek by church leaders may have created difficulties of communication with the local believers. J. Mesnage writes that "The exclusive means of communicating the gospel in Africa was in Latin" (Mesnage 1914: 273).[11] Georges Jehel (2005) also contends that language played an important role when he talks about the absence of a Berber speaking Christianity. A fifth factor is the invasion of the Vandals who stayed in North Africa for almost a century[12] fighting catholic leaders; however, the number of bishoprics did not significantly diminish during their time.[13] Vandals were Arians that were strongly opposed to the Catholic Church's teaching (Maraval 2005). Sixth, the *dhimmi*[14] status of the Christians that pushed many to emigrate or to convert to avoid paying the *jizya*[15] (Jehel 2005). Seventh, the structure of Western Christianity that was different from the Eastern Christianity, which survived longer under Islam, may also explain this decline (Jehel 1999).[16] Finally, there are others

---

10. No one has ever studied how the leadership style affected this decline. The brief study of Augustine's leadership style in chapter 6 may provide some responses, although my study will only focus on his leadership style and not the link between the latter and the decline of the church.

11. Djilani Sergy (1986) believes that the linguistic factor may not have been as crucial for explaining the lack of commitment of the church. He argues that Augustine and other religious leaders used translators and that many people were bilingual if not trilingual in the region.

12. The Vandal kingdom lasted from 442-533 (Cuoq 1984).

13. Christian Courtois (1955) counts 650 catholic and Donatist bishoprics during the time of the Vandals.

14. The term *dhimmi* refers to the status of minority religious groups in Muslim majority lands.

15. *Jizya* is a tax minorities are paying to the governement in some majority-Muslim countries.

16. Georges Jehel (1999) mentions that monasteries were not a common religious structure in North Africa.

such as L. R. Holme (1898) who attribute the decline to solely secular and not religious factors.[17]

While communities outside of North Africa would have had little reason to believe in Christian presence in the region, the existence of Christians has never completely ceased. During the Ottoman period, for example, when captured Christian sailors in the Mediterranean Sea were held in North Africa they attested to having been visited by Catholic missionaries (Friedman 1983; Mantran 1984). There were also European traders during that period in North Africa some of whom were Christians (Renault 1992). But it is only with the French colonization of Algeria in 1830, and the establishment of the Moroccan and Tunisian protectorates, that Christianity started to regain influence in North Africa.[18] During this period, Christianity was represented by the French who migrated to North Africa as well as catholic missionaries like Triniterians, Jesuits, and the *Pères Blancs* (White Fathers) (Renault 1992). According to Direche-Slimani (1994) there was also a Kabyle Christian community in Algeria.[19] Protestant missionaries started to work in North Africa at the end of the nineteenth century (Zwemer 1902). The Eglise Protestante d'Algerie (i.e. the Protestant Church of Algeria) was founded in 1839 followed by other churches in major cities (Blanc 2006). While mainline Protestants essentially ministered to the French community, evangelicals who arrived later were more interested in ministering amongst the Muslim population.[20]

A new decline of the presence of Christianity occurred after independence of the three North African states of Morocco, Algeria and Tunisia at which time the majority of non-Muslims left the country. The Catholic and

---

17. I am indebted to the work of Djilani Sergy (1986) who first pointed me to this author. He uses Holme argument in writing his master's thesis in theology on *Des causes du déclin du christianisme en Afrique du Nord (IIè-XIIè siècles)* (The Causes of the Decline of Christianity in North Africa—second to twelfth century). Djilani Sergy quotes Holme who writes "It is to secular, not religious matters that the historian must turn to discover the reason of the extinction of the African Church" (Holme 1898: 188).

18. At the beginning of colonization, for example, Algeria was predominantly Muslim (Etienne 1989).

19. Karima Direche-Slimani (1994) numbered 1000 Christians in the 1940s.

20. Some examples of missionary organizations which started to work in North Africa at that time are the North African Mission, the Algiers Mission Band, the Methodists, the Mission Rolland and the Mennonites (Hostetler 2003).

Protestant communities kept representatives to care for the needs of the expatriates working in North Africa, but their number remains very small until today.[21]

New Beginnings of the North African Church

In the 1980s, however, there was again a revitalization of the national church. This is how Jean L. Blanc reports the words of an Algerian church leader, Hamid, who played a key role in this new beginning: "Between 1980 and 1990 there were still very few Christians. Suddenly, revival burst out and many men and women came to the Lord. This revival was preceded by a time of fasting and prayer" (Blanc 2006: 19). It is very difficult to give an exact number of church members since these churches do not have a recognized status. Recently a number of churches have become members of the Eglise Protestante d'Algérie (EPA). Other communities have stayed anonymous and autonomous (Blanc 2006). The present number of Christians is very difficult to count because the churches, with leaders and members from a Muslim background, have no official legal status in the country. Some figures claim up to 100,000 while others claim several thousands (Aït-Larbi 2008).

As the church is growing, several internal and external organizations have started to develop leadership-training programs for church leaders. However, there has never been a study that defines the leadership styles of effective North African church leaders. As a result there is an important gap in the understanding of what leadership looks like in this context. I became aware of the need to understand the style of leadership after I co-founded in 1979[22] the organization L'Ami,[23] with the vision to form local

---

21. During a conference, the late Catholic Cardinal Pierre Claverie stated that in 1989 in the diocese of Oran, Algeria, there were four hundred devoted Catholic Church members/goers for a population of six million Muslim Algerians. During that same year the priests numbered twenty-six and the nuns sixty-five in this same region (Claverie 2004).
22. At that time, in the French Protestant context, there was only one yearly gathering for North African believers organized by the North African Mission and a few individuals who had a ministry amongst Muslims.
23. The four goals of L'Ami are (1) sharing the gospel with North African, (2) leadership

fellowships where North African believers living in France could gather for prayer and worship, share common experiences, elaborate new approaches to sharing the gospel with their people, and express their faith in Jesus Christ in appropriate cultural forms. Over the years scores of leaders attended the meetings and received training at L'Ami and many have started their own organizations and fellowships in various parts of France, North Africa and Europe.

Over the years of my ministry, I became aware of shortcomings in the leadership development in the North African Christian context. In 2001, I took a sabbatical to come to Fuller Theological Seminary to pursue a Master of Arts in Islamic studies and Leadership. My final paper was on the topic of Christian leadership in a Muslim context. Although I discovered vast resources on Christian leadership in a variety of cross-cultural contexts very few of them were relevant for North Africa. The research on current Christian leadership in a Muslim North African context was almost non-existent. Most models grew out of Western theories and not a single one grew out of research conducted on the leadership models in the first-generation North African church. The only studies undertaken in this area pertained to conversion and church planting models. Not a single article or doctoral dissertation addressed the leadership styles of the pastors of these emerging churches.

There are several reasons research on the current leadership styles of North African leaders is important. First, there are very few resources on Christian leaders from a Muslim background. We don't know how the Muslim family and society impacts Christian leadership values and behaviors. Second, there have been very few studies conducted on North African historical leaders to identify their leadership styles. Third, the leadership styles of North African pastors have never been described and evaluated. It is not surprising that there is not much data on the current church, since this is a first generation church.

For all these reasons, I believe that my research could strengthen the churches in North Africa and in similar contexts. Historically, most

---

training for North African believers, (3) equipping French churches to reach out to North Africans, and (4) creating communication tools for the North African context.

leadership training models used in North Africa were borrowed from the West. Because no real discussion has taken place on this issue the church, on the one hand, has borrowed heavily from leadership models developed in foreign contexts which are not relevant to the needs of their culture and society. On the other hand, the church has also relied heavily on leaders' natural leadership styles from their cultural and religious context[24] without addressing whether they are faithful to the Bible. I believe that greater effectiveness will flow from leadership styles that are culturally and socially relevant and biblically faithful.[25]

Purpose of Study

This study is a research on common leadership styles for North African religious leaders from historical and cultural perspectives and their influence on their congregations and society for the good. The purpose of my research is to investigate the leadership styles in North African churches in order to better equip church leaders to nurture their congregations and be light and salt in society. My goal is to identity North African Church leadership styles that are currently relevant, biblically sound and influence congregations and society for the good. There are currently between 50,000 to 100,000 known believers in North Africa. I delimited my research to the leaders of congregations formed by North Africans nationals from a Muslim background and who were willing to participate and available to meet with me during my trips to North Africa. Since there are no specific denominations in North Africa for these types of churches, the word "leader" in my study

---

24. For these leaders, the only leadership reference was their own past and what they learned about leadership by watching their parents, their schoolmaster, the *imam* of their mosque, their manager at work and their political leaders. Most of them led their own church with these models in mind.

25. As their biblical knowledge increased, they tried to apply the biblical principles to their ministry but often with no analysis and no missiological reflection on their own context. These leaders were not always aware that they were both affected by their personal heritage as well as by their context of living. All the lessons learned through education, cultural and socio-political context influenced their leadership style without their awareness.

refers to someone who leads Friday church services, teaches the Bible, is a church leader, or leads a local Christian ministry.

CHAPTER 2

An Overview of Contemporary Leadership Theories

In this section, I review current leadership theories in order to understand how they define leadership styles. I will apply the definitions I find in these theories to develop an instrument that will help me explore leadership styles of North African leaders.

I have purposely chosen to briefly describe each theory so that North African church leaders, who may have a limited knowledge of English literature related to leadership, can understand my approach and participate in the definition of their own leadership styles using the data presented in this work.

Great-Man Theory

Great-Man theory in the early 1900s studied the characteristics of influential leaders (Carlysle 1897). It defined the style of extraordinary leaders by looking at their character. This approach provides limited resources for my research for the following reasons. First, my field research focuses on leaders in general without specifically targeting those great leaders such as Augustine, Cyprian and Tertullian. Secondly, great- man theory only considered styles from an ontological perspective looking solely at what is innate in a leader and not the other elements that make up a leadership style as it is theoretically defined today.

Trait-Theory

Trait-Theory (Stogdill 1974) focused on the personality or innate traits of the leader to define his/her style. In my research I do not focus solely on traits for the following reasons. First, traits are resistant to change. Second, personality traits are only one component of any given leadership style. Many successful leaders I interviewed in this region are not chosen because of their innate traits. Since the majority of the churches are first generation churches, leaders are chosen primarily because of their spiritual gifts and their willingness to serve the church. One of the main reasons why leaders do not discriminate between traits is because there are not enough Christian leaders to care for the fast growing number of converts and as a result anyone is welcome to lead as long as he/she possesses the spiritual gifts of preaching, healing, prophecy or teaching. Finally, trait-theory was challenged by many because of the difficulty in finding traits that were consistent across leaders (Stogdill 1948; Mann 1959). Eventually leadership theorists looked at other facets of a leader such as behavior.

Having argued that traits are not the essential elements that define leaders, my field research may provide useful information about personality traits amongst leaders. For example, during my ministry I have learned from North African Christian workers that church leaders need to have a strong personality to exercise their leadership. Therefore is it possible that there is a correlation between strong will and leadership effectiveness? Some scholars have tried to conduct research in this area. For example, Saad Eddin Ibrahim (1982) studied the leadership traits of Egyptian leader Gamal Abd el-Nasser (1918-1970) to understand why he was so effective.[1] But after describing the personality traits of this influential leader, the author is not completely satisfied. Like me, he investigates additional theories that provide ways to look at other factors that may have shaped Nasser's leadership style.

---

1. Ibrahim writes, "In victory and in defeat, in his life and at his death, he commanded an unprecedented sway over the passions, minds and behavior of people from the Arab-Persian Gulf to the Atlantic Ocean" (1982: 30).

Behavioral Theories

Behavioral theories identified that leadership styles are broader than traits and also include recurring qualities, attributes, and behaviors (Hogan quoted by Hugues, Ginnett, and Curphy 2006). This approach provides greater resources for my study because it allows me to research elements of leadership styles through questionnaires and participant observation. As Richard Hughes, Robert C. Ginnett and Gordon Curphy (2006) state, "one advantage of looking at leaders in terms of behaviors instead of, say, personality is that behavior is often easier to measure; leadership behaviors can be observed." In this study I will concentrate on the qualities, attributes and behaviors of leaders.

Contingency Theories

As leadership theory developed, theorists started to broaden the area of research from the individual leaders to his/her followers and context. While in the past leadership effectiveness was measured by the leader, now followers and their context have become important elements of study. Researchers studying leadership ceased solely evaluating personality traits and values of individual leaders and began to also assess their interaction with followers and contexts. In behavioral and contingency theory, researchers investigate "differences in leadership styles or patterns of leadership behavior and their effects" (Bass 1990: 418).

According to contingency theories "leaders should make their behaviors contingent on certain aspects of the followers or the situation in order to improve leadership effectiveness" (Hughes, Ginnett and Curphy 2006: 385). Paul Hersey and Kenneth S. Blanchard (1982) further underlined that leadership style is a function of situation and follower maturity. In their Situational Leadership Model, Hersey and Blanchard, Johnson (1969) highlight the fact that person and situation "are not independent, but rather are interdependent." For example, Victor Vroom (1976) emphasized the importance of looking at the nature of the situation in which the leadership behavior is displaced. By focusing on followers and situation, contingency theories also emphasized the leaders' ability to "change their behaviors as situational and follower characteristics change" (Hughes, Ginnett, and Curphy 2006). These concepts are key to my research. While my study essentially focuses on the description of current leadership styles in North Africa, one advantage of integrating contingent theory to my research is that I can make recommendations to North African leaders that link their leadership to their followers and context.

As both followers and context became key elements to define particular leadership styles, new definitions of leadership styles emerged that enriched leadership studies. By designing the least-preferred coworker (LPC) scale and measuring the leader-follower relations, the task structure and the position power, contingency theorist Fred Fiedler,[2] for example, was able to evaluate in which situation relations-oriented or task-oriented leaders were most effective.[3] This study has been extremely relevant to assess different styles between individualistic countries and more community based ones such as those in North Africa. From my own experience my hypothesis is that North African leaders are more relation-oriented than task-oriented.

This paragraph briefly shows how theorists refined their understanding of leadership styles by creating a plethora of new methods to measure styles and creating new concepts and definitions. Hervey, Blanchard, and Johnson (1969) for example, penned the following definition of leadership style as "the consistent behavior patterns that they [the leaders] use when they are working with and through other people, as perceived by those people."[4] Through their Leader Match approach, Fiedler, Chemers and Mahar studied leadership style and situation control; the latter refers to "the amount of control and influence that the leader has over the group, the task, and the outcome" (1964: 3). And as a third example, the Path-Goal

---

2. Fred Fiedler developed a contingency theory that postulates three key dimensions in leadership effectiveness: (1) leader-member relation, (2) task structure and (3) position-power (Hersey, Blanchard and Johnson 1969).

3. For Fiedler the task-oriented leader is "most likely to be effective in situations that are most favorable or most unfavorable to him or her" and the relations-oriented leader is "most likely to be effective in situations between the two extremes" (Bass 1990: 47).

4. As I will discuss later, this research does not include interviews of followers, although I believe this should be an important element in future research. Since this research is on the first generation of believers, it seems more appropriate to only focus on leaders: their followers are young believes and may not understand the purpose of this research.

theory (Hughes, Ginnett and Curphy 2006: 201) defines leadership behaviors as a function of "intelligence, personality traits, emotional intelligence, values, attitudes, interests, knowledge, and experience."[5] Instead of looking at the leader in a vacuum, all these theories looked at the leader in relationship with followers and contexts.

Contingency theories have several implications for my study. First, they help me evaluate leadership styles by not solely utilizing elements such as personality traits or values, but by drawing resources from behaviors, attitudes and experiences of leaders in specific contexts. Although my research has not included interviewing followers, I have nevertheless asked questions to leaders pertaining to their relationship with their followers. I have also investigated the ministry context of North African leaders.

Second, contingency theories allow me to posit that leaders should be able to adapt to their context.[6] Kenneth K. Killinski and Jerry C. Wofford (1973: 78) rightly say that, "to be more effective, the leader should be able to adapt his style of leadership to the people and the environment in which they operate." Helen Doohan (1984: 166) agrees in saying that "the most effective leaders adapt and augment their responses according to environmental and situational demand." It has been observed that "violation of cultural norms by leaders and managers will result in dissatisfaction, conflict, and resistance on the part of followers or subordinates and, at times, lower performance of leaders, their work units, and their subordinates" (House et al. 2004: 64). Other researchers such as P. R. Harris and R. T. Moran (1989) also underline the fact that leaders must be able to adapt

---

5. The same authors say that, "leaders should make their behaviors contingent on certain aspects of the followers or the situation in order to improve leadership effectiveness" (Hughes, Ginnett and Curphy 2006: 385).
6. Not all contingency theories are equal in the approach of leadership effectiveness. Fiedler's contingency theory has some weaknesses since "the specification of situational favorableness has been vague and variable across studies" (Chermers and Rice 1973: 102). According to Fiedler (1993: 6) himself, there needs to be more studies to understand the interaction between the Least Preferred Coworker (LPC) and the situation control and "to specify how this leads to specific changes in leader behavior." But Fiedler (1993) also points out the stress that can be created by sudden changes in behavior due to the change of situation, and this suggests that for leaders to adapt to a new context, stress and anxiety need to be taken into consideration.

their leadership style to different cultural contexts (which in turn require different behaviors).

How does this last point affect my research? I believe leaders should be able to evaluate whether leadership styles shaped by Western theories are relevant for a context where Islam is dominant. Contingency theories are useful because they explain why some leadership styles may not be effective. Fiedler (1993: 3) posits that, "personality and situational factors interact in generating feelings of uncertainty and anxiety." Could it be possible that these types of human qualities are at work in church leaders that participated in this research? According to my own observation, this is often underestimated in current North African leadership. I want to make church leaders aware of the fact that they are not operating in a vacuum and that they must become aware that the various situations in which they operate must be taken into consideration. I want North African leaders to become aware of what Bass, et al. (1979) underlined when he said that national boundaries make "considerable difference" in leadership style. The concept of effectiveness was first believed to have a universal meaning, but soon, theorists discovered that what is effective in one culture may not be effective in another. Bass (1990: 785) says, "As we move from one culture or country to another, we see systematic differences in what is regarded as important for effective leadership and explanations for why this is so." DePree (1992: 146) suggests that effective leaders, "Understand the context in which people work." Unfortunately, in becoming believers, many North Africans would like to escape the dominant context impacted by Islam. After their conversion, they often feel disconnected from their roots and turn to the West for models of leadership. One of the main reasons I wrote this book is to create awareness about these issues.

I expect that my recommendations may trigger some discussions or debate between church leaders as they will have to wrestle with questions such as "Are Muslim values similar to Christian values and if so, can we adopt them to be more effective as leaders in our context? Are religious values a separate category that cannot be equated with cultural values and be adopted in cross-cultural leadership?" As I have stated before I believe that understanding the context of leadership is essential for its effectiveness. For example, Fiedler and Hersey's contingency theories may help North

African leaders to understand how anxiety and stress affect one's context. Clinton's (1992: 46-47) inflexibility-flexibility continuum, where flexibility is seen "in terms of style range and style adaptability, as well as the ability to change attitudes and plans in light of varying situations" will further equip church leaders to address these issues.[7] There are many more implications of contingency theories that could be highlighted to encourage leadership research in North Africa. Lessons I draw for this current research is that the leaders cannot be studied out of context. In order to best define current leadership styles in North Africa, I must pay attention to the leader, the follower and the context. The data collected on the field cannot be analyzed without understanding these concepts.

Although Fiedler's research provides important resources to my study in highlighting the importance of the situation and the relationship between leader and follower, it nevertheless presents a number of weaknesses. In effect, according to Fiedler (1969), it is not the leadership style that should change but the situation for greater effectiveness. He writes, "We can improve the effectiveness of leadership by accurate diagnosis of the group-task situation and by altering the leader's work environment." In cases where leaders are less effective, he suggests changing "the composition of the group, by including or excluding individuals whose background and language differ from that of the leader" (1969: 241).

Instead of requiring a change of context, other theorists suggest the adaptation of the leader to the context and the followers. I will therefore pay attention to the relationship between follower and leader, as Fiedler, Chermers and Mahar (1964: 36) did when they underlined the importance of "leader-member relations" and "support and trust" of followers. The relationship may vary according to contexts but is still relevant. Fiedler, Chermers and Mahar (1964: 37) say that "some groups traditionally have good relations with their leaders while others traditionally fight their leaders." They also say, "If you have the group's support then you need

---

[7]. Clinton (1992: 47) gives the following suggestions, "If high inflexibility, either engineer situation to fit the leader personality style or move leader to a situation more appropriate to that styles" and "If high flexibility, leader can be trained to learn skills and attitudes to offset personality bent and improve style range and adaptability."

not depend on your position power or task structure to get compliance" (Fiedler, Chermers and Mahar 1964: 27).

My chapter on North African culture shows that North African culture is collectivistic and not individualistic and therefore the leadership style of pastors will be relationship-motivated rather than people-motivated (Fiedler 1993). But the fact that the culture is collectivistic may also be misleading. It may be that leaders emphasize the interpersonal relations in all other activities except leadership.

Finally, another limitation of contingency theories, according to Hughes, Ginnet, and Curphy (2006) is that they received mixed support particularly in field settings. Reasons given by these authors include that findings are based on a false assumption that leaders can accurately assess followers and situation; second, numerous factors affecting leader and follower behaviors are often left out in field settings (Hughes, Ginnett, and Curphy 2006). This should not lead me to discard the theory but rather make me more aware of the difficulties to have valid and reliable data on the followers and the context. More than one research is certainly needed to allow a cross-verification of data from multiple sources.

Transactional Leadership

As contingency theories developed, transactional leadership theories shifted the focus of research primarily on the transaction or exchange between follower and leader. Leaders were encouraged to identify expectations of followers and respond to them (Popper, Mayseless, and Castelnovo 2000). Transactional leaders were usually not able to develop strong emotional bonds with their followers or "inspire followers to do more than followers thought they could" (Hughes, Ginnett, and Curphy 2006: 423). Instead they motivate followers by "setting goals and promising rewards for desired performance" (Hughes, Ginnett, and Curphy 2006: 423). Although this style may exist in North African culture, I foresee that the only reward that North African leaders may expect is an internal one. In a Muslim majority context, being a pastor does not increase their social status. Very few pastors receive salaries and most of the work is based on voluntary participation in the various ministry tasks by followers and pastor. However, it is important to know this theory so that when analyzing the data I collect in my field research I will be able to recognize elements of this theory in the current practices of the church. I will probe the data for narratives or metaphors that express the fact that leaders set goals for followers that bring some type of reward. As I mentioned earlier, it might be that the eternal reward is a very strong incentive for followers.

Another way leaders with a Transactional style may influence followers is by the satisfaction of their needs. This model may prove relevant for my research. In his schema Irving Knickerbocker (1958) said that the dynamic pattern of the relationship between leader and followers is that the latter follow leaders who "provide means for the satisfaction of their needs." In one of my pilot focus groups consisting of North African leaders in North Africa and in Europe, the following question was raised: why are North African leaders, with limited theological training, more effective than those with extensive theological training coming from Europe? One North African leader explained that despite limited theological training North African pastors living among their followers in the same village knew their needs better and were therefore able to meet them. In their sermons they would define the felt needs of the followers and eloquently outline how God and the community could meet them. This is similar to what Knickerbocker (1958: 6) says when he writes, "If the group members see satisfaction of needs in the direction the leader indicates, if he believes the leader will serve as a means for getting those satisfactions, the group members follow." Greenleaf (1996: 14) adds another dimension when he says that, "an important aspect of religious leadership is the nurturing of seekers."

Although I believe that leaders must be able to show they have some control over the means, I also believe that there is a danger in only following the leader because he has this approach. This approach to ministry has led certain leaders to rely heavily on the prosperity gospel teaching. A bad leader could use this to exert detrimental control over followers. This is why the Bible encourages followers to challenge the leader and evaluate his/her actions and words in order to see if the way he/she meets needs is not simply a way to gain more control over followers. It is certainly an aspect of the transactional leadership style that I will revisit as I discuss the data collected in my field research. According to this discussion on transactional theory, the major elements that I will be looking for when I define transactional leadership styles will include concepts such as exchange relationship, meeting needs, rewards, setting goals, status quo, and no major change in the organization or church (see Burns 1978).

Transformational Leadership

Transformational theorists, such as James MacGregor Burns and Bernard Bass, further defined leadership styles. In contrast with the previous theory, they did not look at the transaction between leaders and followers solely in terms of the followers' needs. Instead, they portrayed the leader as a transformational agent and emphasized moral and emotional values (Burns 1978; Ehrlich et al. 1990). Transformational leaders in these theories, encourage followers to do more than they are "originally expected to do" (Bass 1985: 20). By doing so, transformational leaders become role models for their followers.

Bernard Bass (1985), a key theorist after James MacGregor, posited that transformational leaders have charisma, individual consideration and stimulate their followers intellectually.[8] But charisma is not enough (Fry 2003); transformational leaders desire that their followers reach their potential and go beyond self-interests. Transformational leaders also develop "strong emotional bonds with followers" (Fry 2003: 423). Motivation, morality, and emotional attachment are important components of transformational leadership (Burns 1978; Shamir, House and Arthur 1992). The leader not only looks at the self-interests of his/her followers but moves toward transformation of followers and context (Bass 1990). In my field research in North Africa, the various concepts defined in this paragraph such as charisma, strong emotional bonds, motivation and morality, and

---

8. See the difference between "idealized influence" where according to Bass (1985) the leader considers the needs of the follower before his own needs, does not use power for personal gain, has high moral standards and has challenging goals for followers.

transformation of the follower will help me identify various transformational leadership styles.

It is encouraging for my study that Hughes, Ginnett and Curphy (2006) reported that transformational leadership has been observed in all countries. I therefore expect to find transformational leadership in North Africa. Furthermore, several of the features of transformational leadership I have personally observed among leaders during my ministry (such as the importance of the emotional bond and the desire to have a leader who can be imitated as a role model) certainly point to some elements of potential transformational leadership styles.

Visionary or Charismatic Leadership

Another important theory, closely related to transformational leadership seems to reflect what I have observed in North Africa during my thirty years of ministry. This theory, developed by Max Weber (1946)[9] identified the charismatic leadership style[10] and defined three types of authority systems: traditional, legal-rational, and charismatic (Hughes, Ginnett, and Curphy 2006).[11] According to him charismatic leaders have (1) a strong desire to influence others, (2) are role models, (3) set moral goals, (4) have high expectations, (5) are confident in follower's abilities, (6) motivate followers by addressing their needs for esteem, power and affiliation and (7) tie follower's identities to the collective identity of a group or an organization (Weber 1947; Fry 2003). I have noticed that several of these elements were expressed among North African church leaders such as role modeling, setting high expectation, and moral goals.

---

9. Bass (1990: 185) reports how Trice and Beyer summarized Weber's concept of charismatic leadership in five components: "(1) a person with extraordinary gifts, (2) a crisis, (3) a radical solution to the crisis, (4) followers who are attracted to the exceptional person because they believe that they are linked through him to transcendent powers, and (5) validation of the person's gifts and transcendence in repeated experiences of success."

10. This style is a transformational style with certain specifics (Bass and Avolio 1993).

11. Charismatic leadership is sometimes used interchangeably with transformational leadership. This is an unfortunate act.

This leadership style differs from the transactional leadership style in which the importance is placed on negotiating the contract between leader and follower (Burns 1978; Bass 1990: 23). It is transformational because it transforms the "needs, values, preferences, and aspirations of followers to become highly committed to the leader's mission, to make significant personal sacrifices in the interest of the mission, and to perform above and beyond the call of duty" (Shamir, House, and Arthur 1993: 82).

According to Bass (1990), followers of charismatic leaders have a strong desire to identify with them.[12] According to him, "The follower's belief in the solutions comes as a consequence of their faith in the charismatic leader" (Bass 1990). Inspirational leaders will attract people to their goals and purpose, and truly charismatic leaders will attract followers to their person (Downton 1973).[13] Robert J. House and Boaz Shamir (1993: 97) show that "charismatic leaders are visionary" because they bring change in many other areas to their context and in their followers. Charismatic leaders have motivation, a strong vision, charisma, change, and emotional ties with their followers (Hughes, Ginnett, and Curphy 2006). Several Muslim leaders have been called charismatic including (Hughes, Ginnett, and Curphy 2006) Muhammad, the Ayatollah Khomeini and Muhammad Omar. The same study also identifies Jesus, Martin Luther King and Nelson Mandela as charismatic leaders. It is therefore highly possible that my research will identify charismatic leaders.

In times of crisis, followers often put greater hope in charismatic and visionary political leadership rather than in organizations (Hollander 1993). As Terri Scandura and Peter Dorfman (2004: 278) write, "Crisis can provide a need, a need for people to have a leader to look up for guidance."

---

12. Later, Bass (1985) identified four styles: charismatic leadership, inspirational leadership, intellectual stimulation and individualized consideration. Then Bernard M. Bass and Bruce J. Avolio (1993) added contingent reward, management-by-exception and laissez-faire (laissez-faire describes a style in which the leader is minimally involved in decision making and leaves almost total freedom to the follower to plan, lead and organize).

13. It might be possible at the end of my research to make a distinction between inspirational or charismatic leaders. My assumption is that I will find more inspirational leaders, whose followers comply with the directives, rather then charismatic leaders whose followers comply with the person.

One may wonder whether the many challenges and difficulties churches face in Muslim dominant context may not call for this type of leadership.

Based on my experience in North Africa I hypothesize that I will find a charismatic leadership style in the church. That kind of leadership has alternative definitions in a secular context (House and Shamir 1993).[14] In effect, charismatic leadership in a Christian context usually describes the type of leaders that "emphasize the gift of healing, prophecy, and words of knowledge" or some forms of leadership in Pentecostalism (Gill 2000: 173). Leadership theory however describes charismatic leaders as "passionate, driven individuals who are able to paint a compelling vision of the future" (Hughes, Ginnett, and Curphy 2006: 405). The former definition places the emphasis on spiritual capacities and the latter on human capacities. In my research, leaders will be defined as charismatic or visionary when they have vision, human charisma, transform people and structures, have strong emotions, create strong personal attachments with followers, and rhetorical skills (Weber 1964; Tucker 1968).

Autocratic, Democratic and Laissez-Faire Leadership

Power is a concept that has always interested leadership theorists. Hughes, Ginnett, and Curphy (2006: 107) state that, "Some of history's earliest characterizations of leaders concerned their use of power." They then quote two key theorists and their definition of power: first House who defined power as "the capacity to produce effects on others" and Bass who defined power as the "potential to influence others" (House and Bass as quoted in Hughes, Ginnett, and Curphy 2006: 107).

---

14. I will essentially rely for my research on House and Shamir's definition of charismatic leadership which they stated as follows: "We define charismatic leadership as an interaction between leaders and their followers that results in (1) making followers' self-esteem contingent on their involvement in the vision and the mission articulated by the leader, (2) strong internalization of the leaders' values and goals by the followers, (3) strong personal or moral (as opposed to calculative) commitment to these values and goals, and (4) a willingness on the part of followers to transcend their own self-interests for the sake of the collective (team or organization)" (1993: 86).

Kurt Lewin, R. Lippit and R.K. White (1939) defined three styles of leadership that are helpful to evaluate power and influence of leaders. These styles are called autocratic, democratic and laissez-faire. In autocratic leadership, the leader has sole power and does not involve his/her followers in decision-making. Democratic leadership involves a greater participation of the follower (Lewin, Lippit, and White 1939). Laissez-faire describes a leadership style where the leader is rarely involved in the supervision of the work of the follower and leaves him or her much space for individual decision-making, planning, organizing and executing. These three categories will be helpful to evaluate the style of leadership found in North African churches. Although I will not be using the Lewin's leadership style questionnaire to assess the styles, I can still draw from the definitions of these three styles.

A further expansion of these categories are as follows: the commonly used framework of (1) authoritarian versus democratic leadership, (2) participative versus directive leadership, (3) relations versus task-orientated leadership, (4) consideration versus initiating structure, and (5) laissez-faire leadership versus motivation to manage. These definitions again provide good resources for evaluating the data I will collect (Bass 1990). Other ways to categorize styles are directive, manipulative, consultative, participative and delegative (Bass and Valenzi 1973).[15]

The four styles that theorists have defined as concern for task, concern for people, directive leadership, and participative have been researched in North Africa. I was surprised that the research found not only people-oriented

---

15. Bass and Valenzi (1973: 139) give the following definitions of the five categories: "(1) Direction: Telling subordinates what is expected of them, seeing that they work to capacity, emphasizing meeting deadlines, setting standards, ruling with an iron hand, encouraging uniformity, scheduling subordinates' tasks, telling subordinates to follow rules and regulations, changing subordinates' duties without first talking it over with them. (2) Manipulation: Doing personal favors for subordinates, changing behaviors to fit occasion, persuading, promising, making subordinates compete with each other, timing the release of information, making political alliances, maintaining social distance, bending rules, reassigning tasks to balance work load. (3) Consultation: Being candid and open to questions, listening to subordinates, trying out subordinates' ideas, giving advance notice of changes. (4) Participation: Sharing decision-making, making attitudes clear, arranging meetings, putting group suggestions into operation, treating subordinates as equal, being approachable and friendly. (5) Delegation: Exhibiting confidence in subordinates, leaving members free to follow their own course, permitting subordinates to make their own decisions."

leaders, a natural product of the society's communal orientation, but also task-oriented leaders. In addition I was surprised that the research found more evidence of directive leadership than participative leadership (Wright 1996: 36-37). In effect, although the hierarchical model of authority may call for a more directive leadership style, North African leadership is also characterized by leaders who include followers in decision-making through the practice of consultation (*shura*). The reason why the leadership style of North African leaders cannot be labeled correctly may be because Lewin's model does not measure a style that combines personal authority with consultation. This style is different from the participative or democratic leadership style (Triandis 1993). It cannot, however, be labeled autocratic since the decision-making involves the consensus of the community. The North African model may be closer to what Clinton (1992) calls a consensus style in Acts 15 and Acts 16. In this style, Clinton writes, "there is much give and take in arriving at a decision" and the "final decision carries the weight of the entire group." (1992: 66). It may be that new questionnaires should be developed to assess this style. My assumption was that consensus is a common practice in the Muslim world, but I was surprised to find that H. Kabasakal and M. Bodur (1998) said that making decisions by consensus is becoming popular in the West.

TABLE 1: Various Types of Authority

(Adapted from Xavière Remacle)

1. Traditional authority	Custom, family, tribe and religion
2. Rational legal authority	Bureaucratic, impersonal, positional, modernity
3. Charismatic authority	Rooted in a leadership personal quality and attributes; influence because of who you are
4. Interactive authority	Rooted primarily in social interaction with others; participative with the followers; transformational

Servant Leadership

More recently a new style of leadership has been defined. I choose to include the servant leadership style in my discussion of contemporary leadership theories because following my pilot study North African church leaders made so many references to the servant metaphor that I needed to find a framework that would enable me to evaluate it from a leadership perspective. The servant leadership style originally defined by Robert K. Greenleaf (1970) provided a useful model because it emphasizes that leaders look at the interest of the followers instead of their own. According to Greenleaf (1970: 27) the "servant-leader *is* servant first" instead of being leader first. He writes:

> The difference manifests itself in the care taken by the servant-first to make sure that other people's highest priority needs are being served. The best test, and difficult to administer, is: do those served grow as persons; do they, while being served, become healthier, wiser, freer, more autonomous, more likely themselves to become servants? And, what is the effect on the least privileged in society; will they benefit, or, at least, will they not be further deprived? (Greenleaf 1970: 27)

Larry Spears, the CEO of Robert K. Greenleaf Center for Servant Leadership, says, "Greenleaf concluded that the great leader is first experienced as a servant to others, and that this simple fact is central to the leader's greatness." (Spears 2000). Spears continued: "True leadership emerges from those whose primary motivation is a deep desire to help others."

According to Greenleaf (1970) the servant leader has the following characteristics: awareness, conceptualization, empathy,[16] foresight, healing,

---

16. According to Greenleaf (1970: 33), empathy is "the imaginative projection of one's own consciousness into another being." He adds, "the servant always accepts and empathizes, never rejects" (2002: 33). Empathy is closely related to "tolerance of imperfection" and "acceptance" (Greenleaf 1970: 34-35).

listening,[17] persuasion,[18] and commitment to the growth of people, building community, and stewardship. These categories will serve as criteria to define whether servant leadership styles are found in the North African church context from a contemporary leadership perspective.

Greenleaf (1970) has inspired many Christian authors because of the implicit reference to biblical servanthood especially portrayed in Jesus' example (Banks and Ledbetter 2004; Block 1993). Clinton (1992: 46) calls servanthood the basal attitude in a Christian leader. Ken Blanchard and Phil Hodges (2005:12) write that "for followers of Jesus, servant leadership isn't an option; it's a mandate." As will be discussed later, this style is attractive to secular[19] and Muslim theorists (Beekun and Badawi 1999).

Following the publication of Greenleaf's research, many church leaders around the world have been leaning toward the applicability of his findings to church contexts, especially because servanthood seems to resonate well with biblical concepts. Jeff R. Hale and Dail L. Fields, who compared servant leadership in Ghana and the USA (2005), said that although Greenleaf Centers of Servant Leadership have been established on most continents "there is little empirical evidence concerning the applicability of servant leadership across cultures" (2005: 398). These authors go on to explain why it is difficult to use Greenleaf's principles across cultures. I include here only those reasons most applicable to the cultural context I study. First, some cultures do not view followers' willingness to "exercise initiative and direct their own activities" positively (2005: 398); second,

---

17. Greenleaf says, "a true natural servant automatically responds to any problem by listening first." (1970: 31). He expands by saying, "true listening builds strength in other people" (1970: 31).

18. Greenleaf says, "Rather than using their authority to force people to follow, a servant-leader uses persuasion. They are clear and persistent. And while some leaders take on huge institutions, others lead by persuading one person at a time or by taking one small action at a time."

19. Although the theory is attractive to secular theorists, the question of the spiritual element of this style is still debated. Ken Blanchard has said that "servant leadership without a spiritual foundation is just another management technique," and I believe Robert Greenleaf would also agree, even though he argued endlessly about this with friends like Dr. Robert Lynn and retired Episcopal Bishop Simms. Greenleaf simply did not want servant leadership to be seen as a function of only one religious tradition—even Christianity. He also thought the word "God" had become too imprecise to express what he meant, and knew that its use would limit consideration of servant leadership by business organizations and others.

"in higher power-distance cultures, leaders whose followers take initiative on their own without waiting for explicit direction may be seen as weak leaders" (2005: 398); and third, "in cultures which are more collective, followers may not feel comfortable with leaders who emphasize follower individual initiative and creativity because these are viewed as being best accomplished through group discussion and decisions" (2005: 398). I certainly think that these points must be addressed when I analyze my data. I may also find that when church leaders use the metaphor of the servant, they are only thinking of the biblical concept of servant leadership, which may not completely match Greenleaf's model.

The Relationship of the Leader with God

Another variable that secularists do not include is the relationship of the leader with God or an Ultimate Reality. Since I study leaders who have faith in God and who believe God called them to leadership, I need to explore theories that will help me engage this dimension of leadership. Three fields of study are helpful for measuring the relationship of leaders to God: biblical leadership theories, spiritual leadership theories and Islamic leadership theories. They will briefly be discussed in this section.

Biblical Leadership Theories

What makes Christian leadership distinct is the leader's relationship to God, to God's people and to God's task and vision. The research on biblical leadership will highlight this important area which secular contingency or transformational theories do not. By analyzing the Bible and biblical leaders, Christian authors have added their own definitions to leadership theory (McIntosh and Rima 1997; Wright 2000; Clinton 1992; DePree 1992). For example, Max DePree (1992: xi) writes, "Leadership is much more an art, a belief, a condition of the heart, than a set of things to do."

It is important to note that research on Christian leadership draws from secular research. Many Christian leadership researchers draw from secular theories. Edgar J. Elliston, for example, shows the importance of taking the context and the follower into consideration and writes that leadership is "a complex influence process in which leaders and followers interact in a context or a series of contexts over time" (1993: 22). Another example comes from Clinton (1992: 39) when he says "the definitional leadership style of an individual is the behavioral pattern that a leader exhibits when attempting to influence the attitude and action of followers in a given leadership act." In this definition Clinton borrows from secular leadership theorists. As a result this should encourage North African leaders to learn from secular theories as well.

One of the major distinctives of Christian leadership is that it defines God as an agent of change. For example, when personality traits may be very resistant to change, Clinton (1992: 46) writes about servanthood saying, "If this basic leadership value can be changed by God's transforming process, then other values toward task or relationship behavior can also be modified or used for God's purposes." This makes Christian leadership unique compared to secular leadership because God is actively engaged in the process.

Another difference in Christian leadership is the fact that the sacred texts may provide models and values very different from secular models. For example Banks and Ledbetter (2004: 34) write,

> A stark contrast can be drawn between God's and the world's view of leadership. Their relationship may be described as a tension between a purely business model of leadership and one based on biblical models and values. Or it may be expressed in terms of a control-based as opposed to a servant-oriented model of leadership.

Clinton adds that some leadership attitudes and values are only learned from God. He writes, "Servanthood value is not a natural part of any leader's inherited personality bent or culturally determined style. It is learned only through growth as a Christian leader via the power of the Holy Spirit" (Clinton 1992: 82). This is probably why many leaders in North Africa are reluctant to borrow leadership styles from the Muslim community. They believe only God as he is portrayed in the Bible can bring real transformation. Although I agree with Clinton's quote and with my brothers and sisters, I nevertheless believe that God can use leadership styles from other religious contexts and transform them even if they do not honor him. On the other hand God can use cultural models as long as they do not contradict biblical values. For example, the attitude and values of servanthood in Islam may have some common characteristics with Christian servanthood. The same could be said about hospitality or patience both of which are found in Islam and Christianity even if a closer look may reveal some differences in meaning.

Secular leadership and Christian leadership may also be different because what is effective in the secular world may not be regarded as effective in its Christian counterpart. For example, in the Bible there are numerous narratives showing that God's standards of leadership are different from those of humans.[20] Many Christians believe that God is the one who eventually determines the effectiveness of leadership. This issue is subject to debate in the Christian community: to what extent has God given freedom to humans to exercise their opinion on worldly matters and to evaluate effective leadership? I will leave the application of these approaches to the church leaders in North Africa. Although many theorists would not hesitate to assess a leader's effectiveness using human tools, I also believe that Christians should study leadership styles in the church not only to understand how leaders can be more effective, but also how they can be more biblical. I believe that a Christian leader must strive for effectiveness, but not to the extent where he/she denies biblical requirements.

Another crucial question about church leadership is to define whether there are values, attributes or behaviors that are specific to Christian leadership. Some theorists believe that there are specific Christian values in leadership (Banks and Lebetter 2004). Others like DePree list key attributes that are essential for effective leadership such as truth, access, discipline, accountability, respect, hope, justice, tolerance, unity and more (Banks and Ledbetter 2004). Wright (2000: 7) adds to that discussion saying that, "Leadership for Christians is about God, not about us." Bank and Ledbetter (2004: 16-17) talk about being "in line with God's purposes" saying:

---

20. One example is when God chosen David as the future king, and Samuel argues saying that it should be David's older brother (1 Sam 16).

Leadership involves a person, group, or organization who shows the way in an area of life—whether in the short- or long-term—and in doing so both influences and empowers enough people to bring about change in that area. Such leadership may be good or bad depending on the leader's style and the content of what the leader is advocating. From a Christian point of view, it is only when the direction and the method are in line with God's purposes, character, and ways of operating that godly leadership takes place.

In Christian leadership theories various models are often drawn from important biblical characters (Doohan 1984; Clinton 1992; Blanchard and Hodges 2005; Baron and Padwa 1999). For example, Jesus is often quoted as an example whether explicitly or implicitly. Banks and Ledbetter (2004: 108) write, "While he does not often explicitly mention Jesus, Greenleaf regards him as the archetypal leader, focusing primarily on Jesus' distinctive teaching and behavior." Whittington et al. (2005) studied Paul as a model of spiritual leadership and underlined in his life and ministry ten qualities for legacy leadership. I will adopt this approach by asking North African leaders what biblical characters inspire their leadership.

Among the many biblical leadership theories, one in particular stands out for my research because it relates to the cultural context of North Africa. The shepherd metaphor is a biblical one, which various theologians refer to in pastoral theology throughout church history (Gan 2007). Jonathan Gan revisited the shepherd metaphor in the context of pastoral theology using a historical literary approach. His study allows him to define several shepherding functions that are helpful for our research.

First, the shepherd-king figure which includes leading, feeding and protection that are imbedded in tender care and faithfulness to responsibilities. These three functions of the leader "leading, feeding, and protecting" run throughout the Hebrew Bible (Gan 2007: 29). For example, Gan (2007: 87) states that, "There are good shepherds who are like Yahweh, leading the sheep to the right path, protecting them from harm or danger, and feeding them to grow." On the contrary, irresponsible shepherds are careless or sometimes even cruel to the sheep (Gan 2007). It also includes seeking the lost. It is hypothesized here that if church leaders in North Africa look at God as their model, they will be inspired to care for their followers like a shepherd cares for his sheep. However, one must be careful not to equate the model of God with human leadership. No human can compare himself or herself with the covenantal relation of God with his people. Trying to imitate God in this regard can lead to abusing one's leadership role. Therefore, I kindly disagree with Gan when he says that the leader should be a shepherd like God, but I suggest the leader who calls himself or herself a shepherd must place himself and herself under the shepherd-hood of God like his or her followers. Whenever a metaphor of God's leadership style is used in this book to inspire human leadership one must be cautious and not adopt it as an exact parallel. There are characteristics, such as the covenantal love of God, that are uniquely displayed in God.

Second, the shepherd-God metaphor is one where Yahweh is the shepherd whose primary function is "delivering out of distress." This includes restoration, gathering the flock, protecting the flock from harm, feeding and giving rest to the sheep, "assigning the pastures of shepherd and flocks," and ensuring fertility and restoration (Gan 2007: 32-33). Gan contends that every era takes specific forms in the Torah, the former and latter prophetic literature and the writings (i.e. Psalms, Wisdom Literature, and Chronicles). Sometimes the leadership metaphor is connected to others such as the fatherly love of God for His children or to the covenantal relationship between God and humans (Sunderland 1981; Brueggemann 1979):[21]

> The quality of a good shepherd in the Hebrew Bible is one who lives by the word of God. In providing, protecting and feeding, the king, prophet, or priest exercises the judicial role with righteousness and wisdom of Yahweh. All these appointments were set to protect the people spiritually and politically as well as to provide for their living needs, spiritual and physical (Gan 2007).

---

21. I reiterate here the danger of equating the leadership role of God as a shepherd in his covenantal love with the leadership role of a human being. Human leaders can only benefit from this type of love and will never be able to imitate it to the extent that God did.

Metaphors of shepherding also include that leaders must lead with wisdom and knowledge (Gan 2007).

At the end of his book, Gan shows the relevancy of understanding the biblical metaphor of the shepherd for leadership. First:

> The shepherd metaphor elucidates the responsibilities of the kings and rulers, as shepherds to their flocks. The leadership of shepherd provides safety against wild animals and protection from harm to the flock, so the kings and rulers provide safety against enemies and protection from adversaries from the surrounding nations . . . They are responsible for the well-being of their people, as Yahweh is responsible for the welfare and the well-being of his people, Israelites. (Gan 2007: 99)

Third, "The shepherd metaphor exhibits the relationship between the leader and deity, as in relation to the welfare of the people under his leadership . . . as divine representation the leader is responsible to the needs, such as food and protection of the people" (Gan 2007: 99-100). Thus in this study Gan shows the importance of the metaphor of the shepherd to describe the relationship of God to his people, of God to the leader, and of the leader to the people. What Gan teaches helps us identify characteristics of the shepherd leadership style, but the leader who adopts these characteristics should be aware that he is servant of God just as his or her followers and that a parallel with Yahweh's covenant love for his people can lead to serious abuses in leadership.

Another study of the leadership metaphor by a biblical researcher is the work by Timothy S. Laniak (2007). Drawing from the study of biblical texts and an extensive study conducted by observing and interviewing Bedouin shepherds in the Middle East, Laniak describes shepherd leadership using the following three categories as Gan with a slight change of terminology: Provision, Protection and Guidance. In the first category, Laniak includes the following behaviors: called to care, feeding, healing, nursing, finding the lost, gathering the scattered and naming the sheep. Under the second category, Laniak includes watching the flock, recognizing the wolves, facing the lions, gatekeepers, justice, a living sacrifice, sleepless shepherd. In the third category, Laniak discusses issues such as following the leader, working together, authority and decision-making (see table below). Laniak's work is useful for my research because the cultural context is similar to my own and it is a model of integration between cultural and biblical views of shepherding.

TABLE 2: Shepherd Leadership
(Adapted from Laniak 2007)

Provision
Called to Care
Streams in the Desert
Spring Up, O Well
Greener Pastures
Feed My Sheep
The Shepherd Healer
Midwives and Nurses
Lost and Found
Gathering the Scattered
Satisfaction and Restoration
The Staff
Named and Known
Protection
While Shepherds Watch Their Flocks
Recognizing the Wolves
Facing the Lions
The Other Lion
Gatekeeper
Dogs
Justice
The Rod
A Living Sacrifice
Darkness

Guard Yourselves
My Sleepless Shepherd
Following the Leader
Righteous Ruts
Working Together
Indigenous Leadership
Productivity
Reproduction
Think Flock
Finding Good Help
Authority and Abuse
Adaptability and Decision Making
Being There

In looking at the various leadership attributes from the shepherd metaphor one thing that is striking is its resemblance to the *sheikhocratic* leadership style that will be discussed later in this same section.

Spiritual Leadership Theories

Today there is a trend toward adapting spiritual concepts to secular leadership theories (Banks and Ledbetter 2004; Manz 1998; Manz, Manz and Neck 2001). Recently, there has been a move toward more integration between spirituality and leadership as the focus of its study has shifted from the body, emotions and mind to include spirit (Mitroff and Denton 1999). These theories do not equate "spiritual" with "biblical." Fry (2003: 706) writes, "Workplace spirituality and spiritual leadership can therefore be inclusive or exclusive of religious theory and practice." They make sure to state that spiritual leadership is not limited to a specific religion or to religion generally. Fry (2003: 694), who wrote an important article on this issue, continues, "Previous leadership theories have focused in varying degrees on one or more aspects of the physical, mental, or emotional elements of human interaction in organizations and neglected the spiritual component." He defines spiritual leadership, as "comprising the values, attitudes, and behaviors that are necessary to intrinsically motivate one's self and others so that they have a sense of spiritual survival through calling and membership" (2003: 695).²² According to Fry (2003: 717) spiritual leaders motivate followers through "vision, hope/faith, altruistic love, task involvement, and goal identification."

This exchange between the religious and secular world could be another model for my research. In effect, it is my hope that North African leaders will also impact their society with their leadership values, modeling the example of religiously oriented researchers like Stephen Covey (1989), DePree (1992), Greenleaf (1977) and Carlysle (1897) who all have influenced non-religiously oriented leadership theory.

Islamic Leadership Theories

I here describe leadership theories that have been developed by contemporary Muslim theorists who have integrated Islamic leadership principles with current research on leadership to develop specific leadership styles that may be used either in the secular or religious context.

Muslim theorists face similar challenges as Christians as they approach leadership theories. While Christians examine how secular principles can be combined with biblical ones to make a leader more effective, Muslim theorists combine secular with Qur'anic models. They also face the challenge of evaluating what Muslim leaders should reject from secular theories if they want to honor Qur'anic principles.

Compared to the number of theorists in Christianity, the number of Muslim counterparts is much more limited. Although in the field of religious studies there is a plethora of resources on religious leadership (since Islam's nascence), the integration of findings from secular leadership theories is a recent phenomenon. As a result, I will not be able to draw as much from this section as from chapter 1. Furthermore, when Muslim writers integrate modern leadership theories with traditional Islamic ones, they tend to resonate very much with what I explore in chapter 1: the leadership style of Muhammad, caliphs, the imam, etc.

---

22. The author lists many other values under the category altruistic love such as forgiveness, kindness, integrity, empathy/compassion, honesty, patience, courage, trust/loyalty, and humility (Fry 2003).

Having said that the integration of modern and traditional theories has led to the development of several styles that I will discuss here. First, a few researchers in the Islamic studies field believe that the servant leadership style is inherent to Islam. According to Muslims leadership researchers Beekun and Badawi (1999: 15) Muslim leaders are servant leaders because they "seek the welfare [of the followers] and guide them toward what is good." Beekun and Badawi (1999) affirm that the servant leadership style was part of Islam since its beginning.[23] In other words, they posit that Greenleaf has discovered nothing new and that Islam has always considered the leader as a servant.[24] Another theorist, Adnan Aabed (2006: 54) bases his definition of servant leadership on several Qur'anic and Hadith passages to show that leaders are servants (*Sura* 21: 92; Al-Bukhari 2009: 166; Al-Tabri as quoted in Beekun and Badawi 1999[25]).

The weakness of these theories is that the Qur'anic texts and hadiths used to support their theories are very limited. Furthermore, they have no findings from experimental field research. However, since the theorists that adopt and teach this model have a large sphere of influence it may be possible that many Muslims are affected by their teaching.

Second, Muslim researchers have revisited the autocratic leadership style suggesting that in Islam it should best be described as autocratic-*shura* style—which combines autocracy with the practice of consultation in decision-making.[26] Beekun and Badawi (1999: 9) show evidence of the

---

23. The authors (1999: 15) affirm that Islam spoke about servant leadership even before Robert Greenleaf spoke about it in his 1970 book entitled *The Servant as Leader*.

24. They base their statements essentially on one Hadith addressing rulers who must be concerned about the welfare of their followers (*Sahih* Muslim as quoted by Beekun and Badawi 1999). I do not completely agree with these authors. They cannot rely on one Hadith to prove their theory. Concepts of servanthood in Islam, the Bible, and secular leadership theory must be more closely compared and contrasted before one agrees with Beekun and Badawi. But this task is beyond the scope of my research.

25. Al-Tabri as quoted by Beekun and Badawi (1999: 15) says, "Indeed, from among the servants of Allah, there are servants who are not prophets, who the prophets and martyrs will envy. The prophet Muhammad then was asked, 'Who are they, so that we may love them?' He replied, 'They are the people who love each other due to Allah's light, not because of relationship or kinship. They do not fear when the people fear, nor do they grieve when the people grieve."

26. In secular leadership theories, autocratic and democratic leadership styles are mutually exclusive. A leader is either democratic or autocratic. He/she cannot be both at the same time. This is not the case in Muslim leadership theory where an often hierarchical structure

first element. Although they affirm that, "Islam discourages Muslims from actively seeking positions of authority"[27] they also underline that Islam "recognizes the legitimacy of coercive power, at the same time, it makes explicit the conditions under which followers can rise against the use of coercive power by a leader."[28] Zafar Bangash (2000) approaches the balance between power and participation from a slightly different angle when he affirms that Islam regulates power differentiation so that it does not lead to injustice in society. In any case, leaders should not be oppressors according to *sura* 2:124.[29] Muslims base the notion of consultation on Qur'anic texts as well as on practices of respected Muslim leaders such as the caliph Umar who said, "a decision that has been taken without consultation is useless" (Nusair as quoted in Sarayrah 2004: 67). As a result, Muslim leaders promote participation of others in decision-making through *shura* (Nusair as quoted in Sarayrah 2004: 75). Numerous researchers have shown evidence of the use of centralized power combined with consultation in the Middle Eastern or North African world (Ali 2005). According to Ali (2005: 109), in the Arab world,

> The tendency toward consultation does not necessarily mean an absence of the centralization of authority. Several researchers have found that executives in Muslim countries prefer to

---

is combined with a horizontal relation between leader and followers based on consultation.

27. These authors quote a Hadith of *Sahih* Muslim, vol. 3. "The Messenger of Allah (saw) said to me: 'Do not ask for a position of authority, for if you are granted this position as a result of your asking for it, you will be left alone (without Allah's help to discharge the responsibilities involved in it), and if you are granted it without making any request for it, you will be helped (by Allah in the discharge of your duties). They add that in certain exceptions when a leader can request a position such as the prophet Yusus who asked God, "Set me over the storehouses of the land: I will indeed guard them as one that knows (their importance)" (*sura* 12:55).

28. The authors quote a Hadith narrated by Ali 'ibn Abu Talib that relates a case where a leader requires his followers to collect wood, make a fire and throw themselves in the fire. Although this leader appealed "Didn't the Prophet order to obey me," the end of the Hadith reports that Muhammad when asked about this attitude said to the followers "obedience is required only in what is good" (*Sahih* Bukhari, volume 9, Hadith 259).

29. This verse is used by Adalat Khan (2007) to show that leaders should not be oppressors. He shows that Abraham is chosen as a leader but when he asks about his progeny, God says he would not make a covenant with oppressors.

hold on to power by centralization of decision-making and by maintaining close control of management affairs.

Other Islamic researchers have shown a tendency of power sharing and equality in Islam (Ali 2005: 68).[30]

Thirdly, modern Muslim theorists found that the visionary style is important in Islam. Beekun and Badawi (1999: 13) called Muhammad, like all the other prophets, an "ethical charismatic leader" because he "used power to the benefit of mankind, learned from criticism, worked to develop his followers into leaders, and relied on an internal moral standard." Followers are attracted to visionary leaders. According to Ibn Ishaq, Urwa Bin Masud said about Muhammad's followers, "I have seen a people who will never abandon him for any reason; so form your own opinion."[31] Visionary leadership according to Safi is common in the Muslim world. During the decolonization of Algeria (1956-1962), charismatic leaders such as Ben Badis and Abd el-Kader played a major role in the society. The term "charismatic leadership style" is commonly used in Muslim leadership theories to refer to a visionary style. Muhammad, the Prophet of Islam, is considered a charismatic leader; for example in orthodox Islam, it defines the leader as a visionary (Beekun and Badawi 2004). Ali Didier Bourg (1994: 74) for example wrote that *imam* must be "endowed with charisma."

Fourth, leadership theorists in Islam define the guardian leadership style (Beekun and Badawi 1999: 15). For them a leader is a guardian because he is called to "protect his community against tyranny and oppression, to encourage Allah-consciousness and *taqwa*, and to promote justice."

A fifth style to consider is called prophetic-*caliphal* style. Muslims are considered as vicegerents or representatives of God on this earth (*Sura* 6:165). This style draws from the concept of vicegerent or representative of God on this earth described in the Qur'an. Bashir Khadra (1984), from the University of Jordan, Amman, contends that leadership patterns in Islam are drawn from this prophetic-*caliphal* model. He argues that this style

---

30. For further discussion see chapter 4.
31. Ibn Ishaq, as reported by Rahman (1980: 67).

includes personalism, individualism, lack of institutionalism, and the importance of the "great man" (*Sura* 6:165).

Sixth, there are references in modern Islamic theories to the shepherd leadership style. However, from an empiric perspective, there is not much support for this style since most theorists based their findings on the following quote from the Hadith: "According to Islam, every person is the 'shepherd' of a flock (Beekun and Badawi 1999: ix)". There is no further description of this style in Muslim leadership literature except from commentaries of this Hadith.

Seventh, Muslim leadership theorists borrow the transformation leadership style to describe leadership in their context. In Shiism, for example, the imam is the one who effects change. He does so in his "ability to effect change and overcome unforeseen problems: this was made obvious through his supervision of crisis management situations such as wars, famines, epidemics of communicable diseases and similar catastrophes" (Nawafleh 2000).

Eighth, there are non-Muslim theorists who studied the Qur'an and the Hadith in order to define leadership principles for the Muslim community. For example, anthropologist Ernest Gellner (1969: 114) defined '*ulama* as "norm-givers of the community of the faithful; they are the repositories and arbiters of legitimacy." They must bow to the superiority of the ruler but "it does not preclude them to being extremely influential on the general kind of society over which the ruler presides" (Gellner 1969: 115). He concludes "This, I suspect, is indeed the role of the '*ulama* in Islamic society: not very powerful in deciding between one ruler or dynasty and another, they were most influential in determining the general nature of society" (Gellner 1969: 115).

Finally, as we compare relations-oriented and task-oriented leaders, Muslim theorists have defined Muslim leadership has a human-oriented rather than a production-oriented approach (Aabed 2006). This brief overview of Muslim leadership theories provides me with ample models to evaluate leadership in a Muslim context. The eight styles identified in this section are (1) the servant, (2) autocratic-*shura*, (3) charismatic-visionary, (4) guardian, (5) prophetic-*caliphal*, (6) shepherd, (7) transformational and (8) human-oriented leadership. These styles are a good starting point for defining Muslim leadership and evaluating whether they have impacted church leaders in their respective Muslim contexts.

Cultural Approaches to Leadership Styles

In my definition of leadership styles I have on several occasions discussed the impact of culture. The values, beliefs, norms, and ideals that are embedded in a culture affect the leadership behaviors, goals and strategies of an organization (Bass 1990). It is important to explain in greater detail the role of culture in this research. Although North African church leaders operate in a North African context, their leadership training until now has often been Western-based. Because it has been monocultural in its orientation and not receptor-oriented, very few North African Christian leadership models exist that can be used for the contemporary churches. Furthermore, there is an ongoing debate in the church about the borrowing of Muslim forms of leadership to be more effective in broader society. This shows that it is necessary to have a solid understanding of what happens when the style of leadership of one context is borrowed to be implemented in another.

Universal Versus Cultural

The vast majority of contemporary researchers are aware that leadership is impacted by culture although some give more weight to the universal elements while others to the culture-specific factors. For example, Triandis (1993: 168) contended that Fiedler's contingency theory has potential to be universal "with cultural variables functioning as parameters of the theory."[32] In my study of the influence of culture on leadership I agree with House et al. (2004: 15) who says that,

> We understand and expect that the evaluative and semantic interpretation of the term leadership and the ways in which leadership and organizational processes are enacted are likely

---

[32]. Triandis (1993: 169) defines the following theorem: "If a culture is high in X, theory Y works as expected; if a culture is low in X, theory Y must be modified as follows."

to vary across cultures. However, we also expect that some aspects of leadership will be universally endorsed as effective or ineffective.

North African leaders must pay greater attention to their own cultural setting as they evaluate their leadership style. Although there will be commonalities between diverse contexts, there will also be differences that shape the effectiveness of their leadership.

Western Theories Measure Applied Globally

Although research in the field of leadership during the past half-century has essentially been undertaken in North America and Western Europe (Yukl 2002), it is rapidly expanding to new areas around the world today. Nevertheless, the initial framework continues to be Western-based because global research continues to overwhelmingly use theories and instruments developed from research originally conducted with Western informants. There must be a constant revisiting of these frameworks in light of new findings. For example, Triandis (1993: 169) suggests that only a few studies have tested Fiedler's contingency theory in other cultures, and so "we do not know for sure whether the model is universal or works only in cultures similar to those of North America."

In many theoretical frameworks the cross-cultural element is still not completely investigated as is evident of contingency studies. Triandis (1993: 181) states that "the meaning of the leadership situation changes from culture to culture, and if we are to make predictions about how the contingency model will work in other cultures, we need to examine the links between the model on one hand and the cultural variations on the other hand." On the other hand, Triandis (1993: 183) is able to make a number of predictions about differences of leadership using the categories of power-distance, collectivist-individualist as well as uncertainty-avoidance—all of which will be helpful criteria for the analysis of my research.

Cultural Categories For Measuring Leadership Behaviors

Some researchers defined specific categories that help identify cultural differences. Hofstede and Bond (1988) identified: (1) power distance, (2) uncertainty avoidance, (3) individualism versus collectivism, and (4) masculinity versus feminity. A fifth dimension has recently been added to this list, the long- versus short-term orientation (Scandura and Dorfman 2004; Hofstede 2001). The study of North African leaders can show specifically how these cultural dimensions impact their leadership style. For example, we know that North African societies are collectivistic. We can therefore conclude with leadership theorists that the most important attributes of the self are "achievement of one's group, cooperation, endurance, abasement, nurturance, order and self-control" (Hui and Villareal 1989: 319). Triandis (1993: 173) further suggests that in collectivistic cultures, followers expect much from the leader, leaders must give nurturance, and "interest in getting the job done."

Other important areas that may inform my study on North African culture and provide data for the investigation of the situation and follower is the work of Stella Ting-Toomey (1994) on face, work, and shame as well as the work of P. B. Smith and M. F. Peterson (1988) who show how in collectivistic cultures leaders criticize indirectly rather than directly.

Leadership Styles in the Middle East and North Africa

One of the areas most neglected in leadership research is the Arab world. House et al. (2004: 57) write,

> A great deal of effort has been made to compare the leadership styles and requirements of small groups of nations. Usually the comparisons are made amongst the US, Western European, Latin American, and Asian nations. Consequently, more is known about leadership in these regions then is known about leadership in Southern Asian, African, Arab and Eastern European countries.

Today, there is a fresh energy for studying leadership in the Middle East, due in part to the current political events. Modern leadership theory studied some Muslim historical or political leaders using Great-Man or Trait-Theory, but since these theories do not deal with cultural differences (because they posit that great men are "natively endowed with characteristics that cause them to stand out") these studies are not very useful for studying cultural variations (Cooper and McCaugh 1969: 247).

One major source for understanding Arab leadership theory is the GLOBE[33] study. It includes the study of a Middle Eastern cluster including Qatar, Morocco, Turkey, Egypt and Kuwait (House et al. 2004: 187). My study relates to these areas.

The GLOBE study provides considerable data on variation in leadership behaviors across the world. Although Scandura and Dorfman (2004) outline that a number of questions are still not addressed in this research, it is used by some researchers (i.e. Fields) to underline that cross-cultural differences influence the effectiveness of leadership. Unfortunately Fields' study deals with management versus church leadership. It nevertheless provides new ways to look at cultural differences.

The GLOBE study identified the following six global leaders' behaviors that are useful for my research: (1) charismatic/value-based leadership, (2) team-oriented leadership, (3) participative leadership, (4) humane-oriented leadership, (5) autonomous leadership, and (6) self-protective leadership. The study also showed twenty-one primary leaders' behaviors that are universal and eight that are universally viewed as impeding leadership effectiveness (House et al. 2004). It then identified leadership styles that are relevant for the cultural context I study: the authoritative and the *sheikocracy* leadership style. Surprisingly they do not include the charismatic leadership style that has been identified by other authors as relevant leadership style in the Middle East/North Africa region.[34]

---

33. The Global Leadership and Organizational Behavior Effectiveness Program (GLOBE).
34. Ali Damstmalchian, Mansour Javidan and Kamran Alam (2001) studied leadership in Iran. They found further categories not included for the Middle East in the GLOBE such as "family", "humble" and "faithful". Scandura and Dorfman (2004: 297) underline that "one might propose that leadership is both the same and different in the Middle East. And we need to consider each Middle Eastern country separately as we contrast these findings with Turkey." Scandura and Dorfman compared Middle Eastern and American leadership "best practices" and found that the "Middle East is unique is their view of leadership" (2004: 298). According to Kabasakal and Bodur (2002) examined by Colin Silverthorne (2005: 78), professor of psychology at the University of San Francisco, "the relative value of preferred leadership styles was lower indicating that Arab cultures prefer a more balanced, middle-of-the road approach rather than preferring one approach over another at a more extreme level.

Throughout the GLOBE study, one further finds characteristics of various leadership styles. First, Kabasakal and Bodur (1998) showed that in the Arab world (in Qatar, Morocco, Turkey, Egypt and Kuwait) one of the characteristics of effective leaders is team orientation and charisma. Jane Punnett and Oded Shenkar (2004: 307) report findings from Iran, Kuwait, Turkey and Qatar, which indicate "high in-group collectivism." They relate collectivism with "loyalty, pride, cohesiveness, and other in-group collectives" (Punnett and Shenkar 2004: 308).

Second, nepotism (called *wasta* in the GLOBE study) is another characteristic of Arab leadership. In nepotism a leader can influence others because of the family, tribal or personal ties (Neal and Finley 2007). Because it is a common feature in the Arab world, it may also be found in the North African church.

Third, in the Arab context, building trust and relationships are very important to managerial effectiveness (Kabasakal and Bodur 1998: 52). I am predicting that these are two qualities that will be found in North African church leaders. If this is the case, the GLOBE study will allow me to posit that North African leaders have a contextual leadership style. As they demonstrate trust and relationship building they prove to be contingent to followers and context.

Fourth, "an 'outstanding leader' in the Arabic cluster is a person who is able to initiate change and improvement by keeping group solidarity and yet at the same time avoiding nepotism" (Kabasakal and Bodur 1998: 52). In this case, nepotism is seen negatively and counter-productive.

Fifth, according to Dorfman (2004: 308) Middle East leadership styles include attributes such as "familial, humble, faithful, self-protective, and considerate. Paternalistic and autocratic tendencies are found alongside of the desire of a highly considerate, supportive and humble leader" (Pasa, Kabasakal, and Bodur 2001).

Sixth, according to Kabasakal and Bodur (1998) examined by Colin Silverthorne (2005: 78), Professor of Psychology at the University of San Francisco, in the Middle East "Leaders are expected to be competent." They explain further, "the relative value of preferred leadership styles was lower indicating that Arab cultures prefer a more balanced, middle-of-the road approach rather than preferring one approach over another at a more extreme level. Leaders are expected to be competent, and have modest attributes and, at the same time, be a person with a 'miracle' who is able to attain follower's ideals (Abdalla and Al-Homoud 2001).

Seventh, the difference between the autocratic and autocratic-consultative (*shura*) leadership style is not so clear-cut. Other researchers have also found the same results from non-church contexts in the Middle East or North Africa (Ali 1989; Muna 1980). According to Abbas Ali (2005: 109), in the Arab world,

> The tendency toward consultation does not necessarily mean an absence of the centralization of authority. Several researchers have found that executives in Muslim countries prefer to hold on to power by centralization of decision-making and by maintaining close control of management affairs.

The following study may shed further light on this discussion. A comparison between people-oriented and task-oriented U.S. managers and Jordanian and Saudi Arabian managers by Scandura et al. (1999) showed that the people-oriented style for the Middle Eastern sample was not related to job satisfaction and leader effectiveness, but that the task-oriented style was. They concluded that "strong and decisive leadership is expected from an Arab person, hence the effectiveness of setting high goals and standards of performance characteristic of initiating structure, whereas a considerate leader might be perceived as being weak and indecisive" (House, et al. 2004: 64). If this is true, North Africans who live in a people-oriented culture may not model a people-oriented leadership style. This finding needs to be explored further.

Eighth, the GLOBE study (House et al. 2004: 63) shows that in the Arab world the combination of "family and tribal norms in addition to bureaucratic organizational structures fosters authoritarian management practices." According to Jane Punnett and Oded Shenkar (2004: 307), findings from Iran, Kuwait, Turkey and Qatar show "relatively low scores on future orientation and performance orientation." They add, "high power distance scores indicate the acceptance of unequal sharing of power in the society and high in-group collectivism scores indicate the importance of loyalty, pride, cohesiveness, and other in-group collectives" (Punnett and Shenkar 2004: 308).

Ninth, the GLOBE study (House et al. 2004: 63) reveals that the combination of "family and tribal norms in addition to bureaucratic organizational structures fosters authoritarian management practices." In the GLOBE study, team oriented and participative leadership received the lowest score in the Middle East (House et al. 2004: 42).

Tenth, in their study of charismatic and non-charismatic leaders, R. J. House, W.D. Spangler and J. Woycke (1991) showed that the Egyptian and Turkish leaders, Nassar and Ataturk respectively, were charismatic, whereas Nurial-Said of Iraq and Reza Shah Pahlavi of Iran were not. This may explain the change of leadership that took place in that part of the world. The leadership theorist Peter Dorfman commented on the fact that "the context of charismatic leader in the Arab culture returns to the original notion of a divinely inspired gift" (Scandura and Dorfman 2004: 281).

Kabasakal and Bodur (1998) additionally showed that in Arab leadership (in Qatar, Morocco, Turkey, Egypt and Kuwait) one of the characteristics of effective leaders is charisma. However, in the GLOBE study charismatic/value-based leadership received the lowest score (House et al. 2004: 42). According to that research, charismatic/value-based leadership is defined as a "leadership dimension that reflects ability to inspire, to motivate, and to expect high performance outcomes from others based on firmly held core values" (House et al. 2004: 14). One possible discrepancy between my assumptions and their findings is that visionary leadership especially relates to the religious context and not to the management context.

Finally, in researching leadership styles in Arab contexts, Al-Kubaisy found a new style he calls the *sheikocracy* leadership style[35] and defines it as,

> characterized by a patriarchal approach to managing that includes strong hierarchical authority, subordination of efficiency to human relations and personal connections and sporadic conformity to rules and regulations contingent on

---

35. The spelling is not always consistent. Dorfman and House spell it "sheikocracy" leadership style following Al-Kubaisy 1985).

personality and power of those who make them. (House et al. 2004: 63-64)

This style is a combination of "family and tribal norms in addition to bureaucratic organizational structures . . . (which) fosters authoritarian management practices (Al-Kubaisy 1985).[36] This is also sometimes called the paternalistic leadership style (Neal and Finley 2007). It portrays the leader as a father (House et al 2004), one who looks after the needs of the tribe member (Neal and Finley 2007). In North African cultures, this style is called *clientèlisme* characterized by the employees placing themselves under the care of the manager and receiving special attention and privileges. In this model, patriarchal values of honor and shame are dominant (Neal and Finley 2007). House et al. (2004: 63) further developed the study of this style, emphasizing (as Al-Kubaysi has) its caretaking aspect:

> Tribal traditions influence all aspects of life and, as a consequence, managers are expected to act as fathers—viewing their role in a highly personalized manner characterized by providing and caring for employees and favoring individuals within the family and tribe over outsiders. (House et al. 2004: 63)

Over against the relation-oriented style, task-orientedness is a strong component of *sheikhocracy*. According to Dorfman (2004: 308) Middle Eastern countries in general "score quite highly on the 'humane' culture dimension. Kabasakal and Dastmalchian call it relation-oriented in opposition to task-orientedness (Bass 1990). Ali (2005: 108) further states that *sheikhocracy* sanctions personal relations and an open-door policy on behalf of the leader. Dorfman and House (2004: 63-64) state that the paternalistic leadership style is characterized by the "subordination of efficiency to human relations and personal connections."

According to Thomas and Inkson (2004: 128), the *sheikocracy* leadership style also "contains strong elements of personal autocracy." Neal and

---

36. Another study by Kabasakal and Dastmalchian (2001) also refers to this leadership style.

Finfey (2007: 292) underline that the *sheikhocratic* leader often has "near absolute power over subordinates." However, they add that the *sheikhocratic* leader is not a mere autocrate (2007). According to them the *sheikhocratic* leadership style includes a high degree of embeddedness relying on interaction and consultation in which all members of the tribe, whatever their status, are entitled to have a personal audience with the *sheikh*.

According to Dorfman (2004: 308), "Paternalistic and autocratic tendencies are found alongside of the desire of a highly considerate, supportive and humble leader." Ali (2005: 108-109) notices that in *sheikhocratic* models, leaders "might be authoritarian, but their behavior is always tempered by consideration of what is acceptable or not acceptable by the community and the rule of religious law." Dorfman and House (2004: 63-64) add to the "strong hierarchical authority" the importance of "human relations and personal connections." According to Thomas and Inkson (2004: 128) this style "contains strong elements of personal autocracy and conformity to rules and regulations based on respect for those who made the rules rather than for their rationality." They add,

> Rules thus have symbolic importance but will not be implemented if they go against autocratic-tribal traditions: for example the bureaucracy may specify procedures for appointment or merit, but in the event these rules are likely to be ignored. Instead a leader will make appointments based on family relationships and friendships. (Thomas and Inkson 2004: 128)

These findings show that in this style of leadership, near-absolute authority is counterbalanced by attributes such as being supportive, humble, having consideration for others and respecting religious rules in particular. This underlines a type of authority unique to the Arabo-Muslim context that differs from Bass' definition. It resembles more closely to the definition (cited below)—"the interactive authority."

Conclusion

This chapter reviewed leadership theories in order to gain insight into how to define leadership styles. Instead of looking solely at the personality of leaders, this study showed it is important to know the leader's values, behaviors and attributes as well as how he or she makes them contingent to followers and context. Discovering the main characteristics of contingency theory helped me design the framework of my research. As a result, I decided to measure the values, behaviors and attributes of North African church leaders because they are main components of leadership styles. By comparing my findings with those existing models I am able to propose several leadership styles that may be common in North Africa. My conclusions lay an initial foundation on which to build future research to test my suggestions.

This chapter has also outlined the major leadership styles that will serve as criteria for defining those in the North African context. The major styles from current leadership theories include autocratic, democratic, laissez-faire, transformational, transactional, servant and visionary. The study of biblical leadership theories has further provided this study with the shepherd leadership style. Finally, Islamic leadership theories have disclosed the guardian leadership style and the prophetic-caliphal model. Both biblical and Islamic models have adopted these styles from secular leadership theories.

Another significant area highlighted in the study of leadership theories is the influence of culture on leadership styles. Instead of using a Western framework to study leadership styles, I decided to measure attachment styles in North Africa through qualitative research in order to allow the data to emerge from the context and reveal what could be unique to that context. Furthermore, there are universal features in leadership which can be borrowed and adapted to various contexts. From the literature review, I can predict that some of the leadership styles discussed above may be found in slightly altered forms in North Africa.

Finally, in leadership theory, the process of defining leadership styles is ongoing. Depending on the theory, (i.e. great-man theory, in trait-theory or in behavioral theories), the meaning changes. One can assume that the definition will continue to evolve as new contexts are investigated and new principles are developed.

CHAPTER 3

Methodology

This chapter describes the various methods I used to conduct my research. The flowchart included below conveniently explains the various steps of my research and how the methods I used interface with each other. I will briefly explain the various elements of my flowchart and identify when I conducted primary and secondary research. I then discuss how I developed the instrument I used for my field research and how I collected and analyzed the data in North Africa.

My Flowchart

At the onset of my research, I did a review of the leadership literature in order to identify theories that define leadership styles. I then chose the following leadership theories: behavioral, contingency (which takes into consideration the leader, the follower and the context to define a leadership style) and transformational. This process is explained in detail in chapter 2.

Once I had chosen the theories that informed my research of leadership styles, I designed a questionnaire to collect data on them in North Africa. The questions covered the following areas: (1) how does one become a leader? (2) leadership values, (3) how does a leader influence society? (4) how does a leader influence followers? (5) power and influence, and (6) the leader's relationship with God. This process is explained in detail below under "Measuring Leadership Styles." The findings are reported in chapter 8. They represent the results of the primary research and consist of a list of attributes, values and behaviors of current North African leaders.

The study of leadership theories not only provided the definition of leadership styles that helped me frame my questionnaire and interviews but it also enabled me to hypothesize which ones would be relevant to my context. These leadership styles are described in chapter 2 and include the following: autocratic-democratic-laissez-faire, the charismatic-visionary, the *sheikhocratic*, the shepherd, the servant, and the religious. To determine the styles of North African church leaders, I compared the list of attributes, values and behaviors collected with these six leadership styles. I also compared the attributes, values and behaviors from my secondary research on religious, cultural and historical contexts (chapters 4, 5 and 6) with those of North African pastors to determine to what extent their style matches with the religious, cultural and historical patterns. The integration of these various findings will help me make recommendations for leadership patterns of church leaders that will positively impact the church and society.

This doctoral research integrates a variety of methods. The research on leadership theories (chapter 2) and religious and cultural leadership styles (chapters 4 and 5) is secondary research and text-based. The study of North African historical leaders combines historical research (chapters 6). Finally, I do social science research among current North African church leaders using qualitative research. This research is further described in the following found in appendix Q.

Existing Questionnaires?

Once I made the decision to study leadership styles of North African church leaders, the next step was to decide what instruments I would use to measure them. This is when I faced the dilemma of either using standard questionnaires or developing my own research tools. I decided to choose the latter approach for the following reasons.

First, I could not find a questionnaire on leadership styles that was developed from experimental research conducted in North Africa. Until now, the data collected in this region of the world is based on questions that have arisen from observing leadership styles in predominantly Western contexts. As a result, many of these methods appear to be culturally biased.

For example the Multifactor Leadership Questionnaire (MLQ) developed by Bass and Avolio (1993) to measure transformational and transactional leadership styles, was developed in a Western individualistic context. The context I studied, however, is very different. Because I posited earlier that culture and religion shape leadership styles in a unique way, I preferred to use research tools that identify both the cultural and religious context in North Africa. This does not mean that all questionnaires and research tools for identifying leadership styles should be discarded. Several empirical studies have been conducted in Islamic contexts with Western-oriented questionnaires. For example, the "Value for Working Questionnaire" (Flowers, Hughes, and Myers 1975), which evaluated attitudes and behaviors at the work place, was used in Iraq, Iran, Morocco, and Saudi Arabia.[1] According to Ali, this questionnaire, "because of its relative lack of cultural bias . . . is well suited for cross-cultural studies" (Ali 2005: 65). However, the context of that research was far too different from mine to be applicable. That questionnaire was directed to the work place and not to the church. It did not take into account a combination of the variables of this research, including North Africa, the church, Islam, and the Bible. I, on the other hand, preferred to adopt a contextually sensitive approach.

Second, since no empirical data was available for my specific leadership context, I opted for an emic approach in order to let the insiders define the categories rather than imposing foreign grids and frameworks. Recently, some researchers have argued for developing emic or adapting existing questionnaires.[2] Once initial data is collected on leadership styles in the North African church, the next step is to adapt existing questionnaires which I hope other researchers will do in the future. But since my research was first to be conducted in the North African church context, my goal was to impose as little foreign concepts as possible. The thirty-four questions

---

1. This research showed that "in Islamic countries, the prevailing cultural values and norms encourage common and humanistic causes, friendship and harmony, and at the same time stimulate openness, tolerance, trust, and confidence in others to perform their duties" (Ali 2005: 67).
2. For example, Shahin I. Amany and Peter L. Wright (2004) say that leadership theories created in North America may not be relevant in the Middle East. They investigated the use of Bass and Avolio's transformational/transactional leadership model in Egypt and found modification needed to be made to this model for use in the Middle East.

that I designed are very broad and only intended to set some boundaries so that leaders recognize that what I am looking for is information on how leaders lead.

Thirdly, what prevented me from using existing questionnaires was that I am dealing with a first-generation leadership and consequently most church leaders in North Africa have not studied leadership theory.[3] These leaders have not reflected on leadership issues with the kind of theoretical terminology I discussed in chapter 2. They map the world of leadership with their own contextual criteria and this is a good thing because they will not be inclined to use leadership jargon to describe their leadership context. Because I determined this to be a benefit to my study I opted for open-ended interviews and general questions that would allow for the categories to emerge from the narrative instead of being imposed onto it. In the future, further research may use the categories identified in my findings to develop a questionnaire adapted to the context.

Let me end this discussion with two caveats. First, I do not believe it is possible as a researcher to design a research tool that is completely unbiased. I had to make choices when I created the interview questions that may have prevented me from collecting pure emic data. This is why explaining the process of developing the instrument will prove to be so important. This instrument should be improved in the future. Second, I designed a unique research tool. No one else has asked the same questions in the same order and combination. This is the disadvantage of not using sophisticated leadership questionnaires[4] that have been extensively tested for their validity and

---

3. My research does not include doing primary research on the number of leadership books used in North Africa, but my personal observation shows that they are very limited and in many places non-existent. Some organizations are now starting training programs in North Africa using their own Western developed training manuals. For example, the Maxwell Institute of Christian Leadership Training is currently sending trainers to North Africa. However, their training program relies heavily on concepts unfamiliar to an Islamic context.

4. One example of such questionnaire is the one designed by Fiedler, Chermers and Mahar (1964), called the Least Preferred Coworker scale to determine the leadership styles. This eight-point scale allows for the classification of leaders in assessing the qualities that people like or don't like about the least preferred co-worker and defines whether they are task-oriented or people-oriented. Fiedler (1969) defined that leadership will be most effective if three determinants are taken into account, (1) the interpersonal relation between leader and followers, (2) the task structure, and (3) power position.

reliability. Consequently, the leadership styles proposed in the conclusion of this work cannot be considered as final per se; they should be further investigated in the future. Nevertheless, the categories and concepts[5] I collected and used in my conclusion to suggest leadership styles are necessary first steps toward the definition of leadership styles that are culturally relevant and effective to impact the believers and the society for good. These categories and concepts can be considered valid and reliable.

Measuring Leadership Styles

In this section I explain how I developed my instrument to measure leadership styles. Instead of using known leadership styles and their respective questionnaires, I studied their key characteristics which include leadership qualities, values, attributes and behaviors.

What Makes a Leadership Style?

The definition of leadership is the foundational framework for my research and it includes four categories: the leader, the follower, the situation and God. After examining various leadership theories, I formulated the following statements that serve as a framework for my research. While I believe that leadership styles may include some innate traits, they are not central to my research. Styles are broader than traits and include qualities, values, attributes and behaviors some of which are shaped by the beliefs and the culture of the leader. Furthermore, leadership styles include behaviors that may change according to followers and situations.

Leadership theorists defined specific leadership styles as they identified these characteristics in their various and unique combinations. They named the consistent pattern of behaviors they observed as specific leadership styles. Thus, for example, the servant leadership style has the following characteristics: listening, empathy, healing, awareness, persuasion, conceptualization, foresight, stewardship, commitment to growth of others, and

---

5. By categories and concepts I mean the data on leadership values, leadership qualities, leadership behaviors, power and influence, legitimacy and leadership metaphors I collected in my field research.

building community (Spears 2000). These characteristics represent personal and interpersonal values, behaviors, and qualities. It would have been easy to give leaders a questionnaire with these ten characteristics to see whether they match with their leadership style. But since I preferred to not impose a culturally biased framework, I decided to collect "first-level data", which are random leadership qualities, values, attributes and behaviors. I was then able to compare and contrast these personal and interpersonal qualities, values, attributes and behaviors with characteristics from leadership styles to see whether there is any overlap. Thus, the primary data I collected started not from the leadership style but from its specific components.

Questionnaires and Interviews

I measured leadership attributes, values, behaviors and qualities through a questionnaire containing thirty-four items consisting of the following areas: (1) general definitions of leadership, (2) leadership values, (3) leadership behaviors, (4) leadership legitimacy, (5) leadership power and influence, and (6) metaphors of leadership. I have used the same questions for my interviews.

Since my research is based on contingencies theories, the responses cannot be analyzed taking only the individual personality of the leader into account. There are many variables relating to the personal life of the leader, the relationship to followers, to each context and to God. Because this study is a first on leadership in the church, I am aware that my field of investigation is wide-open and extensive. This is why I decided not to interview followers or co-workers. I am aware that interviewing followers is crucial for evaluation regardless of whether the answers of the leader are realistic or idealistic. However, excluding the followers meant that I had to include more questions to the leader about his or her relationship with followers.

The relationship between leader and context was not investigated through the questionnaires but assessed by comparing and contrasting the data collected on the field with the secondary research on biblical, historical, Muslim and North African leadership styles. Once I compared the leadership characteristics of North African leaders with those of various leadership styles from (previous chapters) of biblical, historical and contemporary

North African and Muslim research I was able to assess whether leaders are contextual and biblical.

Leadership Styles in Contingency Theory

Considering the qualities, behaviors, values and attributes in the context of contingency theories broadened the investigation. As a result, contingency theories view leaders in their relation to followers and context. I therefore collected data on personal and interpersonal characteristics. For example, aspects such as the satisfaction of needs and the issue of power are key to understanding the leader-follower relation. Once the data was collected, I was also able to compare it with leadership styles from my research on historical and contemporary North African leaders as well as on Muslim leaders to find out whether leaders were adapting their style to the context. Instead of arguing that leaders must change context to be more effective, I argue that for the greatest effectiveness, leaders should adapt to the North African context.[6] Unfortunately, previous leadership training models in North Africa have often estranged leaders from their own society. I also discuss in this research whether the North African leaders' values, attributes, qualities and behaviors matched biblical models. This is the fourth category that shapes my view of leadership: the relationship of the leader with God. I argue that instead of indiscriminately embracing foreign values, North African leaders should let the Bible, Islam and North African culture shape them. I posit that leaders will be more effective if they both adapt to existing cultural styles and embrace biblical ones.

Behaviors

Behaviors are major components of leadership styles. When leadership researchers realized that personality traits were not sufficient to define a leadership style, they developed Behavioral Theories and started observing the actions or behaviors of leaders. Behavioral theories showed that

---

6. The context studied is complex. For example, traditional society in North African villages may define leadership practices differently than in large cities. Furthermore, the study must take into account that we live in a global world and there is an interface between western and Arab ideas. Today, North African leadership cannot be viewed in isolation. I need to take into consideration that the North African culture is evolving and that there may be a hybridization of leadership styles.

leadership styles include recurring qualities, attributes, and behaviors (Hugues, Ginnett, and Curphy 2006: 201). Fiedler proposed the following definition of behavior as quoted in Bernard M. Bass (1990: 4):

> By leadership behavior we generally mean the particular acts in which a leader engages in the course of directing and co-ordinating the work of his group members. This may involve such acts as structuring the work relations, praising or criticizing group members, and showing consideration for their welfare and feelings.

Therefore, a major part of my field research consisted in finding information on the behaviors of North African church leaders in order to define their leadership styles. The questionnaire contains one specific question about the behavior of leaders.

Behaviors can be measured by qualitative research and are easier to assess than personality traits, which need psychological testing.[7] They are also easier to observe than values.[8] To learn about their behaviors, I asked leaders to describe what they do and how they interact with their followers. Qualities and values are not sufficient to understand a leadership style. Banks and Ledbetter underlined this fact when they discussed how a quality such as faith must become expressed in leadership. They write, "Faithfulness is the concrete expression of faith in the workplace." They suggested that leaders must include in their mission statement "a commitment to being as well as doing" (Bank and Ledbetter 2004: 98-99). If what they say is true, the analysis of actions and skills will provide better information on North African leadership styles than the mere analysis of personality.

---

7. Early theories, such as Great-Man theory or Trait-Theory focused only on inherited aspects of leadership, also called personality traits, at the difference with later theories that stated that actions, behaviors, and styles of leaders may change over time (Avolio 2005; Bass 1990).

8. Leadership theorists Hughes, Ginnett, and Curphy 2006: 199 stated that, "One advantage of looking at leaders in terms of behavior instead of, say, personality is that behavior is often easier to measure; leadership behaviors can be observed whereas personality traits, values, or intelligence must be inferred from behavior or measured with tests." Looking at behaviors makes it easier to use questionnaires and participant observation without resorting to psychological tests.

Behaviors are deeply impacted by culture. As Hugues, Ginnett, and Curphy (2006) write, "leadership behaviors vary depending on country and culture, but they are helpful to study in order to better understand leadership effectiveness in a specific context." Cultural researchers like Triandis (1993: 16) found, "a myriad of ways in which cultures differ." Because I was seeking universal and culturally specific behaviors it is very important for this study that I utilize a qualitative approach.

Behaviors can change. This finding constitutes an important asset for my research. In contrast with traits, behaviors can more easily change. I can therefore posit with J. Robert Clinton that, "leadership style is a dynamic concept" (Clinton 1992: 43). In my recommendations, I argue that because behaviors can change, leaders should adapt their leadership to the context.

Values

Values deeply shape leadership styles (Massey 1979). They constitute another important component of a leadership style that is central to identify in research like mine. Personal values can be defined as, "constructs representing generalized behaviors or states of affairs that are considered by the individual to be important" (Gordon 1975: 2). According to M. Massey (1979), parents, peers, education, media, technology, and religion all contribute to shape people's values. It is therefore foreseeable that North African church leadership values will be uniquely shaped by these various inputs. Furthermore, leadership values take on specific definitions compared to personal ones. Hugues, Ginnett, and Curphy (2006) summarize well five main areas in which values affect leadership including (1) the choices leaders make, (2) the solutions and decisions in problem solving, (3) the perceptions of success, (4) the right and wrong choices, and (5) what are the important things.

Values are important to study for several reasons. First, they have a profound effect on leadership. As stated above, they influence a leader's choices, decisions, and perceptions (Hugues, Ginnett, and Curphy 2006). North African leaders have values that will shape the way they lead. My role in this research is to highlight these values in order to understand North African leadership styles.

Second, values help define the character of leaders including what they think is important and non-negotiable. Ken Blanchard and Phil Hodges (2005: 90) explain that "values are the nonnegotiable principles that define character in a leader." This is well illustrated by Max DePree (1992) when he discusses the importance of integrity as a leadership value. He states that, "Integrity in all things precedes all else. The open demonstration of integrity is essential: followers must be wholeheartedly convinced of their leaders' integrity" (DePree 1992: 10).[9] It will therefore be important in this research to find leadership values of North African church leaders if I want to understand their style. Like DePree, I may find that integrity is a non-negotiable for them or that there are other values that shape their leadership.

A third reason to study values is their tight link to effectiveness. A leader is often judged for his or her values. Terence R. Mitchell shows how leadership values are deeply connected to effectiveness. In writing about leaders in the United States he stated that, "we have serious problems in this country and that some of the causes of these problems can be attributed to the values of our leaders" (Mitchell 1993: 110). In studying North African leadership, I am eager to find out whether leaders understand the values of their context and how their own leadership values affect their effectiveness.

A fourth reason for studying values is to be aware of the effect culture has on them. Culture shapes leadership values, as underlined by Hugues, Ginnett, and Curphy (2006: 154) who write that, "values impact leadership through a cultural context within which various attributes and behaviors are regarded differently—positively or negatively." For example, G. Hofstede (1984) as well as D. Ronen and O. Shenkar (1985) stress the fact that there are different job-related values across cultures. Because North African leaders have received training from Western workers and theorists, one may wonder how their Muslim-shaped values have been taken into account.

A useful theory for addressing cross-cultural issues in leadership training is that of value-based leadership (Hofstede 1980; Kluckhohn and

---

9. Secular leadership theorists have also discussed the importance of the value of integrity (Higginson 1999; Solomon 1992). Christian theorists Banks and Ledbetter (2004: 101) discuss the two extremes of those who believe that integrity is impossible in leadership and others who believe that integrity must be involved in "moment-by-moment practice."

Strodtbeck 1961; and Triandis 1994). This theory asserts that values of collectivities shape behaviors of individuals (Bond and Leung 1993). Since my research is not specifically focused on values, but rather on leadership styles, I will not use this theory as a framework. However, it is useful as it shows me how misunderstandings of people's context and their values may jeopardize effective leadership training. It is one of my assumptions that understanding the cultural and religious context will enhance the leadership of North African church leaders. Some may not be aware that they might operate with values shaped by their Muslim family for example.

Finally, it is important for my research to consider that values are at the core or deepest layer of people's worldviews (Hiebert 1985). Values, therefore, may be as resistant to change as traits. I need to be particularly careful in the way I challenge leaders in the area of values. After exploring the religious, historical and cultural context of leadership in North Africa, I may discover that North African leaders operate in a Muslim majority context without addressing Muslim values. Some leaders may not see the challenges of ministering in a Muslim context with Western leadership values. Others may wonder how biblical values can interface with Muslim values to make leadership more effective. Although I may not be able to address all the challenges of values in cross-cultural leadership, I was encouraged to read the following comment by Wright (2000: 74) who states: "if the culture produces values that are not consistent with the affirmations we make, leaders must slowly and patiently continue to reinforce the stated values until they are embedded in the culture deep enough to last." This statement shows that despite the fact that values are resistant to change, there is a possibility for values to adapt and be transformed. It is not the goal of this research to establish a list of values for effective leadership in North Africa. However, this brief discussion on values has allowed me to highlight one important aspect of my research, which is to be able to define leadership styles by identifying the leadership values of North African believers and those of their context of ministry. After comparing leadership values in the North African, Muslim and Christian context, I may suggest further research that could lead to evaluating the effectiveness of the current leadership styles of church leaders.

In order to define the current leadership values of North African believers, which will help me define leadership styles, I included several questions on values in my interviews:

"What spiritual qualities must the Christian leader have?" (Question 20)

"What are the personal qualities of a Christian leader?" (Question 21)

"What are the values that a Christian leader should have? Are they different from non-Christian leadership values?" (Question 28)[10]

"Is there a list of values common to all Christian leaders?" (Question 29)

Third, specific questions deal with the context and will help show the impact church leaders may have on society:

"What values should a political leader have?" (Question 30)

"What values should the Christian leader display in his family?" (Question 31)

I am aware of the difficulty in measuring values in questionnaires. When people are asked about their values, they often give the ideal values of their culture instead of those they use in their work (Ayman and Hong 1992). A leader may say his/her highest value in leadership is servanthood but he/she may never act like a servant in his/her ministry. Due to these limitations, I will also collect metaphors and narratives that will provide further

---

10. Abbas J. Ali (2005: 64) writes that "values differ from attitudes not in quality, but in depth. Values are determinants rather than the components of attitudes and attitudes are biases while values are metabiases."

information on leadership values. My findings on values will be extremely helpful to define current leadership styles of church leaders.

Leadership Legitimacy

Another important component of the leadership style that must be identified is the legitimacy of the leader. Great-man theory first addressed this issue. According to this theory, leaders may be given their legitimacy from either personal characteristics or a divine appointment. For example, some Christians espouse they were appointed by God to be leaders before they were born. This trumps human legitimacy. Later, leadership theorists found that if the followers do not acknowledge the authority of their leaders, the latter aspect may be less effective. Contingency theory underlines this approach greatly.

Since this is the first research on church leadership in North Africa, I wanted to understand how people felt about their own calling. The point here was to help shed light on their relationship to God and to their followers. Therefore, I asked the following questions:

> "How did you become a leader?" (Question 15)
>
> "Did you receive an education for becoming a leader?" (Question 12)
>
> "Do you think leaders are born or appointed?" (Question 16)
>
> "Do you think one becomes a leader of a church/organization by receiving training?" (Question 17)
>
> "At what age can one become a church leader or a leader of a Christian organization?" (Question 18)

These questions are also very relevant to the socio-cultural context of North Africa. Age, for example, is an important characteristic taken into account in North Africa when choosing a leader. Older leaders usually have more authority and power than their younger counterparts.

Leadership Power and Influence

Power and influence are also important components of a leadership style. For example, in Blanchard's three leadership styles (i.e. autocratic, democratic and laissez-faire) there is a clear difference in how leaders influence their followers and make decisions. As a result, I have included the following questions in my questionnaire to identify how leaders influence followers and how they perceive authority:

"As a leader, what do you expect from followers?" (Question 22)

"How do you make decisions as a Christian leader?" (Questions 23)

"What does it mean for you to have power and influence as a Christian leader?" (Question 25)

"What does spiritual power mean for you as a Christian leader?" (Question 25)

"When should a leader step down and why?" (Question 26)

"What comes to your mind when you think about the authority of the Christian leader?" (Question 27)

"How should a Christian leader influence those who work with him?" (Question 32)

"What story comes to mind when you think of the relationship between those who are leaders and those who are followers?" (Question 33)

Metaphors and Definitions

During my pilot research in North Africa I discovered that while leaders had difficulty providing me examples of church leadership styles, they found it much easier to talk about metaphors and images of leadership. Consequently I decided to collect as many metaphors of leadership as I could. These often gave me significant clues about leadership qualities, values and leadership behaviors.

In order to gather further data, I also asked questions regarding general definitions of leadership. First, I asked North African leaders, "Define what a Christian leader is using a picture, a symbol or a story," (Question 13); second, "What is your favorite biblical passage that talks about a Christian leader?" (Question 14); and third, "What characterizes Christian leaders?" (Question 19).

In response to these questions, leaders gave me substantial and sizeable narratives that I analyzed using grounded theory.

Field Research

The methodology of my research is qualitative. I made a list of thirty-three questions that I administered in the form of questionnaires and interviews. I also audiotaped one conference on leadership which included a panel discussion.

The table below indicates the instruments, the number of informants and the location of my research.

TABLE 3: Instruments, Informants and Location

(Farida Saidi)

Instruments	Methodology	Informants	Location
Questionnaires	Qualitative	15	NAP
Questionnaires	Qualitative	18	North Africa
Semi-Structured Interviews	Qualitative	9	North Africa
Notes from Leadership Conference	Qualitative	9	North Africa

Informants

The respondents were all North Africans. Four of them did not live in this region but were very involved in ministry with their North African community abroad.

The first twelve questions consisted of demographic information such as gender, age, education, and years of experience of the informants. This data will not serve as a variable in this research but may be helpful if later, other researchers want to conduct quantitative research with my findings. I have summarized below the demographic information.

First, there were thirty-four males and eleven females. Their ages vary between twenty-two and fifty-five years old. The average mean is thirty.

Second, the respondents have various roles: nine were pastors, eight were leaders of church activities, seven were elders, one was a professor, and twenty were members of the church. I call them "Timothys" because they are still in training.

Third, out of forty-five respondents only seven answered the question about denomination. The reason for this includes various factors. First, there are no officially registered denominations in North Africa. Second, it may be that respondents did not want to disclose the name of the group they are working with. Third, the way they define themselves is more by connection with people than with church organizations. The three specific organizations or churches named were: (1) Baptist church; (2) Eglise Moissonnante pour Christ (EMC); and (3) chez Ortiz.

Fourth, in regards to location, twenty-seven respondents came from an urban context, sixteen from rural areas and two did not answer this question. When asked about the size of the churches or organizations respondents belonged to, they indicated that membership varied between three and 800 members.

Finally, when respondents were asked how long they worked in a Christian organization, their responses varied between three and twenty-five years. When asked about education, twenty-five graduated from high school, sixteen went to graduate school and four did not respond. When asked about leadership training, twenty-four said they did not receive any leadership training, twenty-one received leadership training.

NAP Conference

I conducted the initial research during a leadership conference in 2006.

During the conference, forty believers from a Muslim background (BMB) gathered for a one-day consultation to discuss the issue of leadership and mentoring. I audiotaped three case studies that were presented as well as the reports of three discussion groups that were held during that day. I also handed out thirty questionnaires to BMBs and received fifteen responses. Some leaders took the questionnaire home but never returned them. The conference gave me the opportunity to do some participant observation that I will include in my description of leadership styles when I analyze the data. I made notes during informal discussions with leaders, recording their comments and insights throughout our table conversations and the presentation of reports during discussion groups.

This is how I introduced the questionnaires. I gave respondents the three page questionnaires and asked them to complete them either at home or during the conference. I also asked them for their permission to use their data for my research. I gave them the freedom to contact me at any stage of my research, including up until the publication of the dissertation, if they wanted me to withdraw any or all of the information they shared. I clearly indicated that they were free to stop the interview process at any moment if they felt uncomfortable and did not want to continue. The strength of the NAP research was that these were key leaders I was able to interview. They had specifically travelled from North Africa to attend this leadership conference and were therefore very motivated to talk and reflect on the issue of leadership. The weakness of the research in NAP is that this was the first questionnaire I was giving and as a result I wish I could have made a few changes to it post conference. However, due to the fact that the people I met do not often travel outside the country I could not have gathered such a distinctive group at another time. I therefore decided to keep the questionnaire as it was and then used it with the rest of the informants I interviewed later in my research.

Visits to North Africa

I made two trips to North Africa where I collected data through questionnaires and interviews. Respondents answered eight questionnaires in French and ten in Arabic. The questionnaires in Arabic were completed by students of a bible school in North Africa. The questionnaires in French were filled in by brothers and sisters I met when I visited churches in North Africa.

This is how I introduced the questionnaires. I gave respondents the three-page questionnaires and asked them to complete them either at home or during the week of teaching. I also asked for their permission to use the data they shared for my research. I gave them the freedom to contact me at any stage of my research including up until the publication of the dissertation if they wanted me to withdraw any or all of the information they provided. I communicated that they were free to stop the interview process at any moment if they felt uncomfortable and did not want to pursue it. After I collected the questionnaire I realized that one of the questions in Arabic was poorly translated and so I discarded the answers to this question.

During another visit to North Africa, I conducted seven interviews with nine people. The respondents were eight men and one woman. All of the respondents were either pastors or elders. They came from different regions of North Africa, with experiences in ministry varying from three to twenty-five years. All were married with several years of Christian experience.

I chose interviews rather than questionnaires because North Africans are very relational and prefer interaction to written questionnaires. The one-on-one interviews helped them express deeper personal feelings about leadership. I found that I collected better data through the interviews and consequently if I were to do the research again, I would only do interviews, particularly because I was trying to identify new categories using grounded theory.

The interviews lasted between one and one and half hours each. All interviews were conducted with one respondent except two interviews with two respondents each. Three interviewees came from a rural context and six from urban ones.

Four interviews were conducted in homes and three interviews in churches. They were conducted in French or Arabic; respondents were fluent in both languages and therefore communication was not an issue. I personally knew six out of nine interviewees from ministry projects we had conducted together. Three respondents, one pastor and two elders, I had never met.

One church leader remained with me during all of the interviews without interfering with the process. He also was my driver. This is how I started the interview sessions. Before recording, I asked for permission to interview the person. I told them immediately that they were free to respond or not to my questions. I also asked them for their permission to use the data they gave me for my research. I stated they were free to contact me at any stage of my research including up until the publication of the dissertation if they wanted me to withdraw any or all of the information they shared. I communicated that they were free to stop the interview process at any moment if they felt uncomfortable and did not want to pursue it. I then opened my tape recorder and asked again for their permission to do the interviews. Their response was recorded. I did the same at the end of the interview.

It was very important to keep the confidentiality of the informants. After the face-to-face interviews, I used other names to protect the identity of the informants. I personally conducted every interview and assured participants that their names would not appear in the dissertation. I also made sure that respondents would not be recognized through contextual information.

Data Analysis

Each interview was recorded, transcribed and then analyzed using the software program Atlas. The questionnaires were recorded and analyzed using the program Word. The questions, which were the same in the interviews and the questionnaires, provided the broad framework of the research. They defined what the respondents said about values, behaviors and qualities, in which relational context they said it,[11] and how they said it.[12] As I was comparing and contrasting the various responses, I looked at the categories that emerged and found certain patterns and frequencies in words, concepts, metaphors and images.

---

11. By context I mean (1) leader-self; (2) leader-follower; (3) leader-God; and (4) leader-society.
12. By "how" I mean (1) metaphors; (2) words; and (3) bible references.

Leadership theories provide numerous leadership styles such as the autocratic, democratic, laissez-faire, charismatic, servant, or shepherd leadership style. Yet no study has defined North African church leadership styles. As I stated earlier, I do not want to impose leadership styles on North African leaders without first investigating their own views on the topic. As a result I only borrowed from my study of leadership broad categories which framed my initial conversations with North African leaders. Although I did not want to influence the informants by using theories not appropriate to their context, I still needed to outline a framework, as suggested by Hughes, Ginnett, and Curphy (2006: 7), who said that "the various definitions [of leadership] can help us appreciate the multitude of factors that affect leadership, as well as different perspectives from which to view it."

The narrative collected has been analyzed in two ways. Some answers were straightforward such as when a leader responded to the question "What is your leadership value?" by saying, "Justice." But for longer narratives I used grounded theory to extract from the text units of meaning that would help me better understand the values, qualities and behaviors of leaders. Like Bass I believe that grounded theory helps discern "the subtleties and nuances involved in the leadership process" (Bass 1990: 887). I respond in this research to the needs expressed by researchers, such as N.W McCall and M.M. Lombardo (1978) who emphasized the need for more ethnographic research on leadership.

I understand, as Glaser (1978) wrote, that I will theorize and write ideas as the categories emerge from the coding of interviews, focus groups and questionnaires. In my coding I will look for both high frequency occurrences and high connectedness between the categories. For example, an initial browsing of the data collected shows that certain words stand out in terms of frequency. Some of these words have been spontaneously quoted by the informants. For example, the word "servant" has been used frequently by respondents even though there are no specific questions on servanthood.

I feel comfortable using grounded theory because other researchers have used it to analyze leadership traits and behaviors. Dail Fields (2005) from Regent University is currently conducting a study of Christian leaders who influenced the world. He uses grounded theory and studies traits, characteristics, and behaviors.[13] Bass explains how qualitative research can be used in leadership studies. He states that "qualitative research is likely to begin with deductions from a theory or a set of general propositions and then to proceed as a detective might to track down patterns, searching for consistencies in the qualitative information" (Bass 1990: 887). I will follow Bass' cues as I proceed.

Descriptive Study

In my research, I am not measuring the leadership effectiveness of North African leaders. I describe their style by looking at their qualities, values and behaviors and matching them with existing leadership styles from the theories presented in chapter 2. This is a descriptive and not an evaluative study. However, in my recommendations I suggest that leadership styles that may be most effective are those who are contingent on the followers, the context and are biblical. The latter is based on the teaching of contingency theory, which posits that leaders must make their behaviors contingent to followers and context.

I assume that if North African leaders do not change some of their styles, they might not be able to adequately serve the church. For example, patience (as a quality) is one of the major leadership traits expected of a Muslim leader. If Christian leaders are not able to demonstrate patience, will they be respected in a Muslim context? As long as patience is also a positive attribute in the Bible (which it is), I believe that Christian leaders should seek to model that attribute.

---

13. These are the words appearing on Field's website "Using a Delphi panel of administrators, academics, and executives, a group of thirteen leaders have been identified who have led society by initiating and implementing world-changing events, organizations, or concepts. Detailed review and analysis of archival information and data is now underway in a search for common themes that help us understand the leadership approaches and behaviors these people used in successfully in changing the world" (http: // www.regent.edu/acad/global/faculty/fields/home.cfm).

Limitations of my Research

I had several challenges as I researched leadership styles. First, it was not easy to measure behaviors, values and attributes by only using questionnaires and interviews. As a result of my own awareness of this difficulty I looked at how leadership theorists researched leadership behaviors. For example, they differentiate between data collected concerning general behaviors over space and time (Ayman and Hong 1992) and specific behaviors observed in a given setting (Ayman and Hong 1992). They call the former leadership traits and the latter leadership behaviors. Since I did not ask informants to indicate behaviors observed in a specific setting or to respond based on their own expectations, ideal behaviors or perceptions, I will not make a clear distinction between trait and behaviors in my findings.

Second, I believe that looking at behaviors, values and attributes must be conducted from several angles. I did not interview followers, which would have given much needed information on their leaders. I also did not include participant observation, which is necessary when one wants to observe behaviors.

Third, many of the informants had not yet reflected much on the topic of leadership. Some had not even received any training in this area. One the one hand, this could be interpreted as a strength since the informants were able to express leadership using their own terms; on the other, the informants were not always prepared to address the leadership context and as a result, sometimes gave general answers.

Fourth, it is a challenge to measure values by asking, "What is your value?" Since I did not use one of the many questionnaires which measured leadership values, I cannot clearly define between quality and value. Because this research is an initial mapping of North African church leadership, I will not consider this issue as a weakness. The data I collected is the first of many more.

Finally, the challenge of this research was to evaluate whether what respondents said about leadership was their actual assessment or an idealization. I did not make this assessment. Based on some discrepancies between the actual practices in the churches I observed during my ministry and the actual responses I collected, I may infer that leaders sometimes presented a more idealistic perspective on leadership. Future research should compare what was said with actual practices in local churches.

Part 2

Styles of Leadership in Islam and North African Culture and History

In this second part of my book, I explore the leadership styles in Islamic contexts and in North African culture and history. The contemporary North African church leaders I study were born and raised Muslim. As a result, they have been influenced by Muslim leadership values either through their family or the Muslim leaders they met throughout their life. It is therefore important to find out if the Islamic context influenced their church leadership style. Chapter 4 identifies leadership styles in Islam through text-based research. In the conclusion of my book I compare and contrast the Islamic leadership styles with what I found in this chapter to define leadership styles of contemporary church leaders.

In chapter 5, I conduct text-based research to find what leadership styles exist in North African culture. I hypothesize that North African church leaders are impacted by their culture despite the fact that some current church leaders may not acknowledge this fact. In the conclusion of this book, I will compare and contrast the list of cultural leadership patterns in North African culture with what I found in the church to define leadership styles of church leaders. I will thus learn whether North African pastors borrow styles from their culture.

Finally, in chapter 6, I present the leadership styles from the study of four historical leaders. In contrast with the two previous chapters, the methodology used in this research stems from social science and requires primary research. As I explained in my methodology chapter, I could not find studies on the leadership styles of these leaders. I therefore conducted primary research using the same questions I asked contemporary church leaders. The challenge of applying this method with text instead of living informants is that I needed to browse an enormous amount of data to be able to locate values and behaviors of these four leaders that would highlight their leadership styles. I will later compare and contrast what I found in this chapter with the values and behaviors of contemporary church leaders to define their leadership styles.

CHAPTER 4

Leadership Styles in Islam

In this chapter, I explore leadership styles in Islam for two major reasons. First, my assumption is that church leaders, whether they know it consciously or not, are influenced by the predominantly Islamic leadership norms of their society. Some aspects of Muslim leadership may shape their values and behaviors. In his research on leadership in the Evangelical Church in Egypt, Samy Hanna Ghabrial noticed how Islam had some influence on the evangelical leadership. He wrote: "The Islamic leadership system has affected the evangelical view on issues like the role of the followers in the leadership process as is present in the *shura* system" (Ghabrial 1997: 94-95). Knowing that Islam may have an influence on the style of North African leaders will be important when I analyze my data on leadership styles in North African churches. In the conclusion, I will compare and contrast what I found in this chapter with my field research in churches to determine whether the religious leadership styles of the Muslim community influence North African church leaders or not.

The second reason for studying leadership in Islam is to find out whether it is possible for church leaders from a Muslim background to retain certain values and behaviors from Islamic leadership when they do not oppose biblical teaching. In other words, it will be important for me to see how the Bible can shape styles from a Muslim context to make North African leaders more effective in their society.

The early stages of my research was not easy because the term "leadership" has a Western connotation and is rarely used in the early texts of Islam. I remember walking into a Muslim bookstore in Paris for my first tutorial and asking the librarian if he could suggest books on leadership in

Islam. His response was blunt: "There is no concept of leadership in Islam. This is a Western concept. In Islam there is no intermediary between God and men. Muslims do not need anyone to stand between them and God when they pray." I am glad this librarian's remark did not prevent me from studying my topic particularly because I later discovered that although the term leadership was not directly quoted in the Qur'an several other terms were used referring to the same concept.

I then reviewed the Qur'an and the Hadith because they are considered to be major sources on leadership by contemporary Muslim researchers (Beekun and Badawi 1999). Instead of looking for terms like leadership or leadership styles, I looked at cognates such as authority, power and influence (Khan 2007).[1] I did not conduct an exegetical study of the text but relied on prominent authors who explored these terms and concepts in the sacred texts of Islam.

To determine leadership styles, I looked first at general values, behaviors and attitudes for successful human endeavor that also apply to leadership (Khan 2007). Second, I tried to find direct references to "authority" or "power." Third, I looked for leadership concepts "reflected in stories about earlier prophets and wise persons in the Qur'an" (Khan 2007: 3). For example, both the Qur'an and the Hadith contain stories of leaders such as Adam, Noah,[2] Moses, David as well as others not mentioned in the Bible, such as Salih[3] or Hud.[4] According to Montgomery Watt these stories are "illustrations of the main Qur'anic conception of the relationship of messenger to community" (1961: 64). Contemporary Muslims rely on them as a resource for leadership styles. Lastly, I studied the life of Muhammad, the Prophet of Islam, who is considered the role model of leadership of the faith and has much to offer to this field of study although his leadership styles have been the subject of great debate throughout the centuries.

Before looking at the sacred texts of Islam and their commentators, I first provide a brief background of pre-Islamic leadership. This will help me

---

1. Adalat Khan (2007: 2) states that Islamic Leadership Principles can be derived from the Holy Qur'an, the Muslim prophets, the caliphs and the pious followers.
2. *Sura* 7:59-64.
3. *Sura* 7:73-79.
4. *Sura* 7:65-72.

examine whether Islam integrated non-Islamic leadership principles that may still influence its leaders today.

Pre-Islamic (jahiliyya) *Leadership*

In this section, I briefly describe the leadership roles of pre-Islamic Arabia in order to understand the leadership principles that may have influenced the development of leadership in early Islam. I also list the leadership values and characteristics of these pre-Islamic leaders. This section will help me identify possible contextual elements in Muslim leadership of first century Islam.

Leadership Roles

The seventh century Arabian Peninsula consisted of nomadic people who pastured camels and sheep, and sedentary dwellers in oases or small towns who were cultivators, traders or craftsmen (Hourani 1991). These social structures shaped leadership[5] uniquely in the following ways.

Pre-Islamic leadership involved respect and honor given by tribal members to a common ancestor (Chelhod 1958; Ibn Khaldun 1967). Hourani explains, "They [pre-Islamic Arabs] were not controlled by a stable power of coercion, but were led by chiefs belonging to families around which there gathered more or less lasting groups of supporters, expressing their cohesions and loyalty in the idiom of common ancestry" (Hourani 1991: 10). Ibn Khaldun demonstrates that this type of Arab Bedouin society encouraged a corporate spirit (*'asabiyya*) (Hourani 1991). Superiority, says Ibn Khaldun, (1967: 101) flowed from group feeling[6]:

> leadership exists only through superiority,[7] and superiority only through group feeling. Leadership over people, therefore,

---

[5]. At that time, the term "leadership" was not used. Authors refer to "government" or "authority" but for the purpose of consistency, I decided to use "leadership" throughout my book.
[6]. To Ibn Khaldun (1967), group feeling results from sharing same blood ties.
[7]. Ibn Khaldun (1967: 203) uses the Arabic term *ghalab* for what is translated by superiority both in Rosenthal's and Monteil's translation.

must of necessity, derive from a group feeling that is superior to each individual group feeling. Each individual group feeling that becomes aware of the superiority of the group feeling of the leader is ready to obey and follow him.

Xavière Remacle further highlights this group feeling that makes Bedouins "not define themselves by their place of residence but by their family ties" (Remacle 2002: 26).

In a context based so heavily on group feeling, individual autonomy threatened the established order (Chelhod 1958). Although chiefs were at the head of tribes, Chelhod posits that the nomads did not consider they obeyed a human being but instead traditions and customs of their clan.[8] The ethos of this society included "hospitality, loyalty to family and pride to ancestry" (Hourani 1991: 10).

Despite the common ancestor and group feeling, the sheikh (chief of the nomadic clan)[9] also played an important role in leadership. In that role he was more or less a type of political leader with spiritual influence. Remacle observes that the Bedouin Arab society was not very hierarchical and adds, "They particularly honor the most influential people and the most charismatic" (Remacle 2002: 119).

The tribal leader combined different roles, which became increasingly separated in sedentary life.[10] Chelhod explains, "The chieftain who, in his role as a poet or *hakam* (arbitrator) had to become a seer, keeps with him the religious emblems of power" (Chelhod 1958: 61). Ibn Khaldun writes, "The restraining influence among Bedouin tribes comes from their sheikhs and leaders. It results from the great respect and veneration they generally enjoy among the people" (Ibn Khaldun 1967: 97).

---

8. Mansour (1975) shows that in pre-Islamic times the customs and traditions became law.
9. The social structure in pre-Islamic Arabia essentially was made up of tribes organized in class (Chelhod 1973).
10. Chelhod (1958: 62), quoting Henri Lammens explains, "Several Arab leaders, such as Zohayr ben Ganab, were both sayyed, orators, poets, ambassadors to kings, prophets, doctors and cavalrymen of their tribes, all at the same time."

The tribal sheikh displayed the virtues of the Arabs, called *muruwah*.[11] Toshihiko Izutsu states that it comprises generosity,[12] bravery and courage, patience, trustworthiness, truthfulness" (Izutsu 2002). Ignace Goldziher shows *muruwah* meant,

> All those virtues, which were founded in the tradition of his people, constitute the fame of an individual or the tribe to which he belongs; the observance of those duties which are connected with family ties, the relationship of protection and hospitality, and the fulfillment of the great law of blood revenge. (Goldziher 2006: 22)

Goldziher further explains that *muruwah* includes loyalty to and self-sacrifice for the sake of everyone connected with one's tribe, as well as right and equity (i.e. a striving for justice).

According to Chelhod (1958) the sheikh was first of all a father figure whose influence expanded with the increase of his offspring. But Chelhod notes that he was also arbiter, supreme judge, and supreme guide. He was chosen by the council of the elders and expected to collaborate with them (Gardet 1981). He led his people into war, and appointed his successor (Chelhod 1958).[13] The council of the elders assisted him as he discussed daily matters pertaining to the rule of the tribe and listened to complaints and advice of its members (Gardet 1981).

The tribal leader made final decisions on war and peace, contracted alliances and interacted with chiefs of other clans (Chelhod 1958). His sovereignty was to be recognized by all and his power[14] lay in the tacit agreement

---

11. Goldziher (2006: 22) explains, "By *muruwwa* the Arab means 'all'."
12. About generosity, Lammens (1914: 235) writes, "in Bedouin thinking... the rich man is perceived to be simply a depositary, a momentary steward of his own fortune; his mission is to distribute it among the needy of the tribe, to use it to practise hospitality, to redeem prisoners and to pay blood money."
13. At some point, the tribal chief had a chief of the army that went to war (Chelhod 1958).
14. Chelhod (1958) believes that during the pre-Islam period, sovereignty was still diffuse. With the start of settlements, nomads included a more diversified vision of leadership and paid allegiance to their family, their tribe, their city and their idols (Chelhod 1958).

of his entire society (Chelhod 1958). According to Gardet (1981) he was both a representative and guide of the tribe or the city. He was also a kind of priest (Chelhod 1958).[15]

Honor and good reputation were key values of these leaders. Albert Habib Hourani confirms this fact as he describes the leaders of nomadic pastoral tribes, "who had little effective power except that which was given them by their reputation in the public opinion of the group" (Hourani 1991: 108). The importance of personal values are further underlined by Chelhod who says about the leader: "A person's authority is fragile: he has to show that he is worthy and back up this claim by brilliant demonstrations of his personal worth, without which he could never claim the obedience of his dependents or aspire to maintain his power over them" (Chelhod 1958: 57). The same author then describes these values saying, "The nomadic chieftain is above all a man who has succeeded in accomplishing and developing in himself all the traditional virtues of an Arab: generosity, hospitality, bravura, clear-sightedness and longanimity (*hilm*)." In another passage, he mentions "eloquence" as the value par excellence and says, "As it is, in these societies where eloquence had always been the most important quality in a leader, he was often considered to be a visionary" (Chelhod 1958: 56).

Bedouin leaders were often considered as having supernatural abilities common to the *sha'ir* (knower) and *kahin* (soothsayer).[16] Several authors remark that these two leadership roles were very similar (Watt 1953; Doutté 1994). The *sha'ir* and *kahin*, sometimes called magicians or sorcerers could predict the future and used magical pronouncements called *saj'*,[17] a "form

---

15. Chelhod (1958: 61) explains: ". . . In a nomadic clan, power is found in the hands of a chieftain who, although he is not a priest, enjoys certain religious prerogatives."

16. There were also many women who had this function, says Doutté (1994). It is actually very important to mention here that in the late seventh and early eighth century the queen of the Berbers, who ruled over all the Berber tribes in the Aurès region, in present Algeria, was called the Kahina. Her real name was Dahiya and she grew up in the North African Djeraoua tribe, which professed Judaism (Fournel 1983: 31). According to Doutté (1994: 31), the fact that Arab historians, the only ones who recorded her story, call her the Kahina, suggest that her leadership role was akin to the pre-Islamic *kahin*, or soothsayer. Furthermore, Doutté (1994: 32) mentions that Procope shows that there were many female prophets among the Berbers at that time.

17. In *Saj'*, the "concluding words of the short sections or lines had an assonance or imperfect rhyme" (Watt 1979).

of rhythmical" prose (Watt 1979: 60-61). Hourani writes, "Soothsayers claimed to speak with the tongue of some supernatural wisdom" (Hourani 1981: 11). This knowledge was not accessible to others (Watt 1953) and their power of divination was believed to come from the *jinn* (Chelhod 1986). They had various functions including predicting the future, arbiters, denouncing murderers, and judge (Doutté 1994).

One of the major differences between the *kahin* and the *sha'ir* is that the latter was linked with a particular shrine (Watt 1979). The *sha'ir* bore this name because he was familiar with "the traditions of his tribe about the noble achievements of their ancestors" (Watt 1953: 60). Watt explains that, "because of his special 'knowledge' the *sha'ir* in early times was often, perhaps usually, the person who decided where and when the tribe was to camp and when it was to move on; he was thus its leader (*qa'id*)" (Watt 1953: 60).

The tribal leader was also a *hakam* (arbiter).[18] Watt identifies this role as a type of leader implying that not all arbiters were actual tribal leaders. Essentially Watt says, "The arbiter had no executive power, but only a certain moral authority, and this was backed by the swearing of oaths and the giving of securities for the carrying out of his judgment" (Watt 1953: 62).

When clans settled in small towns and cities a new type of religious role emerged before Islam.[19] Hourani writes,

> The power of tribal leaders was exercised from oases, where they had close links with merchants who organized trade through the territory controlled by the tribe. In the oases, however, other families were able to establish a different kind of power through the force of religion. (Hourani 1991: 11)

---

18. It is noteworthy that Ali Abderraziq (1994) in his study of the basis of power in Islam underlines that the three major tasks of the early religious leaders in Islam were to teach the Qur'an, to explain Islamic Laws and to arbitrate conflicts between tribes.
19. The use of the term "religious" here does not mean that there was an organized religion in pre-Islamic Arabia. Rather, people believed in local gods, dwelling in natural objects, and good and evil spirits. (Hourani 1991: 11). Xavière Remacle thinks that religion in pre-Islamic Arabia was closer to animism than to polytheism. She mentions, like other authors, this "vague sense of the Sacred, without defining it clearly" and "an invisible universe made up of sacred energy" (2002: 25). She says that this energy, which can also indwell people, was commonly named *baraka* (2002: 26).

These families, which were protected by neighboring tribes, were each respectively the overseer of a specific center of pilgrimage, which had sanctuaries of gods (Hourani 1991: 11). Chelhod explains, "The idol, which is no longer guarded by the ministers of the chieftain, ends up becoming independent from political power. Thus the servant of the temple becomes an important figure: he represents religious power in the eyes of the faithful." Hourani describes other roles of these religious leaders: "a family could obtain power and influence by making skillful use of its religious prestige, its role as arbiter of tribal disputes, and its opportunity of trade" (Hourani 1991: 11).

Cities witnessed a new type of administration and authority called *mala'*. Chelhod explains that this was an assembly similar to the *majlis* of the nomads which was kind of council gathering of the elders of various clans (Chelhod 1958: 75). This is where the decisions about the collective life of the group were made. Decisions were made by consensus or unanimity and the only form of persuasion or coercion was the banishment of the group that did not accept the general decisions (Lammens 1924: 70).[20]

TABLE 4: Pre-Islamic Leadership Roles
(Farida Saidi)

Common ancestor	Unites the clan together
Hakam	Arbiter, judge
Kahin	Magician, poet, soothsayer
Majlis	Council of elder
Mala'	City council
Qa'id	Leader
Sha'ir	Knower
Sheikh	Arbiter, chief of the nomadic clan, power flows from group feeling (*'asabiyya*)

---

20. This habit still seems to influence interpersonal relations in present Muslim communities. When someone becomes an apostate, the way the family and society exercises coercion is to banish him or her from the group.

Influence of Pre-Islamic Leadership on Islamic Leadership

Following this brief description of major leadership roles and functions in the pre-Islamic era, the issue of whether they shaped leadership in Islam is crucial to address. In order to later analyze current leadership styles in the church, it will be helpful to first know what specific aspects of Islam have been borrowed from other cultures, and second, what Muslims feel is uniquely Islamic in their religious leadership styles. I will only be able to address the first issue here, leaving the latter for the end of this chapter following my review of the leadership styles in Islam.

The influence of pre-Islamic leadership on Muslim leadership styles is a subject of much debate. Although the Qur'an makes a number of references to pre-Islamic leadership, it is not ultimately clear in its discussion of the issue. For example, some Qur'anic passages strongly criticize the practices of the Bedouins, such as unbelief (*sura* 9:97) or the lack of zeal (*sura* 98:11), but they never lay blame on the leadership styles. Certain tribal practices such as favoring one's kin were also condemned in favor of justice. Other passages allude to the fact that Muhammad was not a *kahin* or *sha'ir* (*sura* 69:41-42).

The authors I have chosen for this research shed some light on this discussion without coming to complete agreement between them. Watt begins by arguing that "the conception of religious leadership in the Qur'an is very different from that in pre-Islamic times, since it has its center not in the *kahin* or *sha'ir* but in the *nabi* or the *rasul*, the prophet or the messenger" (Watt 1953: 62). However he then points out that some pre-Islamic roles may have been adopted into Islam, such as the function of the *hakam* who "may have influenced the religious leadership exercised by Muhammad" (Watt 1953: 62).[21]

Chelhod seems to agree with Watt and even elaborates a detailed argumentation of how Islam practiced contextualization of leadership. After stating that "Islam marks... a return to nomadism in terms of the function which it creates from chiefdom," he shows the following examples of what Islam adapted from the Bedouin culture: (1) hereditary legitimacy of the

---

21. Watt, despite his oustanding scholarship, was not a Muslim and may only provide an etic approach.

leadership,[22] (2) personal qualities of the leader,[23] and (3) arbitration, modeled from the ancient *hakam* (Chelhod 1983: 16). Chelhod's thesis is that while Islam has deeply changed the social ideal of the Arab Bedouins it has remained very close to the leadership ideals of these same people.

Toshihiko Izutsu also underlines a certain influence of pre-Islamic leadership when he writes that Islam "adopted and revived, in a new form suited to the needs of monotheism, many of the outstanding virtues of paganism" (Izutsu 2002: 74). He continues saying, "There is certain aspect in which we might perhaps speak of the moral aspect of Islam even as a restoration of some of the old Arab ideals and nomadic virtues which have degenerated in the hands of the wealthy merchants of Mecca before the rise of this religion" (Izutsu 2002: 74). The same writer then states that, "Be that it may, we encounter in the Qur'an many of the moral ideals of the desert in the few garments of Islam" (Izutsu 2002: 75). Izutsu concludes however that, "In adopting and assimilating them into its system of moral teachings, Islam purified and freshened them, making their energy flow into certain channels which it had prepared" (Izutsu 2002: 75).

Goldziher furnishes a further example of how pre-Islamic values where integrated into the new religion when he writes, "Islamic teaching was not opposed to a large part of the Arab system of virtues—in particular Islam incorporated into its own teaching the moving loyalty of the Arabs toward those seeking protection" (Goldziher 2006: 23). However, he quickly adds, "Nevertheless there were decisive and basic points in the moral teaching of the Jahiliyya to which Islam was in almost irreconcilable contrast." He then cites a long passage on how the concept of retaliation was transformed in Islam (Golziher 2006: 24-25).[24]

With a slightly different approach Louis Gardet contends that the Bedouin leadership style only influenced its Muslim counterparts in the

---

22. Essentially, Muhammad and the early caliphs were from the leading Meccan tribe of the *qorayshites*.

23. We have discussed above how the tribal leader needed to display a number of personal values that we listed.

24. Golziher (2006: 25) writes, "Muhammed was the first man of their kind who said to the people of Mecca and the unbridled masters of the Arabian desert that forgiveness was no weakness but a virtue and that to forgive injustice done to oneself was not contrary to the norms of true *muruwwa* but that the highest *muruwwa*—was walking in Allah's road."

early years. Later, when the caliphate moved away from Arab lands, this tribal style tended to undergo major transformations (Gardet 1981: 32).

Conclusion

This section has allowed me to underline the following major sources of authority in pre-Islamic Arabia to which Muhammad may have been exposed during his lifetime and which may have influenced his understanding of leadership: (1) common ancestor, (2) sheikh (tribal leader), (3) *majlis* (council of elders), (4) *hakim* (arbiter), (5) *sha'ir* (knower), (6) *kahin* (soothsayer), (7) keeper of the center of pilgrimage, and (8) *mala'* (city council). Some pre-Islamic roles seemed to have disappeared in early Islam such as the *kahin* and the *sha'ir* while others, like *hakam*, have been adopted and transformed. The table in Appendix 1 identifies a specific list of values, attributes and behaviors that will be compared and contrasted later with Islamic leadership characteristics. It also provides significant information on the power and influence of a leader that flows from his blood ties, customs and traditions, group feeling, spirituality and as a result of their visionary function. The table furthers shows that leaders use consultation for decision-making despite the fact that their position makes them so well respected that they often model autocratic leadership. The legitimacy of the leaders, as indicated in the same table, comes from other leaders, heredity, and tacit agreement of the entire society. Finally, four major leadership styles have been identified: the charismatic-visionary leadership style, the sheikh-father, the guide and the priest. The task of arbitration is prominent enough that it practically deserves to be included as a style, but because I have not found enough evidence in the leadership literature to support its inclusion, I leave it for future investigation.

Leadership in Early Islam

We face three major challenges when researching leadership in early Islam. First, as Gustave Edmund von Grunebaum affirms, there is no fully developed theory of law and power in the Qur'an (Gardet 1981). Second, Muhammad died without clearly defining what type of authority would succeed him (Mansour 1975). Third, the word "leadership," as currently used, did not exist in early Islam. However, that does not mean that there are no references to leadership in the Qur'anic texts. Other terms were used instead referring to authority and power, which are key concepts of leadership in Islam (al-Asi 2000).[25] Furthermore, over the years a number of terms such as imam, *qadi*, *fuqaha'*, or *'ulama* were labeled to define the category of "men of religion" who played a greater role in religious leadership than common Muslims (Iogna-Prat and Veinstein 2003: 49). Finally, there are numerous values and qualifications contained in the Qur'an that were borrowed by Muslim leaders with influence.

In this brief overview I look at both Muslim and non-Muslim commentators of the Qur'an, the Hadith and Muhammad's sira to understand how leadership was defined in the early Muslim community. Much is drawn in this discussion from the study of Muhammad's leadership who is a role model for most Muslim leaders (*sura* 33:21).[26]

God's Power versus Human Power

Through the centuries, Islam, just like Christianity, has faced the challenge of defining the nature and legitimacy of religious power (Boulaabi 2005, Gardet 1981, Mansour 1975). The vast majority of Muslim theologians and jurists affirm that God is the source of authority yet they do not address what kind of power human beings have. The Qur'an clearly states that, "The Command rests with none but God" (*sura* 6:57). Power (*hukm*), says Khalifa (E.I. 2CD), belongs to God alone and he does not share it with human beings. God, for instance, is called "Lord of power" (*sura* 51: 58).

If all power belongs to God, how do Muslims then explain the role and influence of Qur'anic leaders? For example, Adam is called "a vicegerent on earth" (*sura* 2:30) and David is claimed to have "brought authority and kingship" (Redissi 1998: 25). Likewise, several Qur'anic passages enjoin

---

25. Boulaabi (2005: 51) lists the terms used in the Qur'an to refer to power as *'amr, mulk, hukm,* imam and sultan.

26. The beginning of this verse says, "Ye have indeed in the Apostle of God a beautiful pattern (of conduct)."

Muslims to obey Muhammad[27] and one in particular commands believers to obey "those charged with authority[28] among you" (*sura* 4:59).[29]

Islamicists have defined the relationship between divine and human power in different ways. For example, Gardet (1981: 35) believes that "not only does this authority derive from God, but there is no other authority than God . . . there can be no true delegation of this authority. . . . God is the only one to have the true temporal authority."[30] He then explains that, "the human intermediary is only an appearance of a sign" (Gardet 1981: 33).

Having defined that all power belongs to God, Muslims agree that some kind of human authority exists even if it is limited. First, Gardet shows the supremacy of God's law over the leader when he says that, "to Muslims belong the duty of obedience toward the earthly chiefs God has given as long as they govern according to Qur'anic laws" (Gardet 1981: 40). Second, Muhammad Khalaf-Allah emphasizes that human authority is primarily "concerned with worldly matters—especially that which deals with security, wars, political, economic, and administrative matters, etc." (Khalaf-Allah 1998: 39).[31] Third, Abderraouf Boulaabi (2005) shows authority

---

27. The expression usually used is: "Obey God, and obey the Apostle" (*sura* 4:59).
28. In Arabic, the term used is *Ulu-l-amr*.
29. Abdullah Yusuf Ali (1934) writes in footnote to *sura* 4:59: "*Ulu-al-amr*: those charged with authority or responsibility or decision, or the settlement of affairs. All ultimate authority rests in God. Men of God derive their authority from Him. As Islam makes no sharp division between sacred and secular affairs, it expects ordinary governments to be imbued with righteousness and stand in the place of the righteous Imam, and we must respect and obey such authority; otherwise there will be no order or discipline. Where, in actual fact, there is a sharp division between law and morality, between secular and religious affairs, as is the case in most countries at the present day, Islam still expects secular authority to be exercised in righteousness, and on that condition, enjoins obedience to such authority."
30. Gardet believes that in Islam, God does not share his power, but that in Christianity, God communicates his authority because he created human beings in his image (Gardet 1981: 35). God does not impart his power and this explains why there is no hierarchy in the religious sphere like there was at certain times in the history of the church. He concludes that, "the difference between the Christian and the Muslim idea of authority does not lie so much in the concept of authority as in the great theological concept of divine government." In Islam, God does not share his authority because this would mean having companions, which is unthinkable in Islam. In Christianity, all power comes from God, but God delegates to humans the temporal power with specific natural guidelines.
31. Having defined these two types of authority, Khalaf-Allah (1998) further explains that religious scholars deal with the first, but their role is limited to explaining the revelation

has evolved in Islam from the theocratic power of Muhammad's time to the polycratic caliphal power under the four rightly guided caliphs to the monocratic dynastic power under the Ummayads and Abbassids.

The most common way the Qur'an defines the relationship between God's power and human power is through the concept of *istikhlaf* (vicegerency). Boulaabi (2005: 47) explains, "the relationship between God's authority and human authority is a 'relationship of *istikhlaf*, a relationship of vicegerency based on an original pact which forms a true contract." He then explains how the prophetic mission becomes simply educational:

> This freedom within the *istikhlaf*, the vicegerency, is the foundation of human responsibility. At this stage, the relationship between divine authority and human authority is direct, thanks to the original pact. It is only much later that the prophetic mission, which is completely educational, comes into play. In other words, humanity, although free, responsible and reasonable, is no longer abandoned to its own devices: it is educated, led, guided by revelation. (Boulaabi 2005)

Boulaabi (2005: 48) shows power and authority are essentially a responsibility that God has given to human beings. Gardet (1981: 35) sees it as God communicating power to human beings.

An important distinct characteristic of Islam compared to some Christian traditions is that it has no sacerdotal status of religious leadership. Most authors would agree that the Muslim community has direct access to the sacred without an intermediary (Boulaabi 2005: 63). As a result, it is the knowledge of the sacred texts that becomes the key criteria for exercising religious leadership. Boulaabi (2005: 63) writes, "Anybody can reach the rank of *mujtahid* or *'alim*. The only condition is the level of knowledge acquired by the person."

---

that has been given by God. No new revelation can be given. In this sense the final authority belongs to God. But Khalaf-Allah further argues that in worldly matters, leaders have more freedom to make decisions and issue new rules as long as they do not contradict the divine revelation. Again, as for the law, the revelation is superior in power to the individual leader.

Authority and Power

To further define power and authority, one has to identify specific terms used in the Qur'an. First, *"amr"* seems to be the term that "best translates the concept of power in the Qur'an" (Boulaabi 2005: 51). He contends that, "The term *amr* (power) was used to cover two concepts: obedience and *shura* which constituted the two terms in the equation of power."[32] *Amr* can be found in nature and in humans as is evidenced by Cragg (1964: 120) who shows that, "The divine *amr* runs through the whole being of phenomena and gives them genesis and continuity." However when it is used with men, "the *amr*, or command of revelatory behest, waits upon the proper submission of humanity. . . it is willed and chosen" (*sura* 32:4-5; 41:12; Cragg 1964: 120).

The following quote is a widely cited leadership passage in the Qur'an which contains the word *amr*:

> O you who have attained to faith! Pay heed unto God, and pay heed unto the Apostle and unto those from among you who have been entrusted with authority; and if you are at variance over any matter, refer it unto God and the Apostle, if you [truly] believe in God and the Last Day. This is the best [for you], and best in the end. (*sura* 4:59)

In Boulaabi's interpretation of this verse, he shows that there is a difference between the authority of God and his prophet and that of the detainers of *amr* (Boulaabi 2005: 51). This third category consists of political and human power that is not related to the sacred sphere (Boulaabi 2005: 51). Thus, it appears that the Qur'an makes a clear distinction between the human authority held by political leaders and the legal authority of God and Muhammad; after the latter's death it is expressed in the *ijma'* (consensus of the community) and by the *'ulama*. Mansour (1975: 30) writes, "Authority is expressed by the majority of the companions, it is their *Ijma'*." Experts of God's law have a different type of power than political leaders. This leads Boulaabi to make the following distinction :

---

32. To show the relevance of the term *amr* for *shura*, Boulaabi quotes *sura* 4:83 and 3:159.

Obedience to God and to the prophet is of a religious nature, while obedience to human power is of a political nature. Thus, nothing in the verse indicates that those who hold power, hold it directly from God or from his Messenger. On the contrary, the Koran makes it clear that those who hold power, the *uli al-'amr*, are well and truly *minkum* among us. (Boulaabi 2005: 51)

It is fair to say from this discussion on *amr* that in Islam, legal authority clearly surpasses executive authority and the consensus of the learned leaders have more weight than the individual ruler.

The second term used in the Qur'an is "*sultan.*" It refers to the power received by Muhammad from God. Redissi (1998) translates it as "authority or tenure". This term was later used to define the Sunni rulers (Kraemers 2001). But its original Qur'anic meaning is that "of argument, proof or reasoning" (Boulaabi 2005: 55). It is sometimes translated as power in the story of Moses (*sura* 11:93) to express his power to fight against tyranny and liberate the community (Boulaabi 2005: 56).

The third term used to refer to leadership in the Qur'an is "*hukm.*" It has the meaning of authority-power and is the most common term used in the Qur'an to refer to issues of government. The major realm defined by *hukm* is the judicature or judiciary power (*sura* 38:22; 2:188; 5:43; Boulaabi 2005). The executive power (*hukm*), according to Gardet (1981: 23), is both civil and canonic. It can only be exercised by an intermediary or by a ruler.[33]

The fourth term found in the Qur'an is *ahkam* and it usually means decision or judgment (Schacht 2001). According to Schacht, this Qur'anic word is used of Allah and the Prophets as well as other men. In its ultimate sense, however, it signals that final jurisdiction belongs to Allah alone because he has given authority to make decisions to his Prophets (*sura* 3, 79; 45:16; 60, 10). He concludes that, "*hukm* comes to mean the authority,

---

33. *Hukm* has also other meanings in the Qur'an that are not important for our study such as judicial decision or rule in regards to religious law (Schacht 2001).

imperium, of the Islamic government and, on the other hand, the judgment of a *kadi* on a concrete case."

Gardet expresses as follow the relationship between various authorities:

> The legislative magisterium (*amr*) belongs only to the Qur'an; the judiciary magisterium (*fiqh*) belongs to every believer who, by the careful and fervent study of the Qur'an, acquires, along with the remembrance of the definitions and the understanding of the sanctions which it gives, the right to apply them. This leaves the executive power (*hukm*), both civil and canonical; it belongs to God alone as the Kharijites will say repeatedly—and it can only be exercised by an intermediary, a sole leader. (Gardet 1970)

The fifth term that helps understand the concept of power in Islam is "*ijma*'" (i.e. consensus of the community). In Islamic jurisprudence, the power of the community became extremely important, although often this power was reduced to a few learned leaders (Laoust 1986).

> *Ijma'* usually means the consensus of the teachers (*'ulama*) in any given period, and, in a special way, the consensus of the Companions. We can add in a secondary and limited way, the decisons recognized by lawyers or theologians from particular schools which are based on the Koran, the *hadith* or the *ijma'* (Gardet and Anawati 1948: 384-385).

Sometimes this community was in competition with the power of the caliph (Mansour 1975: 146). At other times the power of the *ijma'* was in competition with the power of each individual believer whom, according to certain commentators of *sura* 24:55, is granted the status of caliph of God (Mansour 1975: 146). The community's power, however, was always considered important because it could dethrone a leader (Laoust 1986).

Finally, there are terms that when combined, help define Islamic authority. For example, Victor E. Makari (1983) quotes Ibn Taymiyyah who stated, "the exercise of authority is not established in coercion (*qahr*) and awe (*rahbah*) as these may suggest, but on charity (*ihsan*) and on generating willingness and desire (*raghbah*) [to comply]." In the end, each Qur'anic interpreter or jurist will have their specific way of explaining authority and power.

Conclusion

This chapter has briefly outlined the various meanings of the words 'power' and 'authority' in the Qur'an from the perspective of several commentators. While there is widespread consensus in Islam that all power belongs to God, there is diversity of opinions on how this power is transferred to humans. The legal power of God and Muhammad supersedes the executive power of human leaders. Likewise, the authority of the community of religious leaders who know the sacred texts supersedes executive power. Therefore, it appears from this study that the key characteristic of religious leaders is the knowledge of the Qur'an and the Hadith. The Qur'an also shows that political authority has been given to human leaders. Those have received considerable freedom from God to exercise this power as vicegerent of God on earth. At the same time they must always submit to the rule of the Qur'an.

Although Islam believes any believer can lead the regular prayers and that a person with some knowledge of the sacred texts has influence over his or her followers, a variety of leadership roles have emerged within Islam. A human leader's authority is counter-balanced by the following: God, his Law, Muhammad's authority, *ijma'*, *ihsan* and *raghbah*. Coercion and awe should not be used as means of ruling.

Muhammad

Like many Christians who view Jesus as a model for leadership, most Muslim religious leaders are inspired by the leadership styles of Muhammad. Ibn Sa'd (as quoted in Andrea 1904) reported the following statement by Muhammad: "Whoever is not willing to follow my Sunna does not belong to me." It is therefore important to briefly look at how Muhammad exercised his various leadership roles in order to understand how early Islam defined human authority and influence.

Leadership Roles of Muhammad

Muhammad first worked as a trader in Khadijah bint Khuwaylid's trade business. His early leadership values are described by Montgomery Watt (1953: 38) as he says, "when Khadijah heard of the honesty, trustworthiness, and high moral character of Muhammad she invited him to act as her agent on a caravan journey to Syria." Muhammad's leadership style probably combined some of the nomadic values of *muruwah* discussed above, which include "bravery in battle, patience in misfortune, persistence in revenge, protection of the weak and defiance of the strong" (Watt 1953: 74) as well as some of the mercantile values of the Meccan society (Watt 1961). For example, Watt underlines the nomadic influence on Muhammad saying, "The nomadic virtue of fidelity in the keeping of trusts is certainly important, for a certain minimum level of business integrity is necessary in order to inspire that confidence which oils the wheels of trade" (Watt 1953: 74).[34] Watt (1961: 10) then emphasizes the Meccan influence on Muhammad:

> The Meccans were famous for the quality of *hilm*, which is a combination of maturity and self-control, and contrasts with the usual hot-blooded rashness and impetuosity of the Arab. In other words, they were able to smother their feelings where these would have harmed their material interests.

It is evident from biographies of Muhammad that he felt his background had prepared him for leadership. Ibn Ishaq reports, "The apostle of God used to say, there is no prophet but has shepherded a flock. When they said, 'You, too, an apostle of God?' He said 'Yes'" (Guillaume 1955: 72).

Second, when he began to receive the divine revelation in 610, Muhammad became a *nabi* (prophet).[35] According to Gardet (1970), the prophet is the person who receives the revelation (*wahy*). The legitimacy of Muhammad's leadership flows from his prophetic mission. Mansour writes, "It was because Abu-Bakr was the leader of the community that

---

34. Toshihiko Izutsu (2000: 74) said that, "in the pictures of Muhammad which the pious Muslim writers of later ages have left, we often see a typical hero of the Arabian desert."
35. In Arabic, one meaning of the term nabi (prophet) comes from the pile of stones that were put at the crossroads of caravans in the desert and announcing *razzias*.

he had duties which one could describe as being religious, whereas for Muhammad, it was because he had religious duties (a prophetic mission) that he became the leader of the community" (Mansour 1975: 19). No leader after Muhammad was called a nabi; he was the seal of Prophethood (*sura* 33:40).[36] As a result, I will not expand on this role to study leadership for the contemporary church.

Third, Muhammad was a *rasul* (messenger or prophet).[37] Moses was also called *rasul* in the Qur'an (*sura* 7:104), as were Adam, Abraham, Joseph, Isaac, Jacob, David and Jesus.[38] Prophets brought blessings and good things and their behavior and character was proof of their mission (Ibn Khaldun 1967). One significant characteristic of their role is that they brought religion through prayer (Ibn Khaldun 1967). As with the nabi, there are no longer any prophets today and therefore it is not necessary for this study to research the role of the prophet.

Fourth, Muhammad was a *nadhir* or "warner" (*sura* 33:45; 74:2; Watt 1953). The duties of a warner are stated in *sura* 35 verse 24: "Verily, we have sent thee in truth, as a bearer of glad tidings. And as a warner: and there never was a people, without a warner having lived among them (in the past)."[39] Watt (1953: 71) shows that the word "warn" (*andhir*) "describes the action of informing a person of something of a dangerous, harmful, or fearful nature, so as to put him on his guard against it or put him in fear of it." Lane (1863) gave the following meaning to the word *dhakkara* (to remind), used in *sura* 87 verse 9, to describe Muhammad's leadership role: "He exhorted; admonished; exhorted to obedience; gave good advice, and reminded of the results of affairs; reminded of what might soften the heart, by the mention of rewards and punishments" Watt (1953: 63) argues that the activity of a warner is extended to other leaders. He writes:

---

36. Tabari (1980: 336) indicates that Muhammad was called *Al-'Aqib*, which means that he was the last of the Prophets.
37. Watt (1953: 63) suggests that "messenger" is a better translation than "apostle" for this term.
38. *Sura* 7 includes numerous stories of these messengers.
39. Other Qur'anic passages underlining the role of warning are *sura* 74:2 and 87:9. Watt (1953: 71) claims the word *nadhir* is found "more than forty times in the Qur'an."

While the activities of reminding and warning continue to characterize the religious leader as portrayed in the Qur'an, and exemplified at first almost exclusively by Muhammad, they come to be complemented by the activity of the 'messenger' (*rasul*), whom God has 'sent with a message' (*arsala*).

I am therefore expecting to find this role in contemporary leadership.

Fifth, Muhammad was a shahid. He was a witness (*shahid*) and a "Bearer of Glad Tidings" (*sura* 33:45). The next verse says, "And as one invites to God's (Grace) by His leave, and as a Lamp spreading Light" (*sura* 33:45-46). It is important to note that current Muslim leaders are also expected to be witnesses.

Sixth, Muhammad was an administrator, demonstrated most clearly in how he organized the community. Similarly, Muslim leaders are expected to be able to manage and organize. The caliph, Umar, provides an example of being a good administrator.[40]

Seventh, Muhammad was a warrior who had a distinct understanding of how to start and finish wars. There are "extensive reports of *maghazi* ("military expeditions") that Muhammad led or organized and sent out" (Welch 1995: 156). Muhammad is not the only Muslim leader who dealt directly with war. The Qur'an states, for example, that Moses brought victory against the tyrant (Redissi 1998: 25). One of the imam's roles is to call believers to war (Redissi 1998: 37)[41] and the *mufti* (legal adviser) can justify or condemn the recourse to war or establish peace with an enemy. Finally, the caliphs appointed *qadis* (judges) to lead jihad (Ibn Khaldun 1967). "Capability of carrying out the political and military duties of the office" is required from caliphs (Madelung 2001: 3).

Being a man of war, Muhammad is a subject of great debate among Islamicists. Karen Armstrong (2006: 200) expresses this reality when she writes, "Some Muslim thinkers regard the jihad against Mecca as the

---

40. Many Muslim thinkers consider Umar as the founder of the concept of the Islamic state. He organized the Divan, secretariat of the state, established the financial and tax systems, the army, the court system and external state correspondence with foreign powers (Watt 1953).
41. This is why Islam believes the imam must be "sound of mind".

climax of Muhammad's career and fail to note that he eventually abjured warfare and adopted a nonviolent policy." It is clear that one can find in Muhammad's life a wide-spectrum of attitudes toward war. He sometimes sanctioned common customs of the Arabian Peninsula as when he issued the verdict that "all the men of the clan were to be executed and the women and children were to be sold as slaves (*sura* 33:26-27)[42] (Welch 1995: 158). At other times, he decreed truces as he did when he instituted a peaceful treaty between Meccans and Medinans (Welch 1995). One can find in the Qur'an and the Hadith examples of Muhammad both at war and making peace. I acknowledge that there is a wide range of interpretations and because of that I do not argue that Muhammad can only be limited to one set of attitudes and behaviors regarding conflict. It will be interesting to explore how Christians understand this aspect of Muhammad's life and how it influences their involvement in the socio-political sphere.

Eighth, the notion that Muhammad was a miracle maker is a contested one (Goldziher 2003). Tor Andrae (1936) writes, "Mohammed rejected every request to pose as a wonder-worker, and emphatically denied all superstitions in regard to his own person." The same author states that he can only find two instances where Muhammad performed signs and wonders.[43] Others posit that the greatest miracle Muhammad performed was the revelation of the Qur'an (Tor Andrae 1936). Some writers, however, do contend that Muhammad performed miracles. Ibn Khaldun explains miracles (*mu'jizat*) performed by prophets are different from the saint's charisma (*karama*). He writes, "The prophet's miracles are supernatural (journey to heaven, raising up the dead, talking with angels, being lifted up from the ground, going across solid bodies)" (Ibn Khaldun 1967: 143).

Ninth, Muhammad was a true leader. More specifically, he was a tribal leader, who ruled over the various tribal units of his day. Leaders must be able to lead followers toward a goal. For example, Abraham, according to

---

42. Alford T. Welch (1995: 158) writes about this incident: "In this one action of his career, Muhammad followed the customs and expectations of his day rather than his usual magnanimous treatment of his foes after battles and intrigues."

43. The two instances are at the battle of Badr when Muhammad "threw a handful of sand at the enemy in the belief that this magic act would help to gain victory" and Muhammad's "midnight journey to Jerusalem" (Andrae 1938: 251-252).

Islam, led a journey to Mecca (Redissi 1998). Likewise, Muhammad led the early Muslim community toward specific goals.

We have outlined here a number of key roles of Muhammad, which are (1) trader, (2) *nabi* (prophet), (3) *rasul* (messenger), (4) *nadhir* (warner), (5) *shahid*, (6) administrator, (7) warrior and peacemaker, (8) miracle-maker, and (9) tribal leader. This list is not exhaustive but it does help to understand the areas in which Muhammad influenced his followers. Although Muslims are required to imitate Muhammad's leadership, he was the last human to adopt the role of a prophet.

Obedience to Muhammad

There are a number of Qur'anic verses that explicitly discuss the way followers should relate to Muhammad as a leader. What is striking is that God commands followers to obey Muhammad. In effect, the Qur'an says, "Whoever obeys the Messenger thereby obeys God" (*sura* 4:80). Other verses seem to equate obedience to God with obedience to Muhammad (*sura* 4:13-14).[44] How are we to understand these verses in light of Islam's clear distinction between God's power and human power? We already discussed this issue and will only focus here on Muhammad and the obedience that is obliged to him.

First, the fact that followers are called to obey Muhammad does not mean, according to Gardet (1981), that Muhammad was equal to God—obedience after all can only be given to God. Second, Muhammad himself could only be obeyed because he stood in total submission to God (*sura* 42:52) and considered himself a slave of God (Lari 1996). Third, Muhammad's power was temporal (Boulaabi 2005: 63). Fourth, Muhammad was only adhering to what the Qur'anic law ordered and consequently he could be safely obeyed because his followers believed they were actually obeying God's laws and orders (Gardet 1981).[45] Thus, while obeying Muhammad

---

44. *Sura* 4:13-14 read: "Whoever obeys God and His Messenger will be admitted to gardens in which rivers flow [Paradise], therein dwelling forever.... But whoever disobeys God and His Messenger and transgresses His bounds will be admitted to a Fire, therein dwelling forever."

45. Later leaders would be judged as righteous leaders that could be obeyed on this same criteria. Thus, any religious leader, and especially the caliph, as a successor of Muhammad, was not to be considered as an intermediary between God and the believer but rather

was considered normal, his status was not equated with that of God's. On the contrary, obedience to Muhammad was only required from believers because of his status of prophet and his obedience to God's law.

Early Islamic history reports how Muslims expressed their obedience to Muhammad by swearing an oath of allegiance to him. This act is called *bay'a* and was later practiced when Muslims pledged allegiance to other caliphs. The first pledge, called *bay'at an-nisa'* (The Pledge of the Women) was taken by twelve Muslim believers who "made a promise to avoid various sins and to obey Muhammad" (Watt 1953: 145). The second pledge, *bay'at al-harb* (The Pledge of War), was taken by seventy-three men and two women in AD 622 at al-'Aqabah and it meant not only to "obey Muhammad but to fight for him" (Watt 1953: 145).

Ibn Khaldun (1967: 166) explains in detail how the oath of allegiance continued to be practiced in Islam:[46]

> The *bay'ah* (oath of allegiance) is a contract to render obedience. It is as though the person who renders the oath of allegiance made a contract with his amir, to the effect that he surrenders supervision of his own affairs and those of the Muslims to him and that he will not contest his authority and that he will obey him by (executing) all the duties with which he might be charged, whether agreeable or disagreeable.

The same author explains further that the oath, which was first expressed through a handshake, later took on other gestural forms always expressed as certain commitment:

> This customary meaning of the oath of allegiance should be understood. A person must know it, because it imposes upon him certain duties toward his ruler and imam. His actions will thus not be frivolous or gratuitous. This should be taken

---

someone who could be trusted because of his total commitment to God's Law.

46. For example, Ibn Khaldun (1967: 156) shows that "at the death of the Prophet, the men around him proceeded to render the oath of allegiance to Abu Bakr and to entrust him with the supervision of their affairs."

into consideration in one's dealings with rulers (Ibn Khaldun 1967: 167).

Today, other symbols of allegiance may exist between leaders and followers and it will be interesting to see how followers embrace the authority of the leader within the context of the church.

Muhammad's Values

Muhammad displayed a number of values that Muslim leaders later adopted. Some are general values that apply to every Muslim while others specifically deal with leadership. This list is in no way comprehensive and there are differences of opinion regarding what values should be included. However, I have gathered here the most important ones accepted by the majority of Muslims.

First, Muhammad had faith (*iman*). Adalat Khan believes that faith is a key quality of leadership (Khan 2007: 8). It is also a key value for all believers.

Second, Muhammad was generous (*karim*). He was open-handed (Izutsu 2002: 74-75 quoting Ibn Ishaq). The concept of generosity is an important nomadic idea that was adopted with some modifications in the Qur'an. Watt (1953: 75) writes:

> In insisting on acts of generosity it [the Qur'an] was reviving one side of the old Arab ideal, and so building on foundations that were already present in the Arab soul. Acts of generosity, moreover, were relevant to the circumstances of Mecca. At the same time a new sanction was provided for these acts, eschatological reward and punishment.

Although generosity was highly valued by Muhammad as a leader, he did have some issues with the way Arabian customs viewed it. Tor Andrae (1936: 104) shows how Muhammad was critical of the kind of "impulsive and extravagant generosity, just for the mere joy of playing the royal benefactor for a brief moment" that was a hallmark of nobility and chivalrous attitude of Bedouin leaders. Instead, he preferred the gift offering to God, to the spiritual leader,[47] and to the poor and needy (Andrae 1936: 106).

Generosity in the form of *zakat* and *tasakka* became to him and to the Muslim community an integral part of Qur'anic values. Watt (1961) explains:

> Although *tazakka* apparently had no connexion with almsgiving originally, the virtue of generosity was prominent in the earlier passages of the Qur'an, and that of course includes almsgiving. But, as C. Snouck Hurgronje argues, almsgiving was and is not practiced in the East for a socialistic or utilitarian reason but because it is the chief of the virtues.

Third, Muhammad had piety (*taqwa*) (Andrae 1936: 260) which Gardet (1981: 93) translates a "reverential fear." This is not only a key value in Islam but is also important in leadership. Tor Andrea (1936: 260) writes, "The genuineness and sincerity of Mohammad's piety and the honesty of his belief in his religious call, are indisputable." One of Muhammad's greatest legacies to Muslims is his piety.

Fourth, Muhammad, like Joseph, Isaac and Jacob brought science (*'ilm*) (Redissi 1998: 25). Knowledge is very important in Islamic leadership:

> In Islam, one category of men is set apart from the rest of the faithful by their authority and their religious functions. They are "men of God" in a deeper sense, each in their own society. . . . This particular status is conferred on them by a superior knowledge of the most important thing to know: divine revelation as given in the Koran, as well as the actions, deeds and words of him who transmitted it, the prophet Muhammad.

---

[47]. It is interesting to note the regulation found in *sura* 58 verse 13 that seems to indicate that those who visited Muhammad for advise were requested to present some gift. Although there are disagreements about how long this practice was conducted and how much people should give to Muhammad, it will be worth looking at this practice and how it impacts religious leadership in Islam.

Thus, holy men are above all "knowledgeable ones", 'ulamas (Iognat-Prat and Veinstein 2003: 39).

Khuri Fuad (2006: 164-165) gives a detailed definition of *'ilm* saying:

> It must be stressed that this meaning of science[48] is only partially implied in the Arabic term *'ilm*,[49] which in addition, connotes knowledge of the invisible and unresearchable, knowledge obtained through private and particularized means rather than through standardized and universalized ones. *'Ilm* in Arabic conveys the idea of 'certainty' rather than 'predictability' about the ultimate; and *alim* knows what will befall mankind in the future.

All Muslim leaders are required to seek knowledge. Bourg (1994: 74) says the Sunni imam should be competent in religious matters. Mozaffari (1998: 78) says a Shi'a imam must "know the Qur'an and the Muslim traditions."[50] Other types of leaders such as the *qadi*, the *'ulama* or the *faqh* must also have legal knowledge.

Muslim leaders have two ways to acquire knowledge. Some acquire *'ilm* in a methodical study of knowledge gathered and organized by those who preceded them; others gain a direct and intimate knowledge of God (*ma'rifa*) (Iogna-Prat and Veinstein 2003: 39).

Fifth, Muhammad displayed justice (*'adala*). This is significant because in Islam this virtue establishes the legitimacy of the leader's power.[51] According to Tyan (1960), *'adala* is "one of the principle conditions for carrying out public functions." Gardet (1981) explains that the virtue of

---

48. By "this meaning of science" Khuri (2006: 164) means the method that "tries to understand, manipulate and control the 'world', the knowable and researchable."
49. Men of religion in Islam are called *rijal ad-din* (Khuri 2006).
50. In Shi'ism, there are two categories of knowledge required for an imam. The first consists in knowing the Qur'an and the Sunna and be able to draw answers to problems from the text. The second consists in being a skillful political leader that knows well how to lead his community (Mozaffari 1998: 80).
51. The legitimacy of the one who exercises power is founded on his observance of the Qur'anic commandments.

justice (*'adala*) is the required condition for the one who commands and exercises the caliphate (Madelung 2001). In fact, it is one of the four qualities required to become an imam in Sunnism. It is absolutely required from a *qadi* and a *mufti* (Gardet 1981: 140).

The definition of the value *'adala*[52] is widely contested amongst Muslim authors. Generally it describes the state of a person who obeys the moral and religious law (Tyan 1960). *'Adl* also means a "person of good morals" (Tyan 1960).

Sixth, Muhammad showed mercy (*rahma* or *rahim*) (Nawafleh 2000: 18).[53] *Rahma* denotes "kindness, benevolence, an act of kindness, or a favour" (Gimaret 1995). Most of the time *rahma* is used to describe God's mercy in the Qur'an. The word *rahim* is more commonly used for humans and it is an important attribute of religious leaders in Islam. Thus Muhammad was "inviting people with kindness" (Lari 1996; *sura* 16:125). Another leader who displayed charity according to the Qur'an is Jesus (Redissi 1998).

Seventh, Muhammad displayed patience (*sabr*), which, according to Beekun and Badawi (1999: 43), is "one of the defining characteristics of Islamic leadership." Muhammad is often quoted both in the Qur'an and the Hadith as an example of patience in the midst of persecution. For example, Wensinck (1995) in the *Encyclopedia of Islam* writes, "An outstanding example of the Prophet's *sabr* was demonstrated following his suffering at the hands of the people of Ta'if. When the chiefs of Ta'if set the people of the town upon him, instead of seeking revenge, the Prophet prayed for their guidance" (Wensinck 1995). There are several examples of leaders in

---

52. "Etymologically, the term *'adl* is found both as substantive and as an adjective, but with meanings that do not exactly correspond. *'Adl* the substantive, means justice; as an adjective, it means rectilinear, just, well balanced; it thus applies both to beings and to things" (E.I. 2CD).

53. Gimaret (1988: 378) writes, "perhaps the most beautiful elaboration of a Qur'anic remark about the Prophet is found in the concept of *rahma*" such as displayed in *sura* 21 verse 107: "We sent thee not, but as a Mercy (*rahma*) for all creatures." Likewise, when the word is used in connection with other Qur'anic leaders the word mainly refers to God's help toward them. For example, *rahma* is used to describe God's assistance to Moses (*sura* 19:53), to Zachariah (*sura* 19:2) and to Hud and his supporters (*sura* 7:72; 11:58). According to Gimaret (1988: 378) later authorities attribute to *rahma* stronger quality.

the Qur'an that exemplify patience such as Job, Jacob, and Joseph, all of whom showed endurance in the face of tribulations (Wensinck 1995).

The Qur'anic verse that most clearly addresses this value is, "And we appointed from among them leaders, giving guidance under Our command so long as they persevered with patience and continued to have faith in Our signs" (*sura* 32:24). In *sura* 2 verse 155, every believer is required to have patience (Beekun and Badawi 1999: 43).[54] Patience is further defined according to its human or godly origin.[55] The Qur'an defines patience as one of the paths that leads people from darkness to light and as an attribute of morality that is superior to and very different from the daily behavior of many people.[56]

Eighth, Muhammad had wisdom (*hikma*) (*sura* 16:125). Muslim leaders must display this value (*sura* 2:129, 231; 3:81; 4:113). For example, Qur'anic leaders such as Moses, David and Jesus adopted this value (*sura* 2:252; 38:19; 5:110; 43:63; 2:146; 31:11). *Sura* 28 verse 14 says, "When he (Musa) reached full age and was firmly established (in life) We bestowed on him wisdom and knowledge: for thus do We reward those who do good." Beekun and Badawi (2004: 40-41) highlight that wisdom has a practical aspect including the fact that:

> Islam draws a distinction between knowledge (*'ilm*) and one's ability to put this knowledge into practice (*hikmah*). Whereas competence relates more to *'ilm*, the Islamic perspective of

---

54. The verse says, "Be sure We shall test you with something of fear and hunger some loss in goods or lives or the fruits (of your toil) but give glad tidings to those who patiently persevere" (*sura* 2:155).

55. Beekun and Badawi (1999) show there is more than one word to refer to patience in the midst of trials. Patience (*badr*) is for natural disasters, but resolve (*'azm*) and forbearance (*hilm*) are for trials created by humans.

56. The *New Encyclopedia of Islam* gives a number of definitions of patience: "(1) Obligatory (*wajib*) patience—Patience in abstaining from forbidden things and actions, in carry the obligatory duties and in facing adversity beyond your control; (2) Encouraged (*mandub*) patience—Patience in abstaining from disliked things, in performing encouraged worship and in not taking revenge; (3) Forbidden (*mahdhur*) patience—Patience in abstaining from food and drink until death, enduring things that may lead to death, and at the time of fitnah when the Muslims are fighting Muslims; (4) Disliked (*makruh*) patience—Patience in abstaining from physical appetites that causes damage to one's health. (5) Permissible (*mubah*) patience—Patience in abstaining from *permissible but offensive* deeds."

leadership recognized the importance of both, and emphasizes that both should be present for a leader to be effective.

However, when comparing Christian and Muslim notions of wisdom, one must be aware that this value connotes different meanings. Goichon states that the Arabic word *hikma* seems to be closely associated to the Greek word *sophia* (*sojia*). But in the New Testament this form of wisdom is not upheld above other kinds.

Other Leadership Characteristics

Muhammad modeled other leadership qualities that became important for Muslim leaders. They are briefly discussed below.

First, Muhammad displayed charisma. Bourg (1994: 74) posits that the imam must be endowed with charisma. According to Gellner (1981: 26), a saint can acquire a reputation that extends wider than the area of his lineage and his charisma will allow him to become a leader of a religious order thus attracting conversions. However, Hamadi Redissi (1998: 25) underlines some of the dangers of charisma when he talks about imams saying, "charisma is an ephemeral domination when it belongs to extraordinary qualities. When the leader disappears, he leaves the emotional community of faith like an orphan, because the community does not know how to assure the passage of his exemplary ruling to the daily and routine administration."

Second, Muhammad provided behavior modeling. In Islam, leaders influence others by being an example[57]: "O you who are divinely committed! Why do you say that which you do not practice yourself? The worst of you in the sight of Allah is he who says that which he does not practice" (Bourg 1994: 74). Andrae Tor (1936) contends that there are some similarities between Muhammad and Paul in that the latter "expressed the wish that his converts might become like him in all things except his chains." While I agree with Andrae's position I would challenge it slightly. When *sura* 33 verse 31 talks about imitating Muhammad's behavior and says, "A noble

---

57. The importance of influencing followers by being a model as a leader is also emphasized in the Bible and acknowledged by Paul, "Just as you know what kind of persons we proved to be among you for your sake. And you became imitators of us and of the Lord" (1 Thess 1:5b-6).

pattern had ye in God's Apostle, for all who hope in God and in the latter days", it assumes that leaders should imitate Muhammad in submitting to God's law and not their leader because, as in Paul's example, he or she imitated God in Christ.

Third, Muhammad led by *shura* (consultation) as is evidenced by *sura* 42 verse 38, "And consult them in affairs (of moment). Then, when thou hast taken a decision, put thy trust in God" (*sura* 3:159). Although we saw earlier that the believers must obey Muhammad, there is also a duty of consultations on behalf of the leader (Gardet 1981: 34). Likewise Muslim leaders must promote participation of others in decision-making through *shura* (Nusair 1986: 189). Some authors believe this type of consultation is an outgrowth of the pre-Islamic tribal consultative council (Hitti 1987). In either case, this transformed model became deeply rooted in Muslim leadership practices.[58]

Shura is defined as "the process of extensive discussion of an issue from all its aspects and dimensions, selection of the best given views on that issue, and testing of those views to make sure that the best interests of the community are realized" (Abul-Faris 1980: 79). *Shura* implies listening to the followers, which is an important value in Islam. The caliph Umar gives an example of a leader who practiced listening[59] saying that he displayed the ability to include others in decision making by the practice of *shura*.[60] Likewise the Shi'i leader must be able to listen to others (Nawafleh 2000: 18).

There are however some limitations to *shura*. According to the Qur'an, Muhammad would consult with his followers in the conduct of worldly matters when there was no direct revelation for that matter. Muhammad

---

58. From the Qur'anic verses that stress consultation, such as "their [the believers'] communal business is to be conducted through consultation among themselves" (*sura* 36:38), it was decided that selection of the caliph, his dealings and his decision-making, must be conducted by *shura*.

59. In one of his speeches, Umar suggested 40 dinars as an upper limit for the dowry a man pays to his bride. Everything else would be given to the state treasury. A woman from the audience recited a verse from the Qur'an contradicting the caliph's decision. Umar smiled and said: "The woman is correct and Omar is mistaken" (Nawafleh, 2000: 118).

60. Umar said, "a decision that has been taken without consultation is useless" (Nusair 1986: 189).

Khalaf-Allah (1998: 39) believes that *shura* is not possible when a matter directly refers to divine revelation. He writes:

> For if religious matters, like doctrines, worship, what is permitted and what is prohibited, were concerns decided by consultation, then religion itself would have been the work of human beings. Religion is established by God. No one may have an opinion on it, either during the lifetime of the Prophet, peace be upon him, or afterwards.

Khalaf-Allah (1998) shows that the *shura* system is open for adaptation.[61] He writes, "the establishment of such a system [of shura] was one of those matters that God had delegated to Muslims to establish . . . It is up to them to establish it on a basis that is good for the time period in which they live and for the nation to which they belong" (1998: 41-42).

Fourth, Muhammad was humble and shy (Welch 1995: 159).[62] Islamic leadership underlines the importance of humility (Ali 2005: 68). According to leadership research conducted in the Middle East this quality is expected from leaders (Pasa, Kabasakal, and Bodur 2001).

Fifth, Muhammad was modest (Andrae 1936: 259)[63] and not active in the pursuit of material wealth. Lari (1996) states that he "never thinks of material gain."

Sixth, Muhammad was loyal. Izutsu (2002: 74-75) reports how Muhammad was loyal in the keeping of his trusts.

---

61. Khalaf-Allah (1998: 40-41) explains that Muhammad consulted with "Muslims who were with him," "with personal friends," and "his Companions." He gives examples of how this consultation took place: "He would accede to their opinion and would not hold fast to his own opinion" or "he would consult with them on every matter except that which was revealed to him, which he would execute without counsel, and Muslims would help him execute as well," or "the opinion of the majority on the day of Uhud was different from his, and he acceded to the opinion of the majority, which later appeared to be wrong."

62. Welch (1995) quotes *sura* 49 verse 2 for humility and *sura* 33 verse 53 for shyness.

63. Tor Andrae (1938: 259) explains, "Even in Medina Mohammed lived on the whole in rather modest circumstances, and adhered to the moderately ascetic ideal which he defends in the Koran. . . . [T]here is no mention of complaints concerning luxury, splendour, or high living."

Finally, he possessed many other qualities such as sincerity (Lari 1996; *sura* 98:5), trustworthiness (Lari 1996), nobility (Ibn Ishaq, I, 266), truthfulness (Izutsu 2002: 74-75),[64] and serenity of mind (Lari 1996).[65] He was also eloquent and able to "communicate Islamic truths" (Lari 1996).

Critics of Islam nevertheless challenge certain leadership characteristics of Muhammad. First, while one of the chief characteristics of prophets is their chastity (Ibn Khaldun 1965 141), Muhammad has often been depicted as being sensual which seemingly contradicts this value. Those who defend Muhammad argue that he never committed adultery and always remained faithful to the women he married. Second, Muhammad is "told to be harsh in his treatment of those who oppose him" but he is often depicted as gentle and merciful (Welch 1995: 159).[66] Third, some argue that he lacked integrity, which directly contradicts the fact that Islam requires leaders to have integrity. Dalil Boubakeur (1995) underlines in the *Charta of Muslim Worship in France* noting that the Sunni imam must have an exemplary social and moral behavior.

While some of these critiques may be valid, the question remains whether some of these flaws minimize the excellent model that Muslims find in Muhammad. If Muhammad is a role model for Muslims (*sura* 33:21), does he have to be perfect and sinless? Shi'i Muslims believe in the perfection of the leader and his infallibility; in fact, it is one of the three criteria for becoming a successor of Muhammad in Shi'ism (Mozaffari 1998: 78).[67] The list of Muhammad's leadership characteristics by Lari (1996) includes infallibility,[68] bodily perfection and being "protected by God from all sins for he was created for a special purpose." According to Ibn Khaldun (1967),

---

64. Toshihiko Izutsu (2000: 74-75) refers to 'Ali b.Abi Talib who said, according to Ibn Ishaq, Muhammad was truthful of tongue.
65. Evidence comes from *sura* 12 verse 46 and 9 verse 119. In Shi'i Islam, the imam must be a *siddiq* (truthful) (Mozaffari 1998: 78; Nawafleh 2000: 118).
66. Welch quotes *sura* 9 verse 73 and 66 verse 9 to support his statement. The last verse reads "O Prophet, struggle with the unbelievers and the hypocrites, and be harsh with them. Their refuge is Gehenna [Hell], an evil homecoming."
67. The other two are moral integrity and knowing the Qur'an and the Muslim traditions.
68. The infallibility of Muhammad is debated within Sunnism. The infallibility of prophets is an established fact based on reason and tradition. This quality is required for several reasons. The prophets must represent and then present the Revelation without fault or defect. This is their function as guides and good examples to be followed.

however, this is only the nature of the prophets who are free of all sins. Tor Andrea (1936: 252) states that, "Islamic dogma has depicted the Prophet as sinless." However, that does not mean that he is considered perfect in the early texts.

There is also evidence that Muhammad, like other prophets, had to ask for forgiveness.[69] This reality begs the question which leadership behaviors of Muhammad are non-negotiable and subsequently which ones are to be imitated. Each school of Law in Islam has its own understanding of what behaviors are authentic and which ones should be imitated.

Furthermore, Tor Andrae shows that it is often difficult to discern what is genuinely true about Muhammad because of the contradicting statements of some narratives.[70] Andrae notes, for example, that "the descriptions of the poverty and deprivation of the Prophet must be greatly exaggerated" (Andrae 1936: 257). Thus it may be possible that some of the leadership values and behaviors that portray Muhammad as an effective leader may be an idealized. The point here is not to prove these arguments either way but to affirm that most leaders in Islam use them to define their leadership today.

Leadership Legitimacy

Islam emphasizes the importance of legitimacy in religious leadership. The first type in Islam is the divine legitimacy, which is "an essential prerequisite" (Bangash 2000: 2). The second type is human legitimacy. A Hadith states, "God cannot send a prophet who has not the protection of his people." According to Bangash (2000: 2) "leadership in Islam must have both divine as well as popular legitimacy; without the first, it cannot have validity, without the second, it remains unfulfilled."[71] Van Nieuwenhuijze further explains this tension:

---

69. Tor Andrae quotes *sura* 3 verse141 and 7 verses 75-77.

70. He gives the example of some traditions that depict Muhammad as an ascetic character and other traditions that deny it (Andrae 1936).

71. The same author admits that some leaders had divine legitimacy without popular legitimacy. When the second is lacking, the mission of the leader is usually incomplete (Bangash 2000). He puts Yusuf, Dawud, Sulaiman and Muhammad in the category of leaders having both divine and popular legitimacy. This entitled them to become rulers (Bangash 2000).

> Two kinds of authority: both self-imposed as from above-yet in quite different ways-and both begging the questions of legitimacy and legitimation. In merging, they constitute the phenomenon characteristic of the Islamic policy, whether comprehensive or segmentary, namely that of authority as Islamically legitimized power in charge of the conduct of public affairs. Not seldom, legitimacy is tacitly assumed, making it appear as if no problem of legitimation could arise. This however, does not mean that there could be no problem at all. Hence the fascination of the debate, however inconsequential, on the unjust ruler. (Van Nieuwenhuijze 1985: 142)

Leadership qualities and values thus play an important role in the choice of a legitimate leader.[72] Although traditionally the imam's primary qualification was superior knowledge of the Qur'an and Arabic language, the Sunni imam was appointed by the community based on the qualities it witnessed in his life (Bourg 1994).

In some cases, it is not the qualities of the leader that makes him legitimate but his ancestors. The first caliphs were required to be Quraishites and the Shi'i imams were from the line of Muhammad's grandson. The same is true in Sufism. Gellner (1969: 84) shows in the Atlas Mountains of Morocco, that included in the qualifications of the saints (*marabout*) is that they must "be a prophet's descendent (*sharif*)."[73]

The discussion of qualifications naturally leads to the question of leadership training. In other words, must a leader undergo training to be a legitimate leader? Traditionally, there is no official degree specifically designed to train imams because it is widely believed that religious training should be accessible to every Muslim (Bourg 1994). In Islam, any Muslim who masters rudiments of religious knowledge can lead the prayer. However, prayer

---

72. Not only do the leaders need certain qualities and values, but also those who were chosen to elect the caliph. Laoust (1986) states the three characteristics identified by al-Mawardi for a caliph's elector: (1) justice, (2) science, and (3) intelligence and wisdom.
73. The king of Morocco for example claims his legitimacy from being a descendant of Muhammad.

leaders often undergo a specific training.[74] In the past, the Muslim community directly chose its leaders whereas today the State generally appoints imams. Especially in the West, there are now official schools for training imams and in some countries imams are required to have been trained in a recognized school (Boubakeur 1995).

Leadership Roles

This section lists the various roles that exist in leadership in Islam. I have already alluded to some of these roles in the above discussion. The study of these leadership values, qualities and behaviors will further highlight leadership styles in Islam.

General Thoughts about Leaderships Roles

In this study, I am essentially focusing on Sunni Islam which represents the majority of believers in North Africa.[75] The major issue that divided Shi'a and Sunni is specifically the question of leadership. As Khuri (2006: 179) writes, "the controversies that split the Shi'a world are precisely about the lines of descent of imams, the methods of designation and the termination of succession."

Islam did not start with a well-organized religious leadership. Contrary to the wealth of information contained in the Old and New Testaments

---

74. Bourg (1994: 75) describes as following the training program of these religious leaders: "The six-year program includes, first, accurate knowledge of the teachings from the *sira* (life) of the Prophet and the Hadith, and second, knowledge of *fiqh* (Muslim jurisprudence) which includes *Haq an-nafs* (individual rights), *Haq an-nas* (the right of others), and *Haq Allah* (divine right). This teaching is coupled with practical training in orthodox rituals, in language learning and rhetoric. The main topic covered are (1) *Usul ad-din* (the science of religious institutions, (2) *'Ulum al-Qur'an* (The Qur'anic Sciences), (3) *'Ulum al-Hadith* (The Hadith Sciences) and (4) *Usul al- Fiqh* (the foundation of Muslim Law). Thirdly, there is a higher level of education which includes the elements of *'Akida* (faith, theology, God, Angels, Prophets, Eschatology, Resurrection, Free will, etc), the legal and theological schools, orthodoxy, trends, history, philosophy. This third level also includes law, methodology, exegesis, authors, masters and mystical Islam. Modern universities in the Muslim world can add many more topics to the training. . . If there is no university or institute, the imam learns the Qur'an and the Hadith in the mosque. He can also learn *tawjid* (chanting), *tafsir* (exegesis), *fiqh* (grammar, rhetoric) *Khataba* (the art of preaching), and the *Sira* (the life of the Prophet)."

75. Shi'a leadership is different from Sunni leadership in several areas. For example in Shi'ism, "the Prophet is an infallible messenger" and "a medium of revelation" (Khuri 2006: 176).

about how the organization of the religious community, the Qur'anic sources regarding Muslim religious specialists are quite scarce. Mansour (1975) explains that even under the four rightly guided caliphs, there was neither internal religious organization to counterbalance power nor a hierarchy that could control ideas and attitudes in the community. She explains, "The only body of control, the only authority, was a 'vague feeling' in which the masses of Muslims had to participate just as much as the leaders of the community" (Mansour 1975: 21).[76]

In Islam, the concept of "vicegerent" (*khalifa*) describes the leadership of all human beings. The Qur'an states that "It is He Who had made You (His) agents, inheritors[77] of the earth: He has raised You in ranks, some above Others: that He may try you in the gifts he hath given you: For thy Lord is quick in punishment: yet He is indeed Oft-forgiving, most Merciful" (*sura* 6:165). Adalat Khan (2007: 2) builds on this concept to discuss leadership in Islam. He writes:

> As a representative of God himself, human beings are assigned great faculties and qualities which if properly deployed could result in the achievement of miraculous goals. However to reach these goals one needs to follow certain principles and tools which are also known as success or leadership principles.

Since God has granted everyone the possibility to be a leader and because there is no intermediary between God and humans in Islam, some experts, like the Parisian bookstore clerk I met at the beginning of my research, claim Islam has no leadership per se.

Khuri (2006: 166) disagrees arguing that, "The literature on Islam, which focuses mainly on Sunni Islam and always assumes that Islam has no clergy or church, tends to oversimplify the issue." Dominique Iogna-Prat

---

76. Mansour (1975: 21) shows the challenge created by the fact that Islam did not first organize its leadership structures, " to hold power, without having first instituted and organised the specialized class of those who hold power, who are set apart, idealists, men of religion, is to condemn oneself to the possibility of seeing power slipping from one's grasp."
77. The Arabic word translated by "agent, inheritors" in this verse is the word "*Khalifa*" (vicegerent).

and Gilles Veinstein further develop this idea when they say that, "one category of men is set apart from the rest of the faithful by their authority and their religious functions. They are 'men of God' in a deeper sense, each in their own society." This position, according to these two authors,

> "is conferred on them by a superior knowledge of the most important thing to know: divine revelation as given in the Koran, as well as the actions, deeds and words of him who transmitted it, the prophet Muhammad. Thus, holy men are above all "knowledgeable ones", *'ulamas*. (Iogna-Prat and Veinstein 2003: 39)

Iogna-Prat and Veinstein (2003: 39) also describe how intimacy with God confers on certain Sufi leaders a specific leadership role that distinguishes them from the rest of the believers:

> However, this knowledge (*'ilm*) which is methodically acquired from masters who have themselves followed the same program, is opposed to another, which is of a different nature, the intimate and direct knowledge of God (*ma'rifa*), of which the Prophet gave the example, and which is itself obtained thanks to an innate gift or at the end of a programme of initiation.

Caliph

As I stated in the previous paragraph, one of the key leadership issues facing the Muslim community after Muhammad's death was the question of his succession. Sunni Muslims called the successor of Muhammad "caliph" whereas the Shi'i community called him "imam" (Redissi 1998). Because Muhammad died without choosing a successor, the first caliph could only be named a "replacement" of the Prophet in a chronological sense—meaning the one who came after him (Mansour 1975: 19). I will not spend much time discussing this leadership role because the caliphate was abolished in 1923 and as a result does not directly influence present leadership in North Africa. However, some general thoughts about the values and qualities of these leaders will highlight religious leadership styles in Islam.

In early Islam, there were important debates over the qualifications of the caliph. Muslims agreed that the caliph did not have the same prophetic call as Muhammad. According to T. W. Arnold (1922: 885), "the Khalifa is the representative (*na'ib*) of the Prophet, the exponent of the divinely inspired law (*sharia*), and his functions are the protection of religion and the government of the world." Sunnis claim that the caliph must have certain physical qualities (able to hear, see and speak and not be physically handicapped), be adult, sound in spirit, male, and free (Redissi 1998: 38). He must be "just,[78] knowledgeable[79] and capable[80]" (Redissi 1998: 38). The virtue of justice, (*'adl*) insists Gardet (1981: 34), is an indispensable requirement for a caliph. Only if the caliph is just, should he be obeyed (Gardet 1981: 34). Laoust (1986: 29) reports that the imam "must be responsible, a Muslim, free, male, *mujtahid* (jurist), brave, capable of forming an opinion by himself; he must not be deaf, or blind, or mute."

Ibn Khaldun (1967: 167) explains that the imamate is "the supervision of the interests of the Muslim nation in both their worldly and their religious affairs." He calls the caliph "their guardian and trustee" who "looks after their (affairs) as long as he lives." Al-Sa'ad (quoted by Laoust 1986: 29) writes, the caliph is someone who "revives religion, makes sure the Sunna is applied, gives justice to the oppressed and helps each person to recognize his rights".

---

78. About justice, Redissi writes, "It is a twofold virtue: practical and doctrinal. Practical because it consists in not being laxist (*fasiq*) about worship: avoiding committing acts that the Law describes as major sins, absolutely forbidden by the Law, such as murder or theft for example. It is doctrinal, because it consists of not being a heretic in one's thoughts. A fortiori, it is impossible to imagine a guide who is a non-believer or a non-Muslim" (1998: 38).

79. For Redissi (1998: 38) being knowledgeable is: "The requirement of religious knowledge, that is, mastering the four foundations of the Law (the Qur'an, the sunna, the lawmakers' consensus and analogical reasoning) as well as the different branches of this knowledge (law, the Arabic language, etc.) and even including the rudiments of profane knowledge (war, medicine, etc.)."

80. Competence, in this case, means "common sense (*kifaya*): the caliph must have the capacity to judge, the spirit of sagacity necessary for managing the people and dealing with matters. Brave, loyal and and valiant, the imam must also be doted with a political sense which invests power and force in times of war and in times of peace" (Redissi 1998: 38).

There is an ongoing discussion in Islam about whether the imam is an ordinary person or a saint (Redissi 1998: 37). Muslim scholars differ on whether it is enough that he is virtuous (*maftul*) and sound in mind and body, or if he needs to be more than virtuous. In contrast with Sunnism, Shi'i believe the caliph, or imam as they call him, must have a certain personal charisma which allows him to perpetuate the prophesy in the following way: "The imam must be the one who opens the cycle of divine friendship (*wilayat*), following the sealed cycle of prophecy. His mission is to initiate the faithful into the inner sense of the message, an intelligentsia spiritualis which is complementary to the revealed, exoteric message" (Redissi 1998: 36). A Sunni caliph must have science, probity, good judgment and competence (*kifaya*) (Redissi 1998).

In Shi'ism, "the imam is not simply a leader in prayer ... rather, he is the summit of religiosity, the way to salvation and an imitable model in religious actions and behavior. His *sira* (life-style) dictates the precepts for religious action" (Khuri 2006: 180).[81] There is a long list of qualifications for the Shi'i Imam including: (1) vision, (2) courage, (3) endurance, (4) strength, (5) physical fitness, (6) able to do incognito inquiry,[82] (7) empathize with others,[83] (8) good manners, (9) show equality of humankind, (10) austerity,

---

81. Khuri (2006: 180) defines at least three categories of specialists that emerged in Shi'ism: "the *mullas* or *khatibs*, the *mujtahids*, and the *sayyids*. The *mullas* specialize in history and ritual, the *mujtahids* in law and the *sayyids* are simply a genealogical category, non-specialized descendants of imams. Although it is possible to combine these three religious merits in a single personality, as prominent Shi'a leaders often do, the categories themselves are nevertheless separable structures."

82. Umar is an example of a leader that practiced incognito inquiry. Concerned that his governors and principals would carry to him only the good news, Umar perfected the skill of conducting inspection tours in disguise in order to find out what was truly going on in the Islamic state. Umar emphasized the managerial principles of responsibility, accountability and control as exemplified in the following incident. He once asked his confidants: "Assume that I appointed the best of you to govern, and that I urged you to be fair in your dealings, have I assumed my responsibilities in the right manner?" They answered "yes." Omar shook his head and replied: "I disagree. I should watch their actions to make sure that they do what I have asked them to do" (Nawafleh, 2000: 29).

83. The following story reflects Umar's ability to employ this skill: "One day he saw an old man begging for charity. When Omar asked him why he was begging, it turned out that the man was Jewish, and that he was begging in order to be able to pay his taxes and cover his other expenses. 'Oh, my God!' Omar sighed, 'We have taxed you when you were young and we have forgotten you when you got old.' Omar took him to his house where he fed him, and then he ordered his financial officer to pay all aged people a sufficient amount of money that would prevent them from begging" (Nawafleh, 2000).

(11) farsightedness, (12) perceptiveness, and (13) eloquence"[84] (Nawafleh 2000: 118; Madelung 2001). In Shi'ism, "each imam possesses superhuman qualities which raise him above the level of the rest of mankind, and he guides the faithful with infallible wisdom, and his decisions are absolute and final" (Arnold 1922: 885). Furthermore, some kind of "secret knowledge" was communicated to 'Ali from Muhammad and to the other imams after them (Arnold 1922: 885). The imam must be a *sahib* (intimate friend), an *anis* (companion), a *khalil* (close friend) and an *akh* (brother) to the believers (Mozaffari 1998; Nawafleh 2000). He must also show firmness and must have practical ability (Nawafleh 2000). The Shi'i imam must be able to encourage the Muslim community and exhort believers to be faithful to God in their words and deeds (Nawafleh 2000). In Shi'ism, the imam is one who has the "ability to effect change and overcome unforeseen problems: This was made obvious through his supervision of crisis management situations such as wars, famines, epidemics of communicable diseases and similar catastrophes." The ability to affect change is evident in the life of caliph Umar.[85]

Another major difference between Sunnism, Shi'ism and Kharijism lies in the legitimacy of the caliph. The table below shows how each Sunni group chooses their leader from the Quraish tribe, the Shi'i from the family of Muhammad and the Kharijites from anyone within the Muslim community. According to the latter group, "the existence of an imam is not a matter of religious obligation and that at any particular time the community can fulfill all the obligations imposed upon them by their religion, and have an entirely legitimate form of civil administration, without any imam being in existence at all" (Chirane 1994).

From this brief introduction of the role of the caliph we learn that (1) leadership legitimacy can take various forms in Islam, (2) after Muhammad, leaders did not have a prophetic role (i.e. they did not receive direct

---

84. It is worth mentioning here that although "eloquence" may not be valued the same way in some Christian leadership training as it is in Muslim leadership, I found in a nineteenth-century curriculum of French seminaries a course entitled "sacred eloquence" (Prompsault 1849: 426).
85. This was made obvious through his supervision of crisis management situations such as wars, famines, epidemics of communicable diseases and similar catastrophes.

revelations from God), (3) Islam provides leaders that administer the social and political sphere, (4) the leader must submit himself to God and to the Qur'an to be obeyed by his followers, (5) there are certain physical, moral and spiritual qualifications that are required to lead the community, (6) in Shi'ism the imam has supernatural qualities that differentiates him from common people, and (7) the Muslim community can in some cases replace the caliph.

Imam

As we have seen above, following the death of Muhammad in 632, the title of imam was given to the supreme leader of the Muslim community who had both temporal and spiritual power. This was the case for the first four caliphs.[86] Later, Shi'ism gave this title to the leader of its community while Sunnis then replaced the imam by dynasties (Chirane 1994). During the Ottoman Empire the title of "imam" was limited to the worship leaders recognized by the government (Chirane 1994).[87] In Sunni Islam today, the role of an imam is "limited to local functions and is given to those who are leading worship in the mosque and are looking after the spiritual well-being of believers" (Chirane 1994).

According to Ibn Khaldun (1967: 449-450) "the leadership of prayer is the highest of (all) these functions and higher than royal authority as such, which, like (prayer), falls under the caliphate." He continues:

> This is attested by the (circumstance) that the men around Muhammad deduced from the fact that Abu Bakr had been appointed (Muhammad's) representative as prayer leader, the fact that he had also been appointed his representative in political leadership. . . . If prayer did not rank higher than political leadership, the analogical reasoning would not have been sound.

---

86. The first four caliphs are Abu Bakr (632-634), Umar (634-642), Uthman (642-652), and Ali (652-656).

87. In Sunnism, only the rightly guided caliphs "completely fulfilled the conditions of the true *imamate*. Their acts and rulings were binding" (Madelung 2001).

In Sunnism, an imam is "appointed for the five daily prayers, the Friday service, the two festivals, the eclipses of (the sun and the moon), and the prayer for rain" (Ibn Khaldun (1967: 450). Dalil Boubakeur (1995: 50) emphasizes that the imam leads the prayer but is not an intercessor according to *sura* 32 verse 4: "You have none, besides Him [God] to protect or intercede for you."

The role of the imam today is thus restricted to the local sphere. In this sense he can be compared to a pastor. Khuri (2006: 167) distinguishes "between the imam, who derives power from religion, and the emir, who derives it from the use of force and coercion." According to Ali Didier Bourg (1994), the spiritual role of the contemporary imam has the following four elements: he leads the five daily prayers, gives the Friday sermon, issues *fatwas* (legal opinions) for the daily life of the believers, and interacts with the more knowledgeable class of Muslim leaders on questions pertaining to Islam. All these functions make him very accessible to the local believers.

The role of an *imam* may also involve the following: (1) explaining Islam to the believers; (2) teaching the Qur'an to children; (3) teaching Muslim education and moral values; (4) and encouraging the Muslim community and exhorting believers to be faithful to God in their words and deeds (Bourg 1994). Bourg (1994) says that imams have the role of facilitating the transmission of religion and becoming the spiritual reference for local Muslim communities. The imam may teach Arabic and jurisprudence, and is considered as a spiritual leader who often gives advice to believers. He is also engaged in relationships with non-Muslims and conducts *da'wa*. The imam often performs marriages in situations where people do not have access to a Muslim *qadi* (judge).

Bourg (1994) underlines the fact that the imam is not a person that is set apart from the community but rather is a member of it. He must participate in the same realities as the believers (Bourg 1994). To be able to assume his role, Bourg (1994) says the imam should be relational because he needs to show interest in the concerns of the believers.

As we list the various functions of the *imam*, it is clear that the *imam's* role functions closely to that of the pastor. As I later compare Muslim and Christian leadership, I will draw heavily on the leadership style of the *imam* because he has direct contact with the local population, particularly socially, and has significant spiritual influence over them.

Mufti

A *mufti* is "a Muslim jurist capable of giving, when requested, a nonbinding opinion known as *fatwa* on a point of Islamic law" (Nanji 1995: 151). Whereas the role of the *qadi*[88] *is to apply the law*, the *mufti* is to give legal advice, more detailed definitions to specific laws and to provide information where the law is silent or lacks precision (Gardet 1961). Nanji (1995: 151) adds, "the *mufti* came to occupy a mediating position between the *qadi*, the judge who administered the law, and the *faqih* or jurisprudent—that is, between actual courtroom situations where justice was administered and places of learning where the theoretical study of legal texts took place."

Typically there are very few *muftis* and thus it is possible that church leaders will never have personally met a *mufti*. However, the study of their leadership style will still reveal values and behaviors that are common to leadership in Islam. Some duties and functions may be specific to their roles but their values, behaviors and attributes are similar to the other leaders in Islam.

There are several qualifications for becoming *mufti* that are helpful to explore in the study of leadership styles. First, the *mufti* must be Muslim. No Christian can exercise the function of *mufti* in a Muslim context. Second, he must be an adult.[89] Any young man with enough legal knowledge is qualified to become *mufti* (Gardet 1961: 140). Third, the *mufti* must be *'adli* (impartial, just) (Gardet 1961: 140). This value is common in most Islamic leadership roles. Fourth, the *mufti* must have legal knowledge. Nanji (1995: 151) explains that he must possess a "thorough knowledge of established text, traditions, and legal precedents." The *mufti* must be capable of finding in the writings of eminent lawmakers the answer to the legal questions which are addressed to him.[90]

---

88. The *qadi* is defined later in this section.

89. Certain countries raise the age limit for becoming a *mufti*. For example, in Syria, one cannot become a *mufti* under the age of 30.

90. Today, in some countries such as Jordan or Syria, a *mufti* must have a University degree on Muslim law.

Fifth, while technically it is not necessary that the *mufti* be a male, in praxis there are no historical examples of female *muftis*.[91] Sixth, the status of a free man is not necessary. Seventh, a *mufti* must be *halim* (i.e. self-possessed), and calm (*lahu sakina*). He must refrain from issuing a *fatwa* under an emotional state such as out of anger, hunger, sadness, excessive joy, sleep, boredom, excessive heat, painful sickness or any other states that is not within the realm of moderation. Ibn Khaldun (1967: 452) says that, "Muftis must have some restraining influence in themselves that tells them not to undertake something for which they are not qualified, so that they may not lead astray those who ask for the right way or cause to stumble those who want to be guided." Eighth, a *mufti* must have integrity (Nanji 1995: 151). Finally, he must display *lahu waqar* (i.e. to be respectable).

Muftis have a significant influence in the cultural, legal and political sphere (Gardet 1961) much larger than any local pastor would. Their impact on Muslim society is extremely important as illustrated by the following examples: first, the recent decision by the grand-*mufti* of Dubai to authorize women to become *muftis* and exercise a larger influence on society by their legal reflection; second, the grand-*mufti* of Egypt, Ali Gomaa, who "is a prolific author and writer on Islamic issues and he writes a weekly column in the Egyptian al-Ahram newspaper in which he discusses matters of current interest and religion" (Gomaa 2010).[92]

Because of the *mufti's* role in answering legal questions, it is likely for Muslim lawyers to view the *mufti* as God's substitute who knows His will and communicates His instructions; in this sense, he is considered heir of the prophets (Gardet 1961: 139). Today, *muftis* continue to play a major role in the daily life of believers as well as in the higher spheres of power in many Muslim countries. Their legitimacy flows from the human authorities—the former caliphs or contemporary Muslim presidents—who

---

91. There is an ongoing debate within Islam about the possibility for women to exercise the role of *mufti*. Some countries show great openness to such a possibility. In Dubai, the grand *mufti* Ahmed al-Haddad "issued a religious edict or fatwa in February [2010] authorising women to become muftis and in May he called on qualified candidates to apply for a training program that includes instruction in Sharia law and legal thought" (http://www.france24.com/en/node/4916684).
92. Biography of Ali Gomaa, Grand Mufti of Egypt accessed at http://www.aligomaa.net/bio.html.

appointed them. Their leadership style is characterized by their knowledge of the legal texts and their capacity to advise other Muslims in legal affairs. Since the legal issues are usually not the primary concern of church teaching one may wonder if the leadership style of a *mufti* is relevant for the study of church leadership. I posit that it is because in Muslim contexts where legal issues are a common preoccupation, church leaders must be able to prepare Muslim background believers to deal with a religious worldview influenced by legal considerations. The pastor must be familiar with a legal mindset regardless of what he or she teaches about the role of the law in the New Testament.[93]

The *mufti* needs to know his people including their customs, their mischievousness and their tricks. I hope pastors are as knowledgeable of their followers. I also think that a number of the leadership qualifications of the *mufti,* including strong scholarship, integrity, impartiality, self-control, knowledge and respectability, are key for impacting their society. Likewise, it will be interesting to see if similar characteristics are required of pastors.

Qadi

Qadis are judges. Byron D. Cannon (1995: 374) explains, "Throughout Islamic history authority to judge cases between Muslims under the *sharia* was vested in the post of *qadi*, the single judge of the *mahkamah* court." The function of *qadis* started to take its actual form following the four rightly guided caliphs (Mansour 1975: 23). Ibn Khaldun (1967: 452-453) writes, "At the beginning of Islam, the caliphs exercised the office of judge personally. They did not permit anyone else to function as judge in any matter. The first caliph to charge someone else with exercise of (the office of judge) was 'Umar." In early Islam, *qadis* were essentially arbiters of conflicts (Mansour 1975: 23), which may have some similarity with the pre-Islamic role of *hakim* (judge). Ibn Khaldun (1967: 455) explains how the role of the *qadi* has evolved in Islam:

---

93. See the biblical book of Galatians for a discussion on the relationship between law, grace and faith.

> In the period of the caliphs, the duty of judge was merely to settle suits between litigants. Gradually, later on, other matters were referred to them more and more often as the preoccupation of the caliphs and rulers with high policy grew. Finally, the office of judge came to include, in addition to the settling of suits, certain general concerns of the Muslims, such as supervision of the property of insane persons, orphans, bankrupts, and incompetents who are under the care of guardians; supervision of wills and mortmain donations and of the marrying of marriageable women without guardians (*wali*) to give them away, according to the opinion of some authorities; supervision of (public) roads and buildings; examination of witnesses, attorneys, and court substitutes, to acquire complete knowledge and full acquaintance relative to their reliability and unreliability. All of these things have become part of the position and duties of a judge.

Eventually the role of *qadi* was committed to judiciary tasks essentially related to personal status and not to commercial affairs (Mansour 1975).

The legitimacy of the *qadi*'s leadership comes from the caliph and/or a central executive power which delegates to him the judiciary power (Gardet 1961: 136).[94] However, in many Muslim majority countries today, due to the fact that there are sometimes both civil and religious laws, *qadis* do not always reign over the legal field. It is required in Islam that every region has sufficient *qadis*. If a Muslim is the only one in his region he is required to exercise the role of *qadi* (Gardet 1961). The enthroning of the *qadi* traditionally occurs at the mosque. In ancient times, *qadis* exercised their function in the mosque (Gardet 1961).

The qualifications of a *qadi* are as follows. One needs to be a Muslim, to be male, pubescent and free. The *qadi* cannot be deaf or blind. He must

---

94. At the beginning of Islam, the caliphs usually had the office of judges. They did not give this function to anyone else. The first caliph to give this office to someone else was Umar: "He named *Abu-d-Darda* as qadi *of* Medina, *Shurayh* qadi of *Basra* and *Abu-Musa Al-Ash'ari*, qadi of *Koufa*" (Ibn Khaldun 1967: 342)

be learned and just (Gardet 1961: 138).⁹⁵ A *qadi* must "know the Qur'an, the Sunna, the commentators, the canonic law, and be able to resolve a new case by analogy with an older case" (Gardet 1961: 138).

Qadis are also called to impart religious education and knowledge (Mansour 1975: 24). They sometimes lead the prayer or pronounce the Friday *khutba* (sermon). The position of a *qadi* "combines elements both of government power and judicial discretion" (Ibn Khaldun 1967: 455) and should be surrounded by a council of learned jurists. The rule of *shura* (consultation) is very important for this office like it was for the caliph.

Regarding their values and behaviors, "like other public servants the *qadi* . . . need be knowledgeable (*'alim*), just (*'adil*) and competent (*qadir*)" (Makari 1983: 153). Other qualifications are technical and include "personal and technical aptitude (*quwwah* or *qudrah*)⁹⁶ and loyalty (*amanah*)."⁹⁷ Furthermore, "The public servant's character is enhanced by the complementary qualities of mercifulness, fortitude, patience and the avoidance of violence" (Makari 1983: 153).

Muslim *qadis* usually do not deal directly with the Christian community. Mansour (1975: 23) states, "The *qadi* was led, despite himself, to apply Muslim norms. He only had to judge cases involving Muslims. The *'ahl-adh-dhimma*' had their own legal apparatus (which was valid in conflicts relating to personal status)." Usually, Christians living under Muslim rule had their own judges. As a consequence, church leaders should be ready to acquire similar legal skills, since they may have to issue legal opinions to their parishioners.

The study of the role of the *qadi* highlights specific characteristics of Muslim leadership styles. They must adopt similar values and behaviors as the previous leaders presented above. However the way they can best

---

95. If the *qadi* must be just, it is not as strongly required from him to be learned. It is only preferred (Gardet 1961).

96. Makari (1983: 153) explains, "With respect to judicial authority, *quwwah* conveys thorough knowledge of the Qur'an and the Sunna as well as the personal ability to carry out one's judgment. In the arts of warfare, it implies experience, courage, and the cumulative knowledge of war strategy and tactics."

97. Makari (1983: 153) explains, "*Amanah* derives from fearing God, and implies courage and resoluteness in the application of requirements of the law without heeding the slanderous and confused noises of public opinion."

impact their followers is through their legal knowledge and the value of justice and through their piety.

'Ulama

The term *'ulama* refers to the community of learned men who possess particular knowledge (Gilliot 1999). This Arabic term can be translated as "the ones possessing knowledge" and usually refers to the group of men with religious education and religiously related professions. They are specialized in Islamic humanistic culture and have some knowledge of Muslim law (Ajijola 1998: 239). They express the true content of Islam to people and rulers. *'Ulama* have education in the Qur'an, the Sunna and the Sharia. According to Ajijola, *'Ulama* must be able to interpret the principles and laws of Islam in the light of changing conditions (1998: 239). Generally speaking, their most common features are as leaders and guardians of the spiritual wellbeing of their flocks (Van Nieuwenhuijze 1985: 86).

'Ulama "have always constituted a separate, distinct category in Islam" (Khuri 2006: 165).[98] They have considerable power in Muslim countries under Muslim laws. They often cooperate with rulers and influence their politics. The credibility of the *'ulama* however depends on his or her level of independence in relation to their rulers. If they are too close to the rulers, the average lay-Muslim will not trust them (Tore 2003).[99]

According to Gellner (1969: 114), *'ulama* are "norm-givers of the community of the faithful; they are the repositories and arbiters of legitimacy." They must bow to the superiority of the ruler but that "does not preclude them to being extremely influential on the general kind of society over which they ruler presides" (Gellner 1981: 115). He concludes "This, I suspect, is indeed the role of the *'ulama* in Islamic society: not very powerful

---

98. Khuri describes the *'ulama* in Sunni Islam, "They wear distinct and standard costumes, styles of beards and headdresses, which reflect a hierarchy of religious ranks of achievements. They often speak in classical Arabic, punctuating their conversations with Qur'anic verses; their skills in language, religious history and law enable them to play formally definable roles in society. Above all, they consider themselves and are considered by others to be a separate category."
99. The *'ulama* in Sunni Islam are not a very structured body (Van Nieuwenhuijze 1985: 87). In modern States they tend to be less powerful than in the past and become mere spiritual leaders (Tore 2003). However, if they become powerful, they can overthrow governments (Tore 2003).

in deciding between one ruler or dynasty and another, they were most influential in determining the general nature of society" (Gellner 1981: 115).

'Ulama often surpass the imams in knowledge. Ajijola points towards this reality when he says that, "Men being *'ulamas* have education in the Qur'an, the Sunna and the Sharia. *'Ulamas* must be able to interpret the principles and law of Islam in the light of changing conditions, says Ajijola" (1998: 239). Drawing from the study of the sacred texts of Islam, Adalat Khan (1998: 9) writes, "Leadership is a great responsibility and to fulfil this important duty the leader must continuously acquire knowledge as per the above advice[100] put forward more than fourteen hundred years ago by the Prophet Muhammad (peace be upon him)."

It is important to study the leadership style of the *'ulamas* to understand their great influence on the society. In their role and function, they can be compared to theologians with great socio-political expertise and influence. The way they impact their followers flows from their knowledge, their experience, their understanding of society, and their status and their relationship with rulers and other leaders. It will be interesting to explore whether there are Christians playing a similar role in North Africa today.

Conclusions and Recommendations

This chapter has given me significant information on the leadership styles in Islam. I first explored the pre-Islamic leadership styles and found that many values and attributes of the tribal and urban society in Arabia have impacted Islamic leadership. The major models that may have impacted Muhammad and future religious leaders are the sheikh, the *sha'ir*, and the *kahin*. Many of the core leadership values found in Muslim leadership such as patience, loyalty, bravery, or arbitration appear to come from pre-Islamic times. However, most were shaped and adapted to Qur'anic requirements. The major difference between Islamic and pre-Islamic leadership is that the former places leadership and authority under God and the Qur'anic law.

---

100. He refers to a *hadith* of Muhammad, that says, "Seek knowledge from the cradle to the grave."

The leadership styles identified in this section are the *sheikhocratic* leadership style,[101] the charismatic-visionary leadership style and the guardian leadership style. There is a strong focus in pre-Islamic Arabia on the capacity for the leader to arbitrate disputes. In the future, it may be that this behavior will inspire leadership theorists to develop a new leadership style centered on this value. Finally, the fact that Muslim leadership styles may have non-Islamic influence shows that they are not purely religious in that they are influenced by society, culture and historical changes. This may be a convincing argument to show church leaders in North Africa that Muslim leadership styles could be transformed through the interpretive grid of the Bible.

Second, the study of the concept of power in Islam provides ample data on how Islam understands the way leaders influence others. According to Muslim sacred texts the main characteristics of power are: (1) All power belongs to God, (2) God's Law trumps human power, (3) believers can obey Muhammad not because of his personality traits but because he was the recipient of God's revelation and full-heartedly submitted to God's law, (4) all humans are caliphs (vicegerent) and can influence others, (5) executive power, contrary to legal power, is much more flexible and focused on human skills, (6) the prominence of legal authority in Islam, and (7) the knowledge of the Qur'an and the legal texts are the key characteristics of influential leaders in Islam. I can foresee some major differences between Muslims and church leaders in this area of power and authority. There is a major difference in the nature of God and the law that Christians follow. Another difference lies in the fact that Christians also believe that all power belongs to God, and it is reflected in a very specific and unique way in the ministry of Christ. Furthermore legal knowledge may not be seen as a priority in Christian circles, although Christians who live in a Muslim majority country will no doubt want to consider increasing their knowledge of legal issues to better impact their communities and the society in which they live. Finally, there seems to be a major difference in both religions because the idea of mutual submission is central to the Bible whereas its counterpart

---

101. See chapter 2 where leadership theories have already identified this style in the Middle East.

is seemingly absent in Islam, although the practice of *shura* (consultation) may partly express this submission to the community.

Third, from the study of the Qur'an, the Hadith and the *sira*, I was able to better understand the leadership role and style of Muhammad. This section allowed me to define a number of key values of Muhammad's leadership that every religious leader in Islam desires to imitate including faith, generosity, piety, knowledge, justice, mercy, patience and wisdom. Approximately half of them are very similar to the pre-Islamic values, except that the new ones are interpreted through the grid of the Qur'an. Although they appear to have some similarity with biblical values, a more critical evaluation reveals certain differences. For example, the concept of mercy in Islam includes gentleness, kindness, softness, sensibility; but those characteristics may differ significantly from what the Bible says about love as it is taught in Christ. The limited scope of this research will not allow me to compare and contrast the definitions of every value. I leave this to future studies. The exploration of Muhammad's leadership style provides further values, attributes and behaviors. They will be later compared and contrasted with values, attributes and behaviors of North African church leaders.

Finally, I have identified a number of categories of leaders with their roles and values. Amongst them the imam seems to share the closest role to the pastor with primary role as leading prayer. I will closely look at his values and behaviors when I study the leadership styles of North African pastors. But I also noticed that the various leaders in Islam share very similar values and characteristics among themselves which will be useful for my comparative work between leadership in Islam and the North African church.

CHAPTER 5

Styles of Leadership in North African Culture

I present here various North African styles of leadership described from an anthropological and cultural perspective. Cultural theorists help inform me how North African people view power, influence and authority as well as leader-follower relationships. Contrary however to the next chapter that focuses on specific cultural leadership theories I consider here examples from daily life in North Africa. The central assumptions that shape this chapter are based on Sherwood G. Lingenfelter (1986) and Marvin K. Mayers' (2002), assertion that during childhood one "acquires certain forms of behavior, values and modes of living" that become our cultural heritage (1986: 19). The values, beliefs, norms, and ideals that are embedded in a culture later affect the leadership values, behaviors, goals and strategies of organization (Bass 1990). Thus, the reason for looking at culture is to make North African leaders aware that their context has shaped their own leadership in unique ways. The data collected in this chapter is used in the conclusion to evaluate leadership styles in the North African church from a cultural perspective.

It is important to underline at the outset of this chapter that the context of my study is not monolithic. Berber and Arab traditions make up the main North African cultural fabric. They in turn include sub-cultural groups that should not be excluded or misinterpreted. In a 2004 interview with the Boston Globe Emran Qureshi for example critiques Raphael Patai's (1973), *the Arab Mind*, which portrays all Arabs as identical. Qureshi says,

In Patai's case, his methodology was itself based on a fatally flawed set of assumptions—most importantly, that there is one entirely homogenous Arab culture, derived from nomadic Bedouin culture. This ignores both the diversity and history of a people and civilization that extends across dozens of countries, from the Indian Ocean to the Atlantic, and the deeply rooted Arab culture of cities and agricultural communities.[1]

But not only are there Arab and Berber traditions in North Africa, the French also left a significant imprint and today, globalization is inventing new models of leadership (Thomas and Inkson 2004). Like in the Middle East, North African leadership has a contradictory nature in its "desire for modernity, while maintaining traditional cultural values" (Dorfman 2004: 308). I therefore expect to find a diversity of leadership styles from Berber, Arab, French and global influences—all of which shape the cultural mosaic of North Africa.

Socio-political Leadership

In this section, I explore two models of socio-political leadership. The first model provides me with a pattern that exists in various spheres of socio-political leadership. It was first observed in the common form of Middle Eastern and African leadership called sheikhs that has impacted most leaders in that region. The second model, that of Algerian President Boumediène, serves as an example to highlight the first one.

The Sheikh

The sheikh is an important and caring leader in traditional Arabo-Berber cultures. Authors who have studied political leadership in Islam have found that in many Arab countries political leaders have typically ruled using the tribal model in that their leadership values and roles on the state level

---

[1]. Emran Qureshi is not the only one criticizing Qureshi's research. Edward Said in his book *Orientalism* (1979) also accuses Patai of misrepresentations of the Arab mind.

resemble those of the tribe or clan (Bonte, Conte and Dresch 2001). I expect to find this leadership style in the church.

Research shows evidence of a number of qualities and leadership behaviors of the sheikh. According to Sarayrah (2004: 1) "The sheikh's major responsibilities included arbitration of disputes, location of adequate grazing pastures for his tribe's cattle and camels, and defense of its well and livestock against plunderers and rivals." Sheikhs also have a reputation of generosity (Sarayrah 2004: 1; Hitti 1987). According to Sarayrah, the tribal chief was "the oldest, wisest and the most courageous person in his tribe." Sheikhs had to be humble (Ali 2005: 8) and have a listening attitude toward their followers. Another of his characteristics was his loyalty (Punnett and Shenkar (2004: 308).

The sheikh had a very unique type of authority. According to Thomas and Inkson the *sheikocratic* leadership style "contains strong elements of personal autocracy and conformity to rules and regulations based on respect for those who made the rules rather than for their rationality (Thomas and Inkson 2004: 128)". They add:

> Rules thus have symbolic importance but will not be implemented if they go against autocratic-tribal traditions: for example, the bureaucracy may specify procedures for appointment or merit, but in the event these rules are likely to be ignored. Instead a leader will make appointments based on family relationships and friendships.

Neal and Finfey (2007: 292) underline that the *sheikhocratic* leader often has "near absolute power over subordinates." At the same time, however, they say he is not a mere autocrat. Other authors share this view including Dorfman (2004: 308) who says that, "Paternalistic and autocratic tendencies are found alongside of the desire of a highly considerate, supportive and humble leader." Ali (2005: 108-109) notes that *sheikhocratic* leaders "might be authoritarian, but their behavior is always tempered by consideration of what is acceptable or not acceptable by the community and the rule of religious law." Dorfman and House (2004: 63-64) underline that this style includes a "strong hierarchical authority" but also important "human relations and personal connections." This may highlight a type of authority very unique to the Berbero-Arab-Muslim context—one that may differ from authority as it is typically understood in the West.

The community further tempers the power of the sheikh demonstrated by his obligation to consult with the council of his tribe's elders on major issues (Hitti 1974). Sarayrah (2004: 1) explains, "the desert society tends to be democratic and egalitarian, and a Bedouin tends to treat his chief as an equal rather than a boss who has to be obeyed no matter what" (Kennedy 1986). However, the status and rank of being a sheikh still conferred him more authority than individuals in the tribe. Lauren Stephenson, of the College of Education at Zayed University, shows that the power of resources and wealth in present-day United Arab Emirates where "power and decision-making is held by elite families with extensive resources and wealth" (AARE Conference, Sydney, 2005).

Several qualifications seem to stand out in this leadership style. Several authors refer to hospitality as they describe various types of traditional leadership in the Berber society. For example, Robert Montagne speaks about the dignitaries who compete for power in the egalitarian context of some Berber societies. The dignitary who is a successor to the leader "invites the council frequently to his own home to treat its members with great generosity; also he provides huge meals for his friends and dresses with considerable elegance" (Montagne 1973: 59). This leader is called *amghar*[2]: "The *amghar* seeks to utilize his primary resources in order to cut a chiefly figure within the group, and to invite the dignitaries of neighbouring districts to his house in order to create for himself the reputation of a generous man" (Montagne 1873: 60). This behavior parallels what Sarayah and Hitti describe when they say, "He [the sheikh] was expected to be generous and to entertain followers, visitors and guests. A reputation for wisdom and generosity brought more power and influence than the accumulation of wealth and animals" (Sarayrah 2004: 1; Hitti 1974).

According to the preceding definitions one would expect that leaders who function like sheikhs would desire to have resources and wealth as a

---

2. *Amghar* in this context is used for a political leader that seizes power by force, says Montagne. It can also be used according to him to simply refer to the *sheikh* (Montagne 1973: 59)

means of influencing others through sharing them with the community. Their elite position and status in society would thus allow them to make decisions and have power. This model may implicitly shape assumptions in society linking the accumulation of resources and wealth, with increase in power. If this was the case, then church leaders may want to exercise influence over their followers through various means of generosity.

Leadership Patterns of President Boumediène (1932-1978)

I have not had much success in finding resources on political leadership styles in North Africa. However, a short study on Algerian President's Boumediène leadership style is worth mentioning at the end of this chapter. The purpose of studying Boumediène is to initiate an interest in understanding political leadership styles in order to learn about their influence on other leaders in North African society. The primary research I conducted on two other North African political leaders, Ibn Badis and Amir Abd el-Kader, presented in chapter 6 will further highlight the specific styles of North African political leaders.

According to research conducted by Evans and Phillips (2007) we learn the following leadership lessons from President Boumediène. First, Boumediène himself learned rich lessons from other North African leaders such as Ben Bella and Messali. Evans and Phillips (2007: 82) write that the latter had "fallen foul of their opponents because each had projected himself as the great leader—in Arabic *el-Za'im*—a conception of leadership which ran counter to long-standing traditions, notably the village assembly meeting where the elders came together to find a consensus." Boumediène's leadership was more effective because he did not choose to be an *el-Za'im* but rather tried to lead by consensus.

Second, Boumediène did not hesitate from making compromises. Evans and Phillips (2007: 82) write, "Unlike Ben Bella he was careful to reach an accommodation with rival groups, incorporating all the old *wilaya* leaders into the system in order to neutralize opposition." They also add, "In the same way he adopted a conciliatory stance to those associated with the losing coalition of the summer of 1962, going out of his way to make sure some were involved in drafting the new constitution in 1976" (Evans and Phillips 2007: 82). Boumediène adopted a conciliatory style, which gave others a voice. This ressembles closely the practices of sheikhs whom we have studied earlier.

Third, Boumediène used transactional practices to reward followers. He rewarded followers with high positions and good jobs. Evans and Phillips (2007: 82) write, "The trick was to distribute rewards so that the inevitably aggrieved few would always be outnumbered by the preferred many and the distribution of the huge material resources at Boumediène's disposal became a key element of the game." As a result, the same authors say, "The economy underpinned the system since allegiance depended on the expectation of the various factions that they were part of an ever expanding enterprise that would always keep them rewarded" (Evans and Phillips 2007: 82). Here rewards were used to foster and maintain allegiance to the leader. The question of generosity and sharing of wealth has surfaced several times in this research. Christian leaders may want to engage in serious reflection on the specific motivations for sharing wealth. Is it to grain greater influence like village or political leaders, or is it to imitate Christ's love and concern for people in need?

Family Leadership Style

The family is the foundational unit in Muslim societies. In North Africa, the individual's primary identity is as part of a family in which he or she experiences coherent relationships having social, economic, ethical and religious aspects (Boutefnouchet 1982). The family is also "the place where North Africans feel a safe and permanent haven to which they return and can pick up again their abandoned habits and customs" (Zerdoumi 1970: 39). Defining leadership styles in North African families is useful because it highlights the leader's first lessons. As children, for example, they learn from their family how to influence others, who has authority, and how decisions are made.

However, when considering a family to discern leadership styles one must keep in mind the following concern: "Do leadership styles automatically translate from family into the church?" The Palestinian writer and scholar Hisham Sharabi (1996: 35) believes that family values are not necessarily carried over into the larger society. Sharabi compares Japanese and Chinese societies with Arab ones and says that although their values are carried over from the former and substituted for the latter, he does not believe this is the case in Arab societies. He writes that although there are examples of supplanting values in Arab nationalism, these values are "never institutionalized in structures that would insure its translation into actual behavior" (Sharabi 1996: 35). This leaves me with the following question: do leadership values carry over into the church and are they substituted or supplanted in the church? Not every family style may necessarily translate into the church but some may as my conclusion suggests.

Traditional and Contemporary North African Families

Traditionally, North African society has two important structures: The *'ayla* and the tribe (Addi 2004: 1). The *'ayla*, which is the forerunner of the contemporary family, has the following characteristics. First, it is an extended family with several couples and their children living in the same household. Second, it is patriarchal in that the entire group is dependent upon the male head of the family (Addi 2004). The grandfather and father are the leaders of the family.[3] Third, lineage is important with reference to the ancestors (Zerdoumi), which is inclusive of sacred values and defines blood ties (Boutefnouchet 1982: 39). Fourth, this family structure assumes dependence and assistance from its members. It is best described by the concept of *'asabiyya* which means cohesion and describes the social basis of the family. Ibn Khaldun translates this term by "*esprit de corps*" (the sense of being one body) (Boutefnouchet 1982: 39). Fifth, it is a *famille indivise* (joint family) in which the lineage of the male is emphasized. The married sons are closely united so that when the father dies, the elder brother becomes the leader (Addi 2004: 1). This practice protects the family's property. Most North African leaders I interviewed were raised to some extent in this type of family context.

More recently, new forms of family models may have also influenced them. Lahouari Addi (1999: 12), Professor in the Institute of Political

---

3. In the *'ayla* the father had authority over the various sons. The father had authority over the daughters until they left the house when they married.

Science at the Université de Lyon 2 in France, believes that today there is not one but many families with different trajectories. According to him, sociologists do not agree on one single concept or term to describe the modern Algerian family. Some refer to the models as extended or joint while others talk of a diversified model with several types of structures. Addi argues that the current trend is characterized by families developing diverse strategies to adapt to their urban and rural contexts (Addi 1999). Fatima Oussedik quoted by Addi (1999), for example, found five family types in the capital city of Algiers.[4] These transformations show the current family model does not have the same cohesion as the pre-colonial family system (Addi 1999: 41). The makeover tends to create nuclear families that are limited to parents and children.[5] However, compared with other cultural contexts like North America, the extended family still plays a major role in relationships between members.

This brief review of family structure in North Africa would not be complete if I did not pay attention to the very unique relationship between family and society. According to Addi (1999) it is not possible to separate and isolate the family from the social context in which it is integrated since it shapes the social bond through the language and culture it transmits to children. Furthermore, Addi (1999: 208) considers that society is an extension of the family and that there is a tendency to "generalize the family

---

4. These types are the following: (1) The extended neo-patriarchal family including the couple, the single and married children and the grandchildren; (2) the limited neo-patriarchal family including the couple and single children; (3) the nuclear family including the couple and children; (4) the limited nuclear family made up of the children living with one single parent who is widow or divorced; and (5) the para-nuclear family made up of the couple with children living with the in-laws because of the housing crisis.

5. In a recent study of the Algerian family between tradition and modernity, the Algerian authors Fatima Ziani Drid, Miloud Seffari and Belkacem Ziani (2005) underline that the current transformation of the Algerian family affects its basic foundation, its traditional functions and the social relationship existing between its various members. If a basic unit of society such as the family is undergoing basic changes, this dynamic nature of the family also shows that changes are possible within a social structure. I will suggest later in this research that I believe church leaders need to be agents of transformation and must influence not only their church but also their society. I was recently speaking to Korean pastors who were debating this very issue. Many found that they were doing well at impacting their church but were not interested in impacting society. Since many authors are noticing changes occurring in North African society, I want to look at both how these changes impacted leadership styles but also what role leadership played in this transformation.

order to the entire society." This may be an indication that family leadership styles could be present in the church.

Furthermore, according to Addi (1999), North Africa is currently facing a sociological transformation evidenced by the fact that the individual does not solely identify through the kinship system but creates new social groupings outside the family. As he or she maintains a tension between these two social forces they continue to preserve the *habitus communautaire* (Addi 1999: 9). This phenomenon may be observed in the church, where some younger leaders may reject the traditional model of leadership in order to adopt new forms of leadership styles pertaining to new social groupings.

Finally, the fact that religion is shaping North African perspectives on family should not be overlooked. Addi (1999: 15) writes, "The reference to religious norms in the domestic realm seems to want to perpetuate the patriarchal culture and make it sacred so that to prevent the formation of a private sphere around the individual giving him or her an autonomous juridical category." This may be why there is some resistance in changing family patterns. As a by-product, one can observe in North Africa today a resurgence of the traditional patriarchal ideology. According to Addi (1999: 157) political Islam animates the rigid forms of patriarchal ideology ultimately attempting to persuade the individual that society is drifting away from the cultural roots of its ancestors. Some Islamists will use force to bring young and older people back into a patriarchal system. It may appear in my conclusion that forms of patriarchal leadership style exist in the church with tensions between modern and more traditional expressions.

Grandparents Leadership Style

According to Zerdoumi the image of North African grandparents is "*infiniment attachante* (extremely attaching)" (1970: 165). First, that sentiment is widely shared because grandparents are known for their tenderness toward their grandchildren. The grandfather keeps his status of absolute authority in the family but in his relationship with his grandchildren he combines that trait with tenderness and special love (Boutefnouchet 1984). Zerdoumi explains that grandparents have the custom of secretly sneaking candies into the pockets of their grandchildren. They also serve as mediators between parents and children by restraining and softening the severity of punishment (Zerdoumi 1970: 165). In grandparenthood, the focus is thus not so much on education as it is on affection. Zerdoumi (1970: 165) reminds us that the name "*h'anna*," (the word grandchildren use to address their grandmothers) originates with the word "tenderness."

Second, grandparents assume an important role in religious education. According to Zerdoumi (1970: 188) older women have the role to educated young girls in religious matters. Third, the role of grandparents is mainly a supporting and consolidating role. They are the cement of the family, functioning as a refuge and support for the weakest and smallest of its members (Zerdoumi 1970: 165).

Finally, grandparents often assume the role of a mediator and peacemaker. They mediate conflicts between siblings and monitor, as Zerdoumi (1970: 166) contends, that jealousy between older grandchildren and younger ones do not negatively affect family dynamics.

Father Leadership Style

There are a number of characteristics of the role and function of the father in North African Berber and Arab society. These are expressed in the following leadership styles and attributes.

Autocratic Patriarchal System

As I noted earlier, the traditional North African family structure is patriarchal, with the father and grandfather being the central figures of authority. The traditional leadership style of the father is often described as autocratic. As the popular saying goes, a father, who does not give orders, is not a father (Zerdoumi 1970). In traditional settings, the authority of the father is absolute and unconditional confirmed by the name children use to describe their father, "*iah'koum*" (he who gives orders) (Zerdoumi 1970: 163). Children keep a certain distance from him, do not argue, do not raise their gaze, and fear him (Zerdoumi 1970).

At the same time, fathers may often demonstrate positive values (Zerdoumi 1970). Boutefnouchet (1982: 62) believes the Algerian father is different from the *pater familias* of Roman antiquity or the Arab father from the Pre-Islamic era who had ultimate power of death and life over his children. He describes the North African father as someone who must have absolute authority over his children because of the pressure of the social group (Boutefnouchet 1982: 62). But in private the father, says Zerdoumi (1970), tends to be indulgent. He often does not spend much time in the house and lets the mother deal with the education of the younger children. His manner of addressing the children's educational needs is "erratic, without any methodological approach" (Zerdoumi 1970: 163).

On the topic of authority, Zerdoumi (1970) describes an interesting custom observed in traditional settings. Husband and wife don't address each other by their names; in order to call his wife, the husband claps both hands and says *ya mra* (o wife). In this context, daughters are identified with the house (*dar*) when they are in the public sphere (Zerdoumi 1970: 164). The same author further explains that the father expects the son to belong exclusively to him. The son must show that he is proud of his family blood and that he respects his father's authority in every circumstance. He must also show that he serves the family (Boutefnouchet 1982: 78).

Today, the attitude and role of the father is undergoing significant transformation. Lahouari Addi (1999) states that the authority of the father or mother has been altered by modern living conditions[6] in which several nuclear families share the same physical space; subsequently their combined authority is not legitimate enough to entertain the conflicts and interests of the various members living under the same roof. However, this reality does not affect this study because most of the church leaders I researched have been raised in a more traditional setting.

Caretaker

In Muslim settings, the father was traditionally the caretaker and breadwinner of the family. This custom directly flowed from the *nafaqa* prescription in *sura* 4 verse 34 that requires husbands to care for their wives and support them by their means. Zerdoumi (1970) writes that this role of caretaker has inferred to the father the status of absolute master and guide of the family.

---

6. For example, urbanization with the older son moving away from the father's house to the city and only occasionally visiting the village, has changed the power balance between the two. "The reference to religious norms in the domestic realm seems to want to perpetuate the patriarchal culture and make it sacred so that to prevent the formation of a private sphere around the individual giving him or her an autonomous juridical category" (Lahouari Addi 1999 15).

Today, however, mothers and children increasingly participate in supporting the family. According to Addi (1999), this has direct consequences on how the father is perceived. When he loses his role as breadwinner, he also loses his privilege of being the decision-maker. When the father does not work, he maintains strong power, says Addi (1999), but it becomes symbolic and the real power is transferred to the one supporting the family financially in place of the father.

Another way to look at the role of caretaker is to see the father as a protector (Boutefnouchet 1982). His role is to make sure that the family is safe and secure.

Cement of the Group

According to Boutefnouchet (1984), the spiritual leadership role of fathers and grandfathers includes managing the *patrimoine collectif* (collective legacy) of their family. They take charge of maintaining and strengthening the cohesion of the family group and this impacts their daily behaviors and attitudes.

Adopting such a behavior in church may lead pastors to emphasize the needs of the group over those of specific members. In their families they have learned to look at the wellbeing and longevity of group cohesion rather than the specific grievances of individual members.

Decision-Making Style

In pre-Islamic Arabia, the *'ahl* paved the way to the patriarchal family. The protection of the *'ahl* was undertaken by the entire clan. Everyone decided together what decision to make within the clan (Chelhod 1958: 47). Later the father often solely assumed the decision-making role of the family.

Today, decision-making practices within the family usually give priority to its eldest members. It is not done in accordance with the rules of consultation like in *sheikhocracy*. However, those who are younger can find ways to influence the decision. The children often leverage their mother to sway their father's opinion.

Father-Son Relationship

The father-son relationship has very unique characteristics in the North African family that may impact the way pastors lead the church. First, the Algerian family is *agnatique* (Ziani, Seffari, and Ziani 2005). This means that the inheritance is transmitted from father to son thus making the women dependent on the father.[7] Hence being born a boy automatically endows specific privileges of leadership. The boy receives a larger part of the family inheritance that he will supervise and he also provides greater supervision of the family as a result. Power is therefore directly related to gender and hierarchy. This may shape a type of hierarchical and gender-biased leadership style that might be visible in the church.

Second, the father expects the son to be able to be equally skilled in life and to be his right-hand man. This requires mentoring skills that could be very useful for church leaders. Boutefnouchet (1982) underlines the tutorship that the father and owner of the inheritance exercises over his sons. He serves as the ultimate guide (Zerdoumi 1970) for his children.

Third, the father expects his son to support him during old age (Boutefnouchet 1982). In the church, this may be reflected by a greater emotional attachment between leader and follower, where the former desires to invest in the younger follower, as a father would invest in his son. Likewise, there may also be a greater expectation for the younger leader to care and honor the older ones.

Fourth, the relationship of respect between father and son is based on relational inequality. Boutefnouchet (1982) shows that there is a generational hierarchy in North African society. The kind of respect due to the father is a religious and sacred duty. Boutefnouchet goes on to say that the father, being aware of this inequality, will usually compensate in orienting his son's actions by protecting his son socially and teaching him respect. The extent and nature of the respect of son toward father expresses more than filial submission but also familial, social and economic (Boutefnouchet 1982).[8]

---

7. As North Africa experiences demographical changes, this system may change. For example, if families become smaller with only daughters, these laws may become problematic; families in this case give the inheritance to the brother of the father as they currently do (Ziani, Seffari, and Ziani 2005).

8. Lahouari Addi (1999: 19) relates a story that illustrates well the changes encountered

Fifth, the father-son relationship has also influenced the way siblings relate to one another. Commonly, older siblings have authority over younger ones.[9] According to Boutefnouchet (1982) age is the most visible criteria affecting the way siblings relate to one another; it is expressed in the way people speak to one another and behave in the relationship. The older siblings have greater authority and power than the younger ones. In modern times, the older son often becomes the head of the family. According to Addi (1999), when this happens the son continues to protect the honor of the family, cares for the education of his siblings, watches over his sisters, encourages new techniques and new tools, but may limit access of women to the public sphere. Younger siblings always show respect and obey their older siblings in North African families. I wonder how the issue of age and hierarchy affects the leadership styles of the church. Could it be that the example of the older and younger siblings in the parable of the prodigal son may speak more clearly to a North African context than to other cultural contexts?

Mother Leadership Style

Mothers play an important role in the life of North Africans. One tradition for example, contends that North Africans lay their head on their mother's lap when their father dies; but when the mother passes, a person

---

by the patriarchal structure. He tells the story of a sixty-year old Algerian man who spent most of his life in his native village. At independence he must move to the city and was forced to adapt to new living conditions but never feels he fits into this new context. He is embarrassed to watch television when his son and daughter-in-law are present because he grew up with a sense of *horma* (modesty) that taught him never to be in the presence of his father together with his wife. Addi (1999) continues to tell how the daughter-in-law is not ashamed to dress and undress her son in the presence of the father-in-law or to receive letters directly from the hand of the postman. She is different from the women her father-in-law knew who in his village would blush in front of their father, brother or husband (Addi 1999). At the end of this story, Addi (1999: 58) tells that the marginalization of the father does not mean that the patriarchal culture has disappeared from Algeria although it is now the son that has gained more authority than his father.

9. In modern times, the older son often takes on the role of head of the family. According to Addi, when this happens the son continues to protect the honor of the family, he cares for the education of his siblings, he watches over his sisters, he encourages new techniques and new tools, but he may limit the access of the women to the public sphere. Addi writes, "the son-head of the household, reproduces the patriarchal ideology in a social context where the patriarchal family does not exist anymore."

has no place, other than the doorstep, to lay their head. Several *ahadith* of Muhammad also underline the important role of mothers in Muslim societies. Muhammad felt there was no one more important in the family than the mother.

Traditionally the role of motherhood in Islamic countries was to bear children and assure the continuation of the husband's lineage. She preserved the legal hierarchy in the family (Addi 1999). The more children she had, the better her condition was within the *'ayla* of her husband (Boutefnouchet 1982). According to Camille Lacoste Dujardin, being a North African wife naturally meant having a son (quoted in Addi 1999: 72). Although their children were their greatest sphere of influence, the mother's role was not recognized socially since the children received the name of the father and the grandfather (Addi 1999).

In contemporary Algeria, the role of the mother is undergoing transformation. Addi (1999) shows how the mother has an increasing role in the daily management of the household and makes important decisions in regards to marriage, divorce, the pilgrimage to Mecca, the purchase of furniture, and so on. Today the role of mothers is also impacted by the greater involvement of their children in the public sphere, outside the household or the *'ayla*. Addi (1999) reinforces this idea saying that mothers now benefit from resources outside the private sphere because most children do not work within the confines of the household anymore.

The traditional educational style of mothers is described as follows in North African research. First, mothers use blessings and curses to educate their children. Zerdoumi (1970) writes that when threats don't work they utter curses. These threats usually occur gradually typified by embellishments, insults and manifold gestures (Zerdoumi 1970). But it is important to note that mothers often don't take seriously these curses,[10] and according to the same author, they often quickly revert to showering their children with blessings. Zerdoumi adds that curses are used less and less among families in urban contexts (1970).

---

10. Zerdoumi (1970) explains that mothers don't take curses too seriously. These curses are usually on the tip of their tongue, but they don't mean them wholeheartedly. When the anger is gone, mothers quickly ask God to forgive them for pronouncing a curse.

Second, mothers shape children through their gestures, attitudes and taboos (Remacle 2002) through the transmission of popular beliefs, myths, symbols, and legends (Remacle 2002). Their influence is evident through songs, stories and proverbs. Remacle (2002) says that the mother puts the child in contact with culture and religion in an instinctive manner from birth until the time the child goes to school. The child "observes, listens, imitates, participates in daily life, [and] lives in osmosis with the mother" (Remacle 2002: 89).

Third, according to Zerdouni (1970) mothers sometimes have an erratic educational style. In daily life, they may dramatically change from overwhelming tenderness to unleashed fury toward their children.

Fourth, mothers often use mocking as a technique to train wild children. This practice may sometimes also be implemented by siblings, grandmothers or aunts (Zerdouni 1970: 175). Fifth, mothers have an economic role in managing the resources of the family. Sixth, in traditional Islam, older wives gain more authority due to the veneration of their children and therefore have greater freedom to exercise power within the family (Ziani, Seffari, Ziani 2005: 5-6). Thus, older mothers increase their sphere of influence.

Seventh, mothers often play the role of a mediator between father and children. Boutefnouchet (1982) writes that when the son cannot obtain something from the father he often asks the mother to plead his case. When children are afraid of the father's reaction, they usually take refuge with their mother (Zerdoumi 1970). Eighth, mother does everything she can to preserve the cohesion of the group (Addi 1999), thus keeping the family united. I remember witnessing a quarrel between siblings in a family. The mother kept saying to her children, "Stop fighting! You are brothers and sisters!"

Finally, mothers are protectors of the family. They are the "keeper of the temple" which usually means the private sphere (Addi 1999: 38).

North African Family Values

Among the many family values, the ones I underline in the next section are the most specifically North African. They may uniquely shape the leadership styles of North African pastors.

Honor-Respect (Nif)

Honor is a fundamental North African value. Children are raised to honor their parents (Remacle 2002). It is not just their cultural but also their religious duty to do so (*sura* 17:23 and 24; 46:14; 4:36). Zerdoumi (1970: 175) defines *nif* as the positive opinions people have of themselves that they find worth communicating to others. For her, the Algerian boy is extremely sensible to this value (1970). Individuals try to preserve *nif* their entire life. According to Zerdoumi (1970) however, respect has a special meaning in the North African family; children must obey without delay and without arguing.

Honor is also one of the most essential components of interpersonal relations (Zerdoumi 1970: 175) and it is particularly reflected in the husband-wife relation. The prestige of the husband depends on the behavior of his wives, to the point where killing them may sometimes be justified if honor (*nif*) has not been kept (Addi 1999: 45). Traditionally, the wife usually bears the responsibility of preserving the honor of the husband by staying pure and chaste (Mernissi 1983).

According to Zerdoumi, respect in North Africa is deeply connected with fear and therefore she prefers to talk about *respect-crainte* (respect-fear) (Zerdoumi 1970: 167). She explains that children show respect to their father by keeping silent when he speaks and in keep their distance and not engaging in informal talk. Also, according to Zerdoumi (1970: 166), the adult son's behaviors should never express that he has become his father's equal. Instead he should show humility, reserve and restraint.

The concept of *qadr* is directly related to respect-fear. It is deeply connected to the concept of *hachouma* (shame) or even the fear of shame that protects the family from breaking apart (Boutefnouchet 1982: 61). Showing *qadr* to someone means communicating deep respect to that person.

Guemma-Virility

In a patriarchal system where there are clear divisions between gender roles and an emphasis on the father and his male offspring, it is common to find virility as a positive value. The name used in North Africa to express virility is *guemma*. The word goes beyond being male per se and communicates acting like a male and being respected as a male. For example, Addi (1999:

134) says that working husbands will try to avoid speaking of the professional achievements of their wives because they do not want to diminish their male image (*guemma*) in front of others. If he brags about his wife's status, people may say that he has no *guemma*—no sense of honor and values (Addi 1999).

This emphasis on virility also demands an emphasis on masculine toughness. One author, describing the effectiveness of the political leadership of President Boumedienne says, "In a society which placed so much store on male dignity, Boumediene's policies, infused with what Algerians call *redjla* (masculine toughness), struck a deep cord" (Evans and Phillips 2007). Thus the concept of *redjla* takes on a positive value in North African society. There is no place for male "wishy-washiness." Often in the West, this attitude is considered incompatible with virtues such as servanthood or humility. This study may prove this view is wrong. It may be possible to have *redjla*, *guemma* and be a servant leader.

Imitation

North African children are expected to imitate their parents (Renacle 2002). This type of educational approach draws heavily on leading by example. It shapes followers who imitate the actions and behaviors of those in authority reinforcing the idea that people learn less through verbal interactions than through imitating other's behaviors. Zerdoumi (1970: 174) writes, "In the traditional family, the *'ada* is immutably transmitted day by day. The child imitates gestures from those around him or her, he listens to the sayings, tales, proverbs and prescriptions, and internalizes the prohibitions stemming from the family worldview." She adds that this early educational experience is foundational and is much like a spontaneous learning of what is accepted as proper behaviors in society (Zerdoumi 1970).

Another way to view this educational approach is to define it as contextual learning. Nefissa Zerdoumi (1970) writes that girls learn by following the example of other women, listening to their concerns and learning daily lessons. In traditional settings Zerdoumi (1970) notes that girls learn early on to take care of household tasks, receive religious and moral instruction, are taught obsessively and consistently about modesty and the strong rules of virginity.

It is important for this research to look at how learning by imitation in any context impacts the church whereby these rules of good manners permeate the leadership styles of North African leaders. One important leadership behavior defining leader-follower relations is already clearly expressed here: one learns through the behaviors of others more than by being convinced of their arguments. Although nonverbal cues are an assumed way of learning in early childhood, I have noticed that cultures differ on how they influence toddlers. Some cultures use verbal interactions with the toddler to influence his or her behaviors more than others. Could this difference shape two different learning styles in adulthood?

Religious Values

Religion plays an important role in Algerian family practices. Mohammed Ben Cheneb (1897) contends that teaching children the Qur'an is a sign of a parent's piety. He adds that the Qur'an shapes young souls and shapes the various facets of their personalities.[11] Mustafa Boutefnouchet calls fathers and mothers "spiritual leaders" of the family group (Boutefnouchet 1984: 49).

Zerdoumi explains how religion influences education. She says, "all gestures of life will be integrated in a hierarchy: those who are required, those who are recommended, those who are reprehensible and those who are forbidden" (Zerdoumi 1970: 39). It is therefore foreseeable that many church leaders have borrowed religious and family values through their upbringing in a Muslim society even if they questioned some of them at the time of their conversion. I would like to propose that not every family value shaped by Islam is incompatible with church leadership. Some behaviors may need radical biblical transformation while others may need little biblical corrective. For example, respecting one's parents is both important in the Bible and the Qur'an. However, respect for parents may illicit different behaviors in Islam and Christianity. As much as I would like to explore these words, the limited scope of this research prevents me from doing so.

---

11. Ben Cheneb (1897: 24) also refers to a *hadith* that says Muhammad stated : "The one who instructs his son when he is young will be rewarded when he is older. The one who instructs his son will see his enemy eat dust."

Transactional Education

One characteristic of North African education is the non-granting of rewards. Rewards in many parts of the world are given to children in order to encourage them to behave well. In Islamic contexts, these rewards should only be given directly by God or in his name, in order to shape the mentality of the believer (Zerdoumi 1970).

Thus, Zerdoumi believes that Algerians do not use rewards to gratify their children for their good behavior; they leave this to God. Instead they use the concept of reward in the opposite way: they make the child aware that he/she does not deserve a reward because of his/her bad behavior. Seen from this angle, a reward is not meant to shape the personality of children and does not communicate a sense of gratitude toward what was accomplished (Zerdoumi 1970). Nor does it serve as a stimulator for better conduct. Instead the child equates rewards with a negative experience. Zerdoumi (1970: 182) illustrates this practice by quoting a mother who says to her child, "If you are not kind, I will not give you *petit-lait* (*labne*)." This mother would never say, "If you are nice, I will give you some cake" (Zerdoumi 1970). Thus rewards are experienced not as being given but as being withheld.

It may be worth analyzing how church leaders motivate followers to be more effective. What role do rewards play in church leadership? It is only by coming to North America that I realized how much rewards and awards are used to show gratitude and stimulate followers to greater effectiveness. It makes me want to investigate this area further, but due to the limited scope of this research, I will have to postpone this exploration. At this stage of the discussion I can only posit that emphasizing the lack of rewards is the strategy adopted in traditional North African education rather than giving rewards to stimulate followers, but this may also be changing in the modern context.

Shame *(*Hishma *or* Hashouma*)*

The concept of *hishma* (shame) plays an important role in parent-children relations in North Africa. Shame is linked to modesty and the gaze of the other person (Remacle 2002). It is also, according to the same author, rooted in religious beliefs and translates into the education of the individual for maintaining the survival of the group.

In his book, *Honor and Shame: Unlocking the Door,* Roland Muller underlines the importance of this virtue in the Arab culture. He writes, "Every part of the Muslim culture I lived in was based on honor and shame" (2000: 50). To him these values are different from guilt/innocence or fear/power. He explains further, "in order for shame-based cultures to work, shame and honor are usually attached to something greater than the individual. Honor is almost always placed on a group (Muller 2000: 50)."[12]

"In Arab culture, shame must be avoided at all cost. If it strikes, it must be hidden. If it is exposed, then it must be avenged. At all costs, honor must be restored," says Muller (2000: 85). According to him, what makes a person honorable is money, heritage, violence, age and wisdom, charisma, physical strength, strong alliances, bravery and loyalty. These qualities are the hallmarks of persons of honor in the Arab world.

Muller adds an interesting aspect of the discussion on shame which may appeal to the church context of my study saying, "Our Western culture has lost most of our understanding of shame and honor but the Bible is filled with it. The Bible begins with man's fall into shame and ends with his being anointed with glory and honor at God's right hand (Muller 2000: 57)." This may be a new and interesting area to investigate for North African leaders who may find that the Bible is closer to their cultural context than some others.

Religious Education

I have already underlined several educational principles from the North African family that help us understand how North African culture views authority and how to influence other people. Other types of religious education will further inform us on existing leadership styles in North Africa. In traditional Muslim societies, the imams were the first schoolteachers. In North Africa, Qur'anic schools still exist but they are now complemented

---

12. By group he means family, extended tribe, or nation.

by mandatory secular education. I will briefly discuss here the *madrasa* (Qur'anic school) leadership model and religious leadership styles that may influence North Africans as they grow up to become leaders. Several church leaders I interviewed have attended Qur'anic schools in their childhood and have consequently modeled these leadership styles.

Qur'anic School

Islamic education encompasses the Muslim entire way of life. Their lives are permeated by the continual presence of the Qur'an from birth to death (Nasr 1993). It starts when the Muslim child is born and a family member or an imam whispers the *shahada* in his/her ears; it ends with death, when the one who is dying is asked to recite the *shahada*. The entire objective of Muslim education is to shape the mind as well as the soul and the whole person (Nasr 1993: 98).[13] Traditionally the Qur'anic school was the only school that Muslim children attended. Now in many places in the Muslim world, Muslim children attend both Qur'anic and public schools.[14]

The Qur'anic school not only introduces children to the Qur'an but to the basics of religious life and to a mastery of the religious language (Nasr 1993). The traditional image of a Qur'anic school depicts children who are sitting on the floor and the master on a small platform reciting verses of the Qur'an. The children try painstakingly to read what is written on small boards they hold in their hands.

The *Talib*

The main leadership style to be analyzed in this context of religious education is the *talib*, sometimes called *mu'allim*. Traditionally, he was the most educated Islamic person in Islam in his region. Sometimes, the *talib* was the only individual who knew Arabic. His role was to lead the prayers, be

---

13. Nasr (1993: 99) defines several phases in the traditional education of Muslims. The first phase is the one in which mother and father play an important role of educator and teacher in religious matters, in language learning and socialization. Then the child goes to the Qur'anic school, then to the *madrasa* and later to the *jami'a*.

14. According to Remacle, there is an apparent contradiction in the educational approach in Algeria. He says it consists of a combination of "permissivity and severity" (Remacle 2002: 99).

a schoolteacher, wash the corpse of the deceased and lead funerals, marry believers and be a mediator in family conflicts. Let us therefore look at his specific attributes and qualities.

According to the philosopher Ibn Sina, the master or *mu'allim* in charge of education must be chosen very carefully (Nasr 1995: 117). He must be chosen not only for his knowledge but also for his character and the way he will influence that of his pupils. He must be pious, have very high moral standards, a pleasing character and extended knowledge. He must have wisdom and enough discernment to judge with keenness the character of his pupils. He must be able to advise them in the path they want to take for future studies or for their life.

In North African villages the *talib* has many functions. His main role is to teach the Qur'an and some rudiments of Muslim religion. But he is also a personal, spiritual and social adviser for the village people. A good *talib* must be neutral.[15] When the community chooses him, they agree on the amount of his compensation.[16] Usually, the village takes full care of him.[17] He is as much responsible for the education of the children as the parents.

In Qur'anic schools, teaching takes place through repetition. Often the *talib* does not explain the meaning of the Qur'anic verses to children nor do they do learn to write or count. The emphasis is placed on being a good Muslim, performing prayers and knowing the recitation of the Qur'an. But the educational system of the *madrasa* can also demonstrate the following characteristics. First, Zerdoumi (1970: 196) explains that, "The student starts to repeat out loud while he is humming and swinging his upper body back and forth." Second, the authority of the *talib* strengthens the education that the child has already received in his family (Zerdoumi 1970: 196). Third, the child learns to respect the written Qur'anic text (Zerdoumi 1970: 196). Fourth, the child learns to apply the written text to his/her

---

15. In Moroccan villages, the idea was that the *talib* should be from another village so that it would be easier to get rid of him in case of problems, and if he was married, his wife and children did not live in the same village in order to avoid quarrels.
16. Often it did not consist in money but in goods.
17. He received food and lodging from the inhabitants. Often he lived in a room next to the school. On Thursday and on celebrations, children give him a little money (one or two *dirhams*). He is often invited by the villagers and usually receives more invitations than he could accept.

own social context. Al-Jamali (1998: 145) states, "It is through action and participation that his personality is shaped as he [and she] put into practice, in its social context, the principles that are taught to him [or her]." Fifth, pupils learn through the method of observation as well as by reasoning (Al-Jamali 1998; *sura* 35:44; 29:20; 7:179).

Religious education in Muslim contexts involves other characteristics which Al-Jamali (1998: 150-52) explains as the following: (1) the examples of friends and heroes (*sura* 33:21); (2) lessons from history; (3) reasoning (*sura* 16:125); (4) maieutics (*sura* 23:84-90); (5) parables, proverbs and metaphors (*sura* 29:43); (6) an attractive and rhetorical style (*sura* 29:35; 25-68-69; 26:69-89); (7) rewards; and (8) repentance and forgiveness.

The *Wali*

The *wali* (friend, saint, helper or patron)[18] is an important leadership figure for certain branches of Islam, especially Sufism and popular Islam. In North Africa, the *wali* is generally called *marabout*. Later in this section, I will show the role *marabouts* play in contemporary North Africa.

I include the study of this type of leader in the section on culture because it represents a contextual example of religious leadership in North Africa. This does not mean that the other types of leaders studied in chapter 1 are not represented in North Africa. On the contrary, they are very active and make up the majority of religious leadership. However, the *marabouts* are also part of the religious landscape and may have an influence on the way church leaders view leadership. Several of the pastors interviewed come from a region where *marabouts* have been active for centuries. In the rest of this section, I will use the term *wali, marabouts*, or saint interchangeably. But first, let me explain the role and status of *marabouts* in North Africa.

Although there is "no passage in the Qur'an that explicitly recognizes saints or sanctions the institution of sainthood" and only some that emphasize that only God is the "*wali* of the believer,"[19] some Muslims, and especially Sufi commentators, have found some scriptural support for this

---

18. Different terms used in the Muslim world for referring to the concept of saint: saint, *wali, marabout*, peer and so on. Terms vary according to the regions.
19. *Sura* 3:68, 2:107 or 9:116.

leadership role[20] (Clarke 1995: 460). Despite the fact that the Qur'an is against the invocation of saints (*sura* 9:31), Godlziher (2006: 162) argues,

> What a big gap between these notions of primitive Islam and the place saints started to take in the conscience of the believers as soon as the first generation of Muslims was gone and where absolute monotheism of the prophet and the worship of saint led to a complete anthropolatry, to the worship of the living *marabout*."

Iogna-Prat and Veinstein (2003: 39) underline the role of saints by identifying two different ways religious leaders acquire knowledge in Islam. The first acquire it by the study of the religious texts and the second by direct and intimate knowledge of God (*ma 'rifa*). The latter way to gain knowledge was fiercely attacked by the *'ulama* until the development of orthodox Sufism in the ninth century (Iogna-Prat and Veinstein 2003: 49).[21] Throughout history the tensions between these two forms of leadership[22] have existed in times of peace as well as periods of heated conflicts.

There are many types of saints in Islam. It is sometimes difficult to make a clear distinction between popular saints and Sufi saints. Lynda Clarke (1995: 461) explains why, "Sufism has served in the past to absorb local customs and culture and to bring non-Islamic and peasant populations into the fold of Islam. Thus the majority of popular saints are also Sufi saints." As a result, saints in Sufism and popular Islam are often mistaken for the

---

20. Qur'anic verses often quoted are *sura* 10 verses 62, 63 and 65 and 10 verse 3 as well as certain *ahadiths*.
21. Hans Küng (2003: 327) explains further the difference between these two different types of knowledge, "Although, in some manifestations and persons, such mysticism had a revolutionary and offensive element, it was by no means automatically in opposition to the Sharia but sought (like asceticism) to transcend it. The aim was to move from the Islamic Law (*sharia*) on the mystic path (*tariqah*) to the truth (*haqiqah*), to the most real reality, to God. This could be achieved with the help of the three exercises in immersion mentioned above. The aim was not separation from the Islamic community, since a mystic could also belong to one of the law schools. Rather, it was internalization: instead of legal scholarship, work under the guidance of a master, direct knowledge and personal experience of God stood at the centre. This was practical guidance of the soul instead of rational teaching."
22. Iogna-Prat and Veinstein (2003: 48) calls Sufism the "alternative model of *'alim*.'"

same person. There can be places, however, where the distinction is very clear as Gellner (1981: 115) expresses well in the following example:

> Under the general category of Sufism, people tend, for instance, to group together genuine mystics and tribal holy men whose connection with mysticism is minimal . . . this does not mean that the two phenomena are homogeneous and deserve to be classed together, either from the viewpoint of social significance or from that of religious phenomenology.

Saints are leaders that are sometimes more accessible to local believers than other types of religious leaders and therefore have greater influence. Gellner (1981: 115) for example demonstrates that the social structure often influences or limits the role of certain leaders in Islam:

> This limitation is notoriously well attested by the fact that such large segments of Muslim populations look not only, and not so much towards the *'ulama* for spiritual guidance, as they do towards other types of religiously significant groups, whom there is tendency to lump together under the heading of Sufism.

Generally Sufi masters are very much involved in the daily life of the disciples.

Sufi or popular saints have many functions. First, says Dale F. Eickelman (1995: 339), "a *salih* is a person, living or dead, who serves as an intermediary in securing God's blessings (*barakah*) for clients and supporters."[23] The saint has the power to ask for divine blessings in the form of prosperity (Goldziher 2003).

Second, saints have miraculous power.[24] They were typically people capable of doing extraordinary things that no other human being could.

---

23. The same author later explains, "offerings and sacrifices create a bond of obligation (*haqq*) between the pious one and his client" (Eickelman 1995: 339).

24. Ignace Goldziher (2003: 234) has an excellent discussion about the belief in saint's miracles. He argues than none of the four major schools of law condemned it. Goldziher

Saints are able to protect believers from danger (Golziher 2003). Ignace Golziher (2003) explains that the miraculous power of saints manifests itself when they are alive or dead.[25] Miracles performed by saints often define natural laws (Goldziher 2003).[26] To be a saint consists in playing a certain role and/or to be in a certain condition; this definition would include supernatural elements. A saint can only be rationally defined according to what he is doing or what others are doing to him (Gellner 1981).

Third, saints have a special and intimate relationship with God. Goldziher (2003: 168) states, "In the biography of saints, it is not rare to find the mention of a *sakina* which enlightens them, a light that shines around the saint when he prays." Hans Küng (2007: 327) investigates some of the "exercises of spiritual immersion" that Sufi saints practice to get closer to God: (1) the thought of God (*dhikr Allah*) ; (2) listening to poetry and music (*sama*) ; and (3) dance.

Fourth, saints have a certain lifestyle and behaviors that are not so different from what Hans Küng (2007: 327) writes about Muhammad:

> The example of the Prophet as attested in the Hadith led the way for the Sufis: his righteousness and friendliness, his compassion and mercy. He had obtained what the Sufis sought: familiarity with God. Anyone who attempted to imitate the Prophet's career would be capable of attaining a similar familiarity with God.

Sufis actually often took Muhammad as their model: "Sufis turned their back on the luxury of the court, and tried to live as austerely as the Prophet;

---

then presents a list of arguments held by those who are opponents. In summary, those who are against approving saints' miracles say that (1) miracles should only be proofs of prophethood, (2) miracles can lead to sorcery, (3) legal proof looses its authenticity when challenged by miracles, (3) multiplicity of miracles make them look like natural laws, (4) what are the criteria to distinguish between the miracles of saints and the miracles of prophets? (5) loss of prophetic dignity because people other than prophets can do miracles, (6) and difficulty to distinguish between miracles and sorcery.

25. Saints' tombs play an important role in popular Islam. Golziher (2003: 180) writes, "It is the tomb that becomes the object of piety."

26. For a list of twenty categories of miracles performed by Muslim saints, see Ignace Goldziher (2003: 173-176).

they developed a mysticism modeled on his night journey and ascension to heaven" (Armstrong 2006: 200).

Fifth, Sufi and popular saints were often very involved in the life of the local community and demonstrated "a large number of charitable and social achievements" (Küng 2007: 343).

Sixth, as Hans Küng (2003: 343) so eloquently puts it, "Sufism addresses not just the reason but also the heart, the 'eye of the heart', intuitive holistic knowledge, the emotions, the imagination, the disposition, experience and spontaneous, instinctive faith, though some Muslims criticize this as anti-intellectualism."[27] Xavière Remacle (2002: 1530) notes that both Sufi and popular saints emphasize faith and personal experience in that, "This knowledge cannot be communicated through language, but only through a personal experience which transcends the words and that Sufis call the 'flavor', the taste (*dhawq*) in Arabic." Finally, Goldziher says the saint serves as mediator between groups in conflict, serving as court of appeal in the settlement of disputes.

Marabouts in Contemporary North Africa

In North Africa the saints described above are called *marabouts*. Before independence from France, *marabouts* played an important role in the spiritual life of North African people. Rondot (1960) explains that in Kabylia, Algeria, Ben Badis' failure to introduce Reformist Islam limited its impact in that region during the colonial period primarily because of the *Mrabtin*. He also says that they ensured the politico-religious mobilization of the population during the revolution. Observers suggest that the role and status of the *Mrabtin* in Kabylia have undergone a complex transformation (Roberts 1981: 101).

After independence, North African countries became hostile to saint worship. However, it reappeared very strongly in the eighties

---

27. He continues, "they think that a prophetic religion which is meant to be preserved, taught, considered and understood should always depend on scholarly knowledge and methodical rational thought if it is not to lose itself in irrationalism, obscurantism, superstition and a desire for miracles" (Küng 2003: 343).

(Mayeur-Jaouen 2002: 23).[28] In North Africa, *Murabit* (in Arabic)[29] or *Marabout* (in French),[30] is the name given to saints in North and West Africa (Clarke 1995: 461). They are "the pious people who have spread the faith and Muslim fervor to North Africa" (Rondot 1960: 213).

Marabouts[31] were thus always part of the North African landscape. In the 1960s, according to Rondot (1960), it was particularly in the deeply animistic Berber area where saints did the most work. The author explains, "Until today, in the Berber area the *maraboutic* movement is growing." In spite of current criticism by orthodox Islam *maraboutic* practices in rural areas continue to hold a spiritual meaning (1960). In these Berber regions, except for some large urban centers, *maraboutism* remains very active and prominent (Rondot 1960). Today, the two most famous saints in the central Jurjura, a region of Kabylia, are Sidi El Hadj Belkacem, and Sidi El Hadj Mebarek.

The traditional status of a *marabout* was predicated upon his performance of a certain specialist function. The primary function was the religious in nature as illiterate peasants required personal intermediaries with divine power. The miraculous powers of saint are believed to be manifest during life and death. People can refer to them when they are alive or visit their grave (Godziher 2003). Hence popular Islam assumed the form of the worship of the saints (Gellner 1969).

---

28. "In general, an urban religion, will have the tendency to manifest the shamito-semitic of a syndrome manifested as following: (1) insistence put on the writings and therefore instruction; (2) Puritanism, and the absence of sculptures and icons; (3) a strict monotheism; (4) equality between believers, the minimization of hierarchy; (5) absence of intermediaries, absence of excess in worship; and (6) as a consequence, a tendency to moderation and sobriety. The city needs scholars and creates them as *'ulama*, whereas villages and tribes create them as saints. According to Gellner (23), the lower class may need more emphasis on emotion and turn toward religion as a form of knowledge and contemplation but also as a means to soften suffering and escape ordinary life" (Mayeur-Jabouen 2002: 23).

29. The *murabit* may also be called the *wali* in North Africa and was introduced through the Sufi movement (Rondot 1960: 213).

30. The etymology is "he who watches [through the night over his soul]" or "hosts, ascetics and warriors [from the ancient *ribat*]" (Clarke 1995: 461; Rondot 1960: 213).

31. From now on, I will use the term most commonly used in North Africa today which is "*marabout*."

According to Roberts, the *marabouts* were not, of course, an exclusively rural phenomenon; the lower orders of urban society were also illiterate and had similar need of personal intermediaries. In addition to these needs, the *marabouts* served a social function in the cities notably in the provision of medicine and also in the education and instruction of the Qur'an and Muslim law (Hughes, Robert and Curphy 2006).

According to Roberts, the social *mrabtin* functions as the result of (1) absence of literacy for access to the scriptures among urban poor and the entire non-urban population, (2) absence of doctors, (3) absence of teachers, (4) absence of law and order in independent regions. Today the situation is changing but the *marabouts* have still a deep influence on the society in Kabylia. Hugh Roberts writes that the Berber tribal society is everywhere segmented and needs saints to unite these various segments.[32]

It will be very helpful to look at ways pastors acquire knowledge and influence followers in the church to see if there are similar patterns with this form of Islam. Küng provides an interesting example of such an endeavor when he compared Christian religious orders and Sufis and found a lot of similarities.[33] I will try to see later whether church pastors have a leadership style that is closer to a Sufi or popular saint than an *'ulama* by looking at the practices and behaviors as they gain spiritual knowledge and impact followers and society. One noted historical North African leader presented in chapter 6, Abd el-Kader, who was himself a Sufi, will provide us with further understanding of the leadership style of such leaders.

North African *Zawiyas*

In North Africa, the community, which gathers followers of a specific *marabout* or saint, is called a *zawiya*. Certain regions like the Kabyle area of Algeria have a large number of *zawiyas* which are all independent from one

---

32. Bourdieu (1961) echoes this statement and shows how parenthood and genealogy are the only factors that bond the groups together.

33. Some similarities he found are (1) "the ideals of love of God, discipleship, brotherliness and service to fellow human beings", (2) "subordination to superiors (sheikhs)", (3) "a distinctive rule, differing from other rules by virtue of the sheikh and the order, which regulated everything in the smallest detail, from the initiation ceremonial, novitiate and hair-cutting through reflecting on God and 'liturgical' musical arrangements to earning one's living and dying", etc. (Küng 2003 :337).

another. These communities have a large religious sphere of influence in their respective regions (Addi 1999).

The word *zawiya* commonly describes the place of worship where believers gather for the Friday prayer and religious festivals. It is also a place of hospitality for the poor, the needy and the homeless (Bouyerdene 2008). Ultimately, it is a central place for religious training. Many families send their children to *zawiyas* because they know children will be cared for, well fed, and trained in the Qur'an, the Hadith and *Sharia* (Bouyerdene 2008). Typical values taught in *zawiyas* are generosity, benevolence, indulgence, patience, courage and other human values adopted by Muhammad and Muslim saints (Bouyerdene 2008).

Leaders of *zawiyas* are often called *chioukhs*. According to Ibn Khadun (1967), North Africa has produced two types of saints: the village *wali* or *marabout* who performs miracles and the *chioukh*, the founder of a *zawiya*. The latter not only were considered endowed with spiritual blessings but they were well versed in the Qur'an and jurisprudence (Addi 1999). They were usually descendants of Muhammad and displayed along with their knowledge of the religious science, many spiritual powers even over *jinns* (Addi 1999).

Conclusion

In this chapter, I have looked at the various leadership role and styles that emerge from a study on the North African cultures. I was able to identify three main areas in which leadership patterns can be observed: socio-political, familial and the religious. I could have investigated further exploring the public school, the work place with its specific leadership pattern called *clientélisme*, or the new forms of modern social groupings. I leave these studies for the future. The areas I investigated are already showing some common patterns of leadership.

The first area I explored was socio-political leadership. I identified the characteristics of the leadership styles of the most common socio-political leader in this part of the world called the sheikh. This allowed me to create the table in appendix C that I will use later to compare my field data in order to evaluate whether the church leaders have borrowed leadership qualities and behaviors from the sheikh. The following characteristics are notable in this table: (1) a combination of autocratic and democratic leadership styles with the use of consultation for decision making; (2) leader-follower relations that include protection, guarding, supporting, listening, consideration, hospitality, people-orientation and generosity; (3) attributes such as courage, humility, wisdom, consideration, and elegance. There is evidence that the style is hierarchical although the sheikh is very close to his or her followers as he listens and cares for them. Furthermore, although he is at the top of the hierarchy, he consults with other leaders and submits himself to Muslim Law.

The second area I investigated is the family context. A thorough investigation of the family patterns helped me identify key values and attributes that may impact North African church leadership. Although I learned from this research that family patterns do not directly translate into the work place and society, I also found that there is no clear boundary between family and society. Furthermore, family styles of leadership are the first models that shape church leaders. These models, which are transmitted at an age when humans acquire behaviors non-verbally, shape North Africans as well as people in every culture, both implicitly and unconsciously. These models become the foundation of their leadership training and are the most difficult to challenge because they are embedded in deep cultural values. It is therefore of most importance to understand these leadership styles that unconsciously shape the young North African. The study of leadership in the family provided the list of attributes and behaviors that I present in appendix D. This list is compared in the concluding chapter of the book with my findings to assess whether leaders are using family leadership styles. It highlights various traditional leadership characteristics including: (1) autocratic and patriarchal leadership styles; (2) attributes such as care, tenderness, and love; (3) hierarchical model with the grandfather, the father and the older sibling at the top; (4) a strong emphasis on keeping the cohesion and the unity of the family; (5) influencing by being an example, storytelling, non-rewards, setting limits and taboos, requesting obedience; and (6) strong values of shame, honor, respect-fear, and virility.

This list further shows that there are patterns of leadership in the family that allow for peacemaking and mediation. In this type of family, the roles are very well defined. The grandfather adds a greater dose of tenderness to his authority than the father. This despite the fact that in many cases, the father is as tender his grandfather but cannot show it publicly for fear of breaking the rules set by the society. This list also shows leadership styles overlapping with the socio-political style studied in this chapter: (1) leading by being an example; (2) guiding and protecting the followers; (3) virtues of honor, virility, and respect and (4) hierarchical model of leadership. However, it does not show the same decision-making style as the sheikh. The latter leads through consultation but in the family, the decision-maker is usually the father or the mother, depending on the subject, Finally, the list shows that religion plays an important role in education. It shapes what is taught and valued. And because religion is at the core of North African family life many of the values, attributes and behaviors that leaders learned in their early years are both family and also religious.

This conclusion must however be viewed and analyzed in the context of the changes of lifestyles in contemporary North Africa. I have not looked at these transformations since I studied leaders who have been impacted by a more traditional family style. However, in a next study, one should study the contemporary styles of leadership in the family. My guess, from observing the younger generation, is that this type of research would yield data showing a more democratic and egalitarian style in the family.

The third and final area studied in this chapter is the religious leadership style. In chapter 1, I studied the orthodox leadership patterns in Islam. Here, I focused on two kinds of leaders: the *talib* and the *marabout*. The first may be a follower of orthodox or popular Islam. The second is an example of North African leader from popular Islam. After reviewing these styles, I created the following table that I use to compare the data collected in my field research and see how the *talib* and the *marabout* compare and contrast with church leadership styles.

This list yields the following information on North African religious leadership styles. First, the *talib* informs us on how religiously he influences school children and entire villages or urban centers through his teaching. His style has the following characteristics: (1) piety expressed by prayer, respect of the sacred texts, morality, and obedience to the law; (2) knowledge of the sacred texts; (3) teaching by repetition, parables, reasoning, historical lessons, practical applications; and (4) impacting society through giving advice, providing mediation and leading in the regular religious events of the community. Its leadership style is listed in appendix E.

The *marabout* leadership style further underlines the various characteristics listed in appendix 6. The *marabouts* display many of the leadership behaviors that we have studied in chapter 1. However there are several features that distinguish them from orthodox leaders. First their piety takes on a different form. They focus more on the intimacy with God. They talk about a very personal relationship with God that they experience through various practices such as *dikhr*, music or dance. Second, they put a greater emphasis on spiritual power, performing all kinds of miracles and also granting people *baraka*, which makes them very popular. Third, they are very intuitive and emphasize the emotions and the heart in religious matters. Finally, they often are perceived as mediators or intermediaries between a distantly perceived God and God's followers. While they do not make this claim per se, they are often perceived by followers as having greater access (and greater *baraka*) then them. Their presence therefore becomes almost indispensable for experiencing all that God wants to do.

Many of their attributes, values, and behaviors are however similar with the ones I found in chapter 1 when I studied orthodox leaders. For example, *marabouts* (1) are patient, righteous, compassionate, benevolent, generous, and merciful, (2) are deeply connected with their society, (3) teach laws and do mediation, (4) do not cling to wealth but have chosen a simple and austere lifestyle, and (5) know the Qur'anic texts better than their followers in order to be able to teach them and lead the spiritual community.

There is much more that I could have studied in this chapter. North African culture provides an amazing amount of information pertaining to the way people influence others. I believe that this is only the beginning of a process of thorough analysis of the various leadership values, behaviors, and attributes embedded in daily life. Unfortunately, at the onset of my research I found no comprehensive study which could have provided me with a short cut to this conclusion. I therefore expect that future research will sharpen the findings of this chapter.

CHAPTER 6

Styles of Leadership in North African History

My findings on historical North African leaders is addressed in this chapter. I studied two Christian leaders, Augustine (354-430)[1] and Cardinal Lavigerie (1825-1892) as well as two Muslim leaders, Amir Abd el-Kader (1808-1853) and Ben Badis (1889-1940). The reason why these findings appear here and not in previous chapters on secondary research are because no one in the past has researched the leadership styles of these four leaders using a leadership methodology. Many biographical books and articles have been written on their leadership but none specifically addressed what I am researching. I therefore had to browse scores of books and articles where personal and interpersonal values, attributes and qualities of these leaders were discussed in order to organize them in such a way that they could be used to describe leadership styles. I do not claim that I have collected an exhaustive list that allows me to accurately present all the facets of these four leaders' style. However, as I collected the data, I was able to see specific trends and patterns emerge that I am reporting here.

I chose these four leaders because of their large sphere of influence. They had thousands sometimes millions of followers and their legacy is still felt in contemporary North Africa. Although North African church leaders told

---

[1]. I studied Augustine, although I am aware that he was strongly impacted by Roman society and was sometimes disconnected from the local concerns in Algeria. Theologically he was leaning toward the church in Rome more than toward the national church in Algeria which was deeply impacted by the Donatist movement. I will discuss the Donatist influence on the church as well as its specific leadership models in my book.

me they prefer to use Christian leaders as Augustine and Lavigerie as their leadership models, I included the study of two Muslim leaders because they have deeply impacted the North African society both from a cultural and religious standpoint.

I present my findings here by describing briefly the life of each leader and their leadership attributes, and suggest for each figure leadership styles that can be inferred from these attributes. This study provides useful data for evaluating whether contemporary church leaders have leadership styles that match with Augustine, Lavigerie, Abd el-Kader, and Ben Badis and thus, like them, can impact believers and society for good.

Augustine: Theologian and Church Father

In this section, I explore Augustine's leadership style. I selected this North African Christian leader from the fourth century because Algerian society today is reclaiming his legacy. Recently a number of conferences and consultations were held affirming his contributions to society (Liberté 2004). Furthermore the Algerian church leaders I interviewed consider him as a role model. They are proud that in the history of Algeria there was a Christian leader of such stature. Although this leader was born before the arrival of Islam and subsequently cannot be used as a model to compare Islamic and Christian leadership, church leaders relate to him through shared socio-cultural roots. Including Augustine in my research will help me highlight values and attributes of effective leadership in a context religiously different from contemporary Algeria but nevertheless closer to the Algerian church context from a sociological and cultural standpoint than a Western model would be.

Augustine's Life and Legacy

Augustine was born in Thagaste[2] in 354. His entire household was Christian, except his father who was baptized on his deathbed (Markus 1999). Very

---

2. Thagaste was in Numidia, which today would include Algeria, right on the border with Tunisia.

early in his life, Augustine was attracted to studies and research, first learning grammar and rhetoric at Maudoros and later studying in Carthage. He read the writings on Cicero and "gave his allegiance to the teaching of the Manicheans, who seemed to him intellectually more sophisticated" than the Christian Scriptures (Markus 1999: 498). He continued his search for wisdom in Italy, becoming a follower of Christ and a great thinker and writer of the Christian faith (TeSelle 1970).

Augustine is considered as one of the greatest theorists and theologians of Western Christianity. As a church father he laid the foundation of a Christian culture that separated the temporal from the sacred. He influenced leaders like John Calvin, Martin Luther and many other church leaders throughout history.

Although his leadership is greatly praised for the immense success it had throughout the ages, there are some controversial elements that are important to consider as we study his leadership style. The first relates to his theological views such as the relationship between church and state, the doctrine of predestination and his definition of just war. Since it is outside the scope of this study to discuss his theology, I will not do so here. The second relates more directly to his leadership. According to Jean-Claude Eslin (2002) his sphere of influence did not encompass the Eastern Christian world but limited itself to itself to the western region. Today, the religious context in North Africa is influenced by Islam that developed in the East with an Eastern worldview. Augustine's assumptions are influenced by the worldview of the Western Roman Empire and therefore his thesis may not resonate as strongly with the Islamic community. I therefore suggest that models from the Eastern church fathers should also be presented to the church in North Africa because they present patterns of thoughts much more familiar to this part of the world.

The third criticism is made by authors such as Joseph Cuoq (1984) who states that he accepted, albeit reluctantly, to rely on civil authority to fight against various Christian heretical groups. Eslin (2002: 95-96) echoes this criticism when he discusses the use of imperial power by Christian leaders saying:

> Augustine admitted the legitimacy of the imperial power to vindicate the Donatists by the use of power. . . . [A]s they encountered the imperial power, many Donatists committed suicide. . . . [A]nd in the conflict with Pelagius, Augustine also received the backing of the imperial power.

It is interesting to note that the contemporary church in North Africa faces similar dilemmas: how to relate to civil authority; how to relate to foreign powers that may support them; and how to deal with some groups that may divert from sound biblical teaching. The attitudes and decisions of Augustine may be debated but certainly resonate with the contemporary North African church.

Despite all these criticisms, Du Roy (1967: 1056) summarizes his impact as: first, "the influence of his thought and his formulation of doctrine on the greatest of the Latin Fathers who came after him, such as Leon 1 and Gregory 1, as well as on the whole Middle Ages;" second, "the influence of his preaching on preachers of his own age and of the following century;" and third, "the influence he exerted on the whole history of the Christian West through the medium of the 'system' called Augustinianism."

Augustine died around 430 in his late seventies in Hippo.[3] Du Roy (1967: 1041) writes: "By the greatness of his achievement as thinker and theologian, Augustine dominated the Christian tradition of the west, of which he may be considered the founder.

Augustine's Leadership Attributes and Behaviors

No contemporary leadership theorist has examined Augustine's leadership to determine his leadership styles. I therefore read numerous articles and books on Augustine's life and work to collect leadership behaviors, values and attributes. I focused on the attributes, behaviors and values collected through my field data to see whether I could find some similarities and/or differences. As I conducted this study, I saw the following patterns emerge.

First, Augustine had great communication skills to which he gave Christ the credit saying, "Although ill himself, the preacher is a physician, but

---

3. At the time Augustine died, the Vandals had besieged Hippo.

Christ effect the cure" (Lawless 1999: 675).⁴ He was a great preacher and he expressed this sentiment in the following statement:⁵ "Preachers are a sort of singing group, *cytharoedi*, their portable ten-stringed harp or lute is the Decalogue, their new song has God as its author and composer" (Lawless 1999: 675). Preaching was one of the ways he shaped followers.⁶

Second, Augustine believed that the emotional quality of moderation was very important in leadership.⁷ He was aware of the difficulties of rebuking and forgiving and argued for a "just middle" between excess of indulgence and excess of severity (Morel 1954: 67).

Third, Augustine was an educator, a thinker, a teacher and a theologian.⁸ Augustine considered knowledge important and believed that it was a means to encounter God (TeSelle 1970: 341). He had an amazing memory that allowed him to pursue extensive studies of philosophy and more precisely neo-platonicism, which influenced his theology. He was also a prolific writer.⁹

Fourth, Augustine understood some of the challenges of cross-cultural leadership although there is no evidence of how he specifically changed his leadership accordingly. TeSelle (1970: 132) reports that he probably experienced a kind of "cultural shock" in returning from Italy to Africa.

---

4. "While he acts as a trader or broker, the preacher's financial transaction is the cost of himself in an inherently deficient imitation of Christ" (Lawless 1999: 675).

5. George Lawless (1999: 675) expands on the two accounts, the first where Augustine says that "we are ministers of the Word, not ours, but God's, certainly, and our Lord's" and the second where he describes the task of the preacher who: (1) interprets and teaches the divine Scriptures; (2) defends right faith; (3) teaches everything that is good; (4) unleashes anything evil; (5) endeavors to win over individuals hostile to truth; (6) arouses careless individuals hostile to truth; (7) impresses upon ignorant people what's happening; and (8) impresses upon them what to expect. He did it with zeal, ardor, strength, and intelligence, without ever giving up, says Rondet (1954: 55).

6. According to Lawless (1999: 675) Augustine said, "Preaching shapes a congregation, as if in a potter's kiln, in much the same way that the oven of tribulation bakes people. God is the potter" and "They are fathers also in contrast to sons and brothers; both the preacher and his hearers attend school with Christ as their common teacher".

7. Augustine was aware of the difficulties of rebuking and forgiving and argued for a "just middle" between excess of indulgence and excess of severity (Morel 1954: 67).

8. Augustine was an outstanding theologian. His writings have impacted the Western church throughout the ages. TeSelle (1970: 341) calls him "the theologian", because of his massive imprint on the thought of the Church.

9. He wrote sermons, commentaries of the Bible, letters, and treatises. Two of his major works are the *Confessions* and the *City of God*.

Augustine was also aware of the differences that existed in the church on both sides of the Mediterranean Sea (TeSelle 1970).

Fifth, very early in his life Augustine knew that he had a calling for his country. Following his conversion he had a vision for Algeria that prompted him to return to North Africa. He believed that he was called by God to become a leader, which clearly shows that he believed in divine legitimacy of leadership.

Sixth, Augustine believed morality was important in leadership. Augustine expected presbyters to lead a moral life (Fitzgerald 1999: 668).

Seventh, some characteristics of Augustine's personal life include his charity and love.[10] He was always preoccupied by the needs of the church. To Augustine, charity was the greatest commandment and all the other virtues were derived from it.[11]

Eighth, Augustine considered humility as a gift of divine grace, setting the individual above ephemeral earthly greatness (De Labriolle 1955). To him the bishop was to make humility his chief virtue (Lienhard 1999).[12] Rondet et al. (1954: 204) says of him that, "he was the doctor of humility and taught that nothing solid can be built without humility."[13]

Ninth, Augustine worked very hard and made industriousness an important characteristic of his leadership. He had a tremendous energy and worked unceasingly (Morel 1954). Lawless (1999: 676) reports that, "Preaching on successive days was by no means unusual to him." Another

---

10. Augustine defined his duties as a bishop as "love" which is ready to accept death if necessary (Jourjon 1954: 165). He equals the pulpit from which the bishop watches over God's people, ready to die for them, to the cross of Jesus (Jourjon 1954). Throughout his sermons, Augustine underlined God's charity and love. Rondet (1954: 32) shows how Augustine believed Christians could only prove their love for God by the love they had for their neighbors and quotes one of Augustine's statements: "You do not see God yet: in loving your neighbor your eye will become pure and see God."

11. According to Rondet (1954), Augustine celebrated the virtue of charity during his entire life. Morel (1954) also underlines that Augustine's choices were led by the principle of charity.

12. Augustine used to say: "For you I am bishop, with you I am a Christian (Lienhard 1999: 568). He wanted to "disappear behind the Lord and be a perfect mirror of Christ" (Jourjon 1954: 165).

13. When he attended the various church councils, he never sought his own interests but those of Jesus Christ (Rondet 1954: 48).

instance shows the bishop sitting on his cathedra preaching and perspiring under intense summer heat (Lawless 1999: 675).

Tenth, what struck me during this research was that Augustine had so many relational qualities. He understood the importance of communion between followers of Christ.[14] The relational bonds within this community were very strong and he talked about friendship on many occasions.[15] Augustine defined friendship as "the charity that flows from the Holy Spirit" (Lienhard 1994: 210). This type of relationship included listening[16] to his followers and sharing.[17]

Eleventh, Augustine also valued one of the great examples of Jesus' relationship with his followers—servanthood.[18] Augustine considered himself "a servant or a slave" (Lienhard 1999: 668). According to him, a bishop was the people's servant and he strove to avoid being "chief commander of the church", but rather its servant (Jourgon 1954: 158). He was constantly preoccupied by how he could better serve others (Jourgon 1954).

Twelfth, being a caretaker seems to be one of the great characteristics of his ministry. Lienhard (1999: 569) says that Augustine's most telling description of the office of bishop is "*sarcina*, or 'burden', a word for the heavy pack a Roman soldier had to carry on his back." According to Augustine, the bishop is the one who takes care of others[19] and who is attentive to their

---

14. Van Bavel (1999: 170) reports that Augustine's interpretation of the church is primarily Christological.
15. Friends were important to Augustine. He was always surrounded by a group of friends who were ready to talk with him and listen to him, said Liendhard (1994: 210).
16. When believers from religious sects asked him to act as their judge, he listened with compassion and diligence and listened carefully to each party (Rondet 1954: 47)
17. The leaders of the church lived with him, sharing housing and eating together. They also shared their living expenses (Rondet 1954: 50).
18. His ministry was not a means to personal sanctification but rather a service to the believers (Jourjon 1954: 160). He considered that the bishop was a servant in charge of overseeing others, caring for them. Augustine believed that if he could not serve the Christian people anymore as a bishop, it would be better to step down from his role. If peace and unity of the flock were better maintained by him not being leader, he was ready to give up his leadership (Jourjon 1954). During an Episcopal ordination, Augustine said, "We are your servants, we all have only one master. We are your servants in Jesus" (Jourjon 1954: 162). Augustine said, "We are the servants of Christ, the ministers of his word and sacrament" (Lienhard 1999: 568).
19. Although the bishop "carries God's people like a burden," it is actually the Lord's burden. According to Augustine, the bishop's task did not require a program because it

needs. He must display a pastoral vigilance, the kind that must always observe what is happening in the church (Jourgon 1954: 153). His leadership style was closer to a father than a schoolmaster. Augustine said, "Preachers are fathers, not schoolmasters with rod and cane" (Lawless 1999: 675).

Thirteenth, Augustine's love for his followers was such that he was ready to die for his sheep. According to Jourjon (1954: 165) he said on several occasions that the one who wants to lead the sheep must not refuse to die for them (Jourjon 1954: 165).

Fourteenth, during his life he was always church-centered. To him the church "is primarily the active gathering of new humankind into communion with Christ" (Van Bavel 1999: 171).

Fifteenth, Augustine's social characteristics were displayed in his generosity and economic understanding.[20] He never forgot the poor, taking from his own resources to support them (Rondet 1954: 49). He was detached from richness[21] and believed in commonality of property.[22]

Sixteenth, Augustine displayed the skills of a peacemaker although his own views and positions during violent conflicts were not always non-violent. He is the one, after all, who developed the concept of just-war theory! However, when believers from various religious sects requested that he act as their judge, he listened with compassion and diligence to each party (Rondet 1954: 47).

---

was above political functions and did not require a charta because it was too close to the gospel, but could be defined as caring, carrying, and serving others, as well as being a pastor (Jourjon 1954: 152-153).

20. To Augustine, says Ramsey (1999: 879), "rich and poor are not only basically alike but are also, in the divine scheme, dependent upon one another."

21. According to Rondet (1954), Augustine was so poor that he did not have a will at his death. At the same time, he had a balanced position with respect to wealth (Ramsey 1999: 880). Augustine never constructed new buildings. He did not want to burden his mind with this kind of projects. He wanted to be detached from the worries of the times (Rondet 1954: 50). According to him, the leader should not be worried about his material situation. Augustine defined the pastor as a poor man whom the believers must support (Jourjon 1954: 164). Augustine never forgot the poor, taking from his own resources to support them (Rondet 1954: 49).

22. The economic situation of his monastery in Hippo reveals Augustine's concept of property. He argued for a "commonality of property" not just as a monastic ideal but for all believers. Augustine pointed out "the evil effects that private property often has (Ramsey 1999: 880).

Finally, Augustine's spiritual characteristics are prominent in his life. He is well known for his faith[23] and for his love of the Word of God (Lawless 1999: 657). He considered God as a friend and wrote: "And if anyone wants to know God's will, let him become a friend of God (Lienhard 1994: 214). The Bible was the rule, the norm and the mind of Augustine. De Labriolle (1955) describes his practices of mediation, having always the Word of God in his heart. He also was a man of prayer. He studied in depth the various meanings of words referring to prayer (Weaver 1999). He also relied on the Holy Spirit for his life and ministry having the confidence that the Holy Spirit would also assist those who would read his work and would reveal the truth to them (Morel 1954).

Augustine's Leadership Styles

There are a number of lessons that can be learned from Augustine's leadership. First, Augustine influenced others and transformed their lives by communicating knowledge. He was very aware of the importance for leaders to know the biblical text and defend orthodoxy. Today, in the emerging church of North Africa there is a great need for theologians like Augustine. The church is growing very fast and pastors are very active in taking care of the new believers and consequently have less time to write and reflect at the theological level Augustine did. Thus, one way Augustine models how to influence followers is by imparting to them biblical knowledge.

Second, Augustine's way to motivate and influence people was demonstrated in his example to readily give up his life for the church. His commitment as a leader was extremely serious. To him charity, mercy and love were the greatest values of leadership.

Third, leaders can learn from his sense of destiny. He had a strong sense of being called by God and believed in divine legitimacy.

Fourth, Augustine was focused on his ministry rather than on the world. He was ready to give up wealth and an easy way of life to devote himself completely to the church. He was not interested in being famous or earning a lot of money through his elevated position. Likewise the theme of generosity and sharing has been expressed in the previous chapter. One may want

---

23. Augustine expected presbyters to be firm in their faith (Fitzgerald 1999: 668).

to probe further to know how church leaders perceive their place in society and if they value poverty as much as Augustine.

Fifth, Augustine was totally committed to research and communication through teaching and preaching. His extensive writing confirms that he was more than an activist, which is an important corrective for any rapidly growing church which is the danger in overemphasizing its own activism at the expense of serious reflection.

Sixth, Augustine was very pious. He is a model for today's leaders in the way he practiced his spirituality. He was attached to God, rooted in the Bible, and reliant on the Holy Spirit. Most values and behaviors that he adopted are biblical values. In that sense his relationship with God can be best described by intimacy and total dependence on the Trinitarian God.

Seventh, Augustine is a model in the way he related with others. He cared for believers, shared everything with them and was very close to them; he was even ready to die for his followers. He was not individualist, but very community-oriented. It is therefore clear that his style was people-oriented although at times he also appears to be very task-oriented. It may be that in some contexts one does not exclude the other.

Amir Abd el-Kader: Visionary and Father of the Nation

I chose Amir Abd el-Kader because one cannot understand North African history apart from his legacy. He is best known for his involvement in the Algerian war of independence against the French. There are statues of him in numerous Algerian cities and his picture can be found on Algerian currency bills. Algerian society remembers him with gratitude as an outstanding historical leader. Abd el-Kader is also a model for Christian-Muslim relations. Although he was a Muslim leader, I included him in my research on Christian leadership because his leadership style emulates Algerians from all religious backgrounds. I believe the church today can learn from his leadership style in how to reach out to a whole nation.

Amir Abd el-Kader's Life and Legacy

Amir Abd el-Kader was born in 1808 in La Guetna, Algeria.[24] The context where he was born greatly influenced his future leadership style. His father was a *marabout*[25] from the Hachem tribe of West Algeria; his lineage dated back to the prophet Muhammad (Aouli, Redjala and Zoummeroff 1994).[26] In Algeria, those who claim to be descendants of the Prophet have unique religious status and power.

Because of his father's position, Abd el-Kader grew up in a *zawiya*[27] regularly witnessing the visits of believers every Thursday night for dikr[28] and other religious practices. He studied the Qur'an[29] and the Hadith and was trained by his father in the Sufi path. In the Sufi brotherhood he also learned *adab* (good Muslim education), the way to relate with others as Muslim, and the sense of respect and good manners (Etienne and Pouillon 2003).

There are very few books that criticize Abd el-Kader's leadership. Some oppose his leadership style, but for the most part he seemed to live a life that was quite outstanding. Since he was defined as the "father of the Nation," many look at him with respect.

Having said that I will underline certain elements of his leadership that are questionable. Abd el-Kader belonged to several Masonic organizations. For some, this contradicts part of his religious discourse while for others

---

24. La Guetna is not far from the city of Mascara.
25. *Marabout* is a term often used in North Africa and some sub-saharan African countries for a holy man in Islam. A *marabout* is believed to have *baraka* (blessing), can often perform miracles, and has wisdom to lead others in religious matters. A *marabout* sometimes takes on the role of an imam in regions where orthodox Islam is not well established.
26. Descendants of Muhammad are called *chorfa*. This status also implies a number of responsibilities. Often marriages are arranged marriages with alliances that allow for the continuation of the lineage.
27. The term *zawiya* derives from the Greek term *yovia* meaning the cell of a Christian monk, then a small mosque or oratory. The term *zawiya* today is used to refer to a Sufi center of education which focuses upon the writings of a specific Sufi sheikh *(master)*. I have discussed the *zawiya* in the previous chapter.
28. During *dikr* at a *zawiya*, Muslim believers spend the night praying and reciting Qur'anic verses.
29. Abd el-Kader knew the Qur'an by heart at a very early age (Etienne and Pouillon 2003).

this demonstrates his ability to be a bridge between civilizations, powers and religions. Another criticism is that the passion for his vision for Algeria left little room for alternative views.

However, Abd el-Kader's impact was obvious on the society. Chodkiewicz (1962) praised the eminent leadership stature of Abd el-Kader. He was considered an exceptional political figure evidenced by the fact that at one time, the French wanted to make him Emperor of Arabia (Etienne and Pouillon 2003). He was both interested in bringing spirituality to the world and modernity and progress to the Arab world. The majority of his students later became leaders of movements in the mid-twentieth century that led to national independence (Etienne and Pouillon 2003).

From 1855 until his death he lived in the Middle East. Abd el-Kader died in Damascus in 1883 while in exile. He was considered as one of the greatest mystical leaders of contemporary Islam (Etienne and Pouillon 2003).

Amir Abd el-Kader's Leadership Attributes and Behaviors

As was the case for Augustine, no contemporary theorist has examined Abd el-Kader's leadership to determine his leadership styles. I read articles and books on his life and work to collect leadership behaviors, values and attributes. I was not sure at the beginning of my research if I could find many similarities between Abd el-Kader and Christian leaders. But as I collected the data, I found a number of overlapping attributes. I discuss these attributes below.

First, like Augustine, Abd el-Kader was a skilled communicator. He picked up his style of speech when he was a child and used proverbs, parables and *ahadith* when he was older. He was also skillful in poetry. I did not probe for the communication style of North African church leaders when I interviewed them but from Abd el-Kader's experience I learned that the use of poetry, proverbs and traditions are an important rhetorical device leaders should use to influence followers in North Africa.

Second, Abd el-Kader influenced followers through his knowledge. He wanted to "comfort the creatures of Allah by reviving their faith" (Aouli, Redjala, and Zoummeroff 1994: 21).

Third, Abd el-Kader upheld morality. He was the founder of the *khadria*[30] *whose purpose was to increase morality amongst Muslims by following the* Sufi teachings.

Fourth, Abd el-Kader's goal was to weaken human misery (Aouli, Redjala, and Zoummeroff 1994: 21). He was deeply concerned by issues of justice and his religious identity did not disconnect him from the needs of society.

Fifth, Abd el-Kader was also a warrior. When the French conquered Algiers, Abd el-Kader joined the Algerians who then fought the French army. Due to the political situation, and the colonization of Algeria by the French, Abd el-Kader became a soldier—more precisely he became what Aouli, Redjala and Zoummeroff (1994: 93) call a "soldier-monk."[31] Although he was a chief of war, Aouli, Redjala, and Zoummeroff say that he never put this role over that of spiritual leader.[32]

Sixth, Abd el-Kader was a model for Christian-Muslim relations. He had many friends among the Christian religious leaders with whom he talked about theology, morality and piety. He also studied Christianity and Judaism in depth. In 1860, Abd el-Kader was in Damascus during the *Khatti Humayyun* decree and rescued persecuted Christians. Witnesses heard him say, "O Christians, O poor people! Come to me! I am Abd el-Kader, son of Mahi ed-Din the Maghrebian! Trust me and I will protect you" (Aouli, Redjala, and Zoummeroff 1994: 423).[33] Aouli, Redjala, and Zoummeroff (1994: 21) write that Abd el-Kader had "no trace of hostility against people of the book. He deeply respected and venerated Jesus because of his deep love and charity as a prophet of Allah."

---

30. Abd el-Kader's spirituality was influenced by the *khadria*. The branch of *khadria* that was led by the father of Abd el-Kader followed the philosophy of el-Djilali.

31. When Abd el-Kader was captured by the French and sent into exile, his leadership took on a new face. In exile, Abd el-Kader became a spiritual guide in the East and an example for the West (Etienne and Pouillon 2003).

32. Abd el-Kader had the following slogan on his clothes or on a banner: "The victory comes from God and it is near (Aouli, Redjala and Zoummeroff 1994: 101).

33. Abd el-Kader also blamed Muslims for their intolerance and that they did not follow the teachings of the Qur'an accurately. 12,000 to 15,000 escaped death partly because of Abd el-Kader's involvement in this conflict's resolution (Aouli, Redjala and Zoummeroff 1994: 460).

Seventh, Abd el-Kader's legitimacy as a leader flowed from his lineage, from God and from other leaders. His father was a *marabout*[34] from the Hachem tribe of West Algeria. His lineage dated back to the prophet Muhammad (Aouli, Redjala, and Zoummeroff 1994: 32). Early in his life he was aware of the importance he might play in his country. He had several mentors that played a crucial role in his training and his call was confirmed by visions and dreams. Later in life, he did not have to worry about human legitimacy because thousands and thousands of Algerians followed him.

Eighth, Abd el-Kader was humble. Aouli, Redjala, and Zoummeroff (1994: 154) describe him as follows: (1) His ambition was not conquering and (2) glory was not the motivation of his actions.

Ninth, Abd el-Kader's work was impacted by love (Aouli, Redjala, and Zoummeroff 1994: 21). Those who came close to him were impressed by his gentleness. Love is a recurrent theme in this research and Muslim leadership emphasizes many aspects of mercy and love. These words can have a variety of meanings and connotations. A future study should compare love as a leadership attribute in Islam and Christianity to explore what behaviors and models both communities adopt to express love.

Tenth, Chodkiewicz (1962) describes Abd el-Kader as a Bedouin with all the values already mentioned above when I described the sheikh's leadership style. He was known for his bravery (Lacheraf 1965). He was the perfect example of a sheikh who displayed tribal values. Earlier, I studied the leadership style of *sheikhocracy* and Abd el-Kader is an example of someone who has the attributes pertaining to this style.

Eleventh, Abd el-Kader was detached from earthly things.[35] He did not have a love for richness; he was disinterested[36] and poor (Aouli, Redjala,

---

34. *Marabout* is a term often used in North Africa and some sub-saharan African countries for a holy man in Islam. A *marabout* is believed to have *baraka* (blessing), can often perform miracles, and has wisdom to lead others in religious matters. A *marabout* sometimes takes on the role of an imam in regions where orthodox Islam is not well established.

35. Abd el-Kader was detached from earthly things. He had his eyes focused on paradise. He said that only those who do good things, reject impurity and immorality, live eternally (Aouli, Redjala, and Zoummeroff 1994: 20).

36. Aouli, Redjala, and Zoummeroff (1994: 154) describe him as follows: "He was not guided by personal interest."

and Zoummeroff 1994: 154).[37] Aouli, Redjala, and Zoummeroff (1994: 154) describe him as follows: "He was only attached to the earth to do the will of the Almighty from whom he was the instrument." Abd el-Kader was a true Sufi leader who did not put his trust in wealth and earthly richness.

Twelfth, Abd el-Kader showed endurance and perseverance. Many said of him that the numerous difficulties that life brought him enabled him to thrive (Aouli, Redjala, and Zoummeroff 1994: 160). This is a key aspect of Muslim leadership that I discovered in chapter 1. Thus Abd el-Kader was a genuine Muslim leader.

Thirteenth, the way Abd el-Kader influenced others was by modeling and persuasion.[38] He once said, "Never ask the origin of a man, instead explore his life, his actions, his courage, his qualities, and you will find out who he is. If the water from a river is safe, pleasant and soft, it shows it comes from a pure spring" (Aouli, Redjala, and Zoummeroff 1994: 32). This is an amazing statement in a society where people and leaders are often defined by their birth into a particular family. That said, the previous chapters have already revealed how important this type of leadership is in the North African context. Leading by example is a key characteristic of this region, both in the church and the mosque. Abd el-Kader however also emphasized another key aspect of influence, which was the use of persuasion.

Fourteenth, Abd el-Kader was very relational and community-oriented. He enjoyed family and friends (Aouli, Redjala, and Zoummeroff 1994: 439), was close to his followers and had a special relationship with the Algerians. "No one in the Muslim world knows better his own people than Abd el-Kader," said the commander Daumas (Aouli, Redjala, and Zoummeroff 1994: 121). Abd el-Kader also created a new type of community called the *smala*, which included his family, his archives, his workshop and his provisions of war.

Fifteenth, Abd el-Kader played a very important role in society. According to Mostefa Lacheraf (1965), he "reflected as a founder of a modern State." He dealt with issues such as administration, taxes, national

---

37. His father taught him to discard the goods of the earth (Aouli, Redjala, and Zoummeroff 1994: 133).
38. Abd el-Kader preferred using persuasion than attacking first.

currency and justice. Preferring to be called *amir*, he immediately replaced the title of sultan with "*Amir al-Mu'minin* (prince or commander of the believers)" (Aouli, Redjala, and Zoummeroff 1994: 101).

Sixteenth, Abd el-Kader's spirituality was shaped by the *zawia*. Chodkiewicz wrote that Sufism best explains the attitudes of the Amir Abd el-Kader. His Sufi father taught him to reject evil words, pronounce without ceasing the name of Allah, discard the goods of the earth, push away human loves and fear God the most high (Aouli, Redjala, and Zoummeroff 1994: 133).

Seventeenth, Amir Abd el-Kader's faith was deeply impacted by the concept of the unity of God. Aouli, Redjala, and Zoummeroff (1994) report that he taught the concept of the oneness of God under his tent, at the mosque, and when he entered a new city. He devoted himself to spirituality and meditation and he exhorted Muslims to pray for themselves and all humans (Aouli, Redjala, and Zoummeroff 1994). His attachment to earthly things was solely to do the will of the Almighty through him (Aouli, Redjala, and Zoummeroff 1994). He had his eyes focused on paradise. He said: "Observe your religion and the victory will be yours; if you become weak, you will find strength in your beliefs" (Aouli, Redjala, and Zoummeroff 1994: 121). The supernatural played an important role in his spirituality and because of his intense devotional life some called him the "sultan-imam."[39] Abd el-Kader organized his life around prayer, meditation, study and poetry (Aouli, Redjala, and Zoummeroff 1994: 439).

Amir Abd el-Kader's Leadership Style

Although no study yet describes Abd el-Kader's leadership styles, my exploration of his leadership attributes, values and behaviors reveal some patterns that allow me to propose the following.

First, Abd el-Kader was a pious leader who drew his leadership from his relationship with God and his daily spiritual practices. He was totally committed to God, to the Qur'an and the Sunna as well as Sufi spiritual

---

39. The French commander Roche reports that when he was sick he called Abd el-Kader who came to him: "I saw him standing in front of me, his lips seemed to say a prayer, although they did not move, he seemed ecstatic. His longing toward heaven was such that he did not seem to touch the ground" (Aouli, Redjala, and Zoummeroff 1994: 481).

practices. Throughout his life he never valued worldly things above his relationship to God and this lifestyle should challenge the church's sense of spirituality.

Second, Abd el-Kader was a visionary and charismatic leader. He inspired North Africans through his eloquence, life style, and caretaking and made them embrace his vision. His political leadership was preceded by a time of deep spiritual shaping that continued throughout his lifetime.

Third, Abd el-Kader lived a simple life without attachment to the world. This is a very important lesson for the church today especially because certain mission agencies preach a prosperity gospel and motivate leaders with the lure of wealth. Abd el-Kader was not attracted by wealth and prosperity but by a total dependence on God.

Fourth, Abd el-Kader was a transformational leader that wanted to impact not only individual believers, but also an entire nation. Like Augustine, he had a deep love for Algeria. He spent his energy and strength to care for his nation. During his life he tried to unite the various tribes that formed his society around a common goal. Today, some Christian workers have designed models to reach specific ethnic groups without realizing that this might divide the nation. Amir Abd el-Kader sets a good example in that he did not want to divide the nation along ethnic lines, but had its unity in mind.

Fifth, Abd el-Kader was a relational leader. Although he had strong opinions, he was community-oriented and strengthened the bonds between believers. He also respected other religious groups. Even though he fought against the French, he still respected Christians, Jews and atheists. Christian leaders must be reminded that even if they disagree with other groups on theological grounds they can develop the same kind of respect and relationship and be a witness of love and charity.

Sixth, Abd el-Kader influenced others through his knowledge, his teaching and mentoring. Although he did not write as extensively as Augustine, he was aware of the importance of communication—writing extensive letters, conducting research and studying throughout his life.

Finally, Abd el-Kader had a *sheikhocratic* leadership style. He displayed all the attributes and values of a sheikh that we studied earlier such as courage, endurance, consensus, generosity, self-sacrifice, and leading by example.

Cardinal Lavigerie: Contextual Missionary and Communicator

Although he was not a native from North Africa, I chose French Cardinal Lavigerie because of his large sphere of influence in mission during the nineteenth century and due to his impact on Algerians.[40] Lavigerie was one of the first missionaries to North Africa who was aware of the importance of communicating the gospel into context. As I explored his leadership I encountered attributes that are relevant for contemporary North African leaders and others that are not due to the fact he was from a different cultural and religious background. As is the case for the two previous leaders, there is no research on Cardinal Lavigerie's leadership styles; therefore I draw here from studies and biographies where his leadership attributes, values and behaviors are randomly discussed.

Cardinal Lavigerie's Life and Legacy

Cardinal Lavigerie was born in Bayonne, France, in 1825. His family gave him the desire for intellectual study. He learned prayer, catechism, and gospel stories through two female housemaids. Mgr Baunard, his first biographer reported:

> Lavigerie was a hard working person: he was always first when playing games or doing bodily exercises; he often won and sometimes lost but was always ready to take his revenge. . . . He was energetic, ardent, dominating others, able to lead, subjugating and fascinating everyone (Baunard 1896: 5-9).

Lavigerie studied philosophy and theology at the "*Petit Séminaire de Saint-Nicolas du Chardenait.*" The instruction at St Sulpice promoted "a balanced and prudent apostolate which led souls along according to their capacities of the moment" (Burridge 1966: 12). Later, Lavigerie pursued a doctorate in theology and then spent four years in study before entering the priesthood.

---

40. Cardinal Lavigerie knew Abd el-Kader and interacted with him on several occasions.

Early in his life, Lavigerie was exposed to Muslim contexts through his work in the Middle East. Following his bishopric in France he became archbishop and moved to North Africa where he started working with orphans in villages. Despite the fact that the French authorities asked him to exclusively minister to colonists, his passion for cross-cultural mission was not hindered and he founded the Missionary Congregation of the White Fathers or Society of Missionaries of Africa.

His missionary approach was very unique for his time and worth discussing here briefly. Lavigerie's vision of the church was clear. It had to "become part of the life of people as a whole", which according to him was the mark that the church was truly rooted in the country (Burridge 1966: 123). Burridge (1966) posits that Lavigerie's concepts of missionary apostolate stressed community life and adaptation to the country and people being evangelized. Lavigerie defined adaptation as the following: "Adaptation must begin with externals". He advised adaptation to the exterior style of life, in dress and food and in the spirit of Paul who said: "I have become all things to all men, that I might by all means save more" (1 Cor 9:22; Burridge 1966: 104).

Lavigerie always insisted on the necessity of having solid intellectual training to succeed in action. His favorite subject was church history and he was able to use this subject as a resource to reflect on issues of his time. He also reflected, from a political perspective, on the need for reconciliation between the church and the modern world without giving up the traditional faith (Perraudin 1958: 91).

Although Lavigerie's leadership can be described as effective and outstanding in many ways, there are also some negative aspects to it. According to Renault (1992: 121), "In the West, the knowledge of the Islamic world was limited to the period of its downfall" and as a result Lavigerie's understanding of Islam was very limited. Another issue that may have affected his leadership is that Lavigerie sought to reach the Algerian population without a clear call to conversion. Finally, Lavigerie found it difficult to transition from his leadership as a founder of a Christian organization and his successors. Many attribute this to his personality.

His role was not limited to his missionary organization although he spent much time developing its organization and training missionaries. But he was such a relational person that his ties were broader than the missionary order he had founded. He loved to connect with people from all social conditions (Renault 1992: 60) evidenced by the fact he started two orphanages. He preferred to leave the children in their cultural context than to have them adopted by French families.[41]

The governor general of Algeria said that the Lavigerie often told him: "I am the servant of a master whom no one was ever able to confine in a tomb" (Burridge 1966: 195). Burridge (1966: 193) describes the end of Lavigerie's life as follows:

> Unity, charity, zeal, loyalty to the pope, fearless championing of the cause of Christ, total abnegation, reliance on grace, the importance of prayer and humility, this was the atmosphere of the quiet room where this man of the Church was breathing his last, tracing with his finger a tiny cross where his priest had just traced the last anointing.

Cardinal Lavigerie died in 1892 in Algiers, Algeria. At the end of his life, Christ was still the center of his life. According to Burridge (1966: 184), "His own zeal and deepening peace in sacrifice extended into the last months of his life."

Cardinal Lavigerie's Leadership Attributes and Behaviors

The limited scope of this research did not permit me to conduct a comprehensive study of all of Lavigerie's values, qualities and behaviors. However, as I browsed biographies and studies of his life, patterns of leadership emerged that helped me understand why he was so influential. I was able to identify attributes that I also found in other leaders which helped me define his leadership style. I describe them below.

First, Lavigerie had a deep sense of calling expressed by a strong sense of spirituality that grounded his mission as a priest. He only longed to be priest, he said, in order to "be able to join the great enterprise for the

---

41. One of the reasons for keeping the children in their cultural context was that they would encourage their own community later.

salvation of souls with Jesus Christ" (Cristiani 1961: 315). His style clearly expressed divine legitimacy.

Second, Lavigerie upheld moral behaviors, particularly the virtue of chastity. He said: "If a missionary loses this virtue he becomes the dominion of Satan: He thrusts souls into hell and on him falls the anathema uttered by Christ himself" (Burridge 1966: 47). In regards to Christian values, Lavigerie underlined the importance of "a life pure and chaste, of unassailable integrity, of piety." His teaching on sanctification was remarkable.[42]

Third, Lavigerie loved knowledge. Despite the demands of his ministry, he persevered in his own study and personal research. He studied scientific trends and new schools of thought to discern how their insights could impact the church. He took advantage of his trips to Lebanon to study the Eastern Church and became acquainted with other religious communities. Lavigerie was not interested in subjective debates but focused his reflection toward action. He not only loved knowledge but also loved communicating it to others. He was an amazing teacher and educator[43] and an outstanding theologian and great mentor.

Fourth, one of Lavigerie's greatest personal characteristics was his charity[44] (Duval 2000). Lavigerie's Episcopal arms bore the Latin word *Caritas* (charity) (Duval 2000: 17) and another statement explaining that "Faith operates in charity" (Cristiani 1961: 316). Lavigerie believed that love of God and of neighbor should be at the core of his ministry. Charity towards the "infidels" was according to him "the most powerful means of gaining

---

42. Lavigerie said to the missionaries, "You will convert no one, nor sanctify anyone, unless you yourselves first undertake to work steadfastly at your own sanctification" (Burridge 1966: 44-45). He believed that sanctification was important for the individual and for his or her neighbor (Cristiani 1961: 248). Lavigerie continually said of his missionaries, "Saints, I want saints" (Duval 2000: 35).

43. Lavigerie became professor of church history at the Sorbonne in 1854. He was able to use the topics of church history to reflect on current issues. He also reflected on the reconciliation between the church and the modern world without giving up the traditional faith (Perraudin 1958: 91).

44. Lavigerie said, "Charity is the leading weapon, penetrating the hearts. . . . This is the secret of your action: love" (Lavigerie 1950: 53). To explain the kind of love expected from missionaries, Lavigerie (1965: 103) quoted the encounter between Jesus and Peter, when Jesus asked Peter, "Do you love me?" Among all the virtues he considered charity the greatest. He said: At the head of the virtues you must practice charity" (Burridge 1966: 34).

entrance to the hearts of the people" (Burridge 1966: 47). Lavigerie also was prudent and simple. He once said, when he was teaching at the Sorbonne: "I forced myself to combine to the prudence of serpents and the simplicity of the doves, although I share with one of the most outstanding speakers, the opinions of Saint Francois de Sale who wrote somewhere: "My dear Philothée, I would exchange twenty serpents for a dove" (Perraudin 1958: 91).

Fifth, Lavigerie was known for being industrious.[45] According to De Arteche (1964: 141) he was a man who was deeply committed to action, yet governed by an intense interior life. He displayed great zeal[46] in his ministry. Duval (2000: 13) described the working habits of Lavigerie saying: "The life of the cardinal was a storm of activities, travels, struggles of all kind to accomplish tasks that were ever larger and further away . . . he wears action like a piece of clothing; people heard him say: 'If God wanted to send me to hell, he would condemn me to do nothing throughout eternity.'"

Sixth, Lavigerie requested courage from his followers.[47] This quality parallels what Abd el-Kader also expected from his followers. His emphasis on this attribute is reflective of the fact that he was sensitive to the religious and cultural context. An option is that he might have imitated Paul who was often quoted as a model of courage by one of the North African church leaders. Eventually, Lavigerie's personality may have inclined him to this virtue.

Seventh, Lavigerie included his followers in decision making through consultation. He said: "I call the attention of superiors to the fact that they should never decide anything of importance without first getting the missionaries together to discuss it in council, for this is necessary to maintain a sense of solidarity and joint effort" (Burridge 1966: 89). At the same

---

45. Lavigerie was a man "who made his impact by seizing a practical problem and solving it and by hammering home his key thoughts repeatedly as concrete occasion arose," said Burridge (1966: 81).

46. Lavigerie always encouraged missionaries to be zealous. To him, zeal was the perfection of charity (Duval 2000: 67). He reminded them that the apostle is "exclusively the man of God and of souls" (Lavigerie 1950: 84).

47. Lavigerie showed his commitment and zeal by statements such as: "What I now want is men; men animated with zeal for souls, men of courage, faith, and abnegation, to come and join the laborers of the first hour" (Burridge 1966: 134).

time, Lavigerie also insisted on obedience to the rule.[48] Burridge (1966: 47) reports what he said: "Failure to observe your Rule faithfully would certainly bring about the ruin of your mission." But through consultation and obedience, he also viewed power in leadership in the "powerlessness" of the leader.[49]

Eighth, Lavigerie believed a leader must be a model. He said that being an example was the most powerful means of preaching (Burridge 1966: 102). He also added: "Our charity and good example must be such that people will say, 'These are men of God.' Little by little, by the example of a holy life and of charity, you must win the confidence of the people so as to be able to have over them a life-giving influence" (Burridge 1966: 103). There is not a single leader in this research who has not said that leading by example is crucial. Lavigerie was following here a biblical model or perhaps imitating cultural practices in North Africa.

Ninth, Lavigerie's relational qualities were numerous. He was very community-centered exemplified by his policy of sending missionaries in teams of no less than three members (Cristiani 1961: 257). He also believed in the unity of believers.

Tenth, Lavigerie said he was ready to die for his followers (Lavigerie 1950: 320). Lavigerie was convinced of the importance of following Jesus' example and being ready to give up one's life in doing mission work. He said:

> In our relation with the infidels, we must be animated by a supernatural love, we must love them like our Lord loved the apostles; we must be willing to die for them, like Jesus Christ died for his apostles. We must love them, not because of their manners, or because we find them attractive, but because they are a soul needing salvation, a soul that Jesus Christ redeemed by his blood. (Lavigerie1950: 320)

---

48. Lavigerie believed that "Obedience is the supreme law which God prescribes for those who desire to work in union with him for the salvation of souls" (Burridge 1966: 47).

49. Lavigerie said, "The missionaries must above all be convinced of their powerlessness and their nothingness" (Burridge 1966: 101).

As I stated earlier, giving up one's life has become a recurrent theme in this research. Essentially this is a result of the example of Jesus who gave up his life for his sheep. This attitude shows a unique type of relationship between leaders and followers where the leaders ready to give up their lives for their followers.

Tenth, Lavigerie was a peacemaker. He was able to gather people who thought differently. He was a great conciliator and viewed with horror the quarrels between schools of thought which divided Catholics (De Arteche 1964).

Eleventh, Lavigerie insisted leaders should not accumulate wealth. He said: 'Our missionaries may well be content to be better treated than our Lord; he was content with the standard of living of the poorest of the Arabs." He added: "Our mission can only survive if we practice poverty" (Burridge 1966: 46).

Twelfth, Lavigerie's had many spiritual qualities including piety,[50] being attached to God and dependence on his grace.[51] He was a man of faith. His faith consisted not only in accepting the divine teachings but also living by them (Christiani 1961). He stated that "The spirit of faith is indispensable" (Burridge 1966: 46). Lavigerie was also a mystic. He considered that he could not lead souls to God if he did not dwell in God himself (Cristiani 1961). He testified that this love carried him during the hardship of ministry (Cristiani 1961). However he defined mysticism saying "the mystic is the one who understands the divine presence . . . who lives, breathes, fights, suffers and works for God, for his reign, for the salvation of humankind in his son Jesus Christ" (Cristiani 1961: 324). Finally, he was a man of prayer.[52]

Thirteenth, Lavigerie insisted that missionaries be involved in the society. He wanted them "to be solidly grounded in spiritual life and thus

---

50. Lavigerie said, "A missionary who does not practice piety will do no good, he may even do great harm (Burridge 1966: 46).

51. Missionaries "must turn constantly to God, for without grace they will achieve nothing" (Burridge 1966: 101).

52. To Lavigerie, prayer was not just an action but a state: prayer was permanent, and sprang spontaneously; the tongue spoke from the abundance of the heart (Duval 2000: 19).

influence their environment and gradually implant Christianity by productive manual labor, works of mercy, social impact" (Burridge 1966: 17). He stressed the importance of spirituality in mission and desired that the church be perceived by the Algerian population as doing good deeds (Hamman 1966).

Cardinal Lavigeries' Leadership Style

This study has revealed a number of attributes that reflect several leadership styles, which are discussed below.

First, Lavigerie was deeply pious. He had a strong attachment to God, which was reflected in his daily practices. This in turn enabled him to influence his followers through his spiritual life.

Second, Lavigerie's relationship with his followers was deeply marked by love and charity. He was ready to give up his life for his followers and worked hard to strengthen the bond between believers. He believed in unity and community. He also deeply loved those who were not from the church. And he showed concern for those from other faiths.

Third, Lavigerie was very relational in his leadership. The data does not show how task-oriented he was even though it is evident that his ministry was filled with activities. However, the strong emphasis on love and care for believers seems to indicate that he was more relation-oriented than task-oriented. I believe he was able to balance an industrious life and a deep love for followers.

Fourth, like all the other leaders studied thus far, Lavigerie influenced his followers by being an example. While at times he seemed to have an autocratic leadership style, he also stressed the importance of consultation and powerlessness.

Fifth, Lavigerie was a visionary. He was able to impact a large number of followers who were committed to follow the rule of the White Fathers that he had established.

Sixth, Lavigerie deeply believed that he could not influence others without knowledge. He was deeply committed to study, teaching and mentoring. He impacted followers by broadening their sphere of knowledge. His study of contextual mission is an example of the way he impacted the missionary arena.

Finally, Lavigerie cared not only for the church in North Africa but also for broader society. He did not neglect those people who were not part of the church. He took care of the needy and fought for justice and did not shy away from using political means to transform society.

Ibn Badis: Doctor of the Muslim Community

Abd al-Hamid Ibn Badis is one of the most important Muslim religious leaders of modern-day Algeria particularly because of his role in the reformation of Islamic society in the 1920s and 1930s. He was even claimed by some to be the Maghrebian "imam of the century." A close and careful study of his leadership style should therefore enrich the understanding of leadership in North Africa. Despite the fact that there are diverging views about his leadership, some contending he was too radical, he left a lasting imprint on the entire region and some even say the entire Muslim world.

Ibn Badis' Life and Legacy

Ibn Badis was born in Constantine, Algeria, in December 1889 to a prominent religious family.[53] Alghailani (2002: 148) said that his "family had been influential for centuries in the city, and continued to produce great judges and scholars." The first child of his father, Ibn Badis spent his early years at home being educated by his mother; he received a traditional family education where he learned Islamic values as well as North African Muslim social customs (Alghailani 2002). At the age of thirteen, Ibn Badis had learned the Qur'an by heart[54] and led a congregation during the month of Ramadan in a major Constantine mosque (Alghailani 2002).

Ibn Badis was trained in the only major *madrasa* of Constantine in Islamic religious sciences.[55] This education influenced many of his later

---

53. According to Hourani (1983: 369), "This Constantinian family was a descendant of the celebrated Badis Ibn Al-Mansur of the Ziri family. The reign of Al-Mansur's son and successor Al-Muizz (1016-51) established according to Ibn Khaldun, the most prominent historian of North Africa, 'the largest and the richest Berber power in Africa.'"
54. His teacher was Muhammad al-Shaykh al-Madasi, an elderly *'alim* from a neighboring mosque.
55. The teachers continued to promulgate the intellectual tradition from the great centers

decisions in regards to the future of French Algeria (Safi 1993). The various teachers that Ibn Badis had during his years as a student recognized his potential. Alghailani (2002: 151) reports that Hamdan al-Shaykh al-Wanisi, a scholar of tradition and law, "took stock of the great intellectual promises of his pupil and was eager to harness that potential."

Merad (1971: 42) on the other hand stated that the fight against *maraboutism* and "frenchification" (i.e. rendering the society French) constituted the main goals of his life. In 1930, Ibn Badis was elected president of an Association for Education and Learning in Constantine (Alghailani 2002). He then established schools, orphanages, and cultural clubs with the goal, "to teach boys and girls how to uphold their religion, language, and good morals, in addition to channeling funds for Ibn Badis' schools." Ibn Badis was influential to develop a program for the education of Muslims in Algeria.

Ibn Badis' writings and work led to the creation of an organized Islamic movement. Ibn Badis became the leader of the Association of the Muslim Algerian Ulama in 1931 which gave him the opportunity to revitalize and restore Islam in Algeria. This Muslim theologian believed that the aim of Islamic education was to develop a well-ordered society with morally responsible and well-informed people (Alghailani 2002).

Religion was at the heart of Ibn Badis' discourse. For him, it was time for Islam to be viewed as indigenous to Algeria and not a foreign entity. He wanted to reform Islam in Algeria, which was widely perceived as declining. Ibn Badis advocated "the use of certain advances accrued through modernity to aid in this Islamic reawakening" (Alghailani 2002: 160).

Ibn Badis wanted to "purify Islam from Sufi practices" which he held responsible for the decline of Islam (Alghailani 2002: 194). He often showed how "poets disregarded the sources of Islamic Law and violated explicit verses of the Qur'an" (Alghailani 2002: 195). Ibn Badis believed that "the Prophet was a historical model of leadership and a political and spiritual guide, as opposed to the Sufi leaders, whose worldview was extremely myopic" (Alghailani 2002: 196).[56]

---

of traditional learning like Tunis and Qayrawan.
56. In one of his newspapers, *Al-Shihab*, Ibn Badis repeatedly stated that the *marabouts*

Theologian

Ibn Badis wrote a commentary to the Qur'an over a period of twenty-five years (Safi 1993: 76). According to Alghailani (2002: 234), "The core of Ibn Badis' ideas consisted in a total rejection of any idea or system of thought that contradicted the Qur'an and its message. The same author adds, "In almost every statement he made, including political ones, Ibn Badis referred to a Qur'anic passage or its meaning."

Ibn Badis revived Qur'anic *tafsir*.[57] He wrote a commentary on the Qur'an[58] ultimately showing Algerians that the Qur'an is a guide to social economic and political realms (Alghailani 2002).

The enormous influence of Ibn Badis is a well-established fact among scholars across the Mediterranean as well as most distinguished French historians. Ali Merad (1971: 46) recalls the end of his life:

> During the final years of his life, Ibn Badis acts both as a religious and political leader, and as a lecturer. . . . He encounters painful family problems: his only son dies as well as a very dear brother. . . . Added to these pains are difficulties that arose within the Association of the Ulama. Furthermore, he has health problems and dies on April 16th, 1940.

Merad (1971) mentions the titles Ibn Badis received through his life: "the head of the tradition," "the doctor of the community," "the great guide," "the monitor of the community, "the doctor of the century," "the great leader," "the divine master, "the friend of God." All these titles show the extent of Ibn Badis' impact on his country and his people. Safi (1993) reports that he was called father of Algerian nationalism, pioneer of education and teaching, and founder and leader of the reformist movement of Algeria.

---

did not qualify as *'ulama*. He urged them to repent and stop spreading wrong ideas about Islam (Alghailani 2002).

57. Arabic for exegesis.

58. Merad (1971: 12) writes, "the Qur'anic commentary of Ibn Badis constitutes the most important, if not the most unique, doctrinal reference to Muslim reformism in Algeria between the two wars."

Many have commented on his exceptional leadership qualities (Merad 1967). However there are aspects of his leadership that were criticized. Ibn Badis was very severe and intransigent in its interactions with the *maraboutic* organizations. He did not make any concessions because he was convinced of his ideas. Today, some fundamentalist movements such as the Salaffiya have embraced Ibn Badis' ideas.[59] Although many believe Ibn Badis would never have supported the violent actions of contemporary fundamentalists, some of these groups claim him as their leader.

This is how Said Alghailni (2002: 236) summarizes Ibn Badis' ministry:

> From 1914 until his death in 1940, Ibn Badis traveled throughout Algeria to convey his message, giving lectures in clubs and delivering Friday sermons in the mosques. His interests remained focused on the regeneration of his society according to the Islamic creed, although his concerns ranged broadly from those of an educator, intellectual, and spiritual leader to those of a political reformer.

At the end of his life, Ibn Badis says, "We were too busy training and organizing people, we did not have enough time to write books" (Safi 1993: 75).

Ibn Badis' Leadership Attributes and Behaviors

Ibn Badis' life is well-documented. As I explore his ministry legacy and biography I found the following attributes and behaviors that shaped his leadership styles.

First, Ibn Badis had great communication skills. He was an excellent and devoted lecturer[60] and had very good rhetorical and oratorical skills (Merad 1971).[61] He was also a good preacher. He spoke with gentleness (Merad 1971).

---

59. Fundamentalism has deadly implications in Algeria today. During the last decade over 100,000 people have died in Algeria as a result of the tensions between fundamentalists and non-fundamentalists.
60. He grew accustomed to spending most of his day at the mosque, and he preached and lectured on various subjects between prayer times, writes the same author.
61. Ibn Badis used rhetorical and oratorical skills and his wide and deep knowledge of Islamic tradition to address Algerians through Friday sermons, lectures in clubs, lessons

Second, according to Merad (1967), Ibn Badis had a passionate temperament and burned with an extraordinary religious ardor. However, others described him as having self-control.[62]

Third, Ibn Badis was a visionary. He contended that the leader of the *umma* must have vision when he said, "Those who deserve to be at the head of the *Umma*, at its leadership, are those who display vision" (Safi 1993: 96).

Fourth, Ibn Badis was an educator.[63] Ibn Badis believed that education was fundamental for gaining scientific knowledge and Islamic morality (Safi 1993: 74). Ibn Badis started with a small circle in the midst of opposition, but gained an increasingly widening circle of followers. Ibn Badis was also a great teacher. According to Alghailani (2002: 21), Ibn Badis conceived "his mission not to be the writing of books, but the teaching and training of Muslims for the future."[64] And Ibn Badis was very passionate about knowledge.[65] He set as the greatest goal of the Muslim Algerian Ulama he created, "to seek and transmit knowledge and to be concerned

---

in classrooms and mosques where he discussed moral, legal, economic, political and cultural issues alike (Alghailani 2002: 221). Safi (1993) adds to this description that Ibn Badis was a passionate orator and a logical thinker. Safi (1993) reports that his oratory skills developed from 1914 to 1940 while he lectured and taught in the Green Mosque of Constantine.

62. He spoke with gentleness, had self-control and displayed modesty and dignity (Merad 1971).

63. Alghailani (2002) says Ibn Badis was looking for an educational system that would render Algerian Muslims not just informed but creative, dynamic and moral. He insisted on education being based on the Qur'an and the Sunna and not just secular disciplines. His desire was to develop the "social consciousness of every Algerian" (Alghailani 2002: 160).

64. Merad (1971: 42) on the other hand stated that the fight against *maraboutism* and "frenchification" (rendering the society French) constituted the main goals of Ibn Badis' life. In 1930, Ibn Badis was elected president of the Association for Education and Learning in Constantine (Alghailani 2002). He established schools, orphanages, and cultural clubs. Alghailani (2002: 160) states Ibn Badis' goal was "to teach boys and girls how to uphold their religion, language, and good morals, in addition to channeling funds for Ibn Badis' schools."

65. Ibn Badis' writings and work led to the creation of an organized Islamic movement. Ibn Badis became the leader of the Association of the Muslim Algerian Ulama in 1931 that gave him the opportunity to revitalize and restore Islam in Algeria. The *'ulama* believed that the aim of Islamic education was to create a well-ordered society (Alghailani 2002).

with the whole being of men and women" (Alghailani 2002: 185). He was a great intellect and theologian.[66]

Fifth, Ibn Badis was industrious. He was very organized and effective in his work; he was a man of activity and energy (Merad 1971). He always had numerous projects running and his work touched upon many aspects of life (Alghailani 2002).[67]

Sixth, Ibn Badis was also considered as a guide, the monitor of the community. He was a mentor to many.[68] His skills included apologetics and polemics[69] but at the same time he also supported dialogue. Ibn Badis stressed the importance of being in dialogue with opponents.[70]

Seventh, one of the great virtues of Ibn Badis was morality. He had a sincere desire to increase the moral standards of the community and he defined the principles of a moral code in reference to *sura* 17 and 25 (Merad 1971).

Eighth, Ibn Badis had many personal characteristics such as dignity, (Merad 1971: 47) nobility and intuition. He encouraged leaders to anticipate and have foresight.[71] As we have seen, these are common leadership values in Islam.

Ninth, Ibn Badis exhorted believers to have patience, which is an important leadership value in Islam. The Qur'anic references he used to encourage leaders to be patient were *sura* 25:20 and 75 (Merad 1971).

---

66. Ibn Badis pursued an ideology and a methodology of Islam that was unprecedented within the Algerian intellectual milieu of his time. He struck a balance between intellectual analysis and action. He used various media to spread his vision of Islam (Alghailani 2002).

67. Ibn Badis was an excellent and devoted lecturer. Merad (1971: 46) describes his schedule at the end of his life: "The very important number of classes he was teaching at the Green Mosque did not allow much time for rest. His students felt that the master was stretching to the extreme his human capacity".

68. Ibn Badis claimed he was forming leaders for the future. His students have played a major role in Algeria since the 1930s. Those who approached Ibn Badis, says Merad (1971), felt the historical stature and role of this man and felt they participated with him in the shaping of historical events.

69. Ibn Badis wanted to "purify Islam from Sufi practices" that he held responsible for the decline of Islam (Alghailani 2002: 194). He often showed how "poets disregarded the sources of Islamic Law and violated explicit verses of the Qur'an" (Alghailani 2002: 195).

70. Ibn Badis liked direct dialogue, even with his opponents (Merad 1971).

71. "Those who deserve to be at the head of the *Umma*, at its leadership, are those who display vision, have a very accurate intuition, are able to anticipate, are noble, and are able to foresee events" (Safi 1993: 96).

Tenth, Ibn Badis had an acute sense of justice. The theme of justice (*'adl*) and equity (*insaf*) often appear in his writings (Merad 1971).[72] Ibn Badis considered justice as the basis of political life and the practice of power. He was equitable and steadfast.[73] He believed that peace was an important attribute.[74] He also was very attached to the truth[75] and yet was humble—not striving for prestigious positions (Merad 1971).[76]

Eleventh, Ibn Badis was of modest appearance and was often known as a common person (Merad 1971). Alghailani (2002) describes the changes when he started to become a leader: He moved to a small room by the mosque and led an unconventionally modest life and would only use those goods that were of traditional Algerian manufacture.

Twelfth, the way Ibn Badis used power and influence was manifold. He developed a very sophisticated theory of power called "Basis for Power". This theory claims that the power belongs to the *umma* and that the *umma* must be governed by the Muslim Law. Ibn Badis also practiced consultation with his followers.[77] Merad (1971: 215) underlined the central idea of consultation for Ibn Badis when he wrote, "Ibn Badis believes in the quasi-miraculous virtue of political consultation." Ibn Badis proposed leadership that requires a just leader be aided by an assembly of men who are

---

[72]. He studied the meaning of "justice" in its relationship to truth, the respect of people's property, the demand of honesty and the demand of loyalty (Merad 1971). He spoke about justice and integrated it in his actions as a leader.

[73]. Ibn Badis preached and lived according to this value. He also believed that steadfast people would be rewarded by God (Merad 1971). He perceived this quality as the foundation of morality and a sign of the true religion (Merad 1971).

[74]. Ibn Badis insisted that leaders display a spirit of peace (Merad 1971: 174). He saw the positive influence such attitude would have for human relations.

[75]. Merad (1971: 34) says that Ibn Badis had a quasi-mystical attachment to the truth. This love for truth led him to express himself freely, without fear and complaisance.

[76]. Ibn Badis lived according to an advice given by one of his masters, who told him never to aspire for a high public position or to use personal knowledge for acquiring prestige (Merad 1971: 27). Ibn Badis used to say that those who are satisfied with whom they are blind in respect to their imperfections (Merad 1971: 172).

[77]. Ibn Badis considered that political consultation was necessary for the preservation of equity, justice and unity in the community. According to him, consultation allowed citizens to feel personally responsible for their city (Merad 1971). Consultation provided the opportunity for followers to express their solidarity with the leader.

responsible and enlightened (Merad 1971: 215). He was also severe with his opponents,[78] yet at the same time Ibn Badis was also tolerant.[79]

Thirteenth, Ibn Badis had manifold relational skills that enabled him to be community-oriented.[80] Ibn Badis had a strong desire to unify the Muslim *umma* (Safi 1993). His moral reform was aimed at creating a society where brotherhood and solidarity[81] existed (Safi 1993: 87). He believed the *umma* was above the leader and that the latter had to work for unity and solidarity. He stated that "the leaders must obey the *Umma* . . . and no one is allowed to lead the *Umma* without its authorization" (Safi 1993: 94). In his commentary of *sura* 24, Ibn Badis stated that the true believers are those who were able to minimize their personal grievances when they faced a problem of general interest so that the solidarity and unity of the group is not broken by futile considerations (Merad 1971: 213).

Fourteenth, Ibn Badis was generous. To him, true generosity was hidden in the depths of the heart and not in the outward actions. He encouraged believers to be quiet about their generosity (Merad 1971).

Fifteenth, Ibn Badis was very involved in the political life of his country.[82] He felt himself called to serve Islam at all levels of social life and felt called to carry the reformist message from Algeria and beyond (Alghailani 2002).

Sixteenth, Ibn Badis was extremely pious and was even called the "friend of God" (Merad 1971). According to Merad (1971), Ibn Badis' piety had

---

78. Ibn Badis was very severe and intransigent in his interactions with the *maraboutic* organizations. He did not make any concessions. He also was very convinced of his ideas and he did not allow others to think differently.

79. According to Safi (1993), Ibn Badis conceived an Islam of tolerance. "We have forsaken the Qur'an and we established institutions and conventions that we invented; we have forsaken most often the true *hanifyya* full of tolerance, and instead we rely on verbalism and extremism" said Ibn Badis according to Chahine (1971: 231).

80. Ibn Badis shaped a community of believers in Algeria. His desire was for this community to relate by faith to the companions of the Prophet and their followers and be bound by the Sharia law (Alghailani 2002: 235). Ibn Badis considered that the *umma* was above the leader.

81. Ibn Badis emphasized individual responsibility as well as solidarity with the group (Merad 1971: 208). He said that the individual is nothing unless he feels part of a group and is devoted to the group as much as he would be devoted to himself (Merad 1971).

82. Ibn Badis believed that "the Prophet was a historical model of leadership and a political and spiritual guide, as opposed to the Sufi leaders, whose worldview was extremely myopic" (Alghailani 2002: 196).

been influenced by his visits to holy places such as Mecca and Medina and by several mentors he had in influential Muslim centers. Ibn Badis had a deep respect for the Qur'an which he derived from an intelligent study of the Qur'an and the Sunna. He insisted on using simple language in order not to "trouble" the mind of the student and not to create unnecessary problems of comprehension (Merad 1971: 176).

Ibn Badis' Leadership Styles

The study of Ibn Badis' various behaviors and values has underlined numerous leadership styles. First, Ibn Badis was deeply devoted to God and submitted to the law of the Qur'an. His leadership was in total accordance with the core Islamic values of patience, modesty and piety. He deeply influenced his followers through his spiritual lifestyle.

Second, Ibn Badis was a transformational leader and his life bears a legacy of thousands of followers who consider him a reformer of Islam. This is evidenced in the way he influenced his followers through education, teaching and mentoring; he involved them in his decision making through consultation. He never placed himself above the law of God which was given the final word in every decision.

Third, Ibn Badis was a relational leader who was daunted by the many tasks he was to accomplish. He believed in brotherhood and solidarity and was open to dialogue. He had very strong ties with his followers.

Fourth, Ibn Badis was a charismatic and visionary leader and this convinced many who became his followers. He had great rhetorical skills and persuaded others through his intellectual and spiritual argumentation. He was passionate and intuitive as well as an intelligent theologian and politician.

Fifth, Ibn Badis aimed to impact the society for good. He was deeply involved in the life of his country and believed he could bring tremendous transformation to his co-citizens.

Conclusion

The study of two Christian and two Muslim historical leaders of great influence has provided ample resources for investigating the leadership styles of contemporary church leaders. I have found many similarities between them and those I explored in previous chapters. First, I discovered leaders who have deeply impacted people's lives through their piety. They practiced what they preached and attracted many followers to their beliefs as a result. While spirituality played a major role in their leadership, it had diverse expressions. One may wonder how these differences can impact the effectiveness of these leaders.

Second, they all had a strong sense of divine calling, destiny, and vision.

Third, they shared many leadership values with leaders from their own community. To state the obvious, Muslims shared many leadership values common to the Islamic faith while Christians shared values rooted in the Bible. For example, both Augustine and Lavigerie said they were ready to give up their lives for their followers. None of the Muslim leaders made this statement; however their lives indicate self-sacrifice. Does this also include the desire to give up their lives for their followers?

Fourth, all four leaders wanted to impact their own faith community as well as the rest of society for good in order to bring about transformation. Towards that end, they created religious communities that embodied their values.

Fifth, they developed strong bonds between people in their community. Some talked about love and charity; others about solidarity and brotherhood. These terms may have some variation in meaning but all refer to a deep attachment of these leaders with their community.

Sixth, all leaders worked very hard and accomplished a great deal. Industriousness seems to be the hallmark of both Muslim and Christian leaders in this section. With most leadership attributes of this chapter, I have found fascinating connections across areas of study.[83] For example, humility is found in both Christian and Muslim leaders. However, it is not

---

83. By area of study I mean all the areas I studied in this dissertation which are Muslim leadership, Biblical leadership, contemporary church leadership, historical leadership and secular leadership.

highly ranked in the list of Muslim values—instead modesty is considered very important. As a result, the challenge is to understand how modesty differs from humility and how it impacts leadership styles in Islam versus Christianity. This point will be addressed in the chapter where I make recommendations for the importance of a leadership style to be contingent to followers, context and Bible.

I also noticed in the study of the four leaders some differences. First, they did not all have the same role and ministry focus. Augustine was a church father who laid the foundation of a Christian culture and Western theology. Abd el-Kader contributed in the area of shaping unity in the nation. Lavigerie's major contribution was in the domain of ecclesiology and missiology. And Ibn Badis' major impact was in the field of Muslim theological reformation. Their roles probably had varying influences on the formation of their styles.

Second, I noticed some differences in leadership attributes. Although some of them make much sense because they reflect the different cultural and religious contexts, other may be due to the incomprehensive nature of my study. If the scope of this study had not been limited, I could have continued to research all works written on these four leaders including their attributes, values and behaviors. In this case, some discrepancies between leaders may have been explained. For example, justice was only listed once. While I assume that it is an important value for all leaders I can only affirm its importance for the Amir Abd el-Kader. It is not surprising that justice is named as an important Muslim value. What is perplexing is why it is absent in Ibn Badis' study. I suspect that if I were to read more biographies, I would find that value in the life of Ibn Badis. Thus, I only draw in this study from leadership characteristics I found in the work of authors I studied while acknowledging that there may be others in the work of those I have not yet examined. Thus far, what I found is very promising. This chapter has provided useful resources to define North African leadership styles in the contemporary church.

Part 3

Leadership Styles of Current North African Church Leaders

Part 3 includes my findings, integration, implications and recommendations. In chapter 7, I list the leadership values, attributes and behaviors that were given by the North African church leaders. They are organized in such a way that I can compare and contrast them later with the leadership values, attributes and behaviors from Islam and North African culture and history to determine whether North African brothers and sisters were influenced by their context. I include at the end of chapter 7 the biblical leadership models provided by the church leaders. Due to the limited scope of the data on biblical models I recommend that further research should be conducted before drawing significant conclusions.

Chapter 8 is an integration of the various elements of my research. I propose four leadership styles that emerged from my field research findings following a comparison and contrast of leadership styles chosen from the current leadership theories. After these four models are identified with the help of the comparative tables in the appendix, I design another table to compare the attributes, values and behaviors of North African leaders with the attributes, values and behaviors of religious, cultural and historical models from Islam and North African history generally. In my recommendations I explain how these styles may or may not help leaders impact the society and church for good.

CHAPTER 7

Results of Questionnaires and Interviews

In this section, I present the data collected in my field research. The leadership values, qualities, and behaviors collected are listed under the following categories that will help me in the concluding chapter define leadership styles of North African church leaders: (1) leadership values, (2) human qualities, (3) moral qualities, (4) legitimacy, (5) power-influence, (6) relational behaviors, (7) spiritual characteristics (piety), (8) leadership skills, and (9) leadership metaphors. Under these nine categories I organized the characteristics in alphabetical order so that the reader can identify them more easily.

What is presented here are not leadership styles but leadership characteristics; leadership values, qualities and behaviors from existing leadership styles studied in my theoretical section. The final table of this chapter, which lists these characteristics, will be compared and contrasted with those in chapters 1, 2 and 3 in order to suggest leadership styles of North African church leaders.

Leadership Values

In this section I list the responses elicited from the following four questions: (1) Is there a list of values common to all Christian leaders? (2) What are the values that a Christian leadership should have; are they different from non-Christian leadership values? (3) What values should a political leader have? (4) What are values the Christian leader should display in his family life? Respondents were given the questions without further explanation or information, as I did not want to influence the process by providing my own definition of "value."

I classified the responses that church leaders gave in four categories: (1) spiritual values (qualities and behaviors); (2) human values (qualities and behaviors); (3) moral values (qualities and behaviors); and (4) relational values (qualities and behaviors). These categories are mine and were not labeled by respondents. They were chosen to organize the data and make it more accessible to the reader.

I only discuss in this section the values that were quoted at least three times. The rest are simply listed in the table at the end which gives the total of all values given by the respondents. Some respondents indicated more than one value and three respondents did not answer this question.

Finally, the values listed here will appear in other sections of this chapter since respondents quoted them at other occasions. Here, however, they do not simply indicate general qualities or behaviors but core values of church leadership. Therefore, they have to be treated separately from the rest of the responses.

Spiritual Values

Twenty-two responses emphasized the importance of spiritual values (qualities, and behaviors) which could also be labeled as "piety." In this category, "intimacy" and "love for God" ranked first. The words show that leaders value a strong relationship with God (intimacy, passion, love, putting God first, fellowship) combined with submission and fear of God as well as a hatred for idolatry. Practical implications of this strong relation with God is expressed by spiritual behaviors such as the study of the Word, prayer, fasting, obeying God's commands and working for His Glory. Leaders also value a strong dependence on the Holy Spirit that is expressed in the attributes of charisma, gifts of God and miracles.

Human Values

The second main area typified by these values is human characteristics of church leadership. Love was ranked number one (10 times), followed by humility (7 times) and then justice (4 times). The human qualities only quoted once are listed in the table below.

It is worth noticing here the strong emphasis on love. I assume that leaders integrate biblical teaching on love in their leadership. Ten church leaders consider love as a value but another thirty cite love as an integral part of their leadership qualities. The other main values in this category of human qualities and behaviors also seem to flow directly from general biblical values.

Moral Values

The third categories of values relate to moral attitudes and behaviors. Respondents gave many references to such values. Integrity ranked first (7 times), followed by honesty (5 times) and being righteous (5 times). There are many other values that indicate leaders are concerned by holiness and sanctity in their ministry.

I assume that the Bible's high standard of morality may have impacted the leaders. The study of Islamic leadership will reveal whether there is a similar concern by Muslim leaders. Another reason for such an emphasis may be a reaction to a possible lack of integrity that may prevail in the environment of the leader. Whatever the reasons for the search for integrity one has to take into account that North African leaders highly value transparency, honesty, sincerity and righteousness.

Relational Values

Fourteen responses emphasized the importance of relational leadership describing the leader as someone who helps, encourages, supports, forgives, respects, etc. These values express the deep concern and personal involvement they have in their followers' own lives. There is no relational distancing between the leader and the follower but instead a strong human bond.

Unlike the first two sections (see above) no value stood out as most concepts were are only quoted once or twice. But the large number of these relational qualities and behaviors show that church leaders value relationship and caring for their followers. They also seem to integrate the biblical values of forgiveness and servanthood in their interactions with others. The reference to hospitality twice may refer to cultural practices and/or biblical practices.

TABLE 5: Leadership Values
(Farida Saidi)

Spiritual Values	
Intimacy with God	3x
Love God	3x
Prayer	2x
Human Values	
Love	10x
Humility	7x
Righteous	5x
Justice	4x
Faithfulness	2x
Manners (Good)	2x
Mercy	2x
Obedience	2x
Patience	2x
Submission	2x
Wisdom	2x
Moral Values	
Integrity	7x
Honesty	5x
Sincerity	3x
Blameless	2x
Transparency	1x
Relational Values	
Encourager	2x
Forgiving	2x
Helping	2x
Hospitable	2x

Table 5 presents the values quoted at least twice by respondents. A comprehensive list of church leaders' values in alphabetical order is included in appendix 7.

Other Responses on the Question on Values

Further comments from respondents, not included in the table above, seem to indicate that leaders draw from biblical values to describe those in church leadership. First, several Bible verses were given as a response to the question: "What are the values that a Christian leader should have?" (e.g. 1 Tm 3:1-7 and Gal 1:22). Second, while three respondents did not provide the name of a specific value, they instead answered "biblical values" and another said "values from the life of Jesus."

A sub-question to the question on leadership values was "Are they [church leadership values] different from non-Christian values?" Ten respondents indicated that the leadership values of a Christian leader are different from the values of non-Christians; furthermore those values cannot be found outside Christianity. None of the respondents said they were similar. This information does not appear in the table above but should be revisited in my conclusion as I discuss the influence of non-Christian leadership styles on church leadership. Will leaders be open to consider non-Christian values effective in their leadership style, especially if they want to influence society for good and have a contextual approach? The two questions on family and political values do not illustrate further information. In summary, family values should be biblical and political values should not be synonymous with leadership models.[1]

It is also interesting to notice that leaders did not mention power, influence or legitimacy as strong values of leadership. The table above shows only three references to these categories. They will appear and be discussed in a later section because I asked specific questions about legitimacy and

---

1. As stated in the introduction to this section, in my questionnaire there are four different questions on values: (1) Is there a list of values common to all Christian leaders? (2) What are the values that a Christian leadership should have; are they different from non-Christian leadership values? (3) What values should a political leader have? (4) What are values the Christian leader should display in his family life?

power. In summary, when church leaders are asked about their values of leadership, they do not see legitimacy and power as core or central ideals.

Conclusion

This section shows that the majority of leaders I interviewed have leadership values that reflect an intimate relationship with God, a strong and caring bond with followers, and human characteristics influenced by love and biblical principles. There is also a strong sense that the church leadership values are different from non-Christian values and that the Bible is the main source for shaping those of the leaders I interviewed.

Although the vast majority of the responses did not indicate a concern about legitimacy and power, they do give some implicit information regarding these two categories. One can hypothesize that God, the Bible and the quality of the human bond will play a role in legitimacy and power. Finally, it is difficult to assess whether the values church leaders quoted are ideal values or if they are displayed through actual behaviors in the everyday life and activities of the church. Further research is needed to evaluate this issue.

Human Qualities

In this section I have listed all the human qualities of leadership mentioned by leaders throughout the questionnaires and interviews. They were not given in response to specific questions about human qualities but appeared randomly in the answers to questionnaires and interviews. Thanks to Atlas Software I was able to extract these qualities from the text.

I have organized them here in alphabetical order to help facilitate the writing of the concluding chapter on leadership styles. However, the table at the end of the section ranks them by order of importance so that the most common human qualities are easy to identify. If a human quality was listed only once, it does not appear on this list. Whenever respondents explained the meaning of these qualities by examples or stories, I include them in my discussion.

Accountability

Three leaders mentioned they must be accountable to others in their leadership (Int. 6;[2] Q. 30[3] and Anonymous 2[4]) although they gave no further explanations on this human quality. Since I did not probe respondents for a definition I assume the term denotes being liable, responsible and giving an account of one's actions (see Webster Dictionary); otherwise this term may have a more sophisticated meaning related to leadership theories.

I was a little surprised by the lack of reference to this quality. I was expecting that more leaders would refer to accountability since this is a key leadership quality. There may be two reasons for this: first, leaders use another term to describe this same quality or second, it is a core assumption not worth mentioning.

Courage

Ten informants quoted "courage" as an important leadership virtue for North African leaders (Int. 1, 2, 6, 8; and Q. 2, 17, 29, 30, 32 and 36). However, they did not offer examples to describe what this quality means.

This number represents a significant size of respondents. I do not think that all cultures would universally quote "courage" as a key leadership quality. It may be that this quality is culturally bound, which further research in the North African context may help clarify.

Faithfulness

Three respondents said a leader is faithful (Q. 17, 18, 22). They did not give further details about what faithfulness means for church leaders. I have classified this quality under human qualities but it could also fit under a more relational aspect. It may also show that leaders can and should be trusted.

---

2. "Int." stands for interviewee throughout the report of the findings. The two other ways I reference the informants is by using "Q" referring to informants who filled out a questionnaire and "Anonymous" referring to the informants who did not want to be identified. The number following "Int.", "Q", or "Anonymous" is the way I have classified the responses of the interviews and questionnaires.

3. "Q." stands for questionnaire throughout the report of the findings.

4. "Anonymous" means that the person interviewed or who filled the questionnaire did not want to be identified.

At the same time, I do not believe that three respondents are representative of an entire culture. It is therefore important to find other terms that also reflect this quality to be able to posit that faithfulness and trust are key elements of North African church leadership.

Forgiveness

Forgiveness was quoted four times (Q. 10; 21, 27, 28). Respondents have not given further examples of how this translates in the church although it is probably a biblical value.

It is interesting to note that this quality was also named a core value twice in the previous section and should therefore receive more attention in further studies of leadership qualities.

Generosity

Five leaders mentioned generosity as a leadership quality (Q. 6, Int. 2, 8, 9). One brother said, "I visit brothers and sisters. I find out they lack everything and I meet their needs, as much as I can" (Int. 8). Three respondents said, "Generosity is like hospitality."

Generosity will be discussed later as it is reflected in other qualities such as "caretaking." Furthermore, several core values listed in the previous section are closely related to generosity (e.g., "sharing," "being hospitable," or "helping."). It is therefore an important quality worth investigating.

Humility

Humility is an important human quality of North African church leadership. It is the second most often quoted quality after love with twenty-six occurrences (Anonymous 1, 2, Int. 1, 2, 3, 4, 9 and Q. 1, 3, 4, 5, 6, 7, 9, 12, 15, 16, 17, 18, 26, 27, 28, 29, 31, 33, 34). Furthermore, the model of Jesus is quoted fifteen times in relationship with humility. Finally, humility is closely related to servanthood, which is a key leadership quality, as we will see later. One respondent, for example, said that servanthood includes humility. All these responses establish clearly the fact that humility is central to North African church leaders.

Respondents gave many useful comments highlighting the meaning of humility. To learn humility, there is only one school, the school of Christ

(Anonymous 2). Jesus and Moses are symbols of humility (Int. 9). Humility is the hallmark of spiritual power (Q. 18); it is a spiritual quality (Int. 2, 3, and 4). Leaders must be "meek and strong" (Q. 16), not dominate others (Int. 9), put others first (Int. 9), be dead to themselves (Q. 15), not seek their interest (Int. 4, 5, 9 and Q. 12) and, be ready to suffer and die (Int. 6). Sometimes the intensifier "very" was added to the word "humble" (Int.9).

My research confirms the high value of humility for North African church leadership. In effect, seven church leaders quoted humility as a core leadership value, and twenty-six mentioned it as a key human quality of leadership. It is therefore crucial to investigate this quality further to better understand North African church leadership styles.

Justice

The word "justice" is only mentioned three times when applied to the church (Q. 6, 10, 11). Although it is quoted twice as a core value, it still ranks low on the priority list of values and qualities. Respondents gave no specific description or examples of justice.

It will be interesting to reflect later in this book on how the lack of reference to justice will affect contextual leadership especially in a Muslim context that ranks justice very high. The absence of references to justice does not necessarily mean that justice is not practiced among church leaders. It only shows that some other qualities may appear more important to them and therefore worth quoting before justice.

Love and Its Cognates

Thirty-one respondents quoted love as a quality of leadership (Anonymous 1, 5, 10 and Int. 1, 2, 3, 4, 5, 7, 8, 9 and Q. 2, 3, 6, 7, 10, 11, 12, 13, 16, 17, 21, 22, 26, 27, 28, 31, 32, 34, 35, 36). It is the human quality that ranks first for North African church leaders.

The object of love is diverse. Love for the church of Christ (Q. 34), of followers (Int. 4, 5, 7 and Q. 2), of people and country (Anonymous 10), and of neighbors (Int. 4).

Love is further defined by the use of a modifier or intensifier. "True love" like the one displayed by David in the Bible is required from leaders (Int. 8). It is "foremost" love (Int. 4) required from leaders. Leaders must display "deep love" (Int. 1) and one respondent even said the leader must become an "atomic bomb of love." Another said leaders must "love truth without compromise" (Q. 12).

Love for God serves as a means of influencing followers (Int. 2, 8 and 9). For example, "The leader influences others when they see his or her love for God" (Int. 8). According to Int. 5, love is also spiritual quality.

Other attributes mentioned by leaders may form a cluster around love including: "pleasant" (Anonymous 2), "gentleness" (Int.1), "merciful" (Q. 6, 31, 34, 35), "benevolence" (Q. 16), "have a heart" (Q. 1), "slow to anger" (Q. 4), "a lot of grace" (Int. 8), "authority with love" (Int. 9), and "rebuke others with love and gentleness" ( ) Five church leaders talked about "tenderness" (Int. 9, Q. 16, 18, 22, 28).

Finally another cognate of love that has been quoted by eight church leaders is compassion (Q. 1, 4, 6, 11, 12, 18, 28, and 32). I have not probed whether this value (1) has been quoted only in reaction to the lack of love in other contexts; (2) is effectively adopted as a core value of Christian leadership in leadership development; (3) is an ideal value; or (4) how this value is reflected and defined in current leadership in the church.

Loyalty

Two respondents said that a leader must be loyal (Q.6, 13) although they did not explain the specific meaning of this quality.

It may be important to look at other cognates to explore whether loyalty is expressed through different words or expressions. Typically, this is a key quality in North African culture and one would expect leaders to display it. In another study, research may probe for this quality in a questionnaire to see how relevant it is in the church.

Patience

Twenty-one respondents made references to patience (Anonymous 5, 10 and Int. 1, 6, 7, 8 and Q. 1, 3, 5, 6, 7, 9, 11, 16, 17, 18, 21, 29, 32, 35, and 36). Representing almost half of the sample data this human quality ranks as the third most important quality after love and humility.

Sometimes respondents added an intensifier such as "very patient" (Int. 8 and Q. 32). One person noted that a leader must have patience in trials

(Q. 29). Patience should be a hallmark of leaders not just in the context of the church but also in their neighborhoods (Int. 6).

Given the high value church leaders place on patience, it seems natural that they need to think more clearly about how they define it. One also wonders how the biblical notion of patience adopted by church leaders compares and contrasts with its Qur'anic counterpart, which is also a highly valued in Muslim leadership.

Trustworthy

The human quality of trustworthiness has been quoted eight times. A leader should be reliable (Q. 4) and trusted (Int. 2, 5, 9, and Q. 6, 21. 36). Followers, in turn, must trust their leader (Int. 4).

This is an example of a word strengthening the occurrence of another. In effect, this word forms a cluster with other qualities mentioned above such as "loyalty," "faithfulness," and "accountability." It supports the fact that there must be trust between leaders and followers.

Wisdom

Nine North African church leaders said that Christian leadership involves having wisdom (Q. 7, 9, 11, 12, 15, 26, 31, 32). Q. 12 specified what kind of wisdom by saying a leader is "able to judge with God's wisdom."

It can be assumed that since the North African church is an emerging one, leaders may be even more aware than Christians in other contexts of the crucial need for wisdom in the life of the church. The fundamental issue is that its leadership is young and must deal with complex issues, without much history to draw from. In this type of church administration, wisdom is direly needed.

The three most important human qualities for North African leaders are love, humility and patience. All of the values seem to be primarily shaped by the Bible although the cultural and religious contexts certainly play a role as well. These values will be discussed further in the conclusion when I compare and contrast them with qualities from various religious and cultural leadership styles.

Conclusion

In the table below, I listed the major human qualities that have been mentioned by the interviewees. For making the comparison and contrast between church leadership and other leadership contexts studied in this book, I list the human qualities in appendix 8.

TABLE 6: Human Qualities
(Farida Saïdi)

Quality	Frequency
Love	31x
Benevolence (1x)	
Compassion (8x)	
Gentleness (1x)	
Kindness (6x)	
Merciful (4x)	
Pleasant (1x)	
Tenderness (5x)	
Total for cognates of love	26x
Humility	26x
Patience	21x
Courage	10x
Wisdom	9x
Trustworthy	8x
Generosity	5x
Forgiveness	4x
Accountability	3x
Faithfulness	3x
Justice	3x
Loyalty	2x

When ranking occurrences of human qualities, the overwhelming reference to love and its cognates clearly stands out. This is certainly the top human quality expected from a leader. It is interesting to compare this finding with the previous section where love also ranked first as a core value. Many of "love's cognates" such as gentleness, goodness, kindness and mercy are also listed as core values.

Love is closely followed by humility. Here again, it is interesting to notice that humility ranks second as a core value. This is evidence that humility is highly rated in leadership.

What surprised me in looking at the table above is that patience ranked third, while it was only quoted twice as a core value. I cannot explain why, but due to the fact that there are so many references to patience throughout the questionnaires and interviews, it is a value that cannot be overlooked and is certainly shaping the leadership style of North African church leaders.

The other important human qualities that the study highlights are courage, wisdom, generosity, forgiveness, accountability, faithfulness, justice and loyalty. They will all be key components for defining the leadership styles of North African church leaders.

Moral Qualities

In this section, I discuss a specific category called "moral qualities". These relate to the moral choices and behaviors of the leaders. As in the previous section, terms will be listed in the main text in alphabetical order; in the table before the conclusion, they will be listed according to their frequency. When there are specific descriptions of the terms given by respondents, they are included in the discussion.

Blameless

Eight respondents said a leader must be blameless (Int. 2, Q. 13, 34, 33, 36 and Anonymous 2). They explained that the leader must be "blameless within and outside" (Int. 2), "blameless in his conduct" (Q. 36), and "pure of heart" (Q. 34).

When I asked when a leader should step down, the most frequent response was, "when he committed a sin". This combined with references to "the leader must be blameless" (Q 13) points to an understanding of leadership consisting of high moral standards.[5]

This striving for an ideal Christian leadership is also expressed in the responses to when a leader should step down. The most common response given for stepping down is when a mistake is made. As a result, the leader should be fired in the following cases: "unfaithfulness" (Q. 13, 18), "disobedience" (Q. 18, 15), "sin" (Q. 1, 11, 17, 22, 36), "drowning in sin," "serious sin," "serious faults with proof," "grave sins such as adultery or stealing," "moral sins" (Q. 12), "family scandal" (Anonymous 1), "ethical scandal" (Anonymous 1), "divorce" (Anonymous 2), "adultery" (Anonymous 2, 7, Q. 15, 36) and "stealing " (Q. 7, 15, 36).

These examples show how leaders are expected to live a blameless life. One respondent even said, "Someone who walks according to the Spirit of God cannot make a mistake" (Int. 6).

Integrity and Its Cognates

Nine respondents said a leader must have integrity (Int. 3, 5 and Q. 1, 2, 3, 10, 13, 14 and Anonymous 2). One respondent remarked that non-Christians do not possess this value (Q. 14).

The following words may fit in the same category and include transparency (Int. 2, 3, 4, 5), authenticity (Q.18, 26 and 28), honesty (Int. 7 and Q. 6, 9, 12, 17 and 38), truthfulness (Int. 7 and Q. 7, 18, 27), and sincerity (Int. 7 and Q. 9).

Although I was expecting that leaders would emphasize integrity in relation with the church context, most occurrences were directly related to the context of political Muslim leaders.[6] This finding is congruent with values such as honesty and faithfulness. Does this mean that leaders do not feel the need to emphasize these values in their churches? Two ways of un-

---

5. See also the references to integrity in this same section.
6. I asked the question about political leadership values for two reasons. First, I wanted to see whether leadership values are different in the church and outside the church. Secondly it will help me assess how leaders can impact society. In effect, the values that church leaders mention here are the ones that they feel society needs most. If they understand that they can model these values for society, then the society will be transformed according to biblical values. If they believe that political leaders should have integrity, honesty, and faithfulness, this may be where they can impact society the most.

derstanding this finding is to hypothesize that because integrity is part and parcel of the church it is unnecessary to address. Second, Christian leaders often want to be differentiated from socio-political leaders in relation to their values.

Sanctity

According to North African informants, leaders must have a godly life. Leaders must walk in holiness (Q. 18 and 31). They must be consecrated (Q. 18), devoted (Q. 17, 18) and have spiritual maturity (Int. 1 and Q. 6). One respondent quoted Daniel in Babylon "who refuses to be contaminated by the dishes of the king" (Q. 14).

These references to living a holy life correlate with what I found under the section "blamelessness." Clearly, it appears that North African church leaders seek to live a life that honors God.

Conclusion

In the table below I listed the main moral qualities mentioned by the interviewees. The quality that ranked first is integrity. When cognates such as authenticity, honesty, sincerity, transparency, and truthfulness are added to integrity the frequency increases to twenty-eight which shows the leaders' strong support for moral values.

TABLE 7: Moral Qualities

Quality	Frequency
Integrity	9x
Authenticity (3x)	
Honesty (6x)	
Sincerity (2x)	
Transparency (4x)	
Truthfulness (4x)	
Total for cognates of integrity	19x
Blamelessness	8x
Sanctity	7x

The section on moral qualities highlights the importance of integrity, blamelessness and sanctity for North African church leaders.

These qualities can also be related to human qualities discussed earlier such as accountability, trustworthiness, and faithfulness. Furthermore, in the list of core values one can find references to honesty, blamelessness, faithfulness, integrity, sincerity, and transparency. In looking at leadership styles, it will be important to see how forgiveness and patience correlate with the focus on holiness and sanctification.

Legitimacy

In this section I present the responses given when church leaders were asked about how leaders are called. These are questions fundamentally about legitimacy and are crucial to ask if one wants to understand leaders and their relationship to God and to followers. As a result, most leadership theories deal with this aspect of leadership.

I have organized the responses in this section according to the three sources of legitimacy that were given by the respondents. These categories are not borrowed from a specific leadership theory but rather emerged from their context.

Divine Legitimacy

Fourteen respondents stated that God called them without human intervention (Q. 3, 4, 6, 9, 14, 15, 18, 21, 22, 29, Int. 2, 4 and Anonymous 5, 10). These leaders believe in divine legitimacy, believing one can only become a leader when called by God. Respondents used several expressions to talk about divine legitimacy: divine calling and training (Int. 1), and God's calling (Int. 2, 3, 4, 7, 9 and Q. 3, 11, 12, 16, 17, 18).[7]

Several leaders supported this position by giving examples of biblical leaders who were called by God (i.e. Moses (Q. 35)). Q. 9 stated that, "authority comes from God, without the leader seeking it. . . . God elected

---

7. Some of these references include a reference to divine and human legitimacy (see following section). But I included them here to show which words respondents used when referring to God's election.

him/her." This reference to the role of God in leadership is typical of what I observed in North African churches. Leadership is conceived as flowing directly from a specific intervention of God and as a byproduct they have a strong sense of divine election.

Divine and Human Legitimacy

Although divine legitimacy is generally taken for granted, respondents often combined it with human legitimacy. The majority of respondents believe there is both a human and divine intervention in the election of a leader (e.g., Int. 6, 8, 17).

The people who symbolize human legitimacy are the church, elders or other members. More specifically, respondents said the legitimacy of their leadership comes from being appointed or acknowledged by "members of church/organization" (Anonymous 1, Int. 6, 8, Q. 26, 31, 32, 35), by "another leader" (Anonymous 2, Q. 34), by "another leader and by the member of the church/organization" (Q. 2), by "a council of elders" (Anonymous 1, Int. 5, Q. 13), and by "the help of others" (Int. 4, Q. 7).

Self-Appointed Leaders

Human legitimacy might also mean that they believe in their own personal choice to become leaders. I found no evidence of such an attitude, as they did not say their goal in church leadership was to pursue a career. By contrast it was clear from the interviews and questionnaires that the main reason they become leaders was to serve God.

Surprisingly, however, two people responded that they had become leaders "without human intervention" and "a council of elders" (Q. 11, 12). They were somehow self-appointed (emphasis mine). They explained that being called meant having internal and deep convictions without any personal pretention to enter ministry to which one has been appointed by God and later by elders.

During the conference I attended in Malta, the issue of self-appointed leaders was discussed. This topic was raised due to areas in North Africa where the church is sparse some Christian organizations posit that leaders are self-proclaimed in order to meet the needs of a growing number of believers. According to my study, however, this is not how the leaders describe this reality. They would not call themselves "self-appointed" but rather "appointed by God."

However, there is slight evidence that due to the unique circumstances of the church, some leaders may have to take drastic measures including self-proclamation. One respondent said that because he saw the large need and no one was there to care for the church, he decided to become a leader even though he was doing so against his will. He felt he did not have the gifts or propensity necessary for leadership but chose to be one against his will, because he "felt for the church, which was without a caretaker" (Int. 7). Another church leader (Int. 5) said they became the church's "older brothers" and were subsequently forced into leadership because no one else wanted to take up the task.

Conclusion

These references illustrate that church leaders have various views on leadership legitimacy including the following: (1) divine legitimacy, (2) divine and human legitimacy, and (3) self-legitimacy. The first type is the one that receives the largest support. It is evident that church leaders in North Africa strongly believe in divine election. However, this does not mean that they disregard human election; many welcome the advice and decisions of other believers. But there is no leader who believes in human legitimacy alone. God, according to them, is always actively involved in the process of choosing and appointing leaders. Furthermore, leaders do not become so because they feel inclined to by personal choice and desire but rather because they want to serve God and others.

Another important finding is that a few leaders seem to embrace leadership out of necessity. To outsiders these may look like self-appointed leaders but to the North African pastors, this type of leadership legitimacy flows from the needs of the emerging church. These leaders may look like self-proclaimed leaders from the outside but are really "elected" by the pressing needs they see around them.

Power-Influence

In this section I present the findings on how church leaders view power, authority and influence. I draw the responses from the questions relating directly to this issue in the questionnaires and the interviews. I asked church leaders to provide metaphors of authority, to describe how they make decisions and what they mean by authority, influence and spiritual power.

Compared with the other sections, in which informants furnished a word without further explanations, I collected here substantial narratives. Leaders described authority and influence by telling stories or illustrating the word they used with examples. I have therefore decided to include these examples in tables in order to make them more accessible to the reader.

Authority

All North African leaders responded to the question on authority with many examples. They used words such as authority, power, and ruling. Only one North African church leader used the word "influence" (Q. 32) to describe leadership power or authority.[8]

Respondents gave several metaphors to describe the authority of a church leader[9]: (1) king (Int. 8), chief (Q. 30), (3) chief of the army (Int. 1 and Q. 17), policeman (Q. 17), and pope (Int. 7). One respondent insisted only one person should be "in charge" because if a body has "two heads it is a monster" (Int. 7).

Respondents however gave further indications to show authority has limitations including behaving like omnipotent autocratic leaders. A first set of responses emphasized that humility and servanthood are essential components of authority. One informant stated that leaders are not masters but servants (Int. 6). Furthermore, the church leader, according to another informant, "should not be like the worldly leaders who rule over others." One leader explained leadership is "like a pyramid" on in which

---

8. I assume that if leaders had known the current leadership terminology they may have used this term. Or it is possible that they did not use the word "influence" because I did not use it in my questions. This would be worth investigating further.
9. See table below in the same section for further illustrations of these words by informants.

it is reversed like a "v" because the leader is at the base lifting the followers towards the top (Int. 9). Two leaders said that the leader must be humble to have authority (Anonymous 2 and Q. 17). Another stated that they should not dominate followers (Int. 4). One respondent added the followers must be allowed to question the authority of the leader and confront him or her when needed (Q. 2).

In a second set of responses authority means behavior-modeling. For example, followers will respect leaders both because they show a good image or model (Int. 2, 8) and the authority flows out of the leader's testimony and work (Int. 6, 7). According to one informant, authority should be won and not imposed (i.e. leaders must attract followers through the example they set) (Int. 7). In summary, a chief should not be someone that "gives orders and does nothing himself" (Int. 9).

A third set of responses highlight the importance of communicating well. Four leaders reported that authority must involve good communication (Int. 1, 3, 4 and Q. 12) while another said leaders should not manipulate followers (Int. 6). Finally, one informant noted that leaders must gain the right to be listened to (Int. 3).

In a fourth set of responses informants demonstrated that leaders must have a certain sense of organization. For example, one said authority means "putting things in order so that leaders can work" (Int. 2). Another emphasized the fact that leaders must have common sense (Int. 3).

A fifth category underlines the importance of relating well with followers. Pastors should not lead "through violence or yelling but gaining the trust of others" (Int. 9). Informants insisted that the leader must be able to collaborate with others (Anonymous 5, Q. 4, 12, and 30).

Lastly, a major component of authority is the spiritual life of the leader. One respondent indicated that authority means having all the fruits of the spirit from Galatians 5 (Int. 1). One respondent articulated that authority is spiritual (Q. 21) while another North African church leader further specified that God must be the source of authority (Int. 4) based on the Word of God (Q. 31).

TABLE 8: Authority
(Farida Saidi)

Leadership Metaphors		
Chief	3x	Int. 1, Q. 17, 30
Army chief		
"Is in the front, serves others, does not fall back"		
Policeman	2x	Q. 17
Pope	1x	Int. 7
King "who does everything for his people".	1x	Int. 8
Only one leader: "a church with two heads is like a monster"	1x	Int. 7
Humility and Servanthood		
Leaders should not dominate followers	1x	Int. 4
Be humble	2x	Anonymous 2, Q. 17
Not master but servant	1x	Int. 6
A "v" shaped pyramid with the leader at the base lifting followers up	1x	Int. 9
Not dominate	1x	Int. 4
A king that does everything for his people	1x	Int. 8
Not rule over others like the worldly leaders	1x	Int. 7
Followers must be able to question the authority of the leader	1x	Q. 2
Behavior Modeling		
Good model	2x	Int. 2, 8
Testimony and life is an example	2x	Int. 6, 7
Attract followers by their example	1x	Int. 7
Should not give orders when they do not observe these orders	1x	Int. 9
Communication		
Authority involves good communication	4x	Int. 1, 3, 4, Q. 12
No manipulation	1x	Int. 6
Must gain the right to be listened too	1x	Int. 3

Administrative Skills		
Authority is "putting things in order so that leaders can work"	1x	Int. 2
Must have common sense	1x	Int. 3
No dictatorship but no mess	1x	Int. 4
Relational Skills		
Collaboration	4x	Anonymous 5, Q. 4, 12, and 30
Must be able to work in a team.	2x	Q. 13, 18
Lead not "through violence or yelling but gaining the trust of others"	1x	Int. 9
Not imposing authority but winning it.	1x	Int. 7
Spiritual Aspect		
God is the source of authority.	1x	Int. 4
Authority is spiritual	1x	Q. 21
The fruits of the Spirit in Galatians 5	1x	Int. 1
Authority based on the Word of God	1x	Q. 31

In conclusion, the North African leader's view of authority is very unique. It combines elements of autocratic leadership with the use of expressions such as king or master and elements of servanthood, humility, communication and relational skills, being a model, and being spiritual.

Consultation

Leaders underlined the importance of consultation (Q. 2, 3, 4, 5, 12, 22).[10] Two insisted that, "Consultation is the most important thing in leadership" (Anonymous 5 and Q. 35). One leader supported collective deliberation even when there is one person as the head (Int. 7).

---

10. Some respondents used the French word "collégialité" that also expresses the word "consultation" in English but can also be used when there is not one leader who has the role of sheikh.

According to church leaders, consultation requires the following behaviors. First, leaders must be able to listen to others (Anonymous 1 and Q. 21). Second, they must share with others (Anonymous 1, 2 and Q. 8). Third, they must be able to work in a team (Q. 13, 18). Fourth, consultation has a strong spiritual component that must take place under the guidance of God. One respondent said "prayer" must go with consultation (Q. 18) while another insisted the decision must be in accordance with the Word of God (Int. 5). Several stated they ask God to lead them to make decisions together.

Leaders further described their experience of consultation. Second only to sharing is decision-making (Int. 5). While doing the former, leaders ask the advice of others (Int. 7, 9) because, "Discussions are necessary for taking decisions together," (Int. 8). During consultation, leaders try to convince followers of their ideas (Int. 4). Afterward, the leader typically makes the final decision (Q. 36). One informant said, "the leader makes a firm decision" (Int. 4), but that the final decision-making has two characteristics. First, two respondents explained, the leader must make decisions at a good time and the right place, and must make wise decisions in difficult situations (Q. 4, 36). Second, another respondent indicated that, "We do not take decisions unless there is a general agreement. There is no unilateral decision. If one leader does not agree we continue to discuss" (Int. 1).

Opinions vary on whom should be consulted. I received the following answers: those older in faith, other leaders, all members of the church, the board, or elders (Int. 8, 9, and Q. 1, 6, 7, 17, 36). Elders are consulted for their wisdom as is evidenced by the fact that, "Decisions are submitted to the group and the board and "they should ask the advice of elders who are wise and mature" (Int. 4). In some contexts the church is small and consequently consultants are not easy to find. For example, one leader said, "We are four church members, so there are no leaders; it is hard to find a balance, but it is necessary."

TABLE 9: Consultation

(Farida Saidi)

Consultation		
Consultation	9x	Int. 9, Q. 2, 3, 4, 5, 12, 22, An.5, Q. 35
Collective deliberation even when there is one person as the head	1x	Int. 7
Leader must ask the advice	2x	Int. 7, 9
They must be able to listen to others.	2x	An. 1 Q. 21
Consultation Format		
No decision taken until all agree: "If one leader does not agree we continue to discuss"	1x	Int. 1
"Discussions are necessary for taking decisions together".	1x	Int. 8
Sharing	8x	respondents
Shares with others	4x	An.1, 2 Q. 8, 32
Share the vision	1x	Q. 3
Share the burden	1x	Q. 13
Share the tasks	1x	Q. 35
Decision taken together, after sharing	1x	Int. 5
Leader makes a firm decision	1x	Int. 4
Leaders should try to convince others	1x	Int. 4
Leader must take decisions at the good time and the right place and wise decisions in difficult situations.	2x	Q. 36, 4
Consulting Bodies		
The leader must be able to ask for advice from others preceding in faith, other leaders, all members or elders.	4x	Q. 1, 6, 7, 17
Decisions submitted to the group and the board	1x	Q. 36
Ask the advice of elders who are wise and mature.	1x	Int. 4
Ask the council for advice	1x	Int. 8
We are four church members, there are no leaders, it is hard to find a balance, but it is necessary	1x	Int. 7

Spiritual Component		
Prayer and consultation	1x	Q. 18
Decision must be in accordance with the Word of God	1x	Int. 5
They ask God to lead others to take a decision together with the leaders.	1x	Int. 5

These responses demonstrate that leaders place a strong emphasis on consultation when they talk about authority. They desire to include others in their decision-making process which includes discussing, sharing and asking advice; but they make the final decision. Typically they choose older people with greater experience, wisdom and maturity as their consultants.

Another important characteristic in consultation is the importance leaders place on integrating God's advice in their leadership decision. They take much time in prayer, reading the Word and listening to God.

Behavior-Modeling

The interviews and questionnaires clearly show evidence that the way leaders want to influence others through their power and authority is through modeling. This characteristic is strongly supported by twenty-three responses (Anonymous 1, 8 and Int. 1, 3, 4, 5, 8 and Q. 1, 2, 3, 4, 9, 12, 13, 14, 16, 17, 18, 22, 27, 30, 31, 36). A variety of expressions were used to refer to modeling such as, "The follower must be like me" (Anonymous 8) or "Followers must imitate me as a leader" (Int. 8). I have listed the remaining expressions in table 10.

This table not only describes the attitudes and behaviors of human leaders but it also shows that Jesus is considered the greatest model (Int. 4, 7, 9 and Q. 15). The leaders should imitate Jesus so that their followers also imitate Jesus through them.

Therefore, I can posit that according to my findings North African church leaders influence followers by modeling. Church leaders want to be imitated and feel they influence best by the way they model qualities and behaviors. This is summarized when one respondent said, "I influence them

TABLE 10: Behavior Modeling
(Farida Saidi)

Being an Example		
Must be a model for others	23x	An. 1, 8. Int. 1, 3, 4, 5, 8. 9 Q. 1, 2, 3, 4, 9, 12, 13, 14, 16, 17, 18, 22, 27, 30, 31, 36.
Follower must be like the leader	1x	An. 8
Followers must imitate the leader	1x	Int. 8
Leader as an Example		
Good behavior	4x	Int. 5 and Q. 27, 30, 31
Good example leads followers to respect leader	2x	Int. 2, 8
Authority flows out of his testimony and work	2x	Int. 6, 7
Behavior and conduct speak louder than words	1x	Q. 36
Acts must confirm words	1x	Q. 17
Behavior must match words	1x	Q. 13
Daily life must be a witness of their leadership	1x	Q. 3
Model of life	1x	Q. 12
People learn by looking at leaders especially at their behavior when things are tough	1x	Int. 8
Model for the disciples they are leading	1x	Q. 2
They must shine like a light	1x	Q. 16
Tribal chiefs are models	1x	In. 10
People always look at the leaders even if they are not aware of it		
Jesus as a Model		
Jesus is the greatest model	4x	Int. 4, 7, 9 and Q. 15
"I influence them spiritually. I give them a good testimony. I am a model in order that they follow the best model, Jesus-Christ."	1x	Int.9

spiritually. I give them a good testimony. I am a model in order that they follow the best model, Jesus-Christ."

The concept of leading by modeling is not new in mission. This resonates with what the missionary Charles Marsh wrote in his book, *Le Musulman Mon Prochain* (Marsh 1977) saying, "*Il également très important de se rappeler que le message que nous apportons est jugé en fonction de la personne du messager.*"[11] By this he meant exactly what my informant told me: "a leader must model the message by his actions and behaviors."

Conclusion

This section on power and influence has disclosed important aspects regarding how North African leaders understand their leadership. First, it showed that although there is a type of hierarchy in the way leaders understand authority (e.g., king, master, ruler, and pope) they combine it with other qualities such as servanthood, communication, and organizational skills, as well as deep spirituality.

Second, although they express leadership in terms of hierarchy, they place much emphasis on consultation. No followers should expect their leaders to make decisions without consulting elders, boards or the congregation. However, following the process of sharing, discussing and listening, North African leaders are entitled to make decisions. Consultation when connected to a hierarchical view of leadership creates a unique leadership pattern that will be interesting to compare and contrast in the final section of this book.

Third, there is clear evidence that leaders influence others not only through words but also by their example and behaviors. I argue that this approach is a major area of difference between North Africa and North America for example. In the latter region, words sometimes carry more weight while in the former behaviors and actions are of equal, if not more, importance.

---

11. Translation: It is also important to remember that the message we bring is judged according to the personality of the messenger (Marsh1977).

Relational Behaviors

There was no specific question on relational behaviors in my questionnaires but due to the significant number of quotations regarding relationships and leadership I created a specific section on this issue. I report here the various responses referring to relational aspects of leadership that I collected throughout the research.

Caretaking

Twenty-six respondents, two-thirds of the interviewees, said that the leader is someone who takes care of others (Anonymous 8, 10 and Int. 7, 8, 9 and Q. 3, 8, 13, 16, 18, 21, 22, 26, 27, 30, 31, 32, 33, 35 and 36). Sometimes the word "to be concerned" is used instead of caretaking (Int. 9) while other leaders use the word "assist others" (Q. 27, 30) or "meets the needs of others" (Int. 8 and Q. 18, 21, 26, 38, and 30). Leaders are to be more concerned about the needs of others than their own (Int. 9). Finally, respondents also used the word "feeding" for this leadership style. One respondent said leadership is to feed Jesus' sheep (Int. 7), while another said that leaders must feed his followers, help them grow, mature and bear fruits (Int. 8).

As we have seen already in the previous paragraph, the concept of caretaker is often correlated with the metaphor of the good shepherd. North African church leaders are the good shepherds who both "care for their sheep" (Int. 8 and Q. 18, 21, 26, 38, and 30) and give their lives for them. On a number of occasions, North African leaders said they chose the metaphor of the shepherd because of the sacrificial motif.

Leaders assist followers in different ways. Informants said they take care of the spiritual (Q. 1, 26, 21, 36) and practical needs (Int. 2, Q. 13) of their followers. They see everything and take care of the smallest details that followers don't see (Int. 9). The recipients of their caretaking are listed in table 11.

Caretaking is a key behavior of North African church leaders. These leaders are not distant from their followers. Furthermore, they deeply care for them in areas that concern leadership but also in their personal families' lives.

TABLE 11: Recipients Of Caretaking

(Farida Saidi)

Church	Q. 26, Anonymous 10
New converts	Q. 26
Others	Q. 3, 30, 33
Sheep of the flock	Q. 16, 21, 27
Members	Q. 22
Team	Q. 8
Followers	Int. 1, 2, 8

Dying for One's Followers

According to my research, church leaders must follow the example of Christ and be ready to die for their followers. Informants insisted that a leader must first be ready to die for God as well as for others. They used the following expressions: (1) "Give oneself for others" (Q. 16); (2) "gives one's life for his or her sheep" (Q. 21, 26); and (3) must have a "spirit of self-sacrifice" (Q. 6, 29, 36, Int. 7). One informant gave the illustration of Moses, who was ready to die and have his name erased from the book of life for his people, and of Paul who was "ready to die for the brothers" (Int. 1). Another cited the example of Jesus, "the Good Shepherd who gives his life for the sheep" (Q. 27).

According to North African leaders, giving up one's life for a fellow human is different from standard non-Christian values (Q. 16). It is clearly a Christian leadership value and consequently a way to influence others. One respondent argued that self-sacrifice for the sake of others is the best way to influence followers (Int. 1).

I assume that North African leaders are deeply impacted by Jesus' teaching on this issue because they often quote Jesus who gave his life for his sheep. How this relates to practical theology needs to be further investigated. As I indicated above, I do not know to what extent this is an actual practice of pastors particularly since church leaders did not give me practical examples of how they are ready to die for their followers; as a result I cannot posit how this behavior translates in North African churches. Nevertheless, it is striking to learn that this behavior is a crucial example for so many pastors and that the idea of self-sacrifice may be a key characteristic of leadership in this part of the world.

Listening

The characteristic of listening has been abundantly identified in this research. According to twelve North African respondents, listening to others is an important component of leadership (Int. 2, 8, and Q.1, 4, 10, 12, 15, 18, 26, 28 and 35 and Anonymous 5).

Leaders are required to listen in order to understand the needs of followers. Int. 5 says that a "leader should be listening to others . . . and make sure he or she meets their needs as much as possible." Listening involves both understanding (Q. 1, 26) and having a good sense of observation (Int. 8). One church leader gave an example from a tribal chief saying, "people would go to see the chief of the tribe for any kind of problem. Everyone is welcome to visit with him and he listens to everyone who comes" (Int. 10).

This practice of listening is something that would best be probed when interviewing followers and unfortunately, this study did not include them. I hope that in the future, this question as well as others from this section will be asked to followers who are in sufficient positions to evaluate whether leaders have the skills to listen to and meet their needs. Meanwhile, my research demonstrates that leaders have the desire to display a leadership style that includes the practice of listening.

Protection

Several leaders mentioned that a leader must protect his or her followers. Int. 10 painted the picture of broken seashells on the beach that his son brought back to him as a metaphor of how leaders should take care of the broken people: "Each time that followers are broken we want to push them aside, but Jesus does not do that. He imposes the broken one. He wants to restore them and he wants that we help him restore them."

The metaphor of a dog (and not the shepherd) as protector is also useful. When asked to give a metaphor for leadership, Q.10 gave the image of the shepherd's dog which "keeps the flock and defends it when the wolf attacks." Finally, Moses was described as the leader who "carries his people" to protect them (Q. 35).

Conclusion

The various behaviors expressed here show that leaders are deeply concerned by the needs of their followers and want to connect with them. This is not a distant type of leadership relationship like those of the traditional North American and European work environments.

The type of bond between leader and follower is characterized by caretaking, giving up one's life for the follower, listening, and protecting the follower. I assume that deep emotional transactions also occur in this kind of leadership primarily because it seems typical of community-oriented societies. The leader almost acts like a father or a friend. I am wondering if this is a reciprocal relationship where the follower is also expected to care, give up one's life, listen to and protect the leader. If not, this becomes a hierarchical relationship where the follower is depicted as someone in need of the leader's support and may become dependent on him/her.

Spiritual Characteristics-Piety

The title of this section consists of two similar concepts. The title "piety" expresses the leader's devotion to God but since no leader used the word "piety" to express their reverence to God, the more generic term "spiritual characteristics" is introduced to summarize the spirituality of North African leaders. I present here the various words, expressions, images and metaphors used by leaders throughout my research to describe this piety and/or their relationship with God.

Attached to God and Jesus

Nineteen respondents expressed in various forms that a leader must be attached to God (e.g. Int. 1 and Q. 3). Eight respondents further qualified this attachment by the expression "love for God" (Int. 5, 8 and Q. 2, 12, 18, 27, 32, 35). Others expressed this notion by using the expression "intimacy with God" (Int. 3, 7, Q. 1, 2, 21 and 26). Fifteen respondents expressed the attachment to God by saying the leader must have "faith in" God or Jesus (Int. 1, 2, 3, 9 and Q. 3, 11, 15, 16, 18, 22, 26, 28, 29, 33, 36).

Respondents also stated that they are attached to Jesus. They explained that the leader must be "strong in Christ" (Q. 11), a "disciple of Jesus" (Q. 10), "rely on Jesus and nothing else" (Int. 6), and "fix eyes on Jesus" (Q. 30, 32).

The data clearly indicates that the hallmark of leadership is total dependence on God and Jesus. One respondent, for example, quoted David because he "relied on God in every act of leadership" (Q. 1). All the expressions of attachment reflect a deep sense of connection with the divine. They do not explain however what leadership practices enable this attachment. In summary, it is important that we just recognize that the relationship with God and Jesus is very strong, deep, intense and intimate.

Bible-Centered

At least eleven respondents stressed the importance of the Word of God in the life a Christian leader—that the Bible must have a central place in their life and ministry (Int. 2, 3, 5 and Q. 9, 15, 16, 21, 27, 34, 35).

The reference to the Bible can be categorized as following. First, leaders must have a good understanding of the Word (Q. 27); they know it (Q. 21). Second, the Word is their authority: they are founded on it (Q. 2, 27), they submit to it (Q. 34), they are faithful to it (Q. 35), they believe it (Int. 2, 3), and they take it as a reference (Q. 31). Two respondents said it is the "supreme authority" (Q. 15). Third, they put the word in practice (Q. 27), they apply it (Q. 27), all their decisions are based on it (Q. 31), and finally, they teach it (Q. 16).

These various references show that a good number of North African leaders are bible-centered and that they consider the Word of God with great seriousness. The questions did not probe how they study the Bible nor their needs in regards to biblical studies. But I can infer from the data collected that there is a real desire to rely on what God revealed in the Word and communicate it to followers with the greatest faithfulness possible.

Charisma/Filled with the Holy Spirit

Charisma denotes the spiritual power given to leaders by the Holy Spirit. A large number of respondents talked about the importance for a leader to be equipped with the Holy Spirit (e.g. Int. 4, 5, 6, Q. 1, 7, 15, 28, 29, 30,

33, Anonymous 10). One respondent even said, "Somebody who walks according to the Spirit of God cannot make a mistake" (Int. 6). This research thus outlines that a good leader must have the fruits of the Spirit and be filled with the Holy Spirit.

Respondents emphasized their dependence on the Holy Spirit by using various expressions. For example, leaders must be spiritually mature (Q. 29), have the Holy Spirit (Int. 5), have the gifts of the Holy Spirit (Int. 4), be filled with the Spirit (Anonymous 10), live in the Spirit (Q. 7), rely on the Holy Spirit (Q. 29), be led by the Holy Spirit (Int. 1 and 3) and be "in the Spirit" (Int. 3).

This attachment to the Holy Spirit leads to various ministerial expressions including, performance of miracles (Q. 33), [12] analysis of prophesies (Int. 3 and Int. 7), spiritual warfare (Int. 1), supernatural qualities (Int. 6), spiritual discernment (Int. 2, 3, 7, 8 and Q. 2, 3, 4, 7, 12, 13, 36) and the gift of deliverance (Int. 2). All of these skills and qualities are important to North African leaders and interestingly are very similar to those early church leaders cherished as recorded in the book of Acts.

Discernment is one ministry gift that clearly stands out as being a key characteristic of leadership. One respondent for example said, "In difficult situations (deliverance, directives, prophesies) leaders must be able to analyze spiritual things" (Int. 2). Leaders must discern the will of God (Int. 3), the decisions they must make (Q. 4), but they must also "pray and share" (Q. 13).

It is also worth noticing that informants stated clearly that this quality is what distinguishes them from non-Christians. They insisted that spiritual qualities are different from non-Christian ones (Int. 4, 7, 8). Someone even said they are opposite (Int. 4). Furthermore informants insisted that anointing is different between both faiths.

In conclusion, this study shows that there is a strong emphasis in North African leadership regarding the role of the Holy Spirit. The reliance on the Holy Spirit in every aspect of life and ministry is what makes a leader legitimate. I did not investigate here the relationship between church affiliation

---

12. One informant even said all leaders should believe in miracles: "Belief in miracles is a value common to all leaders" (Q. 6)

and the importance given to the Holy Spirit in the doctrinal traditions of the leaders. Nonetheless, what is relevant for my own research is the fact that leaders strongly acknowledge the role of the Holy Spirit and make use of his acts and gifts thus imitating the early church. They also seem to favor discernment as a key spiritual gift in leadership.

Prayer

At least sixteen leaders indicated that a leader must be a man or woman of prayer. Leaders must pray for their followers (Anonymous 1, Q. 8), with their followers (Q. 13, 28, 31, 32), for the healthy spiritual state of the followers (Q. 8), and for the lost (Q. 18). One respondent said, "praying is a way to watch over the people of the flock." It is also a way to worship God (Int. 8).

Respondents offered some indications on how to pray. One informant stated, "leaders must pray without ceasing" (Q. 35); another that leaders must lay hands upon others in prayer (Int. 2). Lastly it is important for leaders to pray for important decisions like choosing an apostle (Int. 10). Leaders are also known as praying more than other believers (Q. 16). These numerous references to prayer highlight a unique aspect of North African church leadership. There is more emphasis on prayer than any other spiritual behavior. This finding confirms what I have experienced in my own interactions with North African church leaders over thirty years. Prayer is a central pillar of their leadership activity.

Submission to God

Five leaders specifically expressed that a leader must submit to God (Int. 1, 2, 4, 6 and Q. 11). Another expression used for submission was "under the authority of the Lord" (Q. 11). A respondent gave a peculiar picture pertaining to submission (Int. 4) saying that someone had the vision of him being the donkey of God. He explained that this refers to the event of Jesus entering Jerusalem on a donkey. This leader stated he wanted to be like that donkey, entering in neighborhoods and visiting family. He viewed his leadership as "Jesus on me." On the other hand, one respondent quoted Jesus entering Jerusalem on a donkey as a model of leadership (Q. 7). Another mentioned he prefers not to submit to the counsel of other church members if they prevent him from submitting to God (Int. 6).

Other qualities found in this research are (a) fearing God (Anonymous 1, 10 and Q. 2, 12), (b) putting God in first place (Q. 9), (c) doing everything for the glory of God (Q. 28, 30, 33 and 35), (d) obeying God (Q. 2, 15, 18, 28, 29 and 30), (e) doing the will of God (Int. 3 and Q. 29, 30), and (f) listening to God (Anonymous 10 and Int. 3, 6 and Q. 28, 32). All these expressions can be correlated with the concept of submission to God. With all these qualities added to the general references listed in the first paragraph, this makes a total of twenty respondents, representing almost half of those interviewed, who referenced submission to God.

Conclusion

The piety and spiritual life of leaders are characterized in this research by the following elements: (1) deep attachment to God expressed by love, intimacy, and faith, (2) bible-centeredness, (3) dependence on the Holy Spirit, (4) prayer of worship and intercession, and (5) submission to God. According to the data collected, leaders in North Africa are deeply spiritual. Their piety is not hidden from their followers as is evidenced in that every aspect of their lives reflects their relationship with God. They take very seriously their day-to-day walk with God, Jesus and the Holy Spirit, all of which translates in various spiritual practices.

Leadership Skills

In this section I briefly describe some leadership skills that have been defined during the interviews and questionnaires. Since many questions were focused on values and behaviors, I did not gather significant information on skills. However, I chose to include here the few that were most commonly mentioned.

Leading

Seven respondents said that a leader is "someone who leads". One respondent said for example that the leader must be "leading members and training them". This skill is further detailed by expressions such as, "He/she walks in front of his flock" and "He/she leads in showing the direction to his people". Moses for example was "leading the people in the desert toward the promised land".

When asked about a metaphor for leadership, one respondent gave the image of the shepherd's dog, which "leads the flock into the sheep's house." It seems that leaders here do not want to equate themselves with Jesus and therefore use one element of the parable to identify with a leadership role but do not identify directly with Jesus. The same may be true when one respondent says that he is the "donkey of Jesus."

Images of animals, I suggest, are used to identify with the role of leadership so as to not equate oneself with the perfect leader, Jesus, and subsequently preserves the submissive element of the human leader submitting to the divine leader. This tension between leading and submitting to the divine leader seems to be a strong characteristic of North African Christian leadership.

Accepting Responsibility

One of the major skills required of leaders in North African churches is "accepting responsibility" (e.g. Int. 7, 8 and Q. 4). Forty-five respondents said that leaders must take responsibility (e.g. Int. 1, 6, 8; Q. 2, 17, 29, 30, 36) showing their courage and hard work. Biblical leaders such as Moses and Abraham were known for having this skill (Q. 29). The image of a father who knows what it means to be responsible is often used to describe the task of accepting responsibility (e.g. Int. 6, 8).

Leaders used several metaphors and illustrations to further describe this skill: (1) the leader must take care of those for whom he is responsible (Int. 7), (2) the leader is like a "beef which carries a yoke" (Q. 22),[13] (3) the leader "is in the front, serves others, and takes on responsibilities and is accountable" (Q. 17), and (4) the leader is responsible for feeding, growing, and making others mature and bear fruits (Int. 8).

---

13. This metaphor could also indicate the submission to God.

Teaching

North African church leaders made several references to teaching their followers. One respondent stated that, "the leader is like a teacher with his pupils" (Q. 30). Another quoted "Apollos, the teacher" in Acts 18:24, as a model of leadership (Q. 33). Respondents showed the importance of teaching the church (Int. 1) the Word (Int. 8 and Anonymous 2 and Q. 12).

There are certain expectations of leaders including that they must teach "rightly" (Int. 8), watch over their teaching (as in 1 Timothy 4:16) (Q. 2) and correctly explain the word of truth (as in 2 Timothy 2:15) (Int. 2). They must have knowledge (Int. 9), be good communicators (Q. 21) and preach the gospel (Q. 31). Finally, leaders make things progress through their teaching (Int. 2) and pick up the missing pieces.

Visionary

Another important skill North African leaders must display is that of being visionaries. Five respondents said a leader must be a visionary (Int. 8, 9 and Anonymous 1 and Q. 2, 32).

Informants used the following expressions to describe the visionary leader. They said, (a) "my vision is to implant churches everywhere" (Int. 8), (b) "the leader has an aim and a vision" (Q. 32), (c) he has a "large vision" (Int. 9); and (d) "he tries to realize a vision with other people" (Q. 32).

Administration

One particular skill was mentioned a single time and because it is very popular in church leadership in other cultures, I believe it is important to mention: management. Only one North African interviewee said that a leader is a good manager of the goods entrusted to him and that he makes fructified (Q. 12).

There could be several reasons why North African leaders did not mention management. First, they lead emerging churches with a majority of new believers that require discipleship training more than anything else. Most churches are in the early stages of organization and often do not have an official permit to legally exist. Many meet in houses or outdoors. It may also be possible that the North African context does not view management skills essential for church leadership. This area should be tested further in future research.

Conclusion

Although church leaders did not mention many leadership skills, it is interesting to discover that nearly all informants indicated that the leader must accept responsibility. The following are possible explanations. First, the church is young and not well-established, therefore, leaders need to work hard and must stick to the task. Second, since the church is not well structured, the leader must consider his ministry as a long-term project that involves hard work. Third, followers may also expect leaders to commit to the church wholeheartedly in order to see it thrive. Further research should ask leaders why they recommend this skill for church leadership.

This section also shows the need for leaders to model and give direction and destination to their followers. Moses and Abraham are key models of leadership because they led followers from point A to point B and were actually present with them in that journey.

This research also reveals the dire necessity for teachers who know the Word and teach it with integrity. These findings are in total agreement with what I have observed during my visits to the North African church prior to this research. Teachers are greatly needed for these emerging churches that consist of thousands and thousands of new believers—all of whom must receive discipleship training.

Another finding is that North African churches desire visionary leaders. The many references to the leader with a vision may point to the visionary style. We will discuss this further in the concluding chapter of this book. Finally, the fact that only one person mentioned management seems to indicate that leaders are preoccupied by many other ministry tasks.

Leadership Metaphors

In the bulk of the data collected, I found a number of recurrent metaphors of leadership that are worth analyzing because they may predict a specific leadership style. These metaphors were either mentioned in response to a specific question or have been used to discuss leadership attitudes and behaviors randomly.

I report these metaphors in this section. Later, in the concluding chapter of this study, I will compare them with the leadership values, behaviors and qualities listed above to suggest leadership styles.

Father Metaphor

Nine respondents used the image of the father to describe their leadership. Leaders must be like the father of a family (Q. 3, 13, 30) or a "daddy" (Int. 8). They must have the quality of a father (Int. 9) or they must be a father or a mother (Q. 12). One informant stated leaders must be like the oldest of the family (Anonymous 2).[14] Finally, a church leader "must be leader like a father whether he/she wants it or not" (Int. 9).

Love is a key element of the father metaphor. One church leader utilized the image of a father to insist that leadership should be motivated by love (Int. 7). The leader's authority flows out of love, said another (Int. 9). And despite the hard work and the conflicts, love encourages leaders to continue in their ministry (Int. 3).

The father metaphor implies that leaders take care of the needs of the followers. One interviewee said that church leaders meet the needs of their followers like a father meets the needs of his children (Int. 8). For example, "a father does not eat before his children have eaten" (Int. 8). The father metaphor is also used to describe the leader who educates followers (Q. 12, Int. 7).

Servant Metaphor

Twenty-three respondents referred to the leader as a servant (Int. 1, 2, 3, 4, 5, 6, 7, 8, 9 and Q. 1, 2, 3, 7, 10, 11, 12, 13, 17, 26, 27, 28, 29 and Anonymous 2). When asked to provide a metaphor for leadership, the picture of a servant immediately came to mind for three respondents. Consequently, leaders must be willing to server others (Q. 11) and have the spirit of a servant (Q. 13). Models of true servanthood are Jesus (Int. 6) and

---

14. In North African society often the oldest sibling takes on the role of the father or the mother.

Moses (Int. 9). Leaders should follow the example of Jesus who came "to serve and not to be served" as in John 13 (Q. 1); he is not a master but a servant (Int. 1); and he gave his life for humanity (Int. 1).

The data collected further illustrates what makes a servant. The servant-leader is described as a restaurant clerk (Q. 1) who is a leader because he/she is not a "master" (Int. 6). Another respondent added that, "All gifts must be used for the service of the church" (Q. 6). Leaders must serve and not take advantage of followers (Q. 12). Int. 4 underlined the greatest person is not the one who attacks others but the one who serves them. Int. 8 stated that serving is a spiritual quality. Q. 1 added, "Spiritual power means serving others."

According to this study, leaders are servants because both leaders and followers are equal before God—"the one that sows the seed and the one who reaps" (Int. 1). No one "is a degree above the other" (Int. 1). The recipients of servanthood are described as "others" (Q. 10, 11, 12, 15, 17, 27, Int. 3, 4, 5), "the brothers" (Int. 4), "believers" (Q. 28), "the North African Church" (Int. 4, 8), "the wife" of the leader (Int. 8), "servant of the team, the church or the organization" (Q. 2), "the people" (Int. 3), and "my family" (Int. 8).

Shepherd Metaphor

Twelve respondents used the metaphor of shepherding to describe a leader (Int. 1, 2, 5, 8 and Q. 8, 14, 18, 21, 26, 36 and Anonymous 2, 8). One respondent said, "Leaders should have the spirit of a shepherd" (Int. 1). Another stated the leader is the "good" shepherd (Q. 21, 26, 36). Jesus is described as gentle (Int. 9), loving (Int. 9) and a loving shepherd. Finally one respondent said the "shepherd" is the best image of a leader (Q. 12).

This metaphor of the shepherd is further supported by Bible passages church leaders cited. One of the most common references indicated by leaders is the passage of John 10 where Jesus is portrayed as a shepherd (Q. 12, 14, 15, 17, 31, and 35). Some quoted specific verses such John 10:11 (Q. 21, 26, 27). Another Bible passage quoted was Psalm 23 (Int. 23).

Due to the fact that I asked for a metaphor instead of a biblical text, there may be two reasons why respondents provided the image of the shepherd. First, it is possible that actual shepherds in North Africa resonate implicitly with the biblical imagery. Second, leaders may have received specific teaching on John 10 by visiting professors or pastors, thus believing this is a key text for their leadership.

Conclusion

The three main leadership metaphors given by the interviewees are of the father, the servant and the shepherd. Consequently, they may predict the type of church leadership styles preferred by the North African. I will discuss them in the concluding chapter of the book when I integrate them with the leadership values, attitudes and behaviors, described by the informants and compare and contrast them with similar occurrences in the historical, cultural and social context of North Africa.

Unfortunately, this research did not probe for detailed illustrations of such metaphors. Further research must provide leaders with opportunities to give explanations as to why they used these metaphors and how they directly relate to leadership styles.

Biblical Leadership Styles

This chapter continues the report of my findings. In Chapter 5, I reported the findings on personal and interpersonal values, attributes, and qualities from the interviews, questionnaires and focus groups. These same research tools also provided information concerning how the leaders explicitly drew from biblical models. These results were drawn from two sources. First, my questionnaire included a specific question on biblical models that influence North African leadership. Second, throughout the research, leaders referred to biblical models and passages even when not probed for biblical examples. This was expected since all the respondents were Christian leaders who naturally drew leadership resources from the Bible. The answers collected helped me better understand the biblical perspective of their leadership and I use them in my concluding chapter to evaluate the biblical base of North African church leaderships. I have included the biblical findings in this chapter.

Among the many biblical characters, there are two leaders, Jesus and Moses, who stand out in the interviews and questionnaires. This seems to indicate that North African leaders consider them as models for leadership.

Jesus

Jesus was quoted nineteen times as a model for leadership—the character most often quoted (Int. 2, 3, 4, 6, 5, 7, 8, 9, 13, and Q. 2, 6, 7, 9, 11, 13, 15, 16, 22, 28).

Respondents chose Jesus because, (1) "The leader must have a character that reflects the image of Jesus," (2) "Jesus must become a model for the leader and must be imitated," (3) "The leader must be like Jesus," (4) "Jesus is considered as the leader 'par excellence,'" (Int. 4, 8, 9, 13) and (5) "Jesus' leadership values must be imitated." He is the symbol of authority (Int. 5).

We see from the table below that, according to North African leaders, Jesus' leadership style includes humility, love, and servanthood, leading by example, power, and communication skills. Jesus is also often portrayed as a shepherd who gives his life for his sheep.

TABLE 12: Jesus' Leadership Characteristics
(Farida Saidi)

Attributes	Examples
Communicator	Int. 6
Humility	Humility Int. 9; the greatest must become the smallest Q.9
Love	The greatest must become the smallest; love for children (Int.2)
Model to imitate	(Int. 4, 5 and Q. 6, 13, 28),
Servant	Washed feet of disciples (Q 1 and Int. 4, 5 and 6)
Powerful	Calmed the storm (Q.16), symbol of authority; he is the symbol of authority (Int. 5)

Moses

After Jesus, Moses was the leader most often quoted (Int. 1, 4, 5, 7, 8, 9 and Q. 3, 8, 9, 15, 26, 28, 29, 35, 36) with fifteen respondents considering him a model of leadership. The table below lists his leadership attributes that inspired North African believers. In summary, Moses' leadership style includes elements of caretaking, humility, love and forgiveness. He is also applauded for his capacity to delegate.

Moses resembles Jesus in many ways. In effect, I found several matching attributes when I compared the leadership of Jesus and Moses. They are both ready to give up their life for followers, have power over the physical elements, accept responsibility and are servants and shepherds. They both love followers and are humble. It seems that North African leaders are attracted to similar attributes in different leaders. This may be a sign that these attributes are significant aspects of their leadership styles.

TABLE 13: Moses' Leadership Attributes

(Farida Saidi)

Attributes	Examples
Caretaker	He takes care of the followers; he carries the people; he was there for his people
Delegation	He delegated; he appoints a successor in Joshua
Forgiveness	He forgives followers when they rebel
Humility	He was humble
Love	Love; he loves his followers to the end, even when they were rebellious
Power	He is a picture of power, calmed the storm, symbol of authority
Responsibilities	He accepts responsibilities to accomplish God's will
Self-Sacrifice for followers	Readiness to die for his people; suffering, ready to have his name erased from the book of life
Servanthood	Service
Servant	Humility; love; forgives when people rebel and is ready to have his name blotted out of the book of life
Shepherd	Willingness to give up his life for his disciples; he carries his followers; suffering; he loves his followers to the end even when they are rebellious

Timothy

Timothy was quoted fourteen times (Int. 1, 2, 3, 5, 6 and Q. 2, 4, 5, 9, 13, 15, 32 and An. 1, 2), barely less than Moses (14 times). However, the difference here lies in the fact that leaders instead quoted passages of the Epistle of Timothy and not Timothy's individual characteristics.

North African leaders quoted various passages from chapter 3, then 4:16 and 2:15 as listed in the table below. The attributes listed in these passages are as follows: be above reproach, the husband of one wife, temperate, self-controlled, respectable, able to teach, not given to drunkenness, not violent but gentle, not quarrelsome, not a lover of money, manage his own family well, not be a recent convert, have a good reputation with outsiders, worthy of respect, sincere, not indulging in much wine, not pursuing dishonest gain, keep hold of the deep truths of the faith with a clear conscience, be tested, have a wife worthy of respect, not malicious talkers but temperate and trustworthy in everything, watch their life and doctrine closely, persevere in them, and stand firm and hold on the teachings passed on to them. This is a clear and extensive list of attributes that fifteen pastors seek to follow intimately.

Before beginning my research, I did not probe whether church leaders had specific teaching on this passage. This may be a reason why they quoted these passages so frequently. One needs to remember that the emerging church in North Africa has not received much training in church leadership. Consequently, it is likely that all the respondents I interviewed have taken the same seminar on leadership.

Paul

Nine respondents viewed Paul as a good model for their leadership (Anonymous 1, 10 and Int. 1, 2, 3, 4, 6 and 8 and Q. 2). Several attributes are similar to the ones quoted above, such as humbleness, love and self-sacrifice—all of which are recurrent attributes in every model of leadership quoted. Other attributes drawn from the study of Paul's leadership are being an adviser or a scholar and having courage.

TABLE 14: Paul's Leadership Style

(Farida Saidi)

Attributes	Examples
Adviser	He gave good advice to Timothy
Courage	He was courageous
Humble	He did not fight for his rights
Love	Love
Scholar	He wrote many books
Self-Sacrifice	His willingness to die for his brothers; he suffered with Jesus; he offered body and soul for Jesus

Other Biblical Leaders

Other biblical leaders quoted are Nehemiah, who was quoted seven times (Int. 2, 8, 9, 17 and Q. 6, 11, 17), David, who was quoted three times (Int. 8, 9 and Q. 1), Joshua who was quoted two times (Int. 1 and 9), Apollos was quoted two times (Q. 33 and Anonymous 2), Joseph was quoted two times (Int. 3 and 5), Abraham was quoted two times (Q. 29 and 30), Peter was quoted two times (Int. 7 and 9), Titus was quoted two times (Int. 1 and 7), Esdras was quoted once, and Philippus was quoted once (Q. 33). Amos (Q.6), Daniel (Int.8), Gideon (Int. 7), Elijah (Int. 9), Priscilla and Aquila (Int. 1) and Samuel (Int. 8) were also each quoted once.

The leadership attributes they model are listed in the table below. Those who were already underlined for previous leaders are leading by example, having spiritual power, accepting responsibilities, forgiving, preaching and teaching followers. Other attributes further highlighting what North African leaders consider as biblical attributes of leadership are: be attached to God, be a builder, foresightedness, lead, listen, obey God, be a soldier, and work hard.

TABLE 15: Attributes Of Miscellaneous Leaders

(Farida Saïdi)

Attributes	Leaders
Attached to God	Abraham (He left his home, family and land to go where God was leading)
Builder	Nehemie, Esdras (he rebuilt the temple)
Forgiveness	Joseph (Forgives his brothers; a strong sense of forgiveness in his heart), Moses
Foresightedness	Joseph (he understood the plan of God for his life)
Leading his followers	Joshua (He led the people toward the promised land)
Listened to	Philippus
Miracles	Philippus
Model	Titus (important model)
Obeyed God	Abraham
Obeyed by his followers	Nehemiah
Powerful	Peter (was powerful, and pushy)
Preacher	Philippus
Responsibilities (accepted)	Abraham
Soldier	Nehemiah (he had the sword in one hand and worked with the other) Joshua (He fought and was the general of an army)
Teacher	Apollos
Worked hard	He did not get tired of building and rebuilding, Moses, Esdras, Nehemie

Conclusion

My field research shows clearly that biblical models influence North African church leaders. Many leadership attributes are drawn from biblical passages and role models. North African leaders do not talk about leadership without quoting the Bible, thus clearly use it as a foundational resource.

Among the many biblical characters two leaders, Jesus and Moses, were most often cited. This indicates that North African leaders consider them as their role models for leadership. It makes sense that Jesus would be the role model of leadership since followers around the world consider him as the best model for believers. However, since not all of Jesus' leadership attributes were quoted, what is important for this research is to identify which ones are significant for church leaders. They will help me identify what leadership styles are attractive to the church context I study. The table above is the criteria of healthy leadership for North African leaders. Of course, since this study was not specifically on biblical leadership styles, there are certainly many more attributes that leaders may have mentioned if time permitted. I am glad however with these initial findings that show me what attributes first come to the mind of believers when they think of Jesus. The importance given to Moses can be explained by the fact that the cultural context of his leadership has many commonalities with North Africa or that his popularity is linked to him being a major Qur'anic leader.

Other major biblical characters of influence are Timothy and Paul. The remaining biblical leaders quoted in the study are less important in the way they shape North African leadership even though they certainly teach valuable lessons to those I interviewed. They are Nehemiah, David, Joshua, Apollos, Joseph, Abraham, Peter, Titus, Esdras, Philippus, Amos, Daniel, Gideon, Elijah, Samuel and Priscilla and Aquila.

It also appears that the book of Timothy is important for leadership training in North Africa, as it was the one most often quoted in my research. The information contained in Timothy is very helpful for my research because it provides me with a clear list of biblical leadership attributes that at least one third of the respondents seem to adopt.

Finally, several leadership attributes are emerging as recurrent in this biblical study. The most common are love, humility, self-sacrifice, leading by example, teaching, spiritual power, accepting responsibility, being a shepherd and being a servant. Other attributes only quoted once remain as significant findings because if probed further, more respondents may claim them. This list is therefore a good initial mapping of the biblical attributes of leadership that are adopted by North African church leaders. I hope it can be expanded in the future.

Chapter Conclusion

The data collected during my research highlights leadership values, behaviors, qualities and metaphors that will allow me to propose leadership styles that are relevant for the North African church context. The table below is a summary of my findings and will allow me to compare and contrast what I have found in the North African church with the historical, religious and cultural context in order to find contemporary church leadership styles that seek the good of the believers and the society.

Instead of presenting the findings in the table below, I have organized them alphabetically so that it will be easier to compare and contrast them with the characteristics of leadership collected in the secondary research on historical, cultural and religious leadership. I have kept the information on the frequency of occurrences but have also added the context in which the value, quality, behavior or metaphor was used. This table therefore shows that the same characteristic of leadership may have been quoted at different occasions. For example, leading by example has been quoted as a leadership value but has also been discussed by leaders when they talked about power and influence. Furthermore, humility is a value for some and a general quality for others.

However, to have a more detailed analysis of the specific examples given by informants the reader should consult the other tables and comments of this chapter for the nine specific areas I studied which are (1) leadership values, (2) human qualities, (3) moral qualities, (4) legitimacy, (5) power-influence, (6) relational behaviors, (7) spiritual characteristics-piety, (8) leadership skills, and (9) leadership metaphors. I will summarize the findings of these nine categories after the table. The table including all the values, attributes and behaviors collected during my field research can be found in appendix 9. This table gives me a good tool to compare and contrast leadership patterns in the North African church with other contexts.

A summary of this chapter shows the following characteristics of North African church leadership. First, leaders have organized the leadership values in spiritual, human, moral and relational characteristics. The spiritual characteristics emphasize personal piety with a focus on intimacy with God, love for God, prayer and fasting, and a Spirit-filled life. The human characteristics highlight love, humility, and justice as the strongest values. Moral values include first integrity, then honesty, righteousness and sincerity (without excluding blamelessness). Finally relational characteristics depict leaders valuing those who encourage, forgive, help and are hospitable. These values are important to know, as they will help us to identify existing leadership styles in our final analysis.

Second, leaders have defined a certain number of human qualities. Those that are most prominent in this research include love, then humility and patience. Three other qualities ranked slightly lower to those mentioned and they include courage, wisdom and trustworthiness. Although justice ranked higher than some other values it is only quoted three times as a general quality. We can already foresee some discrepancy between Islamic societies that rank justice very high and church practices. The human qualities collected seem to already point to a number of existing leadership styles and divert us from others. It is interesting for example to notice that patience is not a value that would necessarily stand out in North America. In this research, however, it is one of the most important human qualities expected from a leader. It is thus clear that already some cultural or religious patterns are emerging.

Third, the study of moral qualities mentioned by North African leaders reveals something quite surprising. It appears that North African leaders set the bar very high in the area of integrity and blamelessness. Many words refer to the moral standard expected from a leader: holiness, honesty, authenticity, transparency, truthfulness, etc. Sanctification is a key requirement in North African leadership. When I suggest leadership styles in later sections, I must remember that North African leadership is demanding in this area.

Fourth, the findings noticeably identify that leaders feel called by God including a great majority that also support human legitimacy. Thus, divine legitimacy and human legitimacy are often combined. However, leaders view God as the ultimate source of their leadership. In only a few cases, leaders said it was necessary they be self-appointed because of the needs in their context and because there was no tangible community to appoint them. It will be interesting to later compare leadership legitimacy in the church with what is practiced in Islam to explore how the context has influenced the appointment of leaders and what leadership style embraces this worldview.

Fifth, power-influence is well defined in the North African church. Authority is based on a hierarchical model that relies heavily on the leader being humble and a servant. An overwhelming number of respondents indicated that leaders must lead by example; a lesser number noted that they should be good communicators with their followers. While administrative skills are certainly needed, informants repeatedly identified that more important is the way leaders relate to followers. They must be able to collaborate and work as a team and their relationships must include the fruits of the Spirit. Furthermore, stating as some leaders did that God is the ultimate source of (spiritual) authority may help minimize any autocratic forms of human leadership. But the unique characteristic of North African church leadership is that it combines spiritual and personal authority with the practice of consultation. North African leaders have clearly explained to me how this consultation occurs. Ultimately, the leader makes the final decision but only when everyone consulted is happy about the process. Of course, since I did not interview followers or the larger community, I cannot state with total assurance that this is how power-influence is practiced on a day-to-day basis in the church. What I can posit however is that this is how leaders conceive of power-influence.

Sixth, leaders model relationship and they expect to take care of their followers. This includes not only specific leadership activities but also every aspect of life. Leaders are like fathers or family members who make sure that the followers' needs are met and that they are protected. Leaders must have the attitude of a listener and know their followers. Eventually one of the greatest characteristics of this relationship is that the leader should be ready to give up his or her life for the follower. This type of relationship is very different from what is expected from a business relationship in North America or Europe. It is very demanding and is follower-centered. Jesus is the ultimate model of how to care for followers, especially in his willingness to die for his sheep.

Seventh, the references to piety depict North African leaders deeply attached to God. This is not only evidenced by the love, intimacy and faith they express in God but also in their submission to Him in their daily walk.

North African leaders spend much time in prayer and fasting and immerse themselves in the Word of God. Also, North African leadership is characterized by numerous references to the work of the Holy Spirit. The majority of the leaders insist that leadership cannot take place without a Spirit-filled life and ministry.

Eighth, leadership skills have only been briefly mentioned. The main leadership skills that emerge in this research which will help me define leadership styles are: (1) the definitions of leading as walking in front of others and pointing toward the destination, (2) accepting responsibility, something that nearly every leader expressed, (3) teaching, which is currently one of the greatest needs in North Africa, and (4) being a visionary. Surprisingly, management is not a leadership skill that is currently identified by leaders.

Ninth, three leadership metaphors have been identified by North African church leaders: father, servant and shepherd. My task in the next chapter will be to find out whether these metaphors contain the same elements as the leadership styles with the same name. This will be very useful in identifying which values, behaviors and qualities collected in this chapter support these leadership styles.

As I conclude this chapter, I remind the reader that the data for this research is based on fifty respondents. Although my conclusions may appear to generalize my findings, it is only valid for the sample of respondents I chose. In a first-generation church, I was only able to identify a few dozen leaders and consequently it is important to keep in mind that this research is only the beginning stages. Many more interviews and questionnaires must be conducted in order to find values, qualities, behaviors and metaphors that reflect the entire population of North Africa. It was however encouraging to find certain agreements on the various leadership characteristics. For example, over thirty North Africans quoted "love" as an important leadership quality. As a result, my future research will certainly probe this quality by including it in a survey questionnaire.

CHAPTER 8

Integration and Implications

In this chapter, I present the integration and implications of this descriptive and evaluative research. The central research issue for this study stated, "What are common leadership styles for North African religious leaders, from historical and cultural perspectives and their influence on their congregations and society for the good?" I first explain here how I compared the values, attributes and behaviors given by North African leaders with the leadership styles from current leadership theories to define four common styles in the North African church. I then explain how comparing the four common leadership styles of North African church leaders with values, attributes and behaviors of religious, cultural and historical leaders (see chapters 4, 5 and 6) help me address the goal of this study, which is to recommend North African church leadership styles that are culturally relevant, biblically sound and influence congregations and society for the good. Finally, I make some recommendations about the use of these leadership styles in the current church.

As a methodology for identifying the styles I designed a table for each where I compare the leadership characteristics (i.e. leadership values, attributes and behaviors) given by the North African church leaders with those that define leadership styles from current leadership theories (see chapter 2). The four tables below are more accurately summarized and the characteristics presented in greater detail in the respective chapters dealing with North African church leadership, secular leadership theories, and religious, cultural and historical leadership.

I designed another table (see Comparative Table of Leadership Characteristics in appendix 10) which includes a comprehensive list of characteristics given by church leaders and compares them with the set characteristics of secular, religious, cultural and historical styles I studied in this research. This last table is designed in such a way that it can be expanded in the future with the responses from a greater sample of respondents to see whether there are other church characteristics that can be found matching those of the various styles I studied in text-based research. I assume that some existing gaps in this table will be filled by later research. The advantage of such a table is that it provides an initial instrument to compare and contrast characteristics from church leaders with religious, cultural and historical styles already defined in the preceding chapters.

The Sheikhocratic Leadership Style

The first leadership style identified by this research is the *sheikhocratic* style. Let me say from the outset that although the characteristics resemble those that define the *sheikhocratic* style from the cultural and historical research, they are not completely identical. Furthermore, none of the church respondents used the word "sheikh" to describe their leadership. However, since characteristics from the sheikh were found in nearly every leadership style in Middle Eastern and North African culture, and because it was modeled by the influential historical leaders Amir Abd el-Kader and Ben Badis, I assumed I would also find it in the church.

My presuppositions were further supported by the fact that secular leadership theorists have identified the *sheikhocratic* leadership style in Middle Eastern and North African countries. Unfortunately, they have not yet developed a methodology to measure it. In light of the limited methodology, I developed the table below that compares the leadership characteristics of the North African church leaders with the leadership characteristics of the *sheikhocratic* leadership style from secular and religious theories. The commonalities discovered led me to conclude that some forms of *sheikhocratic* leadership style exist in the church.

In table 16 I summarize the leadership characteristics of a sheikh from my text-based studies of *sheikhocratic* leadership in the literature, North African culture and historical research, and then compare them with the

TABLE 16: Comparing Church Leadership with the Sheikhocratic Leadership Style

(Farida Saïdi)

Sheikhocratic Leadership Style	North African Church Leadership Characteristics compared with *Sheikhocracy*
Arbitration	No
Autocratic-Consultative	Yes
Behavior Modeling	Yes
Caretaking	Yes
Charisma	Yes
Communication	Yes
Courage	Yes
Father	Yes
Feeding	Yes
Generosity	Yes
Honor and Shame	No
Hospitable	Yes
Humble	Yes
Justice	Yes
Listening	Yes
Loyal	Yes
Patience	Yes
Protective	Yes
Relational	Yes
Self-Sacrifice	Yes
Shepherd	Yes
Support Followers	Yes
Wisdom	Yes

characteristics collected in North Africa to assess the existence of this style in the church.[1] I discovered that a great majority of the characteristics of

---

1. See chapter 2 for a study of *sheikhocracy* in current leadership literature, chapter 5

sheikhocracy are found in the church. This should not be surprising since this style can be found in the society and in influential historical leaders. However, one should be careful is comparing characteristics because church leaders look to the Bible more than to society to shape their leadership. Similar characteristics in this table may have different meanings when used in a biblical context. Future research should test for the meaning of these characteristics in the context of the church.

Caretaking Characteristics

The table above shows the leader as follower-oriented as evidenced by the characteristics of caretaking, being like a father, feeding, generosity, being protective and supportive. The sheikh, the family leaders, and the Arabo-Berber manager are all caretakers of their followers. Likewise, with an overwhelming majority, church leaders said that they must be caretakers of their followers. An important task of the sheikh is to care for the daily needs of the tribe. I have found that church leaders are also deeply concerned by the needs of their followers. One of the biblical examples they favor that has parallels with the sheikh is Moses. They describe him as the leader who "carries his people" (Q. 35) which shows that leaders are protectors of those they lead. This same approach is highlighted by the family leadership style, where a combination of care, love and protection characterizes the family leaders. This way of leading is further illustrated at the work place, where the boss is a paternalistic figure—one who cares for the daily needs of the employees. Augustine and Lavigerie also displayed these qualities, which indicates that leaders influenced by biblical principles can display this style.

Autocratic-Consultative Leadership Style

The sheikh leadership style includes personal autocracy and the practice of consultation. His power is tempered by the consideration for the community and the law. In patriarchal societies, it resembles the leadership style of the father, although within the family the focus is not so much on consultation.

---

for a description of the Middle Eastern and North African sheikh and chapter 6 for the *sheikhocratic* leadership style of Ibn Badis and Abd el-Kader.

I have already discussed in the above section the importance that church leaders lay on consultation. In leadership theory this style requires "embeddedness" (Neal and Finfey 2007). Embeddedness, in turn, requires the skill of listening. North African leaders made ample reference to the behavior of "listening." As I heard their concern about listening to followers, the image of the sheikh inviting the followers to his tent came to my mind. Perhaps the church leaders had a different kind of listening in mind as in the servant type of listening. I wonder to what extent the practice of "embeddedness" is similar to that of "incognito inquiry"[2] practiced by leaders in Shi'i Islam?

It is important to remember that church leaders have a very unique way of understanding authority that may differ from the sheikh. Informants reported that authority should combine good communication, humility, no domination, good sense, servanthood, spirituality, caretaking, the fruits of the Spirit, trust, a capacity to listen, no manipulation, and no verbal abuse. They also believe authority must not be imposed but won and that a bad leader should be confronted. Interestingly, the sheikh also displays some of these attributes even though existing leadership theory labels them as autocratic. This enables me to posit that the term "autocratic" cannot be defined solely by "absolute power" but must be tempered by the above qualities and behaviors that give it a unique form in the North African context. This combination of power and consideration, care and love for the followers, is best expressed in the leadership of the grandparents described in chapter 5. They represent the best picture of humans with absolute authority, who submit to God and the religious laws, the customs and community and at the same time show love, tenderness and care. Perhaps there should be a style called grandparent leadership!

Charismatic-Visionary Leadership style

Another distinctiveness of the sheikh is its charismatic leadership style. Sheikh Amir Abd-el Kader provides a perfect example of this type of

---

2. As I explained earlier, in "incognito inquiry" the leader dresses as a poor person and mingles with his followers to listen to what they say about his leadership. However, this form of listening unfortunately reveals that there is not much trust between the leader and the follower. The leader expects the followers to hide their true feelings about him or her and therefore has to come in disguise to find out the truth about his leadership.

leadership. I posit that this style can also be found in church leadership in North Africa. Although not every leader may be charismatic in the religious sense, there is a clear tendency to emphasize visionary leadership and the attraction of followers by emotional and spiritual characteristics especially in times of crisis. This style has also been evidenced in the political sphere and at the workplace in my research. Therefore, there is strong support in this research for a charismatic-visionary leadership style, which will be further discussed below on the Holy Man Leadership Style.

Community-Oriented

The sheikh is very relational and community-oriented as he cares for the individual and communal needs of his or her followers. I saw earlier that there is high in-group collectivism in Middle Eastern leadership (Punnett and Shenkar 2004: 308). Likewise, church leaders also emphasize this style in that they value people-orientedness, sharing, solidarity, and a high degree of humanness rather than task-orientedness. The quality of the bond between people and followers is very important to them. They are very close to their followers and call them companions, brothers and family. This characteristic of leadership is also strongly supported in the family context. All leaders are required to keep the unity and cohesiveness of the group. Although church leaders have illustrated that they are community-oriented, their responses do not indicate their practices favor the cohesiveness of the group over the needs of the individuals. I believe that this is a key issue for future study since very few Western theories focus on the equilibrium between the needs of a group and the needs of individuals.

One aspect of the communal bond that differs between Muslim and Christian contexts however is the issue of blood ties. There are no references to blood ties in the church. This is a major difference with the traditional sheikh's community or tribe in which the group is united around a common ancestor. Likewise, at the work place in Arabo-Berber contexts the practice of *clientèlisme* and nepotism (*wasta*) favor family, tribal or personal ties. The unique aspect of the contemporary church in North Africa is that it draws people from various backgrounds together. This may change the leadership dynamics and the type of leadership practices drawn from cultural context where blood ties, *clientèlisme* and nepotism are prevalent and can be used in churches in which members are not all relatives. But even with these differences it is evident that there is a strong emphasis of community in the North African church leadership style. I would like to borrow here the word *'assabya* (group cohesiveness) that the sociologist Ibn Khaldun used and I described earlier. It is the term that describes best what I can see in the church. It could become a very unique way to describe the ties within the community and with the leader.

Competence

In Middle Eastern and North African leadership, leaders are expected to be competent (Kabasakal and Bodur 2002). This competence includes courage, loyalty, generosity, hospitality, humility, patience, wisdom, and trust. As is the case with family leaders, the sheikh is also expected to act as a guide, a shepherd and a protector.

There are several characteristics that appear to be similar but might be understood differently in the church and the culture. For example, pastors rank humility very high, not because it is a component of Muslim leadership and *sheikhocracy*, but because Jesus is the definitive role model of humility. Lavigerie and Augustine also exemplified this quality. Humility as described by church leaders was difficult to compare and contrast with references in Islam. Part of the reason is that Muslims prefer the word modesty or moderation. In future research we need to find out what humility means when used in the Islamic and North African cultural context. Likewise, it will also be important to probe the difference between meekness supported in the church and the emphasis on virility, strength and nobility in North African religious and cultural leadership.

Another example of a shared characteristic that may be interpreted differently is patience. This value ranked third after love and humility in the list of church leadership attributes. This is not surprising since patience is a key value both in Muslim leadership and in honor- and shame-based cultures. It was important for me to see that culture is reflected in church leadership. However, before asserting that patience is an effective leadership attribute one must study it more carefully in the Bible.[3] Culture may not be the best standard for transformational leadership.

The notion of accepting responsibilities is a common quality between church leaders and cultural leaders. Church leaders are responsible persons and imitate Abraham and Moses as their role models. These match the paternalistic, the *sheikhocratic* and the North African fatherhood leadership styles where the leader is expected to accept responsibilities. Future research may identify what system holds leaders accountable. Interestingly, church leaders are the only ones who used the term "accountability."

Behavior modeling is another characteristic that is strongly supported by both the church and culture. It is illustrated in the sheikh, the family and the work model. But as we saw earlier, it can also be found in religious leadership styles. One of the leadership styles that clearly stood out in the church data is the fact that leaders lead by being examples. Actions speak louder than words in the North African church, which is a prime example of a contextual practice. Leaders do not deny the use of words, but instead influence others by matching their actions with their words. In the West, although the actions of leaders are important, the emphasis is placed on verbal communication. Training programs developed in the West should include behavior modeling if they want to be effective in a North African context.

Finally some characteristics do not show up in the church list and may be revealed by future research. First, honor and shame were not clearly mentioned in the responses. It may be that these are simply underlining assumptions that shape leadership and therefore don't need to be explicitly addressed. Second, the practice of arbitration, which is of significant importance in the cultural context as evidenced by the sheikh, the grandparents, and the mother, seems to be absent. I was surprised not to find it in the responses of the church leaders. Since the Bible also encourages peacemaking and arbitration, I see nothing that should prevent this quality from being present in the church. Furthermore, it is a model that is very relevant to the cultural context.

---

3. I remind the reader that my research did not include the study of leadership values in the Scripture.

Paternalistic Leadership Style

The paternalistic style has been identified as an important style in the Middle East (Dorfman 2004). It includes as quoted earlier, "strong hierarchical authority, subordination of efficiency to human relations and personal connections, and sporadic conformity to rules and regulations contingent on the personality and power of those who make them" (Dorfman and House 2004: 63-64). I have not found the exact same definition in church leadership but found a clear link with the following statement: "tribal traditions oblige business leaders to behave like fathers, protecting and nurturing employees as they would their children and taking responsibility for the whole business" (Thomas and Kerr 2004: 127).[4] What further supports the idea that church leaders are like fathers to their followers is that over one third of the respondents used the image of the father to describe leadership. I recommend to further research this style that I suggest could be a combination of the paternalistic style and fatherhood in the Berbero-Arab context, which would also draw characteristics from the fatherhood of God in the Bible. This would mean taking elements of the paternalistic leadership style, and adding the affective qualities and behaviors illustrated by the leadership of the North African father, as well as the fatherhood of God illustrated in his relationship with Christ. But for now the sheikh is a better generic term, although it includes a lot of qualities of the father. What the father is to his family, the sheikh is to the tribe.

Strengths and Weaknesses of the *Sheikhocratic* Leadership Style

The strength of this style is that it is culturally relevant making it one of the natural leadership styles of the North African context. In every strata of the society there are elements of the *sheikhocratic* leadership style. It is one of the contextual styles clearly identified by leadership researchers in the GLOBE study (see chapter 2). It contains values that are also reflected in the Bible such as caretaking, generosity or hospitality, although there might

---

4. Also compare with this statement: "Tribal traditions influence all aspects of life and, as a consequence, managers are expected to act as fathers—viewing their role in a highly personalized manner characterized by providing and caring for employees and favoring individuals within the family and tribe over outsiders" (House et al. 2004: 63).

be differences in how these words are understood in their respective contexts. This style has the advantage of being people-oriented and thus has the potential to be transformative. It meets the requirements of contingency theory that I chose for this research in addressing the needs of the followers.[5] *Sheikhocracy* also expects the leader to listen to followers and their needs. Finally, this style is akin to the leadership style of Old Testament leaders such as Abraham or Moses. It is not surprising since these leaders operated in a tribal context, which is the similar to the one that shaped the *sheikhocratic* style.[6] It is much easier for people in a traditional North African context to understand and identify with the leadership styles of Moses or Abraham than it is for a Western Christian. This style strongly supports contingency theory, which posits that the context shapes leadership styles.

But there are also a number of weaknesses that need to be addressed. As I explained in chapter 2 and 5, the sheikh influences followers and includes them in decision making by following an autocratic-consultative model. The advantage is that everyone is listened to. The weakness is that not every leader has the gift of articulating a decision in which all followers feel that their arguments have been taken into account and the decision is for the good of the group. Authoritarian leadership can easily trump the consultative process when the leader does not have the heart of a servant.

The *sheikhocratic* leadership style fits well with a tribal model. But can the church be equated to a tribe? There are at least two reasons why I believe the tribal model is not the ideal one for today. First, North African society has changed. In the introduction I showed how the extended family has replaced the tribe in the North African context. It is not surprising that I found that the *sheikhocratic* leadership style has strong components of the paternalistic leadership style. This makes sense since the grandfathers and the fathers are the successors of the sheikh in modern societies.

Second, the biblical church model is not synonymous with the tribal one. Instead the Bible encourages believers to embrace people from different

---

5. Remember that contingency theory states that leadership must take into consideration not just the leader, as previous theories did, but also the follower and the context.

6. Sheikh is the title of tribal leaders in traditional Bedouin societies in the Middle East.

societal and family contexts. If the church takes the shape of a tribe, how will it be able to impact society and not become inwardly focused?

The *sheikhocratic* leadership model also poses a problem to the church's emerging leaders. In a tribal system, the successor of the tribe is usually the son or a close relative. How does the development of leaders work given this model? While lessons may be learned from Old Testament leaders the key question is whether this is an acceptable model for the current church? This issue needs to be discussed further because it has direct implications for the legitimacy of leaders.

Most church leaders tend to study the nature of God in order to better understand leadership. For example, the servanthood and shepherd models draw directly from the relationship between Jesus and God. Even though I react to this idea, future research should explore whether the Bible presents God as a sheikh. After all, God was never a tribal God. He is the ruler of the entire world. But it is possible that North African brothers and sisters might learn from some characteristics of God that are similar to a sheikh: the sense of hospitality, generosity, listening, and so forth.

Finally, this style should not be limited to men. There are many examples in society and the church where women played the role of a *sheikha* (female sheikh). North African history reports the life of the influential Kahina in its Berber regions. Female church leaders in North Africa have also been significant in the growth of the church. Future research should look more closely at the characteristics of the sheikha and their role in influencing society and church for good.

The Servant Leadership Style

The second style that this research highlights is servant leadership. This style has a theoretical framework developed by Robert K. Greenleaf (1977) and his disciples who emphasized that leaders placed the wellbeing of the followers over their own. They defined eleven characteristics of servant leadership as follows: calling, listening, empathy, healing, awareness, persuasion, conceptualization, foresight, stewardship, growth, and building community. After Greenleaf published his research, many church leaders around the world have readily implemented his findings to various church contexts, especially since servanthood seems to resonate well with biblical concepts. Islam leadership theory has also adopted this style. I have compared and contrasted the eleven characteristics of this leadership style with the North African church leadership data to determine whether North African church leaders are servants according to Greenleaf's theory.

Greenleaf's Categories

In the table below I list the eleven characteristics of Greenleaf's Servant Leadership model and compared them with the characteristics collected in North Africa.

TABLE 17: Comparing Church Leadership with the Servant Leadership Style (Farida Saïdi)

Greenleaf's Servant Leadership Style	North African Church Leadership Characteristics
Awaress	No
Building Community	Yes
Conceptualization	No
Commitment to Growth of Followers	Yes
Empathy	Yes
Foresight	Yes
Healing	Yes
Humility	Yes
Listening	Yes
Persuasion	No
Stewardship	No

Four characteristics from Greenleaf's model are poorly supported by the data from my field research. They are (1) awareness with a few references to "being sensitive" and "perception,"[7] (2) conceptualization, (3) persuasion,

---

7. Greenleaf (1977: 40) describes awareness as "opening wide the doors of perception so as to enable one to get more of what is available of sensory experience and other signals from the environment than people usually take in."

and (4) stewardship. Further research may show that they exist in North African leadership but have not been listed by my sample of respondents.

Seven attributes from Greenleaf's model are supported by the data from my field research, although the terminology may differ. They are (1) humility, (2) community building, (3) empathy,[8] (4) foresight, (5) healing, (6) listening,[9] and (7) commitment to growth of the followers. All these characteristics should be revisited with the informants in order to determine whether their meanings in North Africa are different from Greenleaf's definitions. For example, North Africans are naturally community-oriented and are not in need of Greenleaf's reminder that this is an important characteristic.[10]

Even though the informants do not always use the same terms as Greenleaf they do use words that are close enough that I have accepted them as a relevant. For example, North African leaders never use the word empathy yet I checked the "empathy" column in the table above because they use words such as love, compassion, kindness, pleasant, tenderness, gentleness, mercy, forgiveness, benevolence, have a heart, and graceful—all of which somehow reflect empathy. In a future study I would like to evaluate how the thirty respondents understand the relationship between love and emphathy.

Another example omitted is the characteristic of "foresightedness." According to Greenleaf (2002: 38) "prescience, or foresight, is a better than average guess about what is going to happen when in the future." The fact that eleven informants used the word "discernment" and a few "prophecy" shows there is support for this concept in church leadership. Finally,

---

8. According to Greenleaf (1977: 33), empathy is "the imaginative projection of one's own consciousness into another being." He adds, "the servant always accepts and empathizes, never rejects" (2002: 33). Empathy is closely related to "tolerance of imperfection" and "acceptance" (Greenleaf 1977: 34-35)

9. According to Greenleaf, "a true natural servant automatically responds to any problem by listening first." (1977: 31). He expands by saying, "true listening builds strength in other people' (1977: 31). Listening is also an attribute in Muslim leadership and in *sheikocracy*. I discussed the references related to "listening" from the North African church leaders in the section on *sheikhocracy*.

10. I did not ask any leader about the theory of leadership they knew. I suspect they may have heard about servanthood leadership but have not studied it in detail. This may explain why church leadership did not quote the eleven categories.

healing was absent but I decided that there was enough evidence of caretaking, love, encouragement and transformational practices in the responses of the church leaders, to include it in the list of common attributes.

Biblical "Servant"

I intentionally searched for a style that expressed servanthood because more than half of the respondents used the word "servant" spontaneously in the interviews and questionnaires. It is one of the key metaphors used by church leaders to describe their leadership style. When I noticed the frequency with which it was referenced I decided to investigate servant leadership and discovered Greenleaf's theory very valuable for this purpose. Further support for choosing the servant leadership styles comes from the fact that leaders ranked love as the first leadership quality closely followed by humility. The virtue of humility[11] is a core value of Greenleaf's theory of servant leadership. It is also expressed in the attitude of Jesus when he washed the feet of his disciples (Jn 13), a story often recounted by North African leaders.

There are however several caveats in using Greenleaf's categories. First, church leaders do not know Greenleaf's theory and may have used the characteristics of servant leadership with a different understanding altogether. Second, the biblical passages quoted in this research seem to indicate that church leaders drew their definitions of servanthood from the Bible and not from secular theories. Third, I cannot prove whether servant leadership is an ideal longed for or whether it actually permeates their behaviors. This can only be verified if I measure the behaviors of leaders and interview their followers.

Thus, I believe there is enough evidence from the data that the informants desire to be servant leaders. Using Greenleaf's model, the evaluation of their leadership characteristics demonstrates that their style closely

---

11. In their discussion on servant leadership, Hale and Dail (2007: 398) say that humble leaders are "more concerned about followers receiving recognition for their achievements than receiving accolades for his or her successes." They contend that this is better achieved in lower power-distance cultures' emphasis on "recognition and rewards for follower achievement" which is better appreciated than in cultures with high levels of power distance where "followers may view leaders as a different type of person, without whom achievements in an organization might not be possible" (Hale and Dail 2007: 398).

mirrors the servant leadership style developed by this author. However, the North African church leaders do not point to Greenleaf as a reference but instead look to the Bible for resources on servant leadership. I recommend as a next step to this research to measure how these characteristics are applied in the leaders' ministries.

Strengths and Challenges of the Servant Leadership Style

The strength of using the Servant Leadership Style is that there are many references to servanthood in the Bible. Church leaders can draw resources from the model of servanthood portrayed by Jesus or Paul. The connection made by Jesus between influencing others and serving them is clearly evidenced in John 13. Likewise, the characteristics of servant leadership are further highlighted throughout both Old and New Testaments. The example of the suffering servant in Isaiah 52 and 53 reveals that an interface between leadership and servanthood already existed. Furthermore Augustine and Lavigerie were historical leaders that strongly supported this style. These are valuable examples and models for the church today.

It is encouraging to see that the North African church takes its cues from the Bible and not from secular theories. In doing so, the servant leadership style embodies unique components that do not exist in Greenleaf's model. For example, while biblical love is the key characteristic that North African leaders adopt it is not clearly stated in secular theories of servanthood. Finally, this style being developed is derived from biblical metaphors, which highlight the spiritual component of leadership, which is key to my research.

There are nevertheless a number of challenges to be addressed regarding this style. The context of honor and shame as well as the patriarchal system is certainly not conducive to a servant leadership model. A servant does not maintain a position of influence in Middle Eastern society and therefore is not a model that is very attractive. This style clearly requires people to either adopt the Upside-Down Kingdom approach from Donald B. Kraybill (2003) or investigate the concepts of powerlessness in leadership.

I have found an intriguing way that leaders integrate servanthood in an honor and shame culture. In my observation of the leadership of several pastors over a few decades I have discovered that the combination of seniority and wisdom changes their style and reflects many characteristics of servanthood. It may be that servanthood has different meanings in different context. The challenge lies in finding concepts that are not negating the biblical teaching and models.

It is not always easy to discern if people talk about servanthood in an idealistic manner or if they have actually developed practices of servanthood in their leadership. In chapter 2, I discussed the challenges of adopting Greenleaf's theory in cultural contexts that are different from those in the West. I believe that the more case studies collected and analyzed regarding practical applications of this style in different contexts, the more it will become relevant cross-culturally. On the other hand, it is true that in any culture it is difficult to adopt this style in the leadership context. There are very few cultures in the world—maybe none—where being a servant is a role people aspire to take. Therefore, those who strive for the servant leadership model will need to define very clearly how to assess this role in leadership and how to train people to adopt this style. I believe that Greenleaf has not provided yet a convincing argument for the church. The integration of servant characteristics with leadership characteristics will continue to be a challenge for every culture. I have not demonstrated in this research that North African leaders practice servant leadership. I have only demonstrated that church leaders consider servanthood as an ideal leadership model for their context.

Another challenge this style poses is how much it impacts society. The sheikh seems to have a greater impact on society than the servant. However, in Muslim societies sheikhs display some of the same characteristics inherent to servanthood such as listening, healing, humility or encouraging the growth of the followers. There is therefore some overlap between the two. But the difference of perception certainly becomes evident when the model of Jesus who washes the feet of his disciples is compared with the sheikh who himself has servants to perform this task. Thus, servanthood could become a prophetic transformational model in the North African society as it was during the time of Jesus in Palestine.

But a serious investigation of what constitutes a servant leader must continually be explored if the North African church is to avoid misconceptions. In effect, what does submission and servanthood mean in the religious and cultural context of North Africa? According to the Qur'an, Muslims must submit to God. Does submission to God in the Bible have the same meaning? How does this affect the conception of submission and servanthood in the church?

Greenleaf notes that the servant leader is servant first. The question this leadership style raises is how can and on what basis do people prioritize a passion to serve others over against the need to elevates oneself to a certain position. This is certainly not unique to the North African context as people around the world struggle with this. In regards to my context, it is certainly more rewarding to be a sheikh than to be a servant. But a sheikh who has not a servant heart and attitude certainly cannot pass the test given in John 13. On the other hand, drawing solely from servanthood models in contemporary society may not be the best idea. What Jesus had in mind was a very unique model of servanthood. I am encouraged that the North African church leaders seek a model from a biblical perspective. At the same time, I hope that they will engage in serious exegetical and hermeneutical work to understand what Jesus means for their own context. They also draw resources from the Old Testament, which is helpful and insightful because many texts highlight the characteristics of servanthood, including the suffering servant of Isaiah 53 and the story of Joseph. In doing so they may expand the list of characteristics of servant leadership beyond what Greenleaf has provided.

The Shepherd Leadership Style

The third leadership style identified in this research is the Shepherd Leadership Style. This style is not unfamiliar to biblical leadership theorists—as Laniak and Gan have extensively researched it (see chapter 2). I compare here the characteristics of the shepherd leadership style defined by these two authors with the characteristics collected in my field research to illustrate that this style exists in North African church leadership.

Shepherd Metaphor

When analyzing the data from the church, I was struck by the overwhelming number of references to shepherding; in fact over half of the respondents cited it. Furthermore, nine respondents quoted John 10 were Jesus is portrayed as a shepherd. Half of the respondents stated that their leadership model is Jesus, the shepherd.

As a result, I investigated leadership theories to see if there was such a thing as a shepherd leadership style. While I found some supporting evidence in Islamic leadership theory I discovered stronger support for it in biblical resources. Although several attributes of the shepherd are similar to the sheikh, I intentionally want to separate the two. In effect, when church leaders referred to the shepherd they always used biblical categories of shepherding.

Why did the metaphor of the shepherd clearly emerge in the interviews and questionnaires? Did the respondents know the work of Gan or Laniak? My assumption is that they did not know this literature. Three other possible reasons may be presented. First, over a third of the respondents quoted John 10 and Psalm 23 as key texts for their leadership and the shepherd metaphor is a central element of these two passages. Thus, leaders may have been shaped by the teaching of Jesus and sought to model him, as is a normal practice in North African contexts: followers should imitate the behaviors of the leader. Second, it is possible that church leaders conceived of the metaphor of a non-biblical shepherd is their mind and unconsciously matched it with John 10. This would make sense since shepherds still roam the hills and fields of the regions where these pastors serve. Their cultural and social environment may be more conducive to adopting this imagery from the Bible than it is for those who live in urban areas. To further strengthen this argument, one pastor I interviewed was an actual shepherd before becoming a full time church leader. Third, there are some references in the Hadith about Muslim leaders being shepherds and as a result this concept may have influenced church leaders via the Muslim worldview.

Shepherd Style Characteristics

I compare here the data from North African church leadership with the biblical leadership style defined by two theorists (Gan 2007, Laniak 2007).

According to Laniak the shepherd has two major roles: provision and protection. The data collected in my field research shows that North African leader display these roles. The table I created by studying Laniak has over thirty-five characteristics. I did not find all of them in my primary research. But those listed in the table below are a good summary of what Laniak described. These seven characteristics listed below were all found in the North African church. This is why I can confidently affirm that the Shepherd Leadership style exists in the North African Church.

TABLE 18: Comparing Church Leadership with the Shepherd Leadership Style

(Farida Saïdi)

Shepherd Leadership Style (Gan and Laniak)	North African Church Leadership Style
Caretaking	Yes
Feeding	Yes
Healing	Yes
Justice	Yes
Leading	Yes
Protecting	Yes
Self-Sacrifice	Yes

My first remark concerning this style is that the word caretaking was used by two-thirds of the respondents (see table on caretaking in chapter 7). For North African church leaders, taking care of others, whether it is the followers, the family or society, is highly valued. It shows that leaders are deeply concerned with the needs of their followers. I have already discussed this characteristic of leadership in the *sheikhocratic* leadership style but here this characteristic is embedded in the metaphor of the shepherd illustrated by the church leaders' statement: "the good shepherd cares for his sheep." The leaders care for others as the Biblical shepherd cares for his sheep.

Second, respondents often used the verb "feeding." This category matches with the category "feed my sheep" listed under Laniak's shepherd leadership style. I also found it in the *sheikocratic* leadership style where I listed it under caretaking. I propose that "feeding" should be related to the poorly supported characteristic of "growth" from servant leadership. I would then move "growth" to the strongly supported characteristic category, which would further bolster my argument that servant leadership exists in the North African church.

Third, respondents often used the expression "leading" to talk about the activity of a shepherd. They also quoted Moses who led his people through the desert. This gave me some very useful information on the way leaders understand their role. Here the shepherd expresses concepts such as "moving toward," "standing in the front," and "knowing the destination." This concept could stem from the model of the Muslim imam who stands in front of the believers to lead prayer. There is no desire for standing above others but rather just one step ahead of believers and under God. But my assumption is that North African leaders actually draw this image from biblical models such as Abraham or Moses.

Third, a shepherd is seen as the one who protects. Moses is described as the leader who "carries his people" (Q. 35). Laniak refers to this behavior frequently when he lists characteristics such as "facing the lions," "gatekeeper," "guarding" or "the rod" (see chapter 2). Likewise, church leaders consider these as important leadership behaviors. This is yet another example of a category that is found both in the *sheikhocratic* and shepherd leadership styles. My guess that the reason for the overlap is that traditional sheikh*s* often had flocks they tended to. Likewise in the Bible, this was a common activity that perhaps influenced the way leaders talked about their leadership. As I indicated earlier, it may be that North African church leaders who grew up in a culture where shepherding is still a common professional activity are more familiar with the shepherding image than church leaders in other parts of the world.

Finally, a major characteristic of the biblical metaphor of shepherding is that it includes self-sacrifice. When church leaders used the shepherd image they always included the fact that a shepherd, just like Jesus, must be ready to die for his or her followers. The historical North African leader Augustine exemplified this very fact when he said that he was ready to die for his sheep (chapter 6). Moses and Paul are also quoted as saying they were ready to give up their life for followers. To church leaders, however, Jesus the shepherd remains the greatest leadership model in this area.

This is a very important characteristic of church leaders' perspective on leadership. I believe that the concept and practice of self-giving must be studied in more depth because it seems to be lacking in other parts of the world. A French or American pastor may not say from the pulpit, "I am ready to give up my life for you" whereas North African pastors affirm that they will. I do wonder to what extent this is an ideal value, or whether it is a common practice. I assume that North African leaders are deeply impacted by Jesus' teaching on this issue because they often quote him. How all of this relates to practical pastoral theology needs to be further investigated. Also, it would be helpful to understand how a context shapes the notion of "giving-up one's life" and its relationship to the many references of "self-sacrifice" in the *sheikhocratic* leadership and religious leadership style.

Strengths and Challenges of the Shepherd Leadership Style

There are many advantages in using the shepherd leadership style in the North African church context as this metaphor is tremendously relevant. Most Western people have never seen an actual shepherd in their neighborhood while in North Africa it is commonplace. Several pastors I interviewed have actually been shepherds. As a result, the shepherding metaphor is attractive for cultural reasons. It directly addresses the following three components of contingency theory: the relationship to followers, the relationship to context and to God.

More than any other, the shepherd leadership style highlights the closeness and intimacy between leader and follower. The leader takes care of every need of the follower even to the point of providing physical nourishment. Of course this is a metaphorical image, but it does underline the strong tie that exists between leader and follower.

Finally the shepherding metaphor has the advantage of identifying the leader as one who both serves and leads the group. The way this is carried out in practice may be debated but the fact that the shepherd gives clear directions is something that church leaders value.

There are also a number of challenges that must be addressed if this style is implemented in the church. In a shame and honor culture, the core characteristics of shepherdhood are not particularly attractive as he is usually uneducated and lives a predominantly solitary life. This image might not appeal to someone who is seeking to impact society.

Like with the Servant Leadership Style, a closer examination of the biblical text may highlight characteristics that do not first appear (see chapter 2). The Old Testament portrays the shepherd as someone who is chosen by God for an important task, which may more positively resonate with the honor and shame culture. I therefore recommend the church takes a closer look at the shepherding metaphor of the Old Testament in order to gain additional resources implementing this style in a way that will impact the society and church for good. In order to avoid the danger of using this metaphor as an idealized style, I recommend churches develop best practices of shepherding from a biblical perspective.

In many areas, this style overlaps with the *sheikhocratic* leadership style. The reason why I separated them is because the biblical metaphor of shepherding adds a strong spiritual element. Furthermore, the shepherd leadership style does not offer clear guidelines about decision-making and power. There is a danger for a shepherd involved in intense caregiving and guardianship to become overprotective of the flock. The shepherd must know how the followers can become mature in their faith and ministry without being overly dependent on the shepherd.

Finally, I am encouraged by the fact that North African leaders draw heavily on biblical texts to develop their styles. My study completely omitted exegetical work and so the only biblical evidence I collected came from the interviews. I recommend that the study of this leadership style will continue with greater emphasis on the biblical texts.

The Holy Man Leadership Style

In contrast with the three previous styles, where the characteristics were neatly identified and recorded by secular, Muslim or Christian leadership theorists, I established the following Holy Man leadership style list following extensive research on the religious context in North Africa. These characteristics emerged from interviews and text-based research I conducted in the church (chapter 7), in Islam (chapter 4), in biblical and Qur'anic leadership theories (chapter 2), in traditional religious leadership in North Africa (chapter 5) and in Christian and Muslim historical leadership styles (chapter 6). When I compared the list of the church respondents with biblical models and patterns from their socio-religious context I found strong elements of spirituality and piety. The most helpful way to identify this category is the "Holy Man" style because it corresponds to a religious leader who is close to God and to his followers, has supernatural gifts, is charismatic, a visionary and is divinely chosen. Thus I borrowed this concept from a traditional North African religious model because it has also biblical relevance.

TABLE 19: Comparing Church Leadership with the
Holy Man Leadership Style

(Farida Saïdi)

Holy Man	North African Church Leadership Style
Divine and Human Election	Yes
Autocratic-Consultative	Yes
Charismatic-Visionary	Yes
Piety/Spirituality	Yes
Competence	Yes

Divine and Human Legitimacy

The Muslim community refers to the divine and human election of a leader, as do North African church leaders.[12] Despite these similarities there are also clear differences. First, the understanding of the nature of the God is different between the two faiths. Second, while the concept of anointing is present in both, Christians believe that leaders are anointed by the Holy Spirit whereas Muslims do not. An interesting study would be to compare and contrast signs and wonders as factors of legitimacy in Christian leadership with spiritual power as an element in the leadership of a *marabout*.

Third, Islamic *marabouts* and *kahin* gain their legitimacy through their lineage. Few Christians, however, believe that lineage is important in order

---

12. Only a few talk about being self-appointed.

to become a leader. In this regard, they are similar to the orthodox who obtain legitimacy from the knowledge of the texts. I am surprised however that so few Christian leaders quoted "knowledge" as a characteristic of leadership. In Muslim leadership literature, knowledge of the Qur'an and Islamic law is one of the most prominent criteria for leadership.

Autocratic-Consultative Leadership Style

Islamic leadership includes an autocratic style in conjunction with a unique decision-making approach called consultation. This style does not match the autocratic, democratic and laissez-faire categories; it is in-between autocratic and democratic. The autocratic-consultative style emphasizes leaders' roles in decision-making while at the same time including followers in a participative process. I found similarities and differences when I compared the church context with that of Muslim leadership.

First, North African church leaders tend to have the same style, except that they may accentuate the consultative aspect more strongly and use Western sounding words such as collaboration, teamwork, or agreement. This may reveal their attempt to blend consensus, which is typical in their cultural context with Western teaching on democratic leadership styles.

It is surprising that not only did no one use the term "autocratic" for church leadership but that the informants actually condemned its use in the society. This could be explained in two different ways. First, leaders may have experienced abuse of power in culture or society and do not want to replicate it in the church. Second, the autocratic-consultative leadership style, which is commonly observed in Arab society, might be trumped in the church by concepts such as "servanthood," "giving up one's life for followers," or values such as love and humility. I am of the opinion that the two are not mutually exclusive. In the Old Testament, for example, there are several models of decision-making that are more similar to the autocratic-consultative leadership style than its democratic counterpart—the leadership of Moses being one example.

Second, Christian leaders believe that the authority of the leader must be subordinate to God's. The data collected highlighted that leaders put "God first," "obey God," "listen to God," or do "God's will." Likewise, Muslim religious leaders submit to God and the Qur'an but they also give much weight to Islamic laws to which they submit. Christian informants did not mention laws specifically, which may indicate their emphasis on doctrines and beliefs over legal matters.

Third, in North African contexts, religious education is also a means of power and influence. This is illustrated by the role of the *talib* and the passion Ibn Badis and Amir Abd el-Kader were required to impart knowledge. Christian leaders such as Augustine and Cardinal Lavigerie also had quite an elaborate pedagogical system. This aspect of power was weakly supported by the church respondents although some referenced the importance of teaching.

Fourth, in every Muslim leadership model there is a strong emphasis on competence. The exercise of power is directly linked to a leader's qualities and skills. It is noteworthy that this word was never mentioned in the interviews of church leaders. Reasons for its omission should be investigated in another study.

Finally, other distinct aspects of North African church leaders' decision-making patterns include the powerlessness of the leader, the role of the Holy Spirit and prayer.

Charismatic-Visionary Leadership Style

Both Muslim and Christian leadership styles emphasize a charismatic-visionary aspect. However each respective version is distinct; for example a secular understanding of charismatic leadership is quite different from a Christian one. The latter moves beyond extraordinary human capacities and includes the direct touch of the divine on the acts of a leader. My following comments will help explain how this style is displayed in the church.

First, there were a plethora of references to spiritual power in my field research. When North African leaders used the term charismatic, they essentially meant a leader who has the Holy Spirit and those spiritual fruits and gifts present in their lives. It would be interesting to compare and contrast the role of supernatural gifts with those of traditional spiritual leaders in Islam; the *marabout*, for example, is known for his *baraka* and supernatural power. As I stated before, I do not contend that these gifts and powers are the same in Islam and Christianity but what I find striking is the strong attraction in both cases. Since North African church leaders believe in supernatural manifestations and emphasize piety and closeness with God they have more similarities with leaders of popular Islam than they do with the orthodox. The latter understand charisma as a combination of textual knowledge, piety and miracles they perform.[13] On the contrary, popular religious leaders are known for their charisma, supernatural gifts and piety, as well as for their closeness to God.

Second, North African leaders are visionaries. Respondents used the term visionary in both a secular and spiritual sense. Leaders in orthodox and popular Islam are also visionaries but in their case the spiritual visions differ in nature as those in the church.

Third, while church leaders often talk about "prophecy" the word does not have the same meaning in both contexts. Future research should explore this concept as well as that of charisma. Finally, the research suggests that the charismatic-visionary leadership style is considered effective in the Muslim community, as illustrated by the leadership of Ibn Badis and Abd el-Kader, as well as in the church, and as illustrated by the life of Augustine and Lavigerie.

Piety

In orthodox Islam, the main attributes that define a leader's relationship to God come under the broader notion of *taqwa* (piety). The various categories that define Christian leaders' piety are (1) a deep attachment to God expressed by love, intimacy and faith; (2) Word-centeredness (3) dependence on the Holy Spirit, (4) prayer of worship and intercession, and (5) submission to God.

The first category, attachment to God, is supported in all branches of Islam. In fact, Abdel Kader is portrayed as being "close to God." The difference lies in the way both faiths achieve or portray that closeness with God. When analyzing the responses of church leaders, I was surprised to find that the expressions they used to describe their relationship with God

---

[13]. Muhammad, according to orthodox Islam, performed few miracles; orthodox religious leaders only see miracles as *mu'jiza* (supernatural) and not *karama* (charisma), a word used in popular Islam to describe the supernatural gifts and power that attract people to their leader.

were closer to those used by Sufi and popular leaders than by the orthodox ones. For example, Augustine was called a friend of God as was Amir Abd el-Kader.

The second category, Word-centeredness, is manifest in Muslim and Christian leaders with the primary difference being their sacred texts; for the former it is the Qur'an and the latter, the Bible.

The third category, dependence on the Holy Spirit, underscores a major difference between Muslim and Christian leadership. While church leaders overwhelmingly refer to the Holy Spirit, there is no reference to Him in Muslim leadership.

The fourth category, prayer, receives much support in Christianity as in Islam. Because prayer is one of the key practices of Islam, it is natural that church leaders raised in a Muslim context would be influenced by this behavior; I was not surprised to find it among the top ranking spiritual behaviors. However, one cannot understate the importance of prayer as foundational biblical practice. In summary, this may be a case where a non-Christian cultural and religious behavior helps uniquely highlight biblical teaching.

The fifth category, submission to God, may superficially appear in Islam as more important element because it is a key tenet of the faith. And research on Muslim leadership has clearly evidenced this behavior. Although the terminology might be different, the idea of submission to God (or surrender), however, features prominently among church leaders.

Competence

Numerous values and behaviors have been quoted in this research (see appendix 8). As I compared church leaders with Muslim ones, various similarities and differences emerged. First, there were personal attributes of church leaders quoted more than once that matched those of their Muslim counterparts. These are (1) advisor, (2) behavior-modeling, (3) charity, (4) communication, (5) compassion, (6) courage, (7) generosity, (8) hospitality, (9) humility, (10) justice, (11) knowledge, (12) listening, (13) loyalty, (14) maturity, (15) good manners, (16) mercy, (17) morality, (18) patience, (19) piety, (20) pleasant, (21) preaching, (22) responsible, (23) shepherd, (24) trustworthiness, (25) truthfulness, (26) wisdom, and (27) relational.

A few had some overlap and there are a number of characteristics that are important for the church.

What are the similar attributes that seem to stand out in the above list? Patience is ranked very high in both church and Muslim leadership. I found this very interesting because in the Western world, patience is not highly valued. I argue that these responses may be influenced by the Islamic or North African cultural context. While patience is certainly a biblical value, informants may have prioritized this attribute because it featured prominently in their worldview prior to becoming Christians. Future research should compare and contrast the biblical, cultural and Qur'anic meaning of patience in leadership. It should also explore whether leaders are effectively displaying patience in their congregation or if this is only an ideal value.

The relationship-oriented leadership style is also evidenced in both faiths. Muslims and church leaders value relationship with their followers. Both emphasize companionship, close ties, community, cooperation, goodness, loyalty, listening, and generosity. However, the category "relational," "hospitable" and "caretaking" are only reflected in the leadership of popular Islam. It may appear that the *marabout* is closer to his or her followers than the orthodox leader. Likewise church leaders are very close to their followers.

Other attributes ranking high both in Islam and the church can be clustered in categories including modesty, generosity, and responsibility. As I look at the similarities I am however struck by subtle differences in the meaning of these concepts. For example, when Muslim leaders use the term "humility" they do not think of Jesus but of Muhammad. Therefore the expression of humility is entirely different in each context. I therefore suggest that a future study examines the precise meaning of these concepts and the behavior they elicited in Islam and in the church.

Second, I found important church attributes that are missing in Islamic leadership.[14] The most common ones are: (1) accountability, (2) blamelessness, (3) forgiveness, (4) holiness, (5) meekness, (6) servanthood, (7) integrity, and (8) love. In my initial review of the literature I could not find these

---

14. Sometimes, instead of missing, some attributes are different enough that they cannot really be compared with the ones quoted by church leaders.

terms; however, further research in Islamic literature revealed concepts such as "have probity" and "accept criticism." I also discovered that although love is ranked as the top quality of church leadership it is not totally absent in Muslim leadership. Despite the fact that this term is rarely used, Islam does maintain leadership attributes that are similar to love such as mercy, kindness, gentleness, goodness, friendship, brotherhood, and companionship. Having said that, I believe the attribute "love" as used by church leaders requires special attention. It is not a quality required in most secular leadership styles although it is expressed to some degree in Muslim leadership, Greenleaf's servant leadership, and North African cultural leadership theories. However, it takes on a specific meaning in the church because of its close relationship with Jesus. I assume North African leaders place love as one of the core values of leadership because the Bible teaches about love as the unique mark of Christianity (John 14). By emphasizing love, North African leaders give church leadership a unique shape compared with others in the region.

Likewise, attributes such as holiness and blamelessness may be missing in Islam but can be found to some extent in Muslim leadership within the categories of "morality" and "compliance with Qur'anic laws". To my surprise, although church leaders were the only ones to talk about holiness and accountability, they also discussed integrity in showing the lack of it in the political context. They did not however feel this word was important to characterize church leadership. I was surprised because church leaders set very high moral standards. Several responses indicate that church leaders must be blameless. Muslims maintain a very high moral expectation of their leaders although there are significant differences from their Christian counterparts. A future study should probe the moral failures that lead Muslim leaders to resign.

Third, I have noticed major gaps between the list from the church and Islamic leaders. For example, knowledge of the sacred texts is highly acclaimed in Islam. But that value does not come at the expense of an emphasis on learning from a wide variety of religious and secular sciences. In the present North African church context, leaders are so busy caring for new believers that they do not have time to become well-trained theologians. In the future, this will change. An increasing number of North African

Christian leaders admire historical church leaders like Augustine as models. Nevertheless, the type of knowledge in the church may always be different from the Islamic context especially in the area of jurisprudence. Whereas most leaders should have some knowledge of legal issues in Islam, none of the Christian respondents mentions this as important. This may be an important aspect to consider for the church to be more effective in society. Since Islam deals so much with legal issues, church leaders may want to have some understanding of law from a Christian perspective.

Finally, there are a number of characteristics lacking in the church so far[15] but are important to Islamic leadership. I have organized these characteristics in clusters and discuss them below.

First, the virtue of a simple lifestyle, highly valued by all types of Muslim leaders as well as Augustine and Lavigerie, was surprisingly absent from the church informants. Muslims described this simple lifestyle with words such as "austerity" or "poverty" and quoted Muhammad as their role model. The model of Jesus' simple lifestyle could have inspired church leaders. The reason this did not occur is not clear in this research. A key question that should be raised is what kind of lifestyle is biblically correct and culturally relevant.

Second, the skill of eloquence is missing in the data collected in the church. Every category of leaders in Islam views eloquence as important. Muslim leaders often use rhetorical skills such as poetry in their teaching. Again, perhaps they omitted eloquence for fear that an overdependence on human skill and argumentation (as Paul suggests) is not necessary for the presentation of the gospel. This is something I will investigate further. It might be that church leaders need to demonstrate eloquence to impact society for good.

Third, justice was only quoted four times by church leaders. This reflects a major difference of worldview since most literature on Islamic leadership is shaped by this value. Justice relates to the key behavior expected from every Muslim leader and is key to the arbitration of conflict. Furthermore, every Muslim leader must have knowledge of religious law, with some having more legal education than others. So why is the reference to justice so

---

15. Future research may find them.

weak? There may be two explanations for this: justice is either assumed or Christian teaching on grace trumps that of justice.[16] I would like to suggest church leaders highlight justice when they talk about grace if they desire to have an impact on their society.

Other missing attributes in church leadership that are highly valued by Muslims include moderation,[17] credibility, peacemaking, war-making,[18] self-control, persuasion, rewards and mediation.

For example, patience is highly valued both in Muslim and Christian leadership. But does patience mean the same in both contexts? My research does not test the possible differences. The Holy-Man has been defined by comparing column 1 (pre-Islamic), column 2 (orthodox Islamic), column 5 (*talib*) and column 6 (*marabout*) in order to see how typical religious leadership compares.

This is the first time in this work that I will define specific leadership styles for the church. In the previous chapters I often alluded to leadership styles for the various contexts I studied. As I explained earlier, since I did not use a method developed by leadership theorists to measure a specific style, my study was limited to the exploration of values, attributes and behaviors in the church context that I matched with existing leadership models or styles. My conclusions are in no way final. This is a work in progress. However, this study has helped me develop a framework to continue to collect data and analyze it. It will make things far easier for future studies. The table that compares the various categories of leaders can be regularly updated by doing literature reviews. However, to update the first column, one would have to start new field research because none other has focused on church leadership styles in the North African church.

Based on my study of contemporary leadership theories I hypothesize that if church leadership styles have similarities with North African and Islamic leadership styles they will impact their context and society. They need to be contingent on followers and contexts to be effective. The data in

---

16. Although one must remember here that in grace, there is also justice.
17. Although no church leader quoted this attribute, the historical church leader Augustine did.
18. Although two respondents mentioned the concept of soldier and Augustine was involved in conflicts that led to war with the Donatists.

chapter 6 on four prominent historical leaders who impacted society allows me to conclude that if church leaders want to impact their context, they must adapt their leadership style to match those. However, if these styles are not based on a biblical grid or foundation they will not transform the believers and their community for good. Spiritual transformation can only take place if leaders have styles that match biblical principles. The only data that allows me to probe for biblical values in this research is the information that North African church leaders gave me on the Biblical leaders or passages. This research should be extended in the future to compare and contrast leadership characteristics found in the church with the study of biblical leadership styles. Thus far, two biblical leadership styles were discovered in this research: the servant leadership style and the shepherd leadership style. After comparing the data, I found two others: the Holy Man leadership and the *Sheikhocratic* leadership style. I describe the four of them here.

They are compared and contrasted with the other columns containing data that needs updating as further research is conducted.[19] They present the data collected on the following styles: (1) pre-Islamic leaders, (2) Islamic leaders, (3) the sheikh, (4) family leaders, (5) the *talib*, (6) the *marabout*, (7) biblical leaders quoted by informants, (8) Greenleaf's servant model, (9) Laniak's shepherd's model, (10) the Berbero-Arab leader at work, (11) Augustine, (12) Cardinal Lavigerie, (13) Ibn Badis, and (14) Abdel Kader.

Strengths and Challenges of the Holy Man Leadership Style

The leadership style of North African church leaders is characterized by a deep attachment to God. Leaders influence followers through their piety and spirituality, which is very encouraging. As a result of the leaders' deep

---

[19]. The reason these columns do not present an exhaustive list is because the values, attributes and behaviors of these various categories of leaders is not neatly presented in a book or article but has to be extracted from general works on leadership pertaining to these leaders and their style. Only two styles have a comprehensive list in my book. It is Greenleaf's servant leadership style and Laniak's shepherd leadership style. I want to use this table in the future to probe for terms with blank cells to be able to determine whether the cell is blank because the characteristic does not exist for this leader, or because I have not found it yet in the bulk of the literature on leadership.

commitment to God the Holy Man Leadership Style can be a model for other parts of the world because it defines leaders who love God and others.

North African leaders are also visionary and charismatic. They understand the felt-needs of followers. Meeting the needs of the followers may however create some dependency that leaders must carefully monitor. In times of conflict this type of leadership may create division in the church when the followers view the leader as no longer meeting his or her needs. But overall, this leadership style can only be encouraged in the church when the characteristics that are given by the believers in this research are biblical.

The challenges that need to be addressed in response to this style are the following. If leaders are known for their piety, spirituality and gifting, what are the implications if they ignore those values and rely solely on head knowledge (theological education for example) to influence their followers. Will they have any impact? This reminds me of a recent discussion I had with a church leader which demonstrates that both are important. He reminded me that a few decades ago the church was birthed through dreams, vision, signs and wonders; many people came to Christ because of supernatural manifestations. However, following the churches' experience of opposition, many people not grounded in the Word of God left. This shows that the supernatural, personal piety and the study of the Bible are important. In Islam there is a distinction between popular religious expression, where supernatural manifestations are common, and an orthodox expression where influence flows from the knowledge of the sacred texts and the legal matters. On the contrary the church should combine supernatural manifestations, deep piety and loyalty to the Word of God with its laws and recommendations.

Occasionally the Holy Man Leadership Style could be mistaken for the religious styles of North African majority society. That scenario is possible because values such as patience or compassion are necessary in church and Muslim leadership. I believe however believe that the respective sacred texts have shaped these values in a unique way, and therefore church leaders must look to the Bible to define these religious characteristics. This does not mean that they are entirely different, but it does require serious investigation of the biblical text to highlight what God meant.

Another challenge lies in the fact that the Holy Man leadership style clearly states that the leader is appointed by God. This may affect the leader-follower relation in several ways: the follower may feel that the leader has a higher spiritual status than the followers or the leader may place more emphasis on the relationship with God than he or she does with followers. These tensions can easily be resolved by learning from biblical models how leaders appointed by God served their followers.

The visionary-charismatic style of these leaders may also set them apart from the congregation in regards to their aura and gifting. There is a contextual example of leadership in the Islamic context that equates the charisma of the leader with *baraka*, in which they draw their influence and power from the *baraka* they possess. North African leaders must be aware that some people in their community who observe their gifts may mistake them as *marabouts* or *talibs*. This was Paul's experience when his power was interpreted as coming from Zeus. In such a context, it is important to underline where the blessing comes from.

Finally, one has to ask the question of the impact of such leaders on society. I have noticed that there are shared characteristics between religious leaders in Islam and the Christian community as well as significant differences. Researchers must ask if the leadership characteristics of the Muslims play a role in the way they impact society. If they do, what happens when church leaders do value the importance of these characteristics? For example, church respondents did not emphasize justice, arbitration or dealing with legal matters as much as Muslim leaders did. Does this affect the way they impact society for good? Future research should deal with this issue.

Conclusion

I have used in this section two biblical metaphors, the servant and the shepherd, as well as two leadership roles, the sheikh and the holy man, to characterize the leadership style of North African church leaders I interviewed.[20] These four styles have a combination of characteristics that I

---

20. In effect, when I compared the attributes and styles for the first two categories, I

believe can impact society and church for good. The reason why I am so confident is because the leaders I interviewed have planted many churches and influenced thousands of believers. Their leadership characteristics are very similar to the historical leaders who impacted their society. Although they might not be aware of it, the church leaders are displaying a number of leadership characteristics from their context as evidenced above in this chapter. The major difference between leaders in society and the church is that the latter put God and the Bible first and say they lead according to biblical models. However, the biblical models they choose are very close to their own religious, cultural and societal context.

The identification of these four leadership styles has further highlighted key characteristics that are common to church leaders in North Africa. Leaders are attached to God. They influence others through their piety and spirituality and influence others by modeling behavior. They are people-oriented and great caretakers of their followers. Although they are somewhat task-oriented they combine this with being generous, hospitable, caring, loving and very concerned about the daily needs of their followers.

The North African church leaders are also charismatic-visionary. Perhaps the unfavorable context in which the church grows necessitates people with special charisma. But as leadership theorists know well, there is danger in becoming overly dependent on the leader and forsaking God and his word. The church must keep that balance to grow healthy leaders.

North African leaders influence others and include them in the decision-making by applying an autocratic-consultative leadership style. Autocracy is balanced with consultation as well as the love of the servant leader and the tender care of the shepherd leader. Future research should include followers to see how they experience the consultative process.

Finally, transformative leadership permeates North Africa. This is evidenced by the fact that leaders are clearly follower-oriented and they pray for spiritual transformation for their own lives and the lives of their followers.

---

used categories directly related to men and women who have these roles whereas for the Shepherd and the Servant, these could be actual roles but the way North African leaders were referring to them shows they did not visualize actual shepherds and servants but were referring to metaphors that Jesus was using when he was talking about leadership.

The identification of these four leadership styles also leads me to make a number of recommendations.

First, I recommend these four styles, of course, must be further tested. The way I organized the values, attributes and behaviors in patterns to compare them with other contexts has provided a framework to continue research in this area. It is important to continue to collect data that may reveal characteristics that I have not yet found in the literature review on leadership which could be included in the Comparative Table of Attributes in appendix 10.

Second, there is another style that I see emerging called the paternalistic-familial leadership style. Leaders often create their models from grandparents, parents or older siblings. This style has similar characteristics with the *sheikhocratic* leadership style. I discussed it briefly when I analyzed the leadership style of the sheikh as well as the North African family in chapter 6. Future research should take this style into account. Further resources may also emerge from a style that helps understand religious leadership in a Muslim majority context. This style is called "Prophetic-*Caliphal* Style" and posits that Muslims are vicegerents or representatives of God on this earth.

Third, further research is needed to probe what leaders mean by the attributes they use. Unfortunately, this study does not offer much information or illustration of these terms. Exploring what North Africans mean by generosity, humility, or patience should be the next phase of research. My first guess is that they favor the biblical meaning, but observing their leadership behaviors may reveal that these values are also influenced by their culture and society. Likewise, one should probe Muslim and cultural values for their precise definitions of those presented in this research. This would facilitate the process of comparing and contrasting them.

Fourth, another area that needs further research is to see whether the attributes that informants listed are ideals or real attributes. One can only test this matter by interviewing followers, which I did not do in this research. I make here a strong recommendation that the next step of the research must collect stories and vignettes from followers on each of the major leadership characteristics of North African pastors. This will be the way to find if the characteristics mentioned in this research are ideal or real. The chart in the appendices that indicates the characteristics mentioned by ten respondents and more, could be a good starting point. The discrepancy between ideal and real leadership styles may also apply in Islam. In my first section, I listed a number of leadership attributes from Islamic leadership theory that North African church leaders may not have found in the Muslim leaders they know in their city or village. Their view of the Muslim leader may differ significantly from that of Islamic literature.

Fifth, the choice of contingency theory has helped me posit that if the four styles I found are contingent to the context and the Bible they may impact the believers and the society for good. Thus, the analysis of the contextual and biblical relevance of values, attributes and behaviors, as well as concepts of power, legitimacy and decision-making must continue, in order to prepare leaders for more effective leadership in their context.

Sixth, as I stated in my introduction of the book, I am aware that the current North African society reflects a mix of traditional, modern and postmodern worldviews. This research has not demonstrated which one of these views is best reflected in the responses. Therefore I recommend that future research compares the values collected with values from these three periods to define whether the leadership styles of the North African leaders matches more with traditional, modern, or postmodern worldviews. Readers of this book must be cautious and not believe that the styles I found are effective for every one of these world-views. My inclination however is to say that the styles I found match more closely a traditional-modern context. In effect, the theories and models that reflect my findings (like the sheikh, the imam, the shepherd, etc.) are models from traditional (pre-modern society) with some characteristics of modern societies.

Seventh, my research touched upon womens' issues in a few places but did not focus on the gender similarities or differences in North African church leadership. My respondents included eleven women, which represent twenty-five per cent of the sample. As I compared the responses of male versus female, I did not find major discrepancies and therefore did not divide my responses according to these two categories. However, I recommend future research should look at this issue more closely. Studies should look at how the patriarchal North African society affects church leadership. During my ministry I have observed that God uses many women in leadership roles in the church in North Africa. There are several examples of women starting churches and ministries. However, I have also observed that female leadership has its challenges in a context where male-oriented leadership is very common. Future research should add other female leadership models from history and society to the "mother" leadership style that I studied here to be able to draw the specific leadership characteristics of female leaders and compare them with my findings.

Eighth, the findings provided ample evidence that church leaders have an enormous potential to be mentors and teachers. They are caretakers, close to their followers, and they value behavior modeling. I therefore recommend North African leaders use the findings of this research, which for some may be at the idealistic stage, and use them to train and mentor their followers. I have great confidence that the North African leaders will be very efficient in this role.

Ninth, as I stated in the introduction to this book, I have not started by laying the foundation of a biblical theory of leadership (although I have discussed several in chapter 2). There are many existing biblical perspectives that could be used in mentoring and training leaders that North African church leaders will not find here. It is intentional on my part, because I would like to see the North African brothers and sisters use my findings to biblically reflect on their style. I am looking forward to see how the church will develop their biblical foundation of leadership.

Finally, the major finding of this research is the unique leadership style emerging from the North African church, which is different from any other in the region. The key characteristic for church leaders is love and the greatest model is Jesus. This style combines characteristics of the Sheikh, the Servant, the Shepherd and the Holy Man. It is not disconnected from its context. There remains potential for borrowing or using the common characteristics that exist in other religious and cultural models as long as they remain deeply rooted in the Bible.

APPENDIX A

Pre-Islamic Leadership Characteristics

Characteristic	Definition	Type of Leader
Arbitration	Arbitration of disputes	*Sheikh, hakam, sha'ir*
Blood Revenge	In context of conflict	*Sheikh*
Bravery	*Muruwah*	*Sheikh*
Clear-sightedness		*Sheikh*
Collaboration	Collaborates with other leaders, council	*Sheikh*
Courage	*Muruwah*	*Sheikh*
Eloquence	One of the most important quality of a leader	*Sheikh*
Equity		*Sheikh*
Generosity	*Muruwah*	*Sheikh*
Honor	Honor is a key value of tribal leaders	*Sheikh*
Hospitality	Reputation of hospitality	*Sheikh*
Judgment	Judges between tribes	*Sheikh, hakam, sha'ir*
Justice	*Muruwah*	*Sheikh*
Knowledge		*Sha'ir*
Leadership	Choosing camps for the tribe	*Sheikh*
Listening	Listens to the tribe	*Sheikh*
Longanimity	*Hilm*	*Sheikh*
Loyalty	*Muruwah*, loyalty to family and tribe	*Sheikh*
Patience	*Muruwah*	*Sheikh*
Peacemaking	Initiates peace in times of war	*Sheikh*
Protection	Protects the tribe	*Sheikh*
Reputation	Power given by their reputation	*Sheikh*
Respect	Great veneration among followers	*Sheikh*

Self-Sacrifice	*Muruwah*	*Sheikh*
Supernatural Power	Divination, supernatural wisdom, *saj'*, magic, prediction of future	*Sha'ir, Kahin, Sheikh*
Trustworthiness	*Muruwah*	*Sheikh*
Truthfulness	*Muruwah*	*Sheikh*
Warmaking	Lead the tribe to war, makes final decisions on war and peace	*Sheikh*
Power and Decision-Making		
Ancestor	Pride to ancestry, common ancestor, blood ties	*Sheikh*
Charisma	Spiritual power of leaders	*Sha'ir, Kahin,* sometimes *Sheikh*
Consultation	Assembly, authority of the *mala'*, *majlis* assembly, consensus, unanimity, persuasion and cohesion exercised by banishment	*Sheikh*
Group Feeling	Leadership over people derives from a group feeling, *'asabiyya*, corporate spirit, family ties	*Sheikh*
Majlis	Pre-Islamic tribal consultative council	Tribe
Piety	Political leader with spiritual influence	*Sheikh*
Traditions	Nomads did not obey a human being but traditions and customs of their clan	*Sheikh*
Visionary	The leader was often considered to be a visionary	*Sha'ir, Kahin, Sheikh*
Legitimacy		
Genealogy	Blood lineage	*Sheikh*
Human	Appointed by former leader, council of elder, tacit agreement of entire society	*Sheikh*
Supernatural	Charisma, spiritual power, power given by an ultimate reality or supernatural beings	*Sha'ir, Kahin, Sheikh*

APPENDIX B

Islamic Leadership Characteristics

Characteristics	Definitions	Type of Leader
Administration		Muhammad, Umar
Adviser	Gives advice to followers	Imam
Arbitration	Similar to the pre-Islamic role of *hakim* (judge)	Pre-Islamic Muhammad, *qadis*
Austerity		Shi'i imam
Behavior Modeling	A noble pattern in God's apostle	Muhammad, *rasul*
Blessings		*Rasul*
Bravery		Caliph, pre-Islamic Muhammad
Calm	*Sakina*	*Mufti*
Charisma		Muhammad, imam, saint, Shi'i imam
Common Sense	*Kifaya*	Caliph
Communication		Muhammad
Competence	*Kifaya or qadir*	Sunni caliph, *qadi*
Courage		Shi'i imam
Defiance	Defiance of the strong (Muhammad before Islam)	
Eloquence		Muhammad, Shi'i imam
Empathy		Shi'i imam
Endurance		Shi'i imam
Equality		Shi'i imam
Faith		Muhammad, Muslim leaders
Farsightedness		Shi'i imam

Fidelity	Fidelity in the keeping of the trusts (Muhammad before Islam)	
Firmness		Shi'i imam
Fortitude		*Qadi*
Friendness	*Sahib* (intimate friend), *anis* (companion), *khalil* (close friend) and *akh* (Brother)	Shi'i imam
Generosity	Muhammad was open-handed; gift offering to God and the poor and needy instead of extravagant generosity of the Bedouin leaders, *zakat*, almsgiving	Muhammad, Religious Leaders
Goal-Seeker	Leading followers toward a goal	Muhammad, Abraham
Good Tidings		*Rasul*
Honesty		Pre-Islamic Muhammad
Humility	Muhammad was humble and shy	Muhammad, every leader
Incognito Inquiry		Shi'i leader, Umar
Infallibity	Only in Shi'ism	Shi'i imam
Integrity		Muhammad, *mufti*
Intimacy with God	Intimate and direct knowledge of God, *ma'rifa*	Sufism
Judgment (Good)		Sunni caliph
Jurist		*Mufti, qadi, faqih*
Justice	*'Adala*, obeys moral and religious law, good feelings prevail over bad, practical without laxism, justice to the oppressed, impartial and just	*Qadi, mufti, caliph, faqih* Muhammad
Knowedge	Knowledgeable	*'Ulama, qadi*

Legal Knowledge	Imam can issue *fatwas*, jurist, *mufti*	*Muhammad*, imam
Listening		
Loyalty	*Amana*, Muhammad was loyal in the keeping of his trusts	Muhammad
Manners (Good)		Shi'i imam
Maturity		
Mercy	*Rahma* or *rahim;* kindness, benevolence, act of kindness or favor	God, Jesus in the Qur'an, Muhammad, *qadi*
Miracle-Making	Supernatural, journey to heaven, raising up the dead, talking to angels, *karama*, charisma, saints	Muhammad, saints
Morality	*Hilm*, religious leaders should have integrity in their social and moral life	Muhammad, all leaders
Modesty		Muhammad,
Nobility		Muhammad
Opinion	For an opinion by himself	Imam, caliph
Patience	*Sabr*, core value	Muhammad before Islam, Qur'anic Muhammad, Qur'anic Job, Jacob, and Joseph, every believer, *qadi*
Peacemaking	Call to peace, *qadi* should refrain people from being violent	Muhammad, *mufti*, *qadis*, caliph
Perceptiveness		Shi'i imam
Persistence	Persistence in revenge	Muhammad before Islam
Physical fitness		Shi'i imam
Piety	*Taqwa*, core value	Muhammad

Prayer	Religious leaders are first of all prayer leaders, leading prayer ranks higher than political leadership	*Rasul*
Preaching	Imam gives the Friday sermon	Muhammad, imam, *qadi*
Probity		Sunni caliph
Prophetic	*Nabi*	Muhammad
Protection	Protection of the weak, looks after the affairs of the followers	Pre-Islamic Muhammad, Muhammad under Islam, caliph
Responsible		Caliph
Science	*'Ilm*, methodical study of knowledge, plus knowledge of the invisible God	Muhammad, imam, *'ulama, faqih, qadi*, Sunni caliph
Self-Control	*Hilm*	Pre-Islamic Muhammad, Muhammad, *mufti*
Simple Lifestyle	Muhammad was detached from gain	Muhammad
Sincerity		Muhammad
Social Engagement		Imam, *'ulama*, caliph
Sound in mind and body		Caliph
Strong		Shi'i imam
Teaching	Teaching community, children, Qur'an, Arabic	Imam
Trustworthy		Pre-Islamic Muhammad, Muhammad
Truthful	*Siddiq*	Muhammad
Virtuous	*Mafthul*	Caliph
Violence		*Qadi*

Visionary		Shi'i imam
Warmaking	Call to war	Muhammad, *mufti*, *qadis*, caliph
Warner	*Nadhir*	*Rasul*
Wisdom	*Hikma*, core value, Ability to put *'ilm* in practice	Muhammad, Qur'anic Musa, Dawud, 'Isa, every leader
Witness	*Shahid*	*Rasul, imam*
Power and Decision-Making		
Allegiance	*Bay'a*, pledge of allegiance with Muhammad and caliphs, followers commit to accept the authority of the leader	
Behavior Modeling		*Rasul*
Charity	*Ihsan*, charity in the exercise of authority	
Consensus	*Ijma'*, consensus of the community	
Consultation	*Shura* Muslim leaders must promote participation of others in decision making through *shura*	Muhammad, all leaders, caliphs, *qadi*
Decision-Making	*Ahkam*, decisions or judgments	God and humans
Gift-giving	Sura 58:13 (practice debated)	To Muhammad
Knowledge	Knowledge of the sacred texts is greatest power of leaders; key criteria for exercising leadership	Human leaders
Law	God's law is above human power, Muhammad and caliph are to be obeyed only because they submit to God's law, Legal authority, God, Muhammad, *ijma'*, *'ulama*	

Power-executive	*'amr*, executive power, different from legal power	Humans
Power-God	Everyone must submit to the power of God, even Muhammad	Only God
Power-Judiciary	*Hukm*, judiciary power	Human leaders
Raghbah	Generate willingness and desire to comply	
Respectability	Respectability gives power	*Mufti*
Revelation	Trumps human decisions	Muhammad
Sultan	Power received from God by human leaders	Muhammad, Sunni leader, Moses
Vicegerent	Adam is vicegerent on earth, Muhammad, humans are vicegerents, responsibility given by God to exercise power	Adam, Muhammad, leaders
Legitimacy		
Competence	Qualities and behaviors play an important role in the choice of the leader	
Divine		
Genealogical	Blood ties, early caliphs were Quraishites, Shi'i imams are descendants of Muhammad, saints are *sharif*	
Human	Leader must have the protection of the followers, appointed by the community	*Mufti*, caliphs
Knowledge	Superior knowledge and intimate knowledge of God	

APPENDIX C

The Sheikh's Leadership Characteristics

Characteristic	Definition
Arbitration	Arbitration of disputes
Considerate	Counterbalance autocracy
Consultation	With tribal elders
Courage	Most courageous person of the tribe
Elegance	Dresses with elegance
Feeding	Location of adequate grazing pastures for tribe's cattle and camels
Generosity	Reputation of generosity, brings more power than accumulation of wealth
Hospitality	Competes for power by inviting frequently with great generosity; expected to entertain followers, visitors and guests
Humility	Sheikh is humble
Law	Sheikh must submit to laws
Listening	Listening attitude
Loyalty	
Oldest	
Protection	Defends well and livestock of the tribe
Relational	Counterbalances autocracy
Support	Counterbalances autocracy
Wisdom	Wisest person of the tribe; reputation of wisdom; reputation of wisdom provides more power than accumulation of wealth
Power and Decision-Making	
Autocratic	More authority than people in the tribe
Community	Community tempers the power of the sheikh
Conciliatory	Conciliatory style of Boumediène

Consensus	Consensus is better than being a great leader
Consultation	Sheikh must consult with the council of the tribe's elders
Democratic	Desert society tends to be democratic and egalitarian
Elitism	Elite families have power
Equality	Bedouins tend to treat chief as an equal rather than a boss who has to be obeyed
Hierarchy	Authority is hierarchical
Nepotism	Chooses tribe or family over others
Power (absolute)	Sheikh has absolute power
Rewards	Boumediène used transactional practices and rewarded followers
Rules	Sheikh submits to religious laws and regulations and tradition
Wealth	Power and decision-making hold by elite families with extensive resources and wealth

APPENDIX D

Family Leadership Characteristics

Characteristic	Definition	Type of Leader
Affection	Attaching	Grandparents
Autocratic	Father who does not give orders is not a father; children keep a distance; authority combined with love; authority due to responsibility; when outside social pressure, tends to be indulgent	Father, older sibling
Behavior-Modeling	Through gestures and attitudes; often leads to osmosis; religion education heavily relies on behavior-modeling	Mother, parents
Blessing	Used in education	Mother
Caretaking	Breadwinner	Father, mother, siblings
Consolidation	Cement of the family	Grandparents
Curse	Used in education; often not meant seriously	Mother
Erratic	Erratic educational style, from overwhelming tenderness to unleashed fury	Mother
Guide	Breadwinner	Father
Honor	Respect, *nif*, fear	Family
Indulgence	When not under social pressure	Father
Love	Combined with fear of his authority	Grandparents
Management	Management of household	Mother

Mediator (peacemaker)	Between parent and children, between siblings, mother serves as a mediator between father and children	Grandparents, mother
Master	Because he is the breadwinner	Father
Mocking	Training children through mocking	Mother, other female figures in the family
Peacemaker (mediator)	Between siblings	Grandparents
Piety (spirituality)	Religious education of grandchildren	Grandparents, especially grandmother, mother
Protection	Refuge for the weakest of the family (grandparent), keeping family safe and secure (father), mother is a refuge for children when they fear their father, mothers are the "keeper of the temple"	Grandparents, father
Respect	*Qadr* means "deep respect"	
Reward	Only God can reward. Reverse rewarding	Children
Severity	Punishment	Parents
Shame	*Hachouma*, keeps the bond of the family	Family
Taboo	Used to set limits and used in behavioral modeling	Mother
Tenderness	Toward grandchildren, *h'anna* (grandmother)	Grandparents
Threat	Used in education	Mother
Tradition	Influence through popular beliefs, myths, symbols and legends, songs, stories and proverbs	Mother

Tutor	Tutorship of father toward the son	Father
Unity	Keeps the family united, cohesion	Grandparents, mother
Virility	*Redjla,* masculine toughness and *guemma*, acting like a male	Male
Word of God	Qur'an plays an important role in education	
Power-Decision-Making		
Authority (absolute)	Combined with tenderness, in traditional families authority of the father is absolute and unconditional	Grandfather, father
Caretaking	Power and influence flows from the practice of *nafaqa* (supporting others in the family by one's means or work)	Father, presently also mother and siblings
Collectivism	Needs of family trump individual needs	Family
Decision-Making	Usually the father, although persuasion can be used by other members of the family, but not consultation	
Hierarchical	Relationship based on hierarchy	Parent over children, older over younger sibling, older over younger wife, grandmother over mother
Patriarchal	Grandfather and father are central figures of authority	
Persuasion	Used by family members because there is no consultation	
Submission	Respect to older member of the family expressed by submission	Family

Legitimacy		
Agnatic system	Inheritance transmitted from father to son; power directly linked to gender differences	
Blood ties	Common ancestors	
Patriarchal system	Males play a key role in the family. Authority is counterbalanced by love, care and mentoring	

APPENDIX E

The Talib Leadership Characteristics

Characteristic	Definition
Advisor	Must be able to advise pupils and assess their capacities; personal, spiritual and social adviser for the village
Arabic	Knows Arabic
Character	Chosen for his character and the way he influences pupils
Discernment	Discernment to judge pupils with keenness of character
Eloquence	An attractive and rhetorical style
Knowledge	Traditionally the most educated person of the community; must have extended knowledge
Mediator	Serves as a mediator in the conflicts of the community
Morality	High moral standards
Neutrality	A good *talib* must be neutral in the affairs of the village. He does not take sides
Piety	Must be pious, participates in religious life of the community: prayer, festivals, funerals
Pleasant	Must have a pleasing character
Prayer	Leads the prayer
Teaching	One of the major roles of the *talib*
Word of God	Must know the Qur'an and be able to teach the Qur'an
Wisdom	*Hikma*

Power and Decision-Making	
Authocratic	His authority strengthens the authority of the family
Pedagogy	Examples of friends, heroes, history, maieutic, parables, proverbs, metaphors, participation, and observation
Repetition	Traditionally teaches by repetition
Reasoning	Teaches pupils to reason
Reward	Gives rewards
Social Transformation	Pupils learn to apply Qur'anic texts to their context
Spiritual Transformation	Teaches pupils to respect the Qur'an, teaches them to pray
Legitimacy	
Competence	Chosen for his knowledge of the Qur'an and Arabic and his personal qualities
Human Legitimacy	Chosen by community or the State

APPENDIX F

The Sufi-Marabout Leadership Characteristics

Characteristic	Definition
Austerity	Imitate the austere lifestyle of Muhammad
Benevolence	Show goodness
Blessing	*Baraka*, can secure God's blessings to followers
Compassion	Following Muhammad's example
Courage	Taught in the *zawiya*
Generosity	Like Muhammad, helps the poor and the needy
Holistic	Reason, emotions, spiritual, practical
Hospitality	Through the *zawiya*
Intimacy with God	*Ma'rifa* or direct and intimage knowledge of God is the primary source of knowledge
Intuitive	Intuitive holistic knowledge, emotions, imagination, disposition, experience and spontaneous, instinctive faith, spontaneous
Jurist	Knows Islamic law
Mediation	In times of conflict between communities
Mercy	Following Muhammad's example
Mystical knowledge	Saints are often considered mystics
Personal experience of God	Sufi call it the flavor or the taste of
Patience	Taught in the *zawiya*
Piety	*Dhikr*, prayer, spiritual practices
Protection	Protection of followers in case of danger
Relational	Very involved in the life of followers and community
Righteousness	Following Muhammad's example
Social engagement	Large number of charitable and social achievements

Teaching	Teaching the Qur'an and Islamic law; giving education to school children
Witness	Fervently spread Islam
Word of God	Knows the Qur'an and teaches the Qur'an
Worship and Art	Dance, music, poetry
Power and Decision-Making	
Emotional Power	Sufism addresses not just the reason but also the heart.
Intermediary	Intermediary between God and people-at least in the eyes of the followers
Miraculous power	Saints do extraordinary things
Reward	Followers offer sacrifices and offerings to receive blessings
Legitimacy	
Genealogical	Descendant of Muhammad
Divine	Power comes from God
Human	Followers recognize the spiritual power and give offerings and gifts

APPENDIX G
Church Leadership Values

Value	Frequency
Behavior modeling	1x
Blameless	2x
Charisma	1x
Encourager	2x
Fairness	1x
Faithfulness	2x
Fasting	1x
Forgiving	2x
Gentleness	1x
Goodness	1x
God (called by)	1x
God (fear of God)	1x
God (fellowship with God)	1x
God first	1x
God (seek His glory)	1x
God (intimacy with God)	1x
God (love God)	3x
God (doing His will)	1x
God (passionate for God)	1x
Hate idols	1x
Helping	2x
Honesty	5x
Hospitable	2x
Humility	7x
Integrity	7x
Joy	1x
Justice	4x
Kindness	1x

Lover (of others)	10x
Live by the Spirit	1x
Manners (good)	2x
Meekness	1x
Mercy	2x
Miracles	1x
Obedience	2x
Obey God's commands	1x
Patience	2x
Peace	1x
Perseverance	1x
Personality	1x
Prayer	2x
Respect	1x
Respectable	1x
Responsible	1x
Righteous	5x
Self-control	1x
Servant	1x
Sharing	1x
Sincerity	3x
Spiritual guide	1x
Stimulate	1x
Submission	2x
Support	1x
Temperate	1x
Time (give)	1x
Transparency	1x
Truthful	1x
Wisdom	2x
Word (study)	1x
Word (put into practice)	1x
Works for the glory of God	1x

APPENDIX H

Church Leadership Characteristics Used to Identify Church Styles

Concept	Frequency
Accountability	3x
Administration	1x
Advice-seeker	2x
Authenticity	3x
Benevolence	1x
Blamelessness	8x
Caretaking	26x
Charisma (life in the Holy Spirit)	13x
Courage	10x
Collaboration	4x
Compassion	8x
Communication	6x
Discernment	11x
Faithfulness	3x
Encourager	2x
Fairness	1x
Fasting	1x
Father	9x
Forgiveness	4x
Generosity	5x
Gentleness	1x
God (attached to)	19x
God (faith in)	15x
God (fear)	4x
God (first)	1x

God (glory)	4x
God (intimacy with)	6x
God (listen to)	5x
God (love toward)	8x
God (obey)	6x
God (will)	3x
Goodness	1x
Helping	2x
Holiness	2x
Holy Spirit (dependent on)	11x
Holy Spirit (fruits)	1x
Holy Spirit (live by)	1x
Honesty	6x
Hospitable	2x
Humility	26x
Idol (hatred)	1x
Integrity	9x
Joy	1x
Justice	4x
Kindness	6x
Knowledge	1x
Listening	12x
Love	31x
Loyalty	2x
Manner (good)	1x
Mature	2x
Meekness	1x
Mercy	4x
Miracles	1x
Obedience	2x
Patience	21x

Piety	See God, Word and Holy Spirit
Prayer	16x
Pleasant	1x
Protection	4x
Responsible (+ Moses and Abraham)	45x
Sanctity	7x
Self-sacrifice (dying for followers)	10x
Servant	23x
Sharing	8x
Shepherd	12x
Sincerity	3x
Spiritual Guide	1x
Submission	5x
Supernatural power	10x
Support	1x
Teaching	11x
Temperate	1x
Tenderness	5x
Time-giving	1x
Transparency	4x
Trustworthy	8x
Truthfulness	4x
Visionary	5x
Wisdom	9x
Word-centered	11x
Power and Decision-Making	
Administrative skills	3x
Autocratic	8x
Behavior-Modeling	23x
Communication	6x
Consultation	25x

Humility	26x
Relationship-oriented	8x
Piety	All respondents
Servanthood	
Team-work	2x
Legitimacy	
Divine legitimacy	13x
Human legitimacy	Most combine divine and human 14x
Self-Appointed Leaders	2x

APPENDIX I

Augustine's Leadership Characteristics

Caretaker	Love for God
Charity	Mercy
Good Communicator	Moderation (just middle)
Cross-Cultural Skills	Morality
Dying for Followers	Peacemaker
Educator	Prayer
Faith	Preacher
Father	Relational
Friendship with Followers	Self-Sacrifice
Friendship with God	Servanthood
Generosity	Sharing Wealth
Humility	Spirit-Filled
Industriousness	Thinker
Knowledge	Theologian
Legitimacy (divine)	Word-Centered
Love for Followers	Writer

APPENDIX J
Lavigerie's Leadership Characteristics

Action	Mentor
Attached to God	Morality
Caretaker	Mystic
Charity	Obedience to the Rule
Chastity	Peacemaker
Community-Oriented	Piety
Consultation	Poverty
Courage	Powerlessness
Dwell in God	Purity
Dying for Followers	Relational
Faith	Sanctification
Industrious	Servant
Integrity	Social Impact
Interfaith Relations	Teacher
Knowledge	Team Work
Leading by Example	Theologian
Legitimacy (divine)	Unity
Love of Followers	Visionary
Love of God	Zeal

APPENDIX K

Ibn Badis' Leadership Characteristics

Anticipate	Modesty
Apologetics	Morality
Brotherhood	Noble
Communication Skills	Passionate Temper
Community-Oriented	Patience
Consultation	Peace
Dialogue	Piety
Dignity	Polemics
Equity	Political Skills
Friend of God	Relational
Gentleness	Steadfastness
Generous	Self-Control
Guide	Solidarity
Humble	Teacher
Industrious	Theologian
Intellectual	Tolerant
Intuition	Truth
Knowledge	Unity
Legal Power	Visionary
Mentor	Zeal

APPENDIX L
Abd El-Kader's Leadership Characteristics

- Bravery
- Chivalry
- Communication Skills
- Community-Oriented
- Courage
- Detached from Earth
- Eloquence
- Endurance
- Family-Oriented
- Generous
- Gentleness
- Humility
- Interfaith Relations
- Justice
- Knowledge
- Leading by example
- Legitimacy (blood lineage)
- Legitimacy (divine)
- Legitimacy (human)
- Love
- Meditation
- Morality
- Monk-Soldier
- Peacemaker
- Perseverance
- Persuasion
- Piety
- Political Figure
- Poverty
- Prayer
- Relation
- Respect
- Rhetorical Skills
- Self-Sacrifice
- Sharing Wealth
- Sheikh
- Supernatural Power
- Teacher
- Warrior

APPENDIX M

BIblical Leaders Identified by the Church Leaders

Characteristics	Leaders	Illustrations
Communication	Jesus, Philippus, Apollos	The way he communicated (Jesus), preacher (Philippus), teacher (Apollos)
Humility	Jesus, Moses, Paul	The greatest becomes the smallest (Jesus); He did not fight for his rights (Paul)
Love	Jesus, Moses, Paul	He loves them to the end (Moses)
Sacrificing oneself for others	Moses, Paul	Ready to die for his followers (Moses), ready to suffer for his followers (Moses), ready to have name erased from book of life for followers (Moses); willing to die for others (Paul), sacrifices himself for his people (Paul)
Sacrificing oneself for Jesus	Paul	Offered everything, body, and soul for Jesus (Paul)
Obedience to God	Abraham	Abraham obeyed God who asked him to sacrifice his son
Servanthood	Jesus	Washed feet of disciples (Jesus); loved them to the end even the rebellious (Moses)

Power	Jesus, Peter, Nehemiah, Joshua, Peter, Philippus	Calmed the storm (Jesus), symbol of authority (Jesus); powerful leader, sword in one hand and worked with the other (Nehemiah); metaphor of power (Moses); his people obeyed him (Nehemiah); general of the army (Joshua); powerful leadership style (Peter); pushy leadership style (Peter); made miracles (Philippus)
Delegation	Moses	Delegates, appoints successor (Moses)
Caretaking	Moses	Cares for his people, always there for his people (Moses)
Hard worker	Moses, Esdras, Nehemiah	Rebuilding the temple (Esdras); building and rebuilding the temple (Nehemiah), had a sword in one hand and worked with the other (Nehemiah); accepts responsibilities to accomplish the will of God (Moses)
Forgiving	Joseph, Moses	Strong forgiveness in his heart for his brothers (Joseph); forgives people when they rebel (Moses)
Courage	Paul	He was courageous (Paul)
Academician	Paul	Wrote many books (Paul)
Adviser	Paul	Gave good advice to Timothy (Paul)
Leads toward a goal	Joshua	Led his people to the promised land (Joshua)
Understands plan of God	Joseph	Understood the plan of God for his life (Joseph)
Seeing followers with the eye of God	Joseph	He saw his brothers with the eyes of God (Joseph)
Does the will of God	Abraham	Left his house, family, land to go where God was leading (Abraham)
Followers listen to him	Philippus	

APPENDIX N

Leadership Characteristics Quoted by More Than Ten Respondents

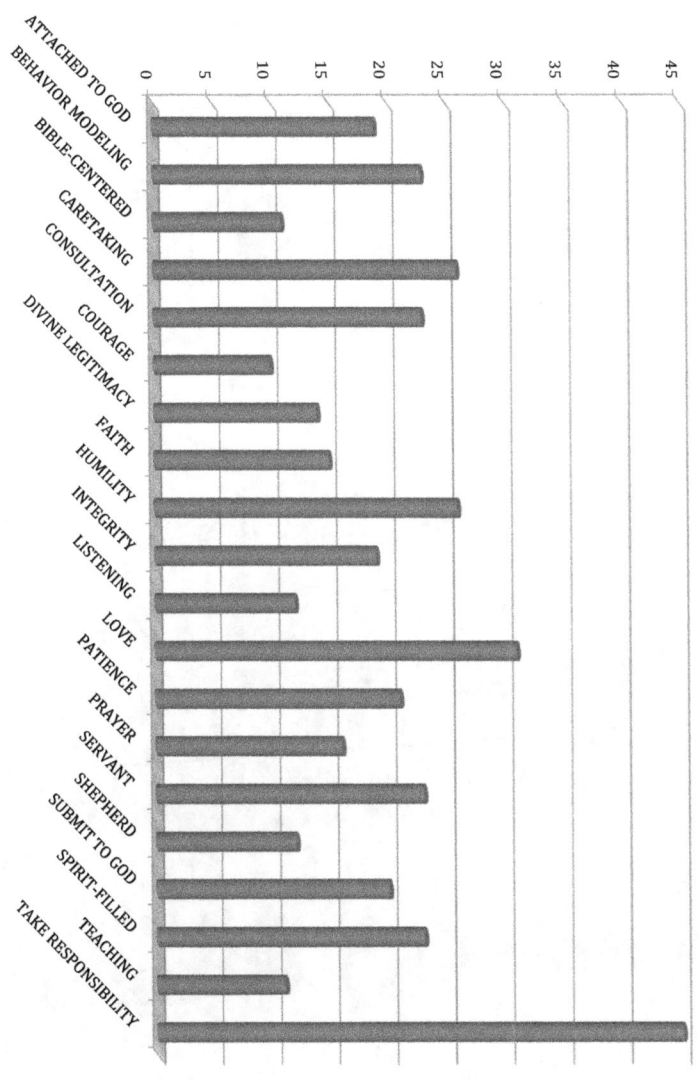

APPENDIX O

Leadership Characteristics of Church Leaders

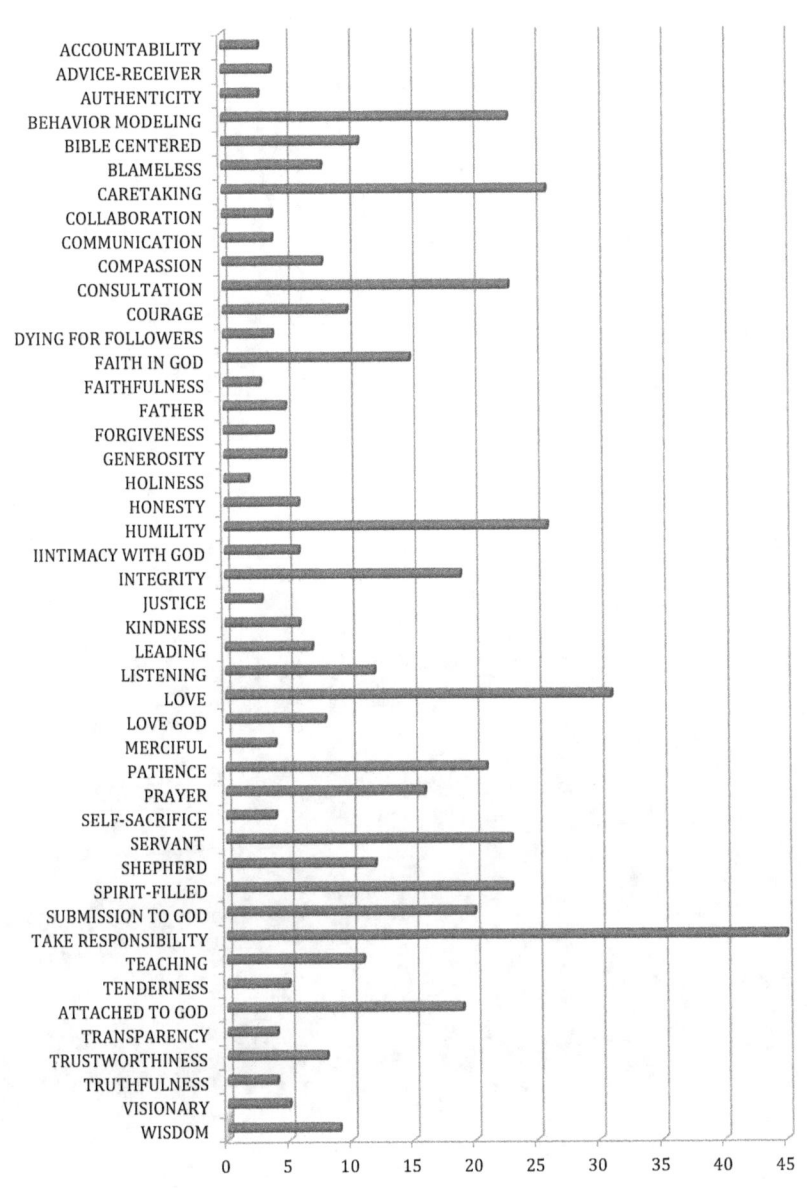

APPENDIX P

Church Leaders' Characteristics Compared with Historical, Religious, and Cultural Characteristics

1=servant
2=shepherd
3=pre-Islam
4=sheikh
5=imam
6=Shi'i leader
7=*wali* in Sunnism

8=*talib*
9=family
10=Augustine
11=Lavigerie
12=Ibn Badis
13=Abd el-Kader
14=church leader

Values, Behaviors, Qualities	1	2	3	4	5	6	7	8	9	10	11	12	13	14
accountability														■
administration					■					■	■	■	■	■
adviser														
adviser-receiver			■							■			■	■
affection									■				■	
allegiance from followers			■											
anti-idolater							■			■				
anticipate														
apologetics										■				
arbitration														
austerity										■		■		
authocratic				■		■							■	
authocratic-consultative			■	■		■	■			■	■	■	■	■
authority-god					■	■	■			■				
awareness	■													
behavior-modeling			■	■	■	■	■	■		■	■	□	■	■

A Study of Current Leadership Styles in the North African Church

Values, Behaviors, Qualities	1	2	3	4	5	6	7	8	9	10	11	12	13	14
benevolence							X							X
blameless														X
blessing			X					X	X					X
blood-revenge				X										
bravery			X										X	
brotherhood									X					
calm						X								
caretaking			X	X	X		X		X	X	X	X	X	
charisma			X	X		X	X	X	X	X		X	X	
charity			X	X	X	X		X	X	X	X	X	X	
chastity											X			
chivalry			X									X		
clear-sightedness			X											
collaboration													X	
common sense						X								
communication								X	X	X	X	X	X	X
community centered	X		X	X	X	X		X	X	X	X	X	X	X
compassion							X							
competence														
conceptualization	X													
conciliatory				X	X									
consensus			X	X	X						X	X		
considerate			X			X								
consultation			X	X	X						X	X	X	
courage			X	X	X	X		X					X	
cross-cultural skills							X			X				
curses							X		X					
detached from earth							X							
dialogue												X		
dignity								X					X	
discernment								X					X	

Appendix P

Values, Behaviors, Qualities	1	2	3	4	5	6	7	8	9	10	11	12	13	14
dying for followers		■								■	■			■
educator														
elegance			■	■										
eloquence														
embededness					■		■			■	■	■		
emotional tie					■	■	■	■	■	■	■	■	■	
empathy	■					■			■			■		
endurance														
encourager														■
egalitarian			■	■								■		
elitism														
equity			■											
erratic										■				
exhortation					■				■		■			
fairness														
faith					■	■	■	■	■	■	■	■	■	■
faithfulness			■						■	■				
family oriented					■	■	■	■				■	■	
farsightedness						■					■	■	■	
fasting					■	■	■	■	■			■	■	
father					■			■				■	■	
feeding	■	■	■	■				■		■			■	
fidelity					■					■				
firmness		■					■		■			■		
forgiving										■			■	
forsightedness	1													
fortitude					■									
friend of god				■		■		■			■		■	
friendship						■					■			
generosity			■	■	■		■		■	■		■	■	
gentleness											■	■	■	

336   A Study of Current Leadership Styles in the North African Church

Values, Behaviors, Qualities	1	2	3	4	5	6	7	8	9	10	11	12	13	14
goal-seeker					X									
god-fearing					X	X	X	X	X	X	X	X	X	X
good judgment					X									
good manners						X							X	
goodness								X						
group feeling														
guardian			X	X										X
guide		X	X	X							X	X		
healing	X	X												
helper						X								
hierachical			X											
holiness											X			
holistic							X							
honesty				X	X	X	X							
honor					X	X		X						
hospitality						X	X	X	X					
humility	X				X					X			X	X
impartiality					X									
infallibility							X							
incognito inquiry														
industriousness										X	X	X	X	
integrity					X					X				X
interfaith relations														
intermidiary: god and follower			X				X							
intimacy with god					X	X	X		X	X	X		X	X
intuitive												X		
joy														
judge			X	X								X		
justice			X	X	X	X	X					X	X	
kindness									X					

Appendix P

Values, Behaviors, Qualities	1	2	3	4	5	6	7	8	9	10	11	12	13	14
knowledge-science														
leading		■		■								■	■	
legal knowledge														
listening	■		■	■			■		■					■
longanimity			▨											
love					■				■	■	■	■		
love god					■	■	■		■	■	■	■		
loyalty				■					■	■	■		■	
master														
maturity					▨									
meditation													▨	
meekness														
mentor										▨		▨		
mercy					■	■	■						■	
miracle making			▨											▨
moderation										▨				
modesty									▨					
mocking														
monocultural			▨											
morality			■	■	■	■	■	■	■	■	■	■	■	■
mystic			▨					▨				▨		
nepotism			▨						▨					
nobility						▨								
passionate									▨					
paternalistic				▨	▨									
patience				■	■	■		■		■	■	■	■	■
peace				■	■		■		■	■	■	■	■	■
pedagogy														
perceptiveness						▨								
perseverance	▨													
persuasion	▨								▨					

A Study of Current Leadership Styles in the North African Church

Values, Behaviors, Qualities	1	2	3	4	5	6	7	8	9	10	11	12	13	14
piety				■	■	■	■	■	■	■	■	■	■	■
physical fitness					■									
pleasant								■						
polemics												■		
political skills														
poverty						■			■					
powerlessness														
practical ability					■									■
prayer				■	■	■	■		■	■	■	■	■	■
preacher				■	■	■		■		■	■	■		■
protection		■	■	■				■	■					
purity								■						■
reasoning														
relational				■	■		■	■		■	■	■		■
reputation					■				■				■	
respectability				■										
responsible				■	■									
reward giving=transactional						■	■							
reward receiving						■		■						
rhetorical skills														
righteous					■									
sanctification											■			
self-control			■		■									
self-sacrifice		■	■				■	■		■	■			
serenity			■											
servant	■								■		■			
severity								■				■		■
shame			■			■								
sharing			■								■			■
sheikhocratic			■											
shepherd				■	■				■	■		■		

Appendix P

Values, Behaviors, Qualities	1	2	3	4	5	6	7	8	9	10	11	12	13	14
simple lifestyle			X		X		X					X	X	
sincerity					X									X
social engagement														
solidarity										X	X	X		
sound mind and body						X								
spirit filled											X	X		
steadfastness										X	X			
stewardship	X													
stimulate														
strong						X				X	X			
submission to others														X
supernatural power			X		X	X	X	X						
supportive				X				X	X					X
teaching					X	X	X	X	X	X	X	X	X	X
team work										X	X			
temperate														
tenderness									X	X	X			
theologian						X				X	X		X	
thinker														
threats at times				X				X						
time-giving									X			X		
tolerant											X	X		
traditions			X											
transformational					X		X	X	X	X	X	X	X	X
transparency													X	
trustworthiness			X	X	X									
truthfulness				X								X		
unity														
vicegerent						X	X					X		
virility			X					X						
virtuous														

Values, Behaviors, Qualities	1	2	3	4	5	6	7	8	9	10	11	12	13	14
visionary			■	■	■		■			■	■			■
war			■	■						■		■		
warner			■	■	■						■			
wisdom			■	■	■	■	■	■						
witness					■	■		■		■	■	■		
word (Bible or Qur'an)				■	■	■	■	■	■	■	■	■	■	
writer										■	■			
zeal					■					■	■	■		

APPENDIX Q

Research Flowchart

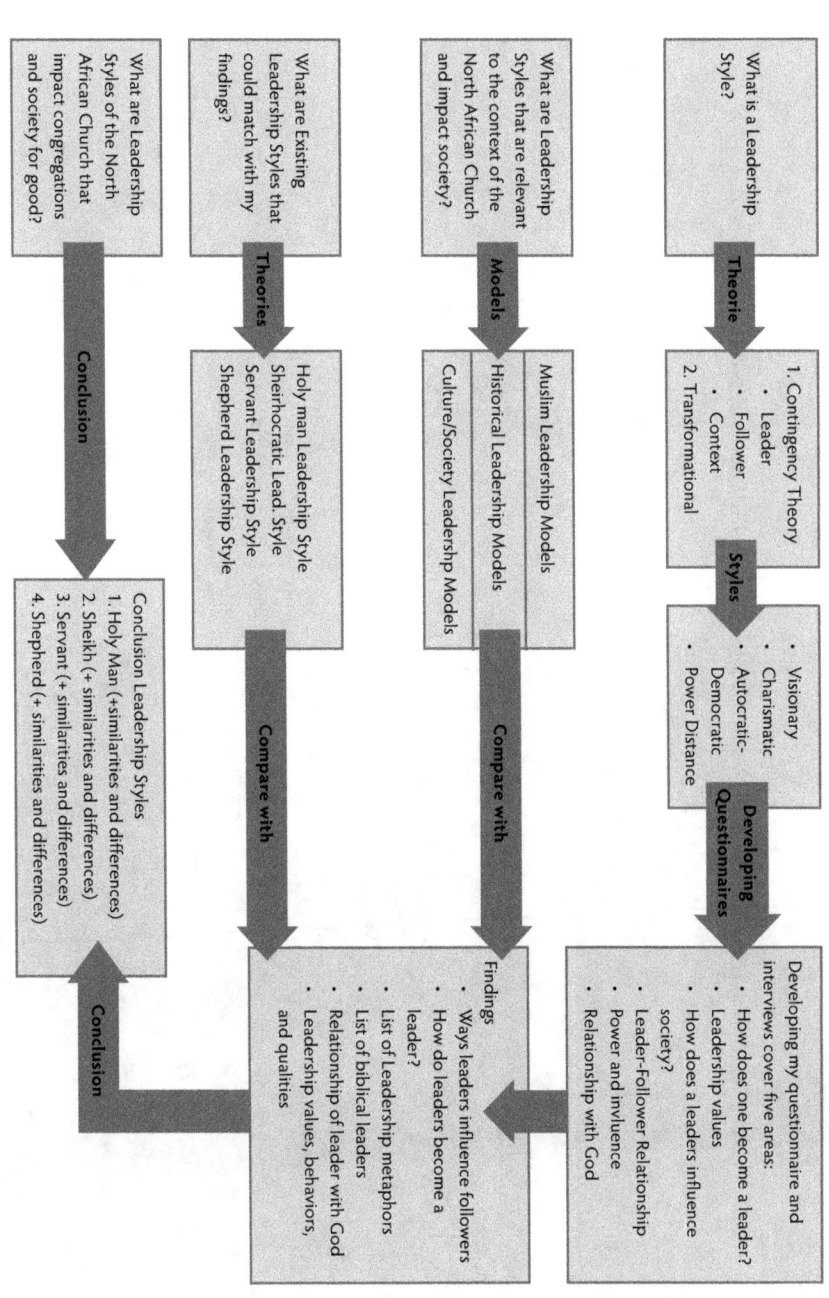

341

GLOSSARY

Arabic Transliteration of Terms

ahkam	decision, judgment
akh	brother
amana	loyalty
amghar	tribal or village leader
amir	prince
amr	authority
anis	companion
baraka	blessing
da'wa	call to Islam
dhimmi	member of a religious minority
faqih	judge
fatwa	legal opinion
fiqh	jurisprudence
fuqaha'	jurist
'adama	sign
'adala	status of justice
'adl	justice
'dli	be impartial, just
'alim	scholar, teacher
'asabiyya	cohesion, group feeling
'ayla	contemporary family
'ilm	knowledge
'ulama	theologian
hadith	tradition
hakam	judge, wise
hakim	just
hikma	wisdom
hilm	patience, longanimity

343

hishma	shame
hukm	authority, supreme executive power
ihsan	charity
ijma'	consensus
imam	religious leader
iman	faith
istikhlaf	vicegerency
jahiliyya	time of ignorance
jihad	struggle
jinn	supernatural being
jizya	tax for religious minorities
kahin	soothsayer
karama	miracle
karim	generous
khadria	brotherhood or community
khalifa	vicegerent
khalil	close friend
maftul	virtuous
maghazi	military expedition
ma'rifa	knowledge
majalis	council
mala'	administration, city council
marabout	holy man/woman
mrabtin	holy man/woman, *marabout*
mufti	legal adviser
muruwa	virtue
nabi	prophet
nadhir	Warner
nafaqa	support of spouse or family
nif	honor-respect
qadi	judge
qahr	coercion

qa'id	leader
raghba	yearning
rahim	gracious
rahma	mercy
rasul	prophet
razzia	quick military raids
sabr	patience
sahib	intimate friend
siddiq	just
shahada	confession of faith
shahid	witness
sha'ir	knower
sharia	path, spring, law
sharif	descendant of Muhammad
sheikh	tribal leader, leader
shura	consultation
sira	narrative, account
sufi	mystical, popular saint
sultan	power
sura	chapter
taqwa	fear and awe
wahy	revelation
wali	guardian
zakat	almsgiving
zawiyya	small mosque or oratory

BIBLIOGRAPHY

Aabed, Adnan
2006 "A Study of Islamic Leadership Theory and Practice in K-12 Islamic Schools in Michigan." Thesis (Ph. D.) Brigham Young University. Dept. of Educational Leadership and Foundations.

Abdalla, Ikhlas A. and Moudy A. Al-Homoud
2001 "Exploring the Implicit Leadership Theory in the Arabian Gulf States." *Applied Psychology: An International Review* 50, no.4: 506-531.

Abderraziq, Ali
1994 *L'Islam et les fondements du pouvoir (Islam and the Foundation of Power)*. Paris: La Découverte/Cedj.

Abul-Faris, Ahmad
1980 *The Political System of Islam*. Amman, Jordan: The Library of the Modern Message.

Addi, Lahouari
1999 *Les mutations de la société algérienne: Famille et lien social dans l'Algérie contemporaine (Mutation of the Algerian Society: Family and Social Bond in Present Algeria)*. Paris: La Découverte.
2004 "Femme, famille et lien social en Algérie." In *Famille et mutations sociopolitiques. L'approche culturaliste à lépreuve*, edited by Azadeh Kian-Thiébaut and Marie Ladier-Fouladi, 71-87. Paris: Editions de la Maison des Sciences de l'Homme.

Aït-Larbi, Arezki
2008 "Les Chrétiens pourchassés en Algérie (Christians Chased in Algeria)." *Le Figaro* (February 25). http://www.lefigaro.fr/international/2008/02/26/01003-20080226ARTFIG00043-les-chretiens-d-algerieen-butte-aux-tracasseries.php (accessed February 2009).

Ajijola, Alhaji Adeleke Dirisu
1998 "Islam, Dialogue, Christianity." In *Liberal Islam: A Source Book*, edited by Charles Kurzman, 239-243. Oxford, UK: Oxford University Press.

Alghailani, Said Ali
2002 "Islam and the French Decolonization of Algeria: The Role of the Algerian Ulama 1919-1940." Thesis (Ph. D.) Indiana University.

Al-Asi, Mohammed
2000 "The Prophet and the Power." In *The Seerah: A Power Perspective*, edited by Mohammed al-Asi and Zafar Bangash. London: The Institute of Contemporary Islamic Thought.

Ali, Abbas J.
2005 "Leadership in the Context of Culture: An Egyptian Perspective." *Leadership and Organization Development Journal* 25, no.6: 499-511.
2005 *Islamic Perspectives on Management and Organization: New Horizons In Management*. Northampton, MA: Edward Elgar Publishing.

Al-Kubaisy, A.
1985 "A Model in the Administrative Development of Arab Gulf Countries." *The Arab Gulf* 17, no. 2: 29-48.

Andrae, Tor
1936 *Mohammed: The Man and His Faith*. Translated by Theophil Menzel. New York: Charles Scribner's Sons.

Aouli, Smail, Ramdane Redjala, and Philippe Zoummeroff
1994 *Abdelkader*. Paris: Fayard.

Armstrong, Karen
2006 *Muhammad: A Prophet for Our Time*. New York: HarperOne.

Arnold, T. W.
1922 "Khalifa." In *The Encyclopaedia of Islam CD-ROM Edition v. 1.0*. Leiden, The Netherlands: Koninklijke Brill. (EI2 CD), s.v.

Avolio, Bruce J.
2005 *Leadership Development in Balance: Made-Born*. Mahwah, NJ: Lawrence Erlbaum Associates.

Ayman, R. and S. Hong
1992 "Gender and Cultural Effects on Expectations of the Ideal Leader: A Comparison between U.S.A. and Korea". Unpublished Manuscript, Illinois Institute of Technology, Chicago, IL.

Bangash, Zafar
2000 "The Concepts of Leader and Leadership in Islam." *Crescent International* (August 16-31). http//islamicthought.org. (Accessed August 2007).

Banks, Robert and Bernice M. Ledbetter
2004 *Review Leadership: A Christian Evaluation of Current Approaches*. Grand Rapids, MI: Baker Book House.

Banks, Robert, and Kimberly Powell, eds.
1999 *Faith in Leadership: How Leaders Live Out Their Faith in Their Work—and Why It Matters*. San Francisco, CA: Matters.

Baron, David, and Lynette Padwa
1999 *Moses on Management: Leadership Lessons from the Greatest Manager of All Time*. New York: Pocket Books.

Bass, Bernard M.
1985 *Leadership and Performance beyond Expectations*. New York: Free Press.
1990 *Bass Bernard and Stogdill's Handbook of Leadership: Theory, Research, & Managerial Applications*. 3rd ed. New York: Free Press.

Bass, Bernard M. and Enzo R. Valenzi
1973 "Contingent Aspects of Effective Management Styles." In *Contingency Approaches to Leadership*, edited by James G. Hunt and Lars L. Larson, 130-157. Carbondale, IL: Southern Illinois University Press.

Bass, Bernard M., P. C. Burger, R. Doktor, and G. V. Barrett
1979 *Assessment of Managers: An International Comparison*. New York: Free Press.

Bass, Bernard M. and Bruce J. Avolio
1993 "Transformational Leadership: A Response to Critiques." In *Leadership Theory and Research: Perspectives and Directions*, edited by Martin M. Chemers and Roya Ayman, 49-80. New York: Academic Press.

Baunard, Louis
1896 *Le Cardinal Lavigerie* (*The Cardinal Lavigerie*). Paris: J. De Gigord.

Beekun, Rafik I., and Jamal Badawi
1999 *Leadership: An Islamic Perspective*. Beltsville, MD: Amana Publications.

Ben Cheneb, Mohamed
1897 *Notion de pédagogie musulmane. Résumé d'éducation et d'instruction enfantine* (*Notion of Muslim Pedagogy : Summary of child éducation and instruction*. Alger, Algeria: Jourdan.

Blanc, Jean L.
2006 *Algérie, tu es à moi: Signé Dieu (Algeria, You Belong to Me: Signed God)*. Thoune, Switzerland: Editions Sénevé.

Blanchard, Ken, and Phil Hodges
2005 *Lead Like Jesus: Lessons from the Greatest Leadership Role Model of All Time*. Nashville, TN: W Publishing Group.

Block, Peter
1993 *Stewardship: Choosing Service over Self-Interest*. San Francisco, CA: Berrett-Koehler.

Bond, M. H., and K. Leung
1993 "The Relationship Between Culture, Individual Valences and Behavioral Intentions." *Journal of Cross-Cultural Psychology* 24:331-338.

Bonte, Pierre, Edouard Conte, and Paul Dresch
2001 *Emirs et présidents (Emir and Presidents)*. Paris: Editions CNRS.

Boubakeur, Dalil
1995 *Charte du culte musulman (The Charta of Muslim Worship)*. Paris: Les Editions du Rocher.

Boulaabi, Abderraouf
2005 *Islam et pouvoir: Les finalités de la Charia et la légitimité du pouvoir (Islam and Power: the Purposes of Charia and the Legitimacy of Power)*. Paris: L'Harmattan.

Bourdieu, Pierre
1961 *Sociologie de l'Algérie (Sociology of Algeria)*. Paris: Presses Universitaires de France.

Bourg, Ali Didier
1994 "L'Université Islamique de France : Un instrument d'intégration pour la seconde génération musulmane (The Islamic University of France: A Way of Integrating the Muslim Second Generation)." *Migrations et Sociétés* 6:71-80.

Boutefnouchet, Mostapha
1982 *La famille algérienne : évolution et caractéristiques récentes (The Algerian Family : Evolution and Recent Characteristics)*. Alger, Algeria :SNED.

Bouyerdene, Ahmed
2008 *Abd El Kader: L'harmonie des contraires (Abd El Kader: Harmony of the Opposites)*. Paris: Seuil.

Brueggemann, Walter
1979 "Covenanting as Human Vocation." *Interpretation* 33:115-129.

Burns, James M.
1978 *Leadership*. New York: Harper & Row.

Bukhari, Sahih
2009 "Compendium of Muslim Texts", Vol. 3, Book 36, Nr. 463. http://www.usc.edu/schools/college/crcc/engagement/resources/texts/muslim/search.html. (Accessed November 2009).

Burridge, W. F.
1966 *Destiny Africa: Cardinal Lavigerie and the Making of the White Fathers*. London: Geoffrey Chapman Edition.

Canard, M.
1965 "Dawa." In *Encyclopaedia of Islam*. New ed. Edited by B. Lewis et al., 168-170. Leiden, The Netherlands: E. J. Brill.

Cannon, Byron D.
1995 "Qadi." In *The Oxford Encyclopedia of the Modern Islamic World*. Vol. 3, edited by John L. Esposito, 374-375. Oxford, UK: Oxford University Press.

Carlyle, Thomas
1897 *On Heroes, Hero-Worship, and the Heroic in History*. Hastings, UK: Owen Press.

Chahine, T.M.
1971 *Le commentaire de Ben Badis dans causeries rappelant la parole du sage et du bien informé (Commentary of Ben Badis in Conversation Recalling the Words of the Wise and the Well Informed)*. Beirut, Lebanon: Dar al-fikr.

Chelhod, Joseph
1958 *Introduction à la sociologie en islam (Introduction to Sociology in Islam)*. Paris: Maisonneuve Larose.
1986 *Les structures du sacré chez les Arabes (The Structures of Sacredness among the Arabs)*. Paris: Maisonneuve Larose.

Chemers, Martin M. and Robert W. Rice
1973 "A Theoretical and Empirical Examination of Fiedler's Contingency Model of Leadership Effectiveness." In *Contingency Approaches to Leadership*, edited by James G. Hunt and Lars L. Larson, 91-129. New York: Academic Press.

Chirane, Abdel Hamid
1994 "La notion d'imam selon l'Institut musulman de la mosquée de Paris (The Concept of Imam According to the Muslim Institute of the Paris Mosque)." *Migrations et Sociétés* 6:65-70.

Chodkiewicz, Michel
1962 *Abd el-Kader: Ecrits spirituels (Spiritual Writings of Abd el-Kader)*. Paris: Edition du Seuil.

Cragg, Kenneth
1964 *The House of Islam*. Encino, CA: Dickenson Publishing Company.

Clarke, Lynda
1995 "Sainthood." In *The Oxford Encyclopedia of the Modern Islamic World*, Vol. 3, edited by John L. Esposito, 460-462. Oxford, UK: Oxford University Press.

Claverie, Pierre
2004 *Petit traité de la rencontre et du dialogue (Small Treatise of Encounter and Dialogue)*. Paris: Cerf.

Clinton, Robert
1992 *Leadership Series: Conclusion on Leadership Style*. Pasadena, CA: Barnabas Resources.

Cooper, J.B., and J.L. McGaugh
1969 "Leadership." In *Leadership*, edited by C.A. Gibb, 242-250. Harmondsworth, UK: Penguin Books.

Courtois, Christian
1955 *Les Vandales et l'Afrique (Vandals and Africa)*. Paris: German Editions.

Covey, Stephen R.
1989 *The Seven Habits of Highly Effective People: Restoring the Character Ethic*. New York: Simon and Schuster.

Cragg, Kenneth
1975 *The House of Islam*. Encino, CA: Dickenson Publishing Company.

Cristiani, Léon.
1961 *Le cardinal Lavigerie, un grand bienfaiteur de l'Afrique, 1825-1892 (Cardinal Lavigerie: A Great Benefactor of Africa)*. Paris: Éditions France-Empire,

Cuoq, Joseph
1984 *L'Eglise d'Afrique du Nord du IIe au XIIe siècle (The North African Church from the 2nd to the 12th Century)*. Paris: Centurion.

Daniel, Robin
1992 *This Holy Seed: Faith, Hope and Love in the Early Churches of North Africa*. Harpenden, UK: Tamarisk Publications.

Dastmalchian Ali, Mansour Javidan and Kamran Alam
2001 "Effective Leadership and Culture in Iran: An Empirical Study." *International Association for Applied Psychology* 50, no. 4 (October): 532-558.

De Arteche, Jose
1964 *The Cardinal of Africa: Charles Lavigerie Founder of the White Fathers*. London: Publishers Sands and Co.

De Labriolle, Saint
1941 *Saint Augustin: La Cité de Dieu (Saint Augustine: The City of God)*. Translated by Pierre de Labriolle. Paris: Garnier.

Decret, François
1996 *Le Christianisme en Afrique du Nord (Christianity in North Africa)*. Paris: Seuil.

DePree, Max
1992 *Leadership Jazz*. New York: Currency Doubleday.

Direche-Slimani, Karima
2004 *Chrétiens de Kabylie, 1873-1954: Une action missionnaire dans l'Algérie coloniale (Christians from Kabylia, 1873-1954: A Missionary Action in Colonized Algeria)*. Alger, Algeria: Bouchène.

Djilani Sergy, Farid
1986 "Des causes du déclin du christianisme en Afrique du Nord: II-XII siècles (Causes of the decline of Christianity in North Africa: 2th-7th Century)." Master's thesis, Faculté libre de théologie évangélique de Vaux-sur-Seine, France.

Doohan, Helen
1984 *Leadership in Paul.* Wilmington, DE: Michael Glazier.

Dorfman, Peter W.
2004 "International and Cross-Cultural Leadership Research." In *Handbook for International Management Research,* 2nd ed., edited by Betty Jane Punnett and Oded Shenkar, 2nd ed., 265-355. Ann Harbor, MI: University of Michigan Press.

Dorfman, Peter W., and Robert J. House
2004 "Cultural Influences on Organizational Leadership: Literature Review, Theoretical Rationale, and GLOBE Project Goals." In *Culture, Leadership, and Organizations: The GLOBE Study of 62 Societies,* edited by Robert J. House, Paul J. Hanges, Mansour Javidance, Peter W. Dorfman and Vipin Gupta, 51-90. Thousand Oaks, CA: Sage Publications.

Doutté, Edmond
1994 *Magie et religion dans l'Afrique du Nord (Magic and Religion in North Africa).* Paris: Maisonneuve.

Downton, J. V.
1973 *Rebel Leadership: Commitment and Charisma in the Revolutionary Process.* New York: Free Press.

Du Roy, O. J.-B.
1967 "St Augustine." In *The New Catholic Encyclopedia,* edited by C. Joseph Nuesse, William J. Hill, Frederick R. McManus, Joseph N. Moody, William A. Wallace and John P. Whalen, 1041-1058. New York: Mc Graw-Hill Book Company.

Duval, Armand
2000 *"Avant tout, la prière: Le témoignage du Cardinal Lavigerie (Prayer before Everything Else : The Testimony of Cardinal Lavigerie).* Paris: François-Xavier de Guibert.

Eickelman, Dale F.
1995 *The Middle East and Central Asia: An Anthropological Approach.* 4th ed. Upper Saddle River, NJ: Prentice Hall.

Ehrlich, S. B., J. R. Meindl and B.Viellieu
1990 "The Charismatic Appeal of a Transformational Leader: An Empirical Case Study of a Small, High Technology Contractor." *The Leadership Quarterly* 1, no. 4: 229-247.

Elliston, Edgar J.
1993 *Home Grown Leaders*. Pasadena, CA: William Carey Library.

Eslin, Jean-Claude
2002 *Saint Augustin : l'homme occidental (St Augustine : The Western Man)*. Paris: Michalon.

Evans, Martin, and John Phillips
2007 *Algeria: Anger of the Dispossessed*. New Haven, CT: Yale University Press.

Étienne, Bruno
1989 *La France et l'Islam (France and Islam)*. Paris: Hachette.

Étienne, Bruno, and François Pouillon
2003 *Abd el-Kader le magnanime (Abd el-Kader : the Magnanimous)*. Paris: Découvertes Gallimard.

Fiedler, Fred E.
1964 "The Contingency Model of Leadership Effectiveness." In *Advances in Experimental Social Psychology*, edited by L. Berkowitz. Vol. 1. New York: Academic Press.
1969 "Leadership: A New Model." In *Leadership*, edited by C. Gibbs, 230-241. Harmondsworth, UK: Penguin.
1993 "The Leadership Situation and the Black Box in Contingency Theories." In *Leadership Theory and Research: Perspectives and Directions*, edited by Martin M. Chemers and Roya Ayman, 1-28. New York: Academic Press.

Fiedler, Fred E., Martin M.Chemers and Linda Mahar
1964 *Improving Leadership Effectiveness: The Leader Match Concept*. New York: John Wiley and Sons.

Fields, D.
2005 "Applying cultural data from the GLOBE study to develop leadership models for Russian organizations." In *Strategies for Effective Leadership: U.S. and Russian Perspectives*, edited by J. Coe, L. Sukhodoyeva, and B. Johnson. Bloomington, IN: Authorhouse

Fitzgerald, Allan D, ed.
1999 *Augustine through the Ages: An Encyclopedia*. Cambridge, UK: Eerdmans.

Flowers, V. S., C. Hughes, S. Myers and S. Myers
1975 "Managerial Values for Working." A Nationwide A.M.A. Survey Report (January).

Friedman, Ellen G.
1983 *Spanish Captives in North Africa in the Early Modern Age*. Madison, WI: University of Wisconsin Press.

Fry, Louis W.
2003 "Toward a Theory of Spiritual Leadership." *The Leadership Quarterly* 14:693-727.

Gan, Jonathan
2007 *The Metaphor of Shepherd in the Hebrew Bible: A Historical-Literary Reading*. Lanham, MD: University Press of America.

Gardet, Louis
1970 *L'Islam, religion et communauté (Islam, Religion, and Community)*. Paris : De Brouwer.
1981 *La cité musulmane : Vie sociale et politique (The Muslim City: Social and Political Life)*. Paris: J. Vrin.

Gardet, Louis and M.-M. Anawati
1948 *Introduction à la théologie musulmane: Essai de théologie comparée (Introduction to Muslim Theology: Writings on Comparative Theology)*. Paris: J. Vrin.

Gellner, Ernest
1969 "A Pendulum-Swing Theory of Islam." In *Sociology of Religion: Selected Readings*, edited by Roland Robertson, 127-138. New York: Penguin.

Ghabrial, Samy Hanna
1997 "The Growth of The Evangelical Churches in Egypt With Reference to Leadership." Unpublished Doctoral Dissertation. Fuller Theological Seminary, Pasadena, CA.

Gill, Kenneth D.
2000 "Charismatic Missions." In *Evangelical Dictionary of World Missions*, edited by A. Scott Moreau et al., 173-175. Grand Rapids, MI: BakerBooks.

Gilliot, Claude
1999 " 'Ulama." In *The Encyclopaedia of Islam CD-ROM Edition v. 1.0*. Leiden, The Netherlands: Koninklijke Brill. (EI2 CD) s. v.

Gimaret, Daniel
1995 *"Rahma."* In *Encyclopaedia of Islam*, edited by C. E Bosworth et al., 398-99. Leiden, The Netherlands: E. J. Brill.
1988 *Les Noms Divins en Islam (The Divine Names in Islam)*. Paris: Le Cerf.

Glaser, B. G.
1978 *Theoretical Sensitivity: Advances in the Methodology of Grounded Theory.* Mill Valley, CA: Sociology Press.

Goichon, A. M.
1971 "Hikma." In *The Encyclopaedia of Islam*. Edited by B. Lewis et al., 377-378. Leiden, The Netherlands : E. J. Brill.

Goldziher, Ignace
2006 *Muslim Studies*. Translated and edited by S.M. Stern and C. R. Barber. London, UK : Aldine Transactions.

Gomaa, Ali
2010 "Biography of Ali Gomaa, Grand Mufti of Egypt." http://www.aligomaa.net/bio.html. (accessed December 2010).

Gordon, L. V.
1975 *Measurement of Interpersonal Values.* Chicago, IL: Science Research Associates.

Greenleaf, Robert K.
1970 *The Servant as a Leader.* Indianapolis, IN: Greenleaf Center for Servant Leadership.
1977 *Servant Leadership: A Journey into the Nature of Legitimate Power and Greatness.* New York: Paulist Press.
1996 *Seeker and Servant.* New York: Pauline Press.

Greenleaf, Robert K., Don M. Frick and Larry C. Spears, eds.
1996 *On Becoming a Servant-Leader.* San Francisco, CA: Jossey-Bass.

Guillaume, A.
1955 *The Life of Muhammad: A Translation of Ishaq's Sirat Rasul Allah.* Oxford, UK: Oxford University Press.

Gülen, Fethullah
      Muslim Society. Cambridge, UK: Cambridge University Press.
      Les saints de l'Atlas (Saints of the Atlas). Paris: Edition Bouchène.
2000 *Prophet Muhammad: Aspects of His Life.* Fairfax, VI: The Fountain.

Hale Jeff R., and Dail L. Fields
2005 "Exploring Servant Leadership Across Cultures: A Study of Followers in Ghana and the USA." *Leadership* 3, no. 4 (November):397-417.

Hamman, A.
1966 *Cardinal Lavigerie: Ecrit d'Afrique (Cardinal Lavigerie: Writings from Africa)*. Paris: Edition Grasset.

Harris, P. R., and R. T. Moran
1989 *Managing Cultural Differences*. Houston, TX: Gulf Publishing.

Hersey, P, Kenneth H. Blanchard, and Dewey E Johnson
1969 *Management of Organizational Behavior: Utilizing Human Resources*. Upper Saddle River, NJ: Prentice Hall.

Hiebert, Paul G.
1985 *Anthropological Insights for Missionaries*. Grand Rapids, MI: Baker Book House.

Higginson, Richard
1999 "Integrity and the Art of Compromise." In *Faith in Leadership: How Leaders Live Out Their Faith in Their Work and Why It Matters*, edited by Robert Banks and Kimberly Powell, 19-33. San Francisco, CA: Jossey-Bass.

Hitti, Philip
1987 *The History of the Arabs*. London: Palmgrave McMillan.

Hofstede, G.
1984 *Culture's Consequences: International Differences in Work-Related Values*. Beverly Hills, CA: Sage.
2001 *Culture's Consequences: Comparing Values, Behaviors, Institutions, and Organizations Across Nations*. Thousand Oaks, CA: Sage.

Hofstede, G., and M. H. Bond
1988 "The Confucius Connection: From Cultural Roots to Economic Growth." *Organizational Dynamics* 16: 4-21.

Hogan, R.T. and A. M. Morrison
1991 "The Psychology of Managerial Incompetance." Paper presented at a joint conference of American Psychological Association-National Institute of Occupational Safety and Health. Washington, DC.

Hollander, Edwin P.
1993 "Legitimacy, Power, and Influence: A Perspective on Relational Features of Leadership." In *Leadership Theory and Research: Perspectives and Directions*. Edited by Martin M. Chemers and Roya Ayman, 29-47. New York: Academic Press.

Holme, L. R.
1898 *The Extinction of the Christian Churches in North Africa*. London: Clay and Sons.

Hostetler, Marian E.
2003 *Algeria: Where Mennonites and Muslims Met (1955-1978)*. Elkhart, IN: Self-Published.

Hourani, Albert Habib
1991 *A History of the Arab Peoples*. Cambridge, MA: Belknap Press.

House, Robert J.
1984 "Power in Organizations: Social Psychological Perspective." Unpublished Manuscript. Toronto, Canada: University of Toronto.

House, Robert J., and Boas Shamir
1993 "Toward the Integration of Transformational, Charismatic, and Visionary Theories. In *Leadership Theory and Research: Perspectives and Directions*, edited by Martin M. Chemers and Roya Ayman, 81-107. New York: Academic Press.

House, Robert J., Paul J. Hanges, Mansour Jividan, Peter Dorfman and Vipin Gupta
2004 *Culture, Leadership, and Organizations: The GLOBE Study of 62 Societies*. Thousand Oaks, CA: Sage Publications.

House, Robert J., William D. Spangler and James Woycke
1991 "Personality and Charisma in the U.S. Presidency: A Psychological Theory of Leader Effectiveness." *Administrative Science Quarterly* 36: 364-396.

Hughes, Richard, Robert Ginnett and Gordon J. Curphy
2006 *Leadership: Enhancing the Lessons of Experience*. Boston, MA: McGraw-Hill.

Hui, C.H., and M. Villareal
1989 "Individualism-Collectivism and Psychological Needs: Their Relationship in Two Cultures." *Journal of Cross-Cultural Psychology* 20: 310-323.

Ibn Khaldun
1965 *La Muquaddima, extrait*. Alger, Algeria: Hachette.
1967 *The Muqaddimah : An Introduction to History*. Edited by N. J. Dawood and translated by Franz Rosenthal. Vol. 1. 2nd ed. Princeton, NJ: Princeton University Press.

Ibrahim, Saad Eddin
1982 *The New Arab Social Order: A Study of the Social Impact of Arab Oil Wealth.* Boulder, CO: Westview Press.

Iogna-Prat, Dominique and Gilles Veinstein
2003 *Histoires des hommes de Dieu dans l'islam et le christianisme (History of Men of God in Islam and Christianisme).* Paris: Flammarion.

Izutsu, Toshihiko
2002 *Ethico-Religious Concepts in the Qur'an.* Montreal, Canada: McGill-Quenn's University Press.

Al-Jamali, M. F.
1998 "Islamic Education." In Les différents aspects de la culture islamique ç L'individu et la société en Islam (The Various Aspects of Islamic Culture: The Individual and Society in Islam). Edited by A. Boudhiba and M. M. al-Dawalibi. Paris: UNESCO.

Jehel, Georges
1999 "Les étapes de la disparition du christianisme primitif en Afrique du Nord à partir de la conquête arabe (The Stages of the Death of Primitive Christianity in North Africa Starting from the Arab Conquest)." http://www.clio.fr/BIBLIOTHEQUE/les_etapes_de_la_disparition_du_christianisme_primitif_en_afrique_du_nord_a_partir_de_la_conquete_arabe.asp (accessed January 2007).

Jourjon, Maurice
1954 "L'évêque et le peuple de Dieu selon Saint Augustin (The Bishop and God's People According to Saint Augustine)." In *Saint Augustin parmi nous (Saint Augustine among Us).* Edited by Henri Rondet, Charles Morel, Maurice Jourgon, and Jules Lebreton, 149-178. Paris: Mappus.

Kabasakal, H., and M. Bodur
2007 "Leadership and Culture in Turkey: A Multi-Faceted Phenomenon." In *The GLOBE Book of In-Depth Studies of 25 Societies,* edited by J. S. Chhokar, F. C. Brodbeck and R. J. House, 833-874. Hove, UK: Psychology Press.

Kabasakal, H., and Ali Dastmalchian
2001 "Introduction to the Special Issue on Leadership and Culture in the Middle East." *Applied Psychology: An International Review* 50, no. 4: 479-488.

Karolia, AbuBakr
2003 "*Taqwa*: A State of Submission." Johannesburg, South Africa, http://www.nuradeen.com/archives/Contributions/Taqwa.htm (accessed July 2006).

Kennedy, Hugh
1986. *The Prophet and the Age of the Caliphates: The Islamic Near East from the 6th to the 11th Century*. New York: Longman.

Khadra, Bashir
1984 "Leadership, Ideology, and Development in the Middle East." *Journal of Asian and African Studies* 19, no. 3-4: 228-239.

Khalaf-Allah, Muhammad
1998 "Legislative Authority." In *Liberal Islam: A Sourcebook*. Edited by Charles Kurzman, 37-45. New York: Oxford University Press.

Khan, Adalat
2007 "Islamic Leadership Principles." In *American Chronicle*. http//www.americanchronicle.com/articles/33073 (accessed February 2008).

Khuri, Fuad I.
2006 *Imams and Emirs: State, Religion and Sects in Islam*. London: Saqi.

Killinski, Kenneth K., and Jerry C. Wofford
1973 *Organization and Leadership in the Local Church*. Grand Rapids, MI: Zondervan Publishing House.

Kluckhohn, F. and F. Strodtbeck
1961 *Variations in Value Orientations*. Evanston, Illinois: Row Peterson.

Knickerbocker, Irving
1958 "The Analysis of Leadership: Leadership: A Conception and Some Implications." In *The Study of Leadership*. Edited by C. G. Brown and Thomas S. Cohn, 3-11. Danville, IL: The Interstate.

Kraemers, J. H.
2001 "Sultan." In *The Encyclopaedia of Islam CD-ROM Edition v. 1.0*. Leiden, The Netherlands: Koninklijke Brill. (EI 2 CD), s.v.

Küng, Hans
2007 *Islam: Past, Present, & Future*. Translated by John Bowden. Oxford, UK: OneWorld.

Laoust, Henri
1986 *Le Califat dans la doctrine de Rasid Rida. Traduction annotée d'al-ilafa au al-Imama al-'u☒ma (Le Califat ou l'Imama suprême)*. Paris : Adrien Maisonneuve.

Lacheraf, Mostefa
1965 *L'Algérie : Nation et Société (Algeria : Nation and Society)*. Paris: Maspéro.

Lammens, P. Henri
1914 *Le berceau de l'islam (The Cradle of Islam)*. Rome: Pontificii Instituti Biblici.
1924 *La Mecque à la veille de l'Hégire (Mecca Before the Hijra)*. Beirut, Lebanon : Imprimerie Catholique.

Lane, Edward William
1863 *Arabic-English Lexicon*. London: Williams and Norgate.

Laniak, Timothy
2007 *While Shepherds Watch Their Flocks : Rediscovering Biblical Leadership*. Matthews, NC : ShepherdLeader Publications.

Lari, Musavi Mujtaba
1996 *Imamate and Leadership*. Qom, Iran: Foundation of Islamic Cultural Propagation in the World.

Lavigerie, Cardinal
1950 *Instructions aux missionnaires (Instructions to the Missionaries)*. Namur, Belgium : Grands Lacs.
1965 *Ecrits d'Afrique (Writings from Africa)*. Paris: Grasset.

Lawless, George
1999 "Preaching." In *Augustine Through the Ages: An Encyclopedia*. Edited by Allan D. Fitzgerald, 675-677. Cambridge, UK: Eerdmans.

Lewin, K., R. Lippit and R.K White
1939 "Patterns of Aggressive Behavior in Experimentally Created Social Climates." *Journal of Social Psychology* 10: 271-301

Liberté
2004 "Colloque sur Saint Augustin à Tizi Ouzou (Colloquium on Saint Augustine in Tizi Ouzou)." *Liberté,* Accessed on line at www.algerie-dz.com/article149.html (accessed October 2008).

Lienhard, Joseph T.
1994 "Friendship with God, Friendship in God: Traces in St. Augustine." In *Augustine: Mystic and Mystagogue*, edited by Frederick Van Fleteren et al., 207-29. New York: Peter Lang.
1999 "Ministry." In *Augustine through the Ages: An Encyclopedia*, edited by Allan D. Fitzgerald, 567-569. Cambridge, UK: Eerdmans.

Lingenfelter, Sherwood G., and Marvin K. Mayers
1986 *Ministering Cross-Culturally: An Incarnational Model for Personal Relationships*. Grand Rapids, MI: Baker Book House.

Madelung, W.
2001 "Imama." In *The Encyclopaedia of Islam CD-ROM Edition v. 1.0*. Leiden, The Netherlands: Koninklijke Brill (EI.2 CD), s.v.

Makari, Victor E.
1983 *Ibn Taymiyyah's Ethics: The Social Factor*. Chico, CA: Scholars Press.

Mann, R. D.
1959 "A Review of the Relationships between Personality and Performance in Small Groups." *Psychological Bulletin* 56: 241-270.

Mansour, Camille
1975 *L'Autorité dans la pensée musulmane : Le concept d'ijma (consensus) et la problématique de l'autorité (Authority in Muslim Thought : The concept of Ijma (consensus) and the Issue of Authority)*. Paris: J. Vrin.

Mantran Robert
1984 *L'Empire ottoman, du XVIe au XVIIIe siècle: Administration, économie, société (The Ottoman Empire from the 16th to the 18th century: Administration, Economy, Society)*. London: Variorum.

Manz, Charles
1998 *The Leadership Wisdom of Jesus: Practical Lessons for Today*. San Francisco, CA: Berrett-Koehler.

Manz, Charles. K R. Marx Manz, and C. Neck
2001 *The Wisdom of Solomon at Work: Ancient Virtues for Living and Leading Today*. San Francisco, CA: Berrett-Koehler.

Maraval, Pierre
2005 *Le christianisme de Constantin à la conquête arabe (Christianity from Constantine to the Arab Conquest)*. 3rd ed. Paris: Presses Universitaires de France.

Markus, Robert A.
1999 "Life, Culture, and Controversies of Augustine." In *Augustine through the Ages: An Encyclopedia*, edited by Allan D. Fitzgerald, 498-504. Cambridge, UK: Eerdmans.

Marsh, Charles
1976 *Impossible à Dieu (Impossible to God)*. Paris: Telos.

Massey, M.
1979 *The People Puzzle: Understanding Yourself and Others*. Reston, VA: Reston.

Mayeur-Jaouen, Catherine
2002 *Saints et héros du Moyen-Orient contemporain (Saints and Heroes in the Current Middle East)*. Paris: Maisonneuve Larose.

McCall, M. W., and M. M. Lombardo
1978 *Leadership: Where Else Can We Go?* Durham, NC: Duke University Press.

McIntosh, Gary L., and Samuel D. Rima
1997 *Overcoming the Dark Side of Leadership: The Paradox of Personal Dysfunction*. Grand Rapids, MI: Baker Books.

Merad, Ali
1967 *Le Réformisme musulman en Algérie de 1925-1940 : Essai d'histoire religieuse et sociale (Muslim Reformism in Algeria from 1925-1940: Essays on Social and Religious History)*. Paris: Mouton et Co.
1971 *Ibn Badis: Commentateur du Coran (Ibn Badis : Commentator of the Qur'an)*. Paris: Geuthner.

Mernissi, Fatima
1983 *Beyond The Veil*. London UK. Sari Book.

Mesnage, J.
1914 *Le Christianisme en Afrique: Origines, développements, extension (Christianity in Africa: Origins, Developments, Extension)*. Vol. I. Paris: Auguste Picard.

Mitchell, Terence R.
1993 "Leadership, Values and Accountability." In *Leadership Theory and Research: Perspectives and Directions*. Edited by Martin M. Chemers and Roya Ayman, 109-136. New York: Academic Press.

Mitroff, I. I., and E. A. Denton
1999 *A Spiritual Audit of Corporate America: A Hard Look at Spirituality, Religion, and Values in the Workplace.* San Francisco, CA: Jossey-Bass.

Montagne, Robert
1973 *The Berbers: Their Social and Political Organization (La vie sociale et la vie politique des Berbères).* Translated by David Seddon. London: Frank Cass.

Morel, Charles
1954 "La vie de prière de Saint Augustin : Le secret de sa force (Saint Augustine's Prayer Life : The Secret of His Life)." In *Saint Augustin parmi nous (Saint Augustine among Us),* edited by Henri Rondet, Charles Morel, Maurice Jourjon, and Jules Lebreton, 57-87. Le Puy, France: Mappus.

Mozaffari, Mehdi
1998 *Pouvoir Chiite: Théorie et Evolution (Shii Power: Theory and Developments).* Paris: L'Harmattan.

Muller, Roland
2000 *Honor and Shame: Unlocking the Door.* Guernsey, UK: XLibris Corporation.

Muna, Farid A.
1980 *The Arab Executive.* Basingstroke UK: Palgrave Macmillan.

Nanji, Azim A.
1995 "*Mufti.*" *The Oxford Encyclopedia of the Modern Islamic World.* Vol. 3. Edited by John L. Esposito, 151-152. Oxford: Oxford University Press.

Nasr, Seyyed Hossein
1993 *L'Islam traditionnel face au monde moderne (Traditional Islam facing the Modern World).* Translated by Gisèle Kondracki. Lausanne, Switzerland: L'Age d'Homme.

Nawafleh, Mohammed
2000 *The Personal and Leadership Characteristics of Omar Bin Al-Khattab.* Amman, Jordan: Majdalawi Publishing.

Neal, M and Jim L. Finley
2007 "American Hegemony and Business Education in the Arab World." *Journal of Management Education* 32: 38-83.

Nusair, Naïm
1986 *Arab Managerial Leadership.* Alexandria, Egypt: The House of Knowledge.

Paşa, F.S., H. Kabasakal and M. Bodur
2001 "Society, Organizations and Leadership in Turkey." *Applied Psychology: An International Review* 50, no.4: 559-589.

Patai, Raphael
1973 *The Arab Mind*. New York: Random House.

Perraudin, Jean
1958 *Entretiens sur la Vie Intérieure du Cardinal Lavigerie (Conversation on the Inner Life of the Cardinal Lavigerie*. Rome, Italy: Pères Blancs.

Prompsault, J.H.R
1849 "Eloquence." In *Dictionnaire raisonné de droit et de jurisprudence en matière civile ecclésiastique*. Vol.1. Paris: Ateliers Catholiques du Petit-Montrouge.

Popper, Micha, Ofra Mayseless, and Omri Castelnovo
2000 "Transactional Leadership and Attachment." *The Leadership Quarterly* 11, no. 2: 267-289.

Punnett, Jane and Oded Shenkar
2004 *Handbook for International Management Research*. 2nd ed. Ann Arbor, MI: Michigan University Press.

Ouitis, Aissa
1984 *Possession, magie et prophétie en Algérie: Essai ethnographique (Possession, Magic and Prophesy in Algeria: An Ethnographic Study)*. Paris: Arcantères.

Qureshi, Emran
2004 "Misreading 'The Arab Mind': The Dubious Guidebook to Middle East Culture That's on the Pentagon's Reading List." *Boston Globe* (May 30). http://www.boston.com/news/globe/ideas/articles/2004/05/30/misreading_the_arab_mind?mode=PF (accessed November 2008).

Rahman, Afzalur
1980 *Muhammad as a Military Leader*. Lahore, Pakistan: Islamic Publications.

Ramsey, Boniface
1999 "Wealth." In *Augustine through the Ages: An Encyclopedia*, edited by Allan D. Fitzgerald, 876-881. Cambridge, UK: Eerdmans.

Redissi, Hamadi
1998 *Les politiques en Islam: Le prophète; le roi et le savant (The Political Leaders in Islam: The Prophet, the King and the Scholar)*. Paris: L'Harmattan.

Remacle, Xavière
2002 *Comprendre la culture arabo-musulmane (Understanding the Arabo-Muslim Culture)*. Lyon, France: Editions Chronique Sociale.

Renault, François
1992 *Le Cardinal Lavigerie (The Cardinal Lavigerie)*. Paris: Editions Fayard.

Roberts, Hugh
1981 "The Conversion of the *Mrabtin* in Kabylia". In *Islam et Politique au Maghreb*, edited by Ernest Gellner et Jean-Claude Vatin. Paris: CNRS.

Rondet, Henri
1954 "La liberté et la grace dans la théologie augustinienne (Freedom and Grace in Saint Augustine's Theology)." In *Saint Augustin parmi nous (Saint Augustine among Us)*, edited by Henri Rondet, Charles Morel, Maurice Jourjon, and Jules Lebreton 199-222. Le Puy, France: Mappus.

Rondet, Henri, Charles Morel, Maurice Jourjon, and Jules Lebreton
1954 *Saint Augustin parmi nous (Saint Augustine among Us)*. Le Puy, France: Mappus.

Rondot, Pierre
1960 *Islam et les Musulmans d'aujourd'hui (Islam and Today's Muslims)*. Paris: L'Orante.

Ronen, S., and O. Shenkar
1985 "Clustering Countries on Attitudinal Dimensions: A Review and Synthesis." *Academy of Management Review* 10: 435-454.

Safi, Hammadi
1993 "Abdel Hamid Ben Badis entre les exigences du dogme et la contrainte de la modernité (Abdel Hamid Ben Badis between the Requirements of Dogma and the Constraints of Modernity). " In *Penseurs Maghrébins Contemporains (Contemporary Maghrebian Thinkers)*, edited by M. Y. B. Retnani, 73-99. Casablanca, Maroc: EDDIF.

Safi, Louay
2005 "Visionary Leadership: Vision, Communication, Empowerment, and Discipline." http://www.lsinsight.org/articles/Current/Leadership.htm (accessed November 2007).
2006 "Leadership and Education." ISNA Leadership Development Center. http//www.ildc.net (accessed November 2006).

Saïd, Edward
1979 *Orientalism*. New York: Random House.

Sarayrah, Yasin Khalaf
2004 "Servant Leadership in the Bedouin Arab Culture." In *Global Virtue Ethics Review* 5, no. 3: 58-79.

Scandura, Terri A., M. A. Von Glinow and K. B. Lowe
1999 "When East Meets West: Leadership 'Best Practices' in the United States and the Middle East." In *Advances in Global Leadership*. Vol. 1. Edited by W. Mobley, M. J. Gessner and V. Arnold, 235-248. Stanford, CT: JAI Press.

Scandura, Terri A., and Peter Dorfman
2004 "Leadership Research in an International and Cross-Cultural Context." *The Leadership Quarterly* 15, no. 2: 277-307.

Schacht, J., B. Lewis and Ch. Pellat
2001 "*Ahkam*." In *The Encyclopaedia of Islam CD-ROM Edition v. 1.0*. Leiden, The Netherlands: Koninklijke Brill. (E.I 2), s.v.

Shahin, Amany I., and Peter L. Wrigth
2004 "Leadership in the Context of Culture: An Egyptian Perspective." *Leadership and Organization Development Journal* 25, no. 6: 499-511.

Shamir, Boas, Robert J. House, and Michael B. Arthur
1992 "The Motivational Effects of Charismatic Leadership: A Self-Concept Based Theory." *Organizational Science* 4, no. 4 (November): 577-594.

Sharabi, Hisham
1996 *Le néopatriarcat (The Neopatriarcat)*. Translated by Mercure de France. Oxford, UK: Oxford University Press.

Silverthorne, Colin
2005 *Organizational Psychology in Cross-Cultural Perspective*. New York: NYU Press.

Smith, P. B., and M. F. Peterson
1988 *Leadership, Organizations and Culture*. Newbury Park, CA: Sage.

Solomon, R. C.
1992 *Ethics and Excellence: Cooperation and Integrity in Business*. New York: Oxford University Press.

Spears, Larry C.
2000. "On Character and Servant-Leadership: Ten Characteristics of Effective, Caring Leaders." *Concepts and Connections* 8, no. 3.
2003 "Understanding the Growing Impact of Servant-Leadership." In *The Servant-Leader Within: A Transformative Path*, edited by Robert K. Greenleaf, Hamilton Beazley, Julie Beggs, and Larry C. Spears, 13-28. New York: Paulist Press.

Stogdill, Ralph M.
1948 "Personal Factors Associated with Leadership: A Survey of the Literature." *Journal of Psychology* 25:35-71.
1974 *Handbook of Leadership: A Survey of Theory and Research*. New York: The Free Press.

Sunderland, R. S., ed.
1981 *A Biblical Basis for Ministry*. Philadelphia, PA: Westminster Press.

TeSelle, Eugène
1970 *Augustine, the Theologian*. New York: Herder and Herder.

Thomas, David and Inkson, Kerr
2004 *Cultural Intelligence*. San Francisco, CA: Berrett-Koehler Publishers.

Tilley, Maureen A.
1996 *Donatist Martyr Stories: The Church in Conflict in Roman North Africa*. Liverpool, UK: Liverpool University Press.
1997 *The Bible in Christian North Africa: The Donatist World*. Minneapolis, MN: Fortress Press.

Ting-Toomey, Stella, ed.
1994 *The Challenge of Face Work*. New York: Suny Press.

Tore, Kjeilen
2003 " '*Ulama*." In *Encyclopedia of Orient*, http://www.Lexicorient.com (accessed January 2007).

Triandis, Harry C.
1993 "The Contingency Model in Cross-Cultural Perspective." In *Leadership Theories and Research: Perspectives and Directions*, edited by Martin M. Chemmers and Roya Ayman, 167-188. New York: Adademic Press.

Trice, H. M., and J. M. Beyer
1986 "Charisma and Its Routinization in Two Social Movement Organizations." *Research in Organizational Behavior* 8: 113-164.

Tucker, R. C.
1968 "The Theory of Charismatic Leadership." *Dædalus* 97: 731-756.

Tyan, E.
1960 " *'Adl.*" In *Encyclopaedia of Islam*. New ed., edited by H. A. R. Gibb et al., 209-210. Leiden, The Netherlands: E. J. Brill

Van Bavel, Tarsicius J.
1999 "Church." In *Augustine Through the Ages: An Encyclopedia*. Edited by Allan D. Fitzgerald, 169-176. Cambridge, UK: William B. Eerdmans.

Van Nieuwenhuijze, Christoffel
1985 *The Lifestyles of Islam: Recourse to Classicism Need of Realism*. Leiden, The Netherlands: E.J. Brill.

Vroom, Victor
1976 "Can Leaders Learn to Lead." *Organizational Dynamics* 4 (Winter): 743-769.

Watt, W. Montgomery
1953 *Muhammad at Mecca*. Oxford, UK: Clarendon Press.
1961 *Muhammad: Prophet and Statesman*. Oxford, UK: Oxford University Press.
1991 *Muslim-Christian Encounters: Perceptions and Misperceptions*. Oxford, UK: Routledge.

Weaver, Rebecca H.
1999 "Prayer." In *Augustine Through the Ages: An Encyclopedia*, edited by Allan D. Fitzgerald, 670-675. Cambridge, UK: Eerdmans.

Weber, Max
1946 "The Sociology of Charismatic Authority." In *From Max Weber: Essays in Sociology*, edited and translated by H. H. Gerth and C. W. Mills, 245-252. New York: Oxford University Press.
1947 *The Theory of Social and Economic Organization*. Edited by T. Parsons, and translated by A. M. Henderson and T. Parsons. New York: Free Press.

Welch, Alford T.
1995 "Muhammad: Life of the Prophet." In The *Oxford Encyclopedia of the Modern Islamic World*. Vol. 3. Edited by John L. Esposito, 153-161. Oxford, UK: Oxford University Press.

Wensinck, A. J.
1995 *"Sabr."* In *Encyclopaedia of Islam*, edited by C. E Bosworth et al., 685- 687. Leiden, The Netherlands: E. J. Brill.

Whittington, J. Lee, Tricia M. Pitts, Woody V. Kageler and Vicki L. Goodwin
2005 "Legacy Leadership: The Leadership Wisdom of the Apostle Paul." *The Leadership Quarterly* 16, no. 5: 749-770.

Woodberry, J. Dudley
1979 "The Footprints of Moses in Arabia." Personal Address, June 15, 1979.

Wright, Walter C.
1996 *Mentoring: The Promise of Relational Leadership*. Carlisle, UK: Paternoster Press.
2000 *Relational Leadership: A Biblical Model for Leadership Service*. Paternoster Press: Carlisle UK.

Yukl, Gary A.
2002 *Leadership in Organizations*. 5th ed. Upper Saddle River NJ: Prentice Hall.

Yusuf Ali, Abdullah
1934 *The Holy Qur'an: Text, Translation and Commentary*. Beltsville, MR: Amana Publications.

Zerdoumi, Nefissa
1970 *Enfants d'hier: L'éducation de l'enfant en milieu traditionnel algérien (Children of Yesterday: The Education in the Algerian Tradition)*. Paris: Maspéro.

Ziani Drid, Fatima, Miloud Seffari and Belkacem Ziani
2005 "La famille algérienne entre tradition et modernité (The Algerian Family Between Tradition and Modernity)." http://iussp2005.princeton.edu/download.aspx?submissionId=50843.International (accessed March 2008).

Zwemer, Samuel M.,
1902 *Raymond Lull*. New York: Funk & Wagnalls.

Index

accountability x, 32, 120, 211, 215, 217, 220, 264, 284-285
administration xi, 88, 110, 121, 181, 215, 241
administrative skills 254
adviser 101, 155, 248
affection 142
allegiance 85, 104-105, 138, 169
ancestor 83-84, 91, 262
apologetics 197
arbitration 90-91, 130, 135, 264, 286, 290
art 30, 116
austerity 120, 286
authenticity 159, 218-219, 253
avoidance
    uncertainty avoidance 45
behavior modeling xiv, 110, 230, 264, 294
benevolence 108, 163, 214, 269
blamelessness 219-220, 253, 284-285
blessing xvii, 177, 180, 290
blessings 100, 147, 158, 163
blood revenge 85
blood ties 83, 91, 139, 262
bravery 85, 99, 130, 153, 180
brotherhood 177, 199-201, 285
caretaker 143-144, 173, 222, 232
caretaking x, xi, xiv, 50, 183, 212, 232-233, 235, 247, 260-261, 265, 270, 275, 284
character 13, 33, 64, 99-100, 114, 128, 155, 246
characteristics
    social 174

charisma x, 22, 24-25, 41, 47, 49, 102, 110, 120, 153, 206, 236, 282, 290-291
charity 98, 108, 120, 172-173, 175, 179, 183, 186-189, 191, 201, 283
clear-sightedness 86
collaboration xvii, 280
collectivism 45, 47-48, 262
common sense 119, 224
communication 6, 9, 72, 170, 176, 178, 183, 195, 224, 226, 231, 246, 261, 264, 283
community
    community-oriented xi, 176, 181, 183, 199, 235, 262, 269
compassion 38, 159, 173-174, 214, 269, 283, 289
competence xi, xii, 109, 119-120, 263, 281, 283
conciliatory 137
consensus 4, 27, 88, 95-98, 119, 137, 183, 280
considerate 47-48, 51, 135
consultation x, xiv, 26-27, 39-40, 48, 51, 71, 91, 111-112, 128, 132, 144, 164-165, 188-189, 191, 198, 200, 226-229, 231, 254, 260-261, 280, 291
context
    social 140, 146, 156, 245
control
    self-control 45, 99, 126, 196, 287
courage x, 38, 85, 120, 128, 163-164, 181, 183, 188, 211, 217, 240, 248, 253, 263, 283
curse 147

Damascus 178-179
decision-making 26-27, 36, 39-41, 48, 91, 111, 136, 144, 165, 227, 229, 278, 280-281, 291, 293
defiance 99
delegation 26, 93
destiny
  sense of 175
dialogue iv, 197, 200
dignity 150, 159, 196-197
discernment 155, 237-238, 269
educator 154, 171, 187, 195-196
elegance 136, 164
eloquence 86, 121, 183, 286
empathy 28, 38, 59, 267, 269
endurance 45, 109, 120, 181, 183
equality 41, 120, 161
equity 85, 198
faithfulness x, 33, 62, 211-212, 215, 217-218, 220, 236
farsightedness 121
fasting 8, 206, 252, 255
feeding 33-35, 232, 240, 260, 275
fidelity 99
firmness 121
forgiveness x, 38, 90, 114, 156, 207, 212, 217, 220, 247, 269, 284
forgiving 171, 249
fortitude 128
friend
  friend of God 175, 194, 199, 283
friendship xviii, 57, 120, 173, 285
gentleness 132, 180, 195-196, 214, 217, 269, 285
God
  love for 172, 206, 214, 235, 252
  love of 34, 162, 187
  obedience to 96, 103-104
  submission to xi, 103, 238-240, 273, 282-283
God first 206, 280
goodness xvii, 217, 284-285
group feeling 83-84, 91
guardian 41-42, 52, 119, 131
guide 39, 85-86, 91, 119, 143, 145, 179, 193-194, 197, 199, 263
hierarchy 93, 117, 129, 145-147, 151, 161, 164, 231
holiness 207, 219-220, 253, 284-285
holy man xii, xiv, xv, 177, 180, 262, 278-279, 288-290, 294, 341
honesty 38, 99, 106, 198, 207, 218-220, 253
honor 32, 38, 50, 83-84, 86, 145-146, 149-150, 153, 164-165, 264, 271, 277-278
hospitality 32, 84-86, 136, 163-164, 208, 212, 263, 265, 267, 283
impact
  social 191
incognito inquiry 120, 261
indulgence 163, 171
industriousness 172, 201
infallibility 113
intermediary 82, 93-94, 96-97, 103, 117, 158
intuition 197
joy 105, 125
judge 85, 87, 119, 123-124, 126-128, 155, 173-174, 215
judgment 87, 96-97, 120, 128
jurist 98, 119, 124
kindness 38, 108, 132, 217, 269, 285
knowledge
  legal 107, 124, 129, 131
leader i, vii, 6, 8, 10-11, 13-17, 19-26, 28-36, 38-41, 45, 47-52, 55, 58-64, 66-69, 73-75,

84-87, 90-91, 93-94, 97-103, 105-108, 110-111, 113-115, 117, 120-123, 130-132, 134-139, 145, 150, 156, 162-163, 165, 168, 172-176, 179-183, 189, 193-196, 198-200, 205-207, 209, 211, 214-218, 220-224, 226-227, 229, 231-244, 246, 251, 253-255, 260-264, 266, 269, 272-277, 279-282, 284, 286-291, 293, 341

transformational 183, 200

leadership

  metaphor xi, 28, 30, 33-35, 37, 232, 234, 240, 243-244, 252, 274-278

  paternalistic xi, 50, 265-266

  paternalistic leadership style xi, 50, 265-266

  prophetic-caliphal style 41, 292

  Servant Leadership vii, xi, xiv, 28-30, 39, 59, 267-268, 270-273, 276, 278, 285, 288, 341

  sheikhocratic xi, xiv, 37, 51, 56, 131, 135, 183, 258-260, 264-267, 275-278, 288, 292

  shepherd leadership style xi, xiv, 35, 42, 52, 74, 273-275, 277-278, 288, 341

  skill 255

  transactional vii, 20, 22, 24, 57

  transformational vii, 22-23, 264

  value 31, 46-47, 57, 64, 66, 74, 76, 86, 105-106, 108-111, 113, 124, 129, 131-132, 149-151, 176, 197-198, 202, 206-207, 209, 212-215, 217-218, 233, 237, 252-253, 262-263, 270, 277, 284-286, 290, 294

legitimacy

  divine x, xii, 35, 67, 93-95, 99, 106, 112, 114, 116, 118, 120, 158, 161, 171-172, 174-175, 187, 190, 194, 201, 220-222, 236, 240, 253, 279, 281

  human viii, ix, x, xii, xiv, 18, 25, 32, 34, 37, 49-51, 67, 82, 84, 92-96, 98, 103, 109, 112, 114, 117, 125, 131, 136, 158, 162-163, 179-180, 182, 197-198, 205-207, 210-217, 220-222, 229, 233, 240, 252-254, 265, 279, 281, 286

lifestyle

  simple 28, 166, 183, 188, 200, 286

listening x, 26, 29, 59, 111, 135, 150, 159, 164, 173, 229, 231, 234-235, 239, 261, 267, 269, 272, 283-284

longanimity 86

love for 35, 172, 174, 180, 183, 191, 198, 206, 213-214, 235, 252, 261

love for followers 191

loyalty x, 38, 47-48, 83-85, 90, 128, 130, 135, 153, 186, 198, 214-215, 217, 263, 283-284, 289

man

  holy xii, xiv, xv, 177, 180, 262, 278-279, 288-290, 294, 341

management 29, 41-42, 46, 48-50, 121, 147, 241-242, 255

master 7, 9, 143, 154-155, 157, 173, 177, 186, 194, 197, 226, 231, 244

mature i, 227, 232, 237, 240, 278

mediator 142, 148, 155, 160

meditation 182

meekness 263, 284
mentor xvii, 187, 197, 294
mercy 108, 132, 159, 175, 180, 191, 217, 269, 283, 285
metaphor
    servant xi, 28, 243
miracle 48, 102
moderation 125, 161, 171, 263, 287
modesty 146, 150, 152, 196, 200, 202, 263, 284
Montagne, Robert 136
morality 22, 93, 109, 166, 172, 179, 196-198, 207, 283, 285
Moran, R.T. 17
Morel, Charles 171-172, 175
Moses xi, xiv, 82, 96, 100-101, 108-109, 213, 220, 233-234, 240, 242, 244, 246-248, 251, 260, 264, 266, 276, 280
motherhood 147
Muller, Roland 153
Myers, I. B. 57
mystic 157, 190
Nasr, Seyyed Hossein 154-155
Nawafleh, Mohammed 42, 108, 111, 113, 120-121
Neal, M. 47, 50, 135, 261
nepotism 47, 262
nobility 105, 113, 197, 263
noble 87, 110, 197
nursing 35
Nusair, Naim 40, 111
obedience 40, 86, 93, 95-96, 100, 103-104, 164, 166, 189
opinion 32, 41, 86, 105, 112, 119, 124, 127-128, 144, 280
Ottoman
    period 7
Oussedik, Fatima 140
Padwa, Lynette 33

paganism 5, 90
Pasa, F. S. 47, 112
path-goal theory 16
patriarchal 49-50, 139, 141-144, 146, 149, 164, 260, 271, 293
patriarchal system 141-142, 149, 271
Paul xi, xiv, 15, 33, 110-111, 185, 188, 233, 248-249, 251, 271, 276, 286, 290
peace 85, 101-102, 112, 119, 130, 157, 173, 186, 198
peacemaker 103, 142, 174, 190
peacemaking 165, 264, 287
Pentecost 3
perceptiveness 121
Pères Blancs 7
Perraudin, Jean 185, 187-188
perseverance 181
persistence 99
persuasion 29, 59, 88, 181, 267-268, 287
Phillips, John 137-138, 150
physical fitness 120
poetry 159, 178, 182, 286
polemics 197
political figure 178
politics 129
Popper, Micha 20
poverty 6, 114, 176, 190, 286
power
    legal 98, 131
power distance 44, 48, 270, 341
powerlessness 189, 191, 271, 281
    supernatural 86-87, 102, 122, 159, 182, 189, 237, 279, 281-282, 289
prayer x, 8-9, 100, 115, 120, 122-123, 128, 132, 163, 165, 175, 182, 184, 186, 190, 195, 206,

227, 229, 238-239, 252, 255, 276, 281-283
preacher 170-171, 195
preaching 14, 116, 170-173, 176, 189, 249, 283
probity 120, 285
Prosperity Gospel 21, 183
protecting 33-34, 145, 165, 235, 265
protection x, 33, 35, 85, 90, 99, 114, 119, 144, 164, 234, 260, 275
Provision 35, 162, 275
Punnett, Jean 47-49, 135, 262
Ramsey, Boniface 174
reason
  reasoning 96, 119, 122, 156, 166
Redissi, Hamadi 92, 96, 101, 103, 106, 108, 110, 118-120
Redjala, Ramdane 177-182
relation 16, 34-35, 40, 58, 61, 129, 149, 189, 206, 218-219, 290
relational ix, x, 72-73, 123, 145, 173, 181, 183, 186, 189, 191, 199-200, 205-207, 211, 226, 232, 252-253, 262, 283-284
relation-oriented 16, 50, 191
relationship-oriented 284
Remacle, Xaviere 27, 84, 87, 148-149, 152, 154, 160
Remacle, Xavière 27, 84, 87, 148-149, 152, 154, 160
Renault, François 7, 185-186
repetition 155, 166
reputation 86, 110, 135-136, 248
respectability 126
revelation 93-94, 99, 102, 106, 111-113, 116, 118, 131
revitalization 8
reward 20-21, 24, 105, 109, 138, 152
rhetoric 116, 169

rhetorical skills 25, 200, 286
Rice, Robert W 17
righteousness 34, 93, 159, 207, 253
Rima, Samuel D. 30
Robert, Hugh xvii, 15, 24, 28-29, 39, 63, 136, 162, 267
Rondet, Henri 171-174
Rondot, Pierre 160-161
rule 51, 85, 96, 98, 128, 135, 162, 175, 189, 191, 223
sacrifice 35, 186
Safi, Hammadi 41, 193-197, 199
Safi, Louay 41, 193-197, 199
sanctification 173, 187, 220, 253
sanctity x, 207, 219-220
Sarayrah, Yasin Khalaf 40, 135-136
Scandura et al. 48
Scandura, Terri 24, 45-46, 48-49
science 56, 80, 106-107, 115-116, 120, 140, 163
self-sacrifice 85, 183, 201, 233-234, 248, 251, 276-277
severity 141, 154, 171
shame 45, 50, 149, 152-153, 164, 264, 271, 277-278
Shamir, Boaz 22, 24-25
Sharabi, Hisham 138-139
sharing 8-9, 26, 41, 48, 83, 137-138, 173, 175, 212, 227, 229, 231, 262
sheep 33-35, 83, 174, 190, 232-233, 240, 246, 254, 275-276
sheikh viii, xii, xv, 51, 84-85, 91, 130, 134-136, 162-165, 177, 180, 183, 226, 258, 260-267, 272-274, 288, 290, 292-294, 303, 341
Shenkar, Oded 47-49, 64, 135, 262
shepherd xi, xiv, xv, xvii, 33-37, 42, 52, 56, 74, 232-234, 240,

244-246, 251, 255, 263, 267, 273-278, 283, 288, 290-291, 293-294, 341
shepherd metaphor xi, 33, 35, 37, 244, 274
sincerity 106, 113, 207, 218-220, 253
Smith, P.B. 45
sociological transformation 141
soldier-monk 179
solidarity 47, 188, 198-201, 262
Spears, Larry 28, 60
spirituality
    characteristic 47-48, 67, 94, 98, 100, 115, 152, 172, 181, 229, 234, 237, 240, 252, 254, 262-264, 269, 271, 275-277, 280, 288, 294
    transformation 22-23, 31, 42, 140-141, 143, 147, 151, 160, 200-201, 288, 291
    value 31, 46-47, 57, 64, 66, 74, 76, 86, 105-106, 108-111, 113, 124, 129, 131-132, 149-151, 176, 197-198, 202, 206-207, 209, 212-215, 217-218, 233, 237, 252-253, 262-263, 270, 277, 284-286, 290, 294
Stephenson, Lauren 136
stewardship 29, 59, 267, 269
stimulate 22, 57, 152
Stogdill, Ralph M. 14
Strodtbeck, F 65
submission xi, 95, 103, 131-132, 145, 206, 238-240, 254, 272-273, 282-283
Sufi 118, 156-162, 177, 179, 181-182, 193, 197, 199, 283
sultan 92, 96, 182

support xvii, xviii, 19-20, 39, 42, 91, 113, 142-143, 145, 156, 170, 174, 219, 222, 235, 253, 255, 262, 269-270, 274, 283
task-orientedness 50, 262
teacher 154, 171, 187, 192, 196, 241
temperate 248
tenderness 141-142, 148, 164-165, 214, 261, 269
Tertullian 4, 6, 13
TeSelle, Eugene 169, 171-172
Thagaste 168
theologian ix, 6, 168, 170-171, 187, 193-194, 197, 200
thinker 169-171, 196
Thomas, David 50-51, 134-135, 265
Tilley, Maureen A. 5
Timothy xi, 35, 241, 248, 251
Ting-Toomey, Stella 45
tolerance 5, 28, 32, 57, 199, 269
tolerant 199
Tore, Kjeilen 129
Trait-Theory vii, 14, 45, 53, 62
transparency 207, 218-220, 253
Triandis, Harry C. 27, 43-45, 63, 65
tribal traditions 50, 265
tribe 50-51, 85-87, 90, 121, 135-136, 139, 153, 177, 180, 234, 260, 262, 265-267
trustworthiness 85, 99, 113, 215, 220, 253, 283
truth 32, 100, 157, 171, 175, 198, 214, 241, 261
truthfulness 85, 113, 218-219, 253, 283
Tucker, R. C. 25
unity 32, 164, 173, 182-183, 186, 189, 191, 198-199, 202, 262
Valenzi, Enzo R. 26
Van Bavel, Tarsicius J. 173-174

Vandals 6, 170
Van Nieuwenhuijze, Christopher 114-115, 129
Veinstein, Gilles 92, 107, 118, 157
vicegerent 41, 92, 117, 131
Villareal, M. 45
violence 128, 153, 224
virility 149-150, 164-165, 263
visionary vii, ix, xi, 23-25, 41, 49, 52, 86, 91, 176, 183, 191, 196, 200, 241-242, 255, 262, 279, 282, 289, 341
warner 100, 103
warrior 101, 103, 179
Watt, Montgomery 4, 82, 86-87, 89, 99-101, 104-106
wealth 112, 116, 136-138, 166, 174-175, 181, 183, 190
Weaver, Rebecca H. 175
Weber, Max 23, 25
Welch, Alfort T 101-102, 112-113
Wensinck, A. J. 108-109
Whittington, L. Lee 33
witness 101, 183
Wofford, Kenneth C. 17
worship 9, 109, 112-113, 119, 122, 157, 160-161, 163, 238-239, 282
Wright, Walter C. 27, 30, 32, 57, 65
writer 90, 125, 138, 169, 171
Yukl, G. A. 44
zeal 89, 171, 186, 188
Zerdoumi, Nefissa 138-139, 141-143, 145, 147-152, 155
Ziani, Drid 140, 145, 148
Zoummeroff, Philippe 177-182
Zwemer, Samuel M. 7

www.ingramcontent.com/pod-product-compliance
Lightning Source LLC
Chambersburg PA
CBHW061704300426
44115CB00014B/2557